THATCHERISM: PERSON

Also by Kenneth Minogue

THE LIBERAL MIND
NATIONALISM
THE CONCEPT OF THE UNIVERSITY
ALIEN POWERS: The Pure Theory of Ideology

Also by Michael Biddiss

FATHER OF RACIST IDEOLOGY: The Social and Political Thought of
Count Gobineau
THE AGE OF THE MASSES: Ideas and Society in Europe since 1870
DISEASE AND HISTORY (*with F. F. Cartwright*)
GOBINEAU: Selected Political Writings (*editor*)
IMAGES OF RACE

Thatcherism: Personality and Politics

Edited by

Kenneth Minogue

Professor of Government
London School of Economics and Political Science

and

Michael Biddiss

Professor of History
University of Reading

MACMILLAN
PRESS

First published 1987

Published by
THE MACMILLAN PRESS LTD
Houndmills, Basingstoke, Hampshire RG21 2XS
and London
Companies and representatives
throughout the world

Printed and bound in Great Britain at
The Camelot Press Ltd, Southampton

British Library Cataloguing in Publication Data
Thatcherism: personality and politics.
1. Great Britain—Politics and
government—1979–
I. Minogue, Kenneth R.   II. Biddiss,
Michael D.
320.941   JN231
ISBN 0–333–44724–7 (hardcover)
ISBN 0–333–44725–5 (paperback)

Contents

Notes on the Contributors

Digby Anderson is Director of the Social Affairs Unit, London.

Michael Biddiss is Professor of History at the University of Reading.

The Rt Hon. Baroness Elles (**Diana Elles**), MEP for Thames Valley, was formerly Vice-President of the European Parliament.

S. E. Finer is Emeritus Fellow, All Souls College, Oxford.

Julius Gould was Professor of Sociology at the University of Nottingham, and is now Chairman of the Trustees of the Social Affairs Unit, London.

Peter Hennessy is Co-Director of the Institute of Contemporary British History and a Visiting Fellow at the Policy Studies Institute, London.

David Marquand is Professor of Contemporary History and Politics at the University of Salford.

Kenneth Minogue is Professor of Government at the London School of Economics and Political Science.

Philip Norton is Professor of Government at the University of Hull.

C. F. Pratten is Fellow of Trinity Hall and Senior Research Officer, Department of Applied Economics, University of Cambridge.

Preface

The essays in this volume originated from a conference held under the auspices of the journal *Government and Opposition* at the London School of Economics (LSE) in the autumn of 1986. The seven papers delivered on that occasion have been revised for publication by their authors in the light of the discussion which they prompted and of events up until late November 1986. Both the Introduction and the essay by Philip Norton (Chapter 2) have been written specially for this volume. In this book, the contributors have not sought to express any collective view of Thatcherism. Each speaks only for himself or herself. We hope, however, that the collection will prove all the more valuable precisely by virtue of the variety of opinions and approaches that it offers.

All those who gave papers at the conference benefited from the distinguished company of others who participated in the discussion sessions: Mr Vernon Bogdanor, Professor E. A. Gellner, Professor G. Ionescu, Professor G. W. Jones, Professor Isabel de Madariaga, Dr J. G. Merquior, Dr Roger Morgan, Professor Geraint Parry and Baroness White. We are grateful to Mr Brendan O'Leary, whose record of the proceedings has been available to the contributors during the process of revising papers. In organizing the essays for publication we have been fortunate to have the advice and assistance of a number of colleagues associated with *Government and Opposition*. As editors, we wish most particularly to record our warm appreciation of all that Mrs Rosalind Jones has done towards the preparation of this volume.

KENNETH MINOGUE
London School of Economics
MICHAEL BIDDISS
University of Reading

Introduction: The Context of Thatcherism
Kenneth Minogue

First, the logic of the expression: fusing the name of a person with a doctrinal suffix is an ugly process which can only be defended on the ground that politics is pre-eminent among human activities in being a playground for persons who stand for something. But even in politics, it is rare for practitioners to be promoted to the status of an 'ism'. The career grade in such promotions is to adjective, as in 'Churchillian' or 'Heathite'. Mrs Thatcher seems to be unique among British prime ministers in making it to the top. How can we explain this unlikely event? The main reason is a widespread conviction that she has introduced something new and significant into British political life, and my main business in this introduction will be an attempt to explain this conviction. But there is a further point: 'Thatcherism' as an expression is largely the creation of Mrs Thatcher's enemies. They need a focus, and being intellectuals, would hardly be satisfied with merely disliking a person. They disapproved of everything she stood for: hence – Thatcherism.

The appropriate context for understanding an office-holder is the institution within which he holds the office; the context of a person standing for an idea must be wider. I shall take the context of Thatcherism to be the development of liberal democracies in the twentieth century, and I can only do it in terms of a story about whose details there will certainly be endless disagreement. A possible version runs as follows: liberal democracies (most of them in Europe and America) were created in the nineteenth century by extensions of the franchise, and turned in the twentieth century (when not occupied with wars) to a concern with integrating all their members into something like a genuine community. In formal terms, politicians spoke about 'the poor', the 'disadvantaged' and the 'underprivileged', but the actual content of these expressions varied according to changes in society. Early on, the poor were construed as the industrial working class, but later it was the unemployed, racial minorities, the physically handicapped, women, the inner cities, and

so on. This concern led to the development of a rhetoric of compassion based upon the idea of social justice, a rhetoric which (among other things) went far to usurp the spirituality of the churches. Social democratic postures could become an alternative to the private charitable endeavours of the past, endeavours soon superseded by the invention of a whole array of rights which, taken together, added up to whatever was the current form of social integration. In this way, liberal democracies became welfare states.

This grand process of our civilization contained many strands, and it is worth disentangling a few of them. Perhaps we should put first the political calculation that if something were not done about the poor, they would become disruptive. Enemies of liberal democracy emphasize this form of realism, and no doubt it played a part, though I would judge it a relatively minor part. A second element was the rhetoric of caring and compassion which led politicians to describe what they were doing in terms of a generalized sympathy for those who suffered from some disadvantage or other. This strand had developed out of another element, inherited from earlier centuries and usually going by the name of 'socialism'. It was socialism as an ethical commitment which gave a colouring to the whole process. Next we must mention the administrative ingenuity of the expanding civil service, an ingenuity sharpened by the experience of war, by which the power of the state could be brought to bear on how the economy could be controlled, resources redistributed and services supplied to the needy. And finally, perhaps most fundamental of all, was a grand passion for transforming society in terms of an idea, rationalizing it, tidying it up, above all, making it fit a vision. Both the ends and means of this vision were subject to endless controversy, but a basic impulse of this character infused the whole endeavour.

The British landmarks of this quite general historical process are all familiar: the Lloyd George budget of 1909 was the real beginning of redistribution, while the public corporation, as perfected by Herbert Morrison, was the device by which British governments sought to dominate the economy in such a way as to clip the wings of profit-seeking industrialists. The Beveridge Report elaborated a rational form of social security and inspired the Labour government of 1945–51. Thereafter, so long as the Western world remained buoyant, governments of all complexions sustained and extended the edifice. Indeed, British governments extended it, even when economic circumstances were difficult, up to, and to some extent even after, 1979. Consensualism about social integration in the form of basic

equality was to domestic policy what bipartisanship was to foreign, and the consensuality went by the name of Butskellism. It is perhaps a measure of Mrs Thatcher's stature that the names of two men – Butler and Gaitskell – were needed to supply a name for the attitude she set out to contest.

Socialism in 20th-century liberal democracies was thus an administrative expedient, an ethical commitment, an attitude of mind, and also a solution to what seemed to be the main problem of political life. It seemed like the next logical step after the reform of the franchise, a move from political rights to economic. But it had a further dimension. Those socialists in whom the grand vision of social transformation had most taken root were impatient of constitutional limitations and political processes which could all too easily (they believed) be dominated by power and wealth. These revolutionaries dreamed of taking over the whole resources of the community – both real and personal – so as to bring the vision about.

The result was that, for something like a century, most liberal democracies operated a one-and-a-half party system. One of the dominant parties usually supported parliamentary democracy wholeheartedly, but the other was somewhat split between those for whom socialism was a proposal to be implemented piecemeal with the support of a democratic electorate, and those whose real aim was to seize power in order to implement the vision. Sometimes this element of national politics was almost outside the party system altogether, as in the Communist Parties of France and Italy. In the British Labour Party over long periods this element was very carefully excluded, though it had a continuing life in some of the rituals of the party, and considerable power in the trade unions. This curious half of the notional two-party system led for the most part a shadow existence, unable to step forward successfully in its own colours, because no electorate in its senses would vote away its own powers in order to submit to the domination of enthusiastic visionaries making an implausible claim to be the working class. In the United States, communists went by the name of 'socialists' and socialists by the name of 'liberals', in another version of that unavoidable chamelionism by which a static vision tried to come to terms with the dynamic process of liberal democratic politics.

In all of these strands of social improvement, there was no room for the kind of classical liberalism Mrs Thatcher was to affirm because most people took it for granted that leaving society and the economy alone merely resulted in misery for large numbers of people. The

injustices of a capitalist society could only be corrected by the deliberate intervention of the state. The emerging formulation of the idea was that people ought to be able 'to take control of their own lives'. From about the 1960s onwards, however, it became clear that many of the existing devices of socialism had merely substituted bureaucratic fashions for inherited inequalities – tower blocks for slums, as it were – and as a result new ideas such as participation came to be seen as better ways of implementing the idea. But few people doubted the basic premise that political idealism meant having a social vision – indeed, a plan.

The real context of Thatcherism is to be found in the troubles which came to afflict this vision in the 1970s. They became evident at two levels, and Britain was exemplary, indeed rather advanced, at both levels. The most obvious level has been described as 'the crisis of the Welfare State'. From 1951 onwards, governments had, it might plausibly be suggested, been bribing electors and attempting to solve social problems at the expense of piling burdens on manufacturing industry. But the oil crisis of the 1970s, combined with the inflationary consequences of too fluent a recourse to Keynesian expedients, began to produce a quite new situation. Confident reformers of the 1950s had assumed that capitalist productivity was irresistibly on its way to the land of Cockaigne; only distribution was a serious political question. Now, however, the machinery began to falter, and liberal democratic stagnation was put in an altogether more alarming light by the realization that in Asia a new economic challenge, of menacing efficiency, had arisen.

Earlier in the century, there had been a vogue for contrasting young nations and old, the up-and-coming have-nots and the status quo powers. Even at that time Britain was already familiar with living in a world full of young, thrusting competitors; it now became clear that Britain's fate merely anticipated that of Europe and America. And once the problem had been posed in these terms, at this second structural level its explanation seemed clear enough. The great achievements of the liberal democracies had occurred when the scope of government was small and when productivity responded to eonomic incentives. But, over the decades, creative vitality had diminished. There was, of course, controversy about the extent to which the arrival of the Germans and the Americans on the world economic stage at the end of the last century had or had not been facilitated by some overall governmental design; and there were those who saw in the Japanese miracle less of sheer economic

creativity than the guiding hand of MITI. But there was no doubt that in the relatively stagnating West, governments were increasingly taxing the efficient in order to subsidize the inefficient. Firms on the edge of bankruptcy found that, as a substitute for increasing efficiency, they could mobilize their workers as voters in order to extract regulatory protection, or even direct subsidy from their governments. Those with a taste for medical metaphors diagnosed a form of economic arteriosclerosis. The lithe and responsive economy of earlier decades had been replaced by a static system bent above all on warding off rather than responding to challenges from afar.

When grand visions fail, there are only two possibilities: one is to take reality by the scruff of the neck and *make* the vision work; the other is to abandon visions altogether. The first option can be seen being fitfully attempted by the Labour government of 1974–9, and it operated largely in terms of the participatory theory which had recently become dominant in socialist circles. But it is difficult for a government to make participation work, and what was actually attempted was a form of corporatism called 'the social contract'. Workers and businessmen, the trade unions and the Confederation of British Industry were called into consultation with the government in order to agree the terms for, most notably, an incomes policy. Since the thing called 'consensus' had failed, it must be recreated by way of things called 'negotiations', which, in this period, seemed to be rationality itself. But this was the rationality of a state which had evidently overreached itself in trying to determine everything, right down to what workers ought to be paid. What few people observed at the time was that this kind of corporatism greatly resembled what the despised Fascist movements had attempted earlier in the century: it was clearly a declaration of the bankruptcy of the representative system of government. It amounted to a recognition that the representative capacity of Members of Parliament was too weak to sustain a government of such ambitions, and needed supplementation by some functional expedient which would bring into the political process those who spoke for the producers. But this expedient merely compounded an evident unreality inseparable from the grand vision itself, for the officials of the Trades Union Congress and the Confederation of British Industry were themselves no less remote from the people than the members of the House of Commons itself. They could not deliver the promises they made, though they could certainly collect on the concessions they extracted. Such a piling of unreality upon unreality crumbled in the winter of 1978–9, when

workers in many industries, but especially in those public services supposedly devoted to the good of the nation, responded to the promise of the grand vision with the immemorial cry: 'Where's mine?'

It was by no means a new idea that what lay at the root of all these troubles was the growth of the state. The Conservatives when in opposition in the late 1960s had veered in that direction under Edward Heath, who had been the hero of the repeal of resale price maintenance. But Heath in power had sold the pass. The man who, after the Conservative defeat of 1974, underwent a Damascus Road conversion to classical liberal principles was Sir Keith Joseph, who proceeded to stomp the country and transform its political atmosphere so that, when the 'winter of discontent' came in 1978–9, attitudes had already changed. But the key figure in this doctrinal relay race was Mrs Thatcher, who not only took up these ideas and ran, but took the Conservative Party with her. And it was clear that while they came primarily in the guise of ideas about the economics of inflation, their real appeal lay to highly traditional moral convictions such as Mrs Thatcher had absorbed from her background and had held ever since she was a Young Conservative. This fact has had an important consequence for the way her conduct has been interpreted. Although she has rejected the entire 'logic' of a grand vision to be imposed upon modern society, she has been criticized as a highly 'ideological' politician (and therefore basically unconservative) because she has rejected the pragmatism in which the grand vision had cloaked itself. However, the real principles guiding her political posture are in fact moral rather than social.

Much of the significance of Mrs Thatcher's 1979 triumph lay in its timing. Two elements in the political calculation of the time supplied the urgency that turned a policy into something not far from a crusade. The first of these was the problem that, as a result of the Keynesian expedients favoured by both parties, the number of people on the public payroll (including local government) kept on increasing. With every down-turn in Britain's economic fortunes, governments borrowed to subsidize failing industries, increased local authority spending and augmented the numbers of civil servants. The danger loomed of a country in which sheer voter-interest might entrench in power governments who would push this cycle to inevitable disaster. The second urgency lay in the belief that North Sea oil would provide the incumbent governments of the 1980s with such resources that they would be enabled both to bribe electorates

for a decade or more, and ward off until too late the necessity for a major structural overhaul of economic practices.

The rhetorical core of Mrs Thatcher's appeal was thus the belief that Britain had long been lost to a kind of narcissism by attending to the luxuries of social integration without noticing that developments in the wider world were threatening catastrophe. While not repudiating the basic decencies of welfarism, Mrs Thatcher argued that economic realism, as the precondition of any desirable element of social integration, must come first. In time, this message came to be overlaid by elements of melodrama: the patriotism of the Falklands war, and the image of Mrs Thatcher as a Prospero scourging a band of Council Calibans,[1] the rump of the socialist revolutionary movement which was surviving these hard times in redoubts opened up by local government reorganization. But the basic appeal was always a form of realism based on economics.

Realism is, of course, not a policy but an idiom of political argument, and *any* policy can be supported on realist grounds. Welfare policies can be advanced with the realist argument that the marginalized will tend to unsettle the state unless they are provided for. Most socialists, however, preferred to talk of welfarism in moralistic terms, and too much moralism, by veering towards unreality, is an ideal background for a passionate realism. After too much sickly compassion, there is something unmistakeably refreshing, even bracing, about a realist call to the sterner forms of duty, and no one who ignores this transformation of the moral and rhetorical atmospherics of British politics in the late 1970s will have understood Thatcherism. To her enemies this realism was a regression back to what Tony Benn called 'the jungle', subjecting the British people to the selfishness of big business. But this view does not accommodate the fact that Mrs Thatcher's realism also had a moral appeal; indeed, the economic and the moral shaded into each other. At its lowest level, it was the simple moral lesson that you can't spend more than you earn. At a slightly more complex level, it was the argument, which came to be called 'monetarism', that excessive government spending causes inflation, an argument of great appeal to many people for whom one of the major stabilities of life was undermined when the pound in their pockets bought less and less with every passing month. At a more sophisticated level still, this became the

---

[1] Certainly Stephano seems to have heard about the Arts Council: 'This will prove a brave Kingdom to me, where I shall have my music for nothing' (*The Tempest*, III, 2, 156–7).

policy of the public sector borrowing requirement and got lost in the technicalities of how to describe money supply. What it meant in practice was a government bent on cutting government expenditure, amid a constant wail of interest groups asserting that desirable services were being (as the point was put in a notably uneconomic way) 'underfunded'.

It is always difficult, and perhaps impossible, to isolate the individual from the currents of thought and feeling within which he or she swims. But among the more plausible counterfactuals of this century is the argument that without Churchill, and without de Gaulle, the history of Britain and France would be significantly different. It seems almost equally plausible to suggest that the same is true of Mrs Thatcher. Some of the decisions she took, and persistence in some of the policies she espoused, are hard to imagine had the responsibility been on any other shoulders. Her opponents in the notable dramas which it has been her vocation to provoke were none of them insignificant, but each served merely to exhibit her mettle. Each of them failed in part because of a significant unreality in the cause he stood for: General Galtieri because his invasion of those islands in the South Atlantic was primarily a gambit in domestic politics, Michael Foot because the Labour Party's two halves seemed to have lost contact with political reality, and Arthur Scargill because in the end no one could seriously pretend that it was wise to continue draining the nation's wealth to support uneconomic pits. But individuals are only important in politics because they stand for something beyond themselves. Mrs Thatcher stands for the diminution of governmental power and the enhancement of economic vitality, and it is not the least of the paradoxes of her period of rule that the project of diminishing goverment has often led to an actual increase in the range of governmental intervention; and that the attempt to create an 'enterprise culture' has led to a weakening of some of the subsidized economic life inherited from an earlier period. Between the programme and the transformation many shadows fall. But the essence of what has happened lies in the detail and that is the concern of the chapters which follow.

1 Thatcherism: Concept and Interpretations
Michael Biddiss

Early in 1986 *The Times* reported that, from the latest poll of visitors to Madame Tussaud's waxworks, Margaret Thatcher had emerged as the most popular political figure on display; it added, however, that she was also runner-up to Hitler under the category 'Hate and Fear'. A few months previously Sir Keith Joseph had remarked that 'My eyes light up at the sight of her, even though she's hitting me about the head, so to speak'.[1] These may be masochistic trivia, but they hint at deeper truths about the nature and power of the impact made by the ideas and personality of Britain's first female prime minister. Not only does she seem determined to surpass Asquith's record for longest continuous service by a 20th-century premier (as she will do in January 1988), but she has already achieved the distinction, unique amongst holders of that office, of witnessing her own eponymous 'ism' being firmly established in contemporary political discourse. Many of her supporters have come to find the label of 'Thatcherism' almost as convenient as her opponents have done, despite the divisions between them over its precise meaning, and certainly over the worth of her aims and achievements. There is thus today a large measure of agreement that 'Thatcherism' can be usefully employed to denote, if not a rigorously systematized ideology then at least a certain set of values and a certain style of leadership, and that these have been promoted by an exceptionally forceful personality, put to work at a critical epoch in British history, and directed towards dismantling many leading features of the particular form of political consensus developed over the post-war period.

VALUES AND STYLE

Commentators of all persuasions acknowledge that Mrs Thatcher's own values have their deepest roots in Grantham – in the family grocery, and in the civic activities of (to use her own words) 'a father who had a conviction approach'.[2] As Hugo Young and Anne Sloman observe in their valuable collection of interviews about 'the Thatcher

1

Phenomenon' (originally broadcast on radio), there is a marked wholeness about her formation, 'a very close identity between her public and her private character, her personal origins and her political performance'.[3] Sir Douglas Wass, for example, recorded his perception of the crucial link between her upbringing as the daughter of a small trader operating in the uncertain economic circumstances of the 1930s and her 'deep feeling for small businessmen and people who are staking their livelihoods on their activities'.[4] It is widely accepted that Mrs Thatcher has sought – with a quite exceptional directness – to make publicly felt the impact of her own particular experience and convictions. She depicts that task as being fundamentally moral: 'Economics are the method; the object is to change the heart and soul'.[5] She has thus presented herself as the champion of those keenest to exercise personal responsibility, to exhibit self-reliance and initiative, to maintain the traditional structure and role of the family, and to recognize the demands of duty as well as the allure of 'entitlements'. In political terms, such concerns have been most evident through the commitment to reverse the triumph of collectivist over individual values by effecting a reduction in the powers of the state whose intervention, according to *The Right Approach* (the seminal Conservative statement during the early phase of Mrs Thatcher's leadership), 'must be strictly limited to defined purposes, justified by particular circumstances rather than by doctrinaire theories'.[6] As for economic aspirations, these have included the promotion of thrift, the defence of 'sound' rather than 'suitcase' money, the matching of effort to appetite, the provision of positive incentives rather than of negative cushioning, the privatization of state-owned industries, the encouragement of calculated risk-taking within the context of a market freely responsive to patterns of individual choice, and an increase in the number of those with a propertied stake in social order.

One of the most remarkable features of Mrs Thatcher's quest to establish such a 'neo-Smilesian' culture and morality of enterprise has been her willingness to put at a discount that concern for equality which has been so pervasive in recent decades, not least among the ranks of a *bien pensant* bourgeoisie perhaps mildly remorseful about its own advantages. As *The Right Approach* frankly proclaims: 'Conservatives are not egalitarians. We believe in levelling up, in enhancing opportunities, not in levelling down, which dries up the springs of enterprise and endeavour and ultimately means there are fewer resources for helping the disadvantaged'.[7] Nor, in the Thatch-

erite perspective, is this deemed to be the only economic and moral
failing of egalitarianism; it is condemned also for its reliance on what
Sir Keith Joseph and Jonathan Sumption have called 'one of the
central prejudices of modern British politics, the belief that it is a
proper function of the State to influence the distribution of wealth for
its own sake'.[8] What rends the fabric of a nation is, on this
interpretation, not the existence of classes as such; rather, divisions
are caused by those (such as socialists) who calculatedly foment
antagonism between classes by use of the destructive force of envy
and by a misreading of the psychological as well as economic
dynamics behind sustained growth and real social cohesion. This is
one of the contexts in which Mrs Thatcher's supporters have found
most irksome the pretensions of the Labour Party to hold a monopoly
over the politics of care and moral concern, while that same body has
been itself so much to blame for developing a society 'where
compassion has become a sort of code-word for inaction'.[9] The
enterprising alternative depends on the recreation of that ethos, once
praised by Tocqueville, in which the British had 'the courage to seek
prosperity, freedom to follow it up, the sense and habits to find it,
and the assurance of reaping the benefit'.[10] Only on that basis might
economic well-being, social cohesion, and a due sense of patriotic
pride be properly restored and nurtured.

As a prophet of national redemption, Mrs Thatcher might well
have found in Augustine of Canterbury (though scarcely, according
to her taste, in his latest archiepiscopal successor) a somewhat less
incongruous patron than St Francis. Certainly the style in which her
values and instincts have been expressed has often revealed a quasi-
religious intensity, and even intolerance. As Monica Charlot rightly
observes: 'She has a messianic side'.[11] It is precisely this which seems
to have enhanced her attractiveness to some, while discomforting
others – including such Tories as remain attached to their trad-
itionally sceptical habits of mind. From the Labour ranks Peter
Shore declares that 'She has articulated right-wing moral convictions
in a more formidable and more committed way than any leader of the
right in post-war Britain'; and Denis Healey, with a further hint of
admiration, has dubbed her 'La Passionara of middle-class privilege'.[12]
The Soviet caricature of the 'Iron Lady', quickly made current in the
West, already conceded an awareness of that strength of personality
which in and beyond the Falklands war was to become projected as
the basis for a 'resolute approach' to any problem in hand. Even
before General Galtieri gave her the opportunity to become quite

literally so, there was something of the crusading war leader in Mrs
Thatcher – qualities of response to an hour of crisis which prompted
comparison with Lloyd George and Churchill among her 20th-century
predecessors, and even with de Gaulle. Her bearing amidst the blitz
of the Grand Hotel in Brighton elicited, quite properly, an altogether
wider and less ambivalent admiration. Without such toughness –
allied to an unusually forceful determination not simply to profess but
also to implement the promptings of inner certainty – the values of
Thatcherism would have proved far less formidable in action. Thus
conveyed, however, they have seemed all too frequently marked by
strident obstinacy and narrowness of outlook. As Ferdinand Mount
observed at the outset of her premiership, albeit with the delicacy of a
sympathetic associate, there is in Mrs Thatcher 'a certain impatience
with subtlety of feeling, a lack of sympathy with people unlike her,
and a definitely limited range of experience'.[13] Such defects help to
sustain an almost Manichean vision of the world, in which those who
are not for her are crudely numbered among the forces of darkness,
and where every manifestation of opposition, doubt, or compromise
is liable to moral condemnation.

This is the atmosphere in which Mrs Thatcher has presented her
values as a radical challenge to the post-war British political
consensus, and not least to its language and the priorities of the
agenda. At the root of the malaise, as thus perceived, lay the policies
pursued by Attlee and his colleagues between 1945 and 1951 on the
basis of Keynesian economics (including a commitment to 'full
employment') and of Beveridge's positive approach to the challenge
of comprehensive welfare provision. Yet, as indicated by the growth
of 'Butskellism' over the next decade or so, subsequent Conservative
administrations proved more willing to adapt than properly to
dismantle the corporatist structures built by Labour. According to
the Thatcherite analysis, this indicates that Tories, too, had been
seduced into endorsing collectivist notions of social morality; that
they had mistakenly treated the Sirens of the new *bien pensant*
Butskellite establishment as the true interpreters of the people's
voice; that they had engaged in a pointless quest to find somewhere
between folly and common sense a still more profitable 'middle way';
and that consensus on those terms had amounted to a betrayal,
however unwitting, of authentic Conservative tradition. The party's
'wets' have of course had ample cause to wonder, conversely,
whether Mrs Thatcher's own counter-proclamation of the need for a
'conviction approach' might itself represent a far more significant

discontinuity in Tory development. Whatever the merits of that controversy, it is arguable that the Thatcher government installed in 1979 cannot take all the credit – or, viewed otherwise, all the blame – for eroding the Butskellite legacy. The latter's continuing appropriateness was already being called into question under the impact of the oil shock of 1973–4. In his provocative comparative study of the Anglo-American 'politics of decline', Joel Krieger observes that 'It was far easier before the political implications of the global recession of the 1970s were as obvious as they are today, and before Reagan and Thatcher, to be lulled by the seeming permanence of the thirty-year reign of Keynesianism'.[14] Moreover, as Ronald Butt stressed in his 1986 Summer Address to the Centre for Policy Studies, the advance of the fundamentalist Left within the Labour Party and the political behaviour of the trade unions between 1974 and 1979 have also to be accounted as major threats to the particular kind of consensus evolved since 1945.[15] James Callaghan's experiences at the hands of the International Monetary Fund in 1976 and over the issue of 'ungovernability' through the 1978–9 'winter of discontent' show how strong was the strain which inflation and union demands were already exerting on the old framework. The elements of continuity between his Labour administration and the early years of its Tory successor were greater than either party leadership found it comfortable to concede. 'The first UK monetarist government', Peter Jackson starkly declares, 'was, in fact, a Labour government'[16] – albeit with the important reservation that it moved into this posture less out of deep conviction than because of *force majeure*.

How, then, was Mrs Thatcher's own stance arrived at? The testimony assembled by Young and Sloman shows well just how early came the formation of her unwavering commitment to Conservatism: when she went on from Grantham to Oxford it was the only thing that her college principal found interesting about her, and its fervour was already such as to suggest her disbelief in the merits of mere consensus.[17] Even so, her route to power involved four years' service as a major spending minister, at Education, during which there was scant seismic trace of any distinctively Thatcherite volcano ahead. As Young and Sloman comment, 'In Mrs Thatcher's years of uncomplaining servitude to Ted Heath's quite different economic policy, the prejudices may have been latent, but the opinions went unexpressed. More than anything it was a political accident, the fall of the Heath government in 1974, which made her stock her mind with something new'.[18] If her instincts already urged her to have no further truck with

the ex-prime minister's Conservatism of technocratic compromise, her own formulation of an alternative strategy still required a great deal of more intellectual refinement. To that end, the 12 months preceding her victory in the party leadership contest of February 1975 seem to have been spent in quite intensive contact (personal or through their writings) with such mentors as Alfred Sherman, Alan Walters, and Friedrich von Hayek. Her path towards macroeconomic monetarism was, however, made harder by the habit which Peter Jay has described as that 'of preferring her grocer's daughter's micro-economic reflexes and values to any economic theory'.[19] All observers agree that the most crucial influence on her was exercised by Sir Keith Joseph who during those same months appears himself to have had the experience of being 'born again'. According to his own testimony: 'It was only in April 1974 that I was converted to Conservatism. I had thought that I was a Conservative but I now see that I was not one at all'.[20] When (to general surprise) it was Mrs Thatcher who emerged to challenge and trounce Mr Heath in the first round of the leadership ballot, Sir Keith Joseph was her sole front-bench supporter. It is clear that neither this triumph nor her still more decisive win over William Whitelaw in the second round, signified any general conversion of Conservative MPs to some conception of Thatcher*ism* which was, in any case, still only quite imperfectly formed.[21] David Butler and Dennis Kavanagh state: 'She was very much an intruder'; put another way (by Peter Riddell), she prevailed 'principally because she was not Edward Heath'.[22] At that point, as Christopher Patten recalls, 'it was much more a peasants' uprising than a religious war. It was seen much more as the overthrow of the tyrant king rather than as a great ideological shift'.[23] By the time of the Conservatives' return to power four years later this change of leadership had assumed, retrospectively, an altogether greater significance. It now portended a real possibility that through the 1980s it would be a radicalism of the Right, not of the Left, that would set the principal items of agenda in British politics.

RADICAL CONSERVATISM IN ACTION

The Labour defeat of 1979 gave Thatcherism its opportunity, not its national endorsement. As the Nuffield study of the election concluded, it was lost by the outgoing government rather than won by

the incoming opposition: 'The Conservatives were well placed to
catch the plum that fell into their laps. But it was the Labour
movement that shook it off the tree'.[24] Most of the task of
transforming attitudes thus still lay ahead. As premier, Mrs Thatcher
set herself objectives as radical as those which featured on Attlee's
agenda. In many ways her programme developed as a mirror image
of his, with Conservatism reassuming its proper function as a project
of reversal rather than as a lame endorsement of the fallacy of
inexorable unidirectional progress, and with a redefinition not just of
its methods but also of its fundamental goals. In Butt's words: 'If 1945
represented a constitutionally achieved revolution in political structure, 1979 began a constitutionally achieved counter-revolution'.[25]
There were lessons to be learned from the current experience of
Raymond Barre's administration in France (dating from 1976), but
the agenda of Mrs Thatcher's Conservatism proved still more
ambitious. 'What really mattered', Rudolf Klein observes 'was not
what the state did for the people, but what the people did for
themselves. For the first time since 1945 Britain actually had a
Government which took pride in stressing how little it could do,
instead of emphasizing how much it would do. Economic crisis had
created a minimalist political ideology in its own image, just as
economic growth had created a maximalist political ideology'.[26] In
practice, of course, the outcome has proved more complex – and,
indeed, very disappointing to many of the supporters who were naive
enough to take Mrs Thatcher entirely at her word. It is no simple
matter, especially under the international conditions of the late 20th
century, to fulfil a project of radical, counter-revolutionary, Conservatism according to such minimalist principles. However well-
intentioned the scheme of shrinkage, that radicalism may have to rely
– at many points and even into the medium term – upon a firm
dirigisme and some enhancement of executive power. Tension
between the values and the manner of their implementation is all the
more likely when leadership lies with a singularly forceful character
practising what Riddell calls 'a highly personalised style of government'.[27]

The paradoxically 'statist' elements in Thatcherism have been
recently interpreted by Krieger as less a means towards genuinely
minimalist ends than something altogether more intrinsic to the
phenomenon – and, indeed (within a quite different institutional
structure) also to its US correlate. For him the ways in which
President Reagan and Mrs Thatcher operate:

point to a theoretical blind spot – and raise crucial issues about
the political consequences of an unusual introjection of state
power... Both have used free market ideology as a potent
mechanism for taking politics above the traditional interplay of
interests, and both are the chief executives of powerfully *dirigiste*
states – states which are not readily subject to the arrangements of
the post-war settlement ... [or] the traditional interplay of
Keynesian coalitions.[28]

On this reading, with its attribution of calculatedly 'de-integrative'
strategies, the two leaders share the motto *divide et impera*. Certainly
in the specific British context those sceptical about taking all the
minimalist rhetoric at face value have supported their case by
interpreting Thatcherism as meaning, for example, an erosion of the
local authorities' capacity to act as a check upon the centralised
power (abolition of the GLC and the other metropolitan councils,
together with greater central control over financial and curricular
aspects of schooling) or a negative approach to issues of civil liberty
and 'open government' (treatment of Sarah Tisdall and Clive Ponting
in awkward contrast to that of the condoned Westland leakers).[29]

Mrs Thatcher's own performance can suggest, to a sympathetic
observer such as Martin Holmes, that she is 'not averse to the
exercise of the Prime Ministerial power right up to its legitimate
constitutional limits'; gauging her more harshly, as Michael Heseltine
did at the height of the Westland row in January 1986, she may even
be thought sometimes to go beyond them.[30] That affair confirmed
how Thatcherism's penchant for using authoritarian means towards
allegedly benign ends has manifested itself particularly in the
premier's conduct of Cabinet government. In the midst of the
Westland dispute, David Owen attacked her 'total contempt' for the
democratic basis of the Cabinet.[31] At the very least, as Peter
Hennessy's new and penetrating study makes plain, she conducts the
affairs of her 'Conviction Cabinet' in a radically different way from
Attlee's 'collecting the voices'.[32] During Mrs Thatcher's early period
of power the 'wet' wing of her party was strongly represented within
the senior ministerial team. By the eighth year, however, the balance
was different. The roster of the 'doubters' who had withdrawn or
been dismissed from the Cabinet had become impressive in quantity,
and even in quality. Mrs Thatcher has exploited with unusual
directness what Lord Bancroft calls 'the grovel count',[33] and has
attained an unusual measure of personal dominance over most of her

ministers. Her organization of key components in the mechanism of government – such as *ad hoc* groups being preferred to formal Cabinet committees, the enhanced role accorded to the Downing Street Private Office, and the ambiguous pluralism sustained in the functions allocated to Sir Robert Armstrong (which were complex enough even before his curious performance at the Sydney trial devoted to Peter Wright's book about MI5) – has been directed towards strengthening her scope for autonomous action. This has been most evident in regard to external affairs – as Peter Riddell has traced in general and as her own imperious handling (even post-Westland) of the anti-apartheid sanctions issue at the Commonwealth mini-summit of August 1986 has recently demonstrated.[34] Hennessy's conclusion that Mrs Thatcher has not yet (in Julian Critchley's idiom) 'handbagged' traditional Cabinet government beyond recognition needs to be balanced with the evidence which he has also accumulated to support his reasonable finding that she has nonetheless flouted much of its spirit and given its conventions their greatest hammering since the epoch of Lloyd George.[35]

The clearest declared objective for the exercise of the authority thus inherited or augmented has been economic recovery. Dismissing Keynes's distinction between the principles of domestic and national financing, Mrs Thatcher herself has never repented of preaching prosperity via 'the homilies of housekeeping or the parables of the parlour'.[36] Her approach has been most successful in two broad areas. While eschewing any formal incomes policy that might have enshackled her government to 'corporatist' collaboration with such bodies as the CBI and the TUC, Mrs Thatcher has managed to reduce the rate of inflation to a level approaching that of other leading economies. She has also made significant progress in her project of 'popular capitalism': growing home ownership (boosted particularly by council house sales), wider patterns of shareholding (especially as an effect of the privatization of state-run industry), and enlargement in the numbers of small businesses and of the self-employed. On the debit side, her government has so far failed to achieve its professed aim of cutting public spending – not least because it has also presided over huge growth in the ranks of those whose joblessness produces a direct charge on the social security budget as well as driving up less easily accountable costs in terms of illness, crime, social divisions, and a general deterioration of human capital. The Saatchi electoral slogan of 1979, 'Labour isn't working', stigmatized a figure of 1.2 million out of work; by late 1986

this had risen (despite regular reductive 'technical adjustments' of an increasingly ingenious kind) to around 3.2 million. Mrs Thatcher appeared to blame the administrations of James Callaghan, Harold Wilson, and indeed Edward Heath for helping to create the earlier situation, while absolving herself from any direct responsibility for the later and graver one. All her opponents find implausible the related denials, such as Martin Holmes endorses, that there is no significant trade-off between the drive towards lower inflation and a rise in unemployment, which has attained levels not explicable simply by world recession.[37] Some critics go much further, arguing that higher unemployment is actually *intended* to serve a positive function – the 'de-integrative' campaign, in Krieger's idiom – within the scheme of Thatcherism. Such a phenomenon, asserts John Hall, 'can ... be understood [only] in *political* rather than in purely economic terms. It is designed to restore the stick to capitalism by means of unemployment'.[38]

The central issue here has been the reduction in the power of the trade unions. Mrs Thatcher's own 'loathing' for them (James Prior's term)[39] has been expressed in her determination – at once political and economic – to legislate on such matters as picketing, the closed shop, and strike balloting, and to free government (as well as the market) from the inflationary blackmail constantly imposed by previous corporatist collaboration with the union 'barons'. If it is unfair to claim that her regime has created higher unemployment precisely for the purpose of undermining their resistance, the grave rate of joblessness has nonetheless proved a much bigger factor than any series of statutes in enabling Thatcherism to put the unions on the defensive, to prompt transformation in the attitudinal 'culture' of workers, and to restore to managers the right to manage. David Marquand is correct (for the present at least) in observing that, 'as in the 1930s, the *simpliste* notion that unemployment radicalizes the working class has turned out to be the reverse of the truth'.[40] Mrs Thatcher has enjoyed considerable success in appealing to rank-and-file unionists over the heads of their more extremist leaders. For that (and for much else) the miners' strike of 1984–5 was *locus classicus*.[41] The ability of the government (aided by its surrogate, Ian Mac-Gregor) to take on, divide, and defeat the NUM – Edward Heath's bane – was an indicator as to how far the climate of industrial relations had altered during the decade since Mrs Thatcher became Conservative leader. In Arthur Scargill she had an adversary every bit as inflexible and dedicated to 'conviction' approaches as herself,

and every bit as prepared to treat the struggle as a *political* matter of crucial significance, testing the effectiveness (even the legitimacy) of an extra-parliamentary defiance of the government. Between them, battle was conducted in a mode of reciprocally intensifying toughness. Her victory over him – and indirectly over a Labour Party leader whose stature was diminished as he ran out of fence to sit on with regard to such violence and intimidation as came from the striking miners' side rather than from other quarters – appears, for the immediate future, to have reduced the problem of 'ungovernability' to a secondary importance.

THE UNFINISHED REVOLUTION

To what extent, however, has Thatcherism succeeded in its wider and self-professed project of changing a nation's 'heart and soul'? How applicable still is the conclusion, reached by Ralf Dahrendorf in his 1982 Reith Lectures, that 'it is the cultural alienness of this approach which is most likely to defeat it'?[42] What store should be set by a patriotism which seems to involve the Procrustean project of racking the British into conformity with the American, or the German, or the Japanese work-ethic? How fair is Peter Shore's judgement of Thatcher herself, that 'she wins arguments, she defeats opponents, but she doesn't convince them'?[43] By June 1983 she had made such personal impact that, according to the Nuffield study, 'Thatcherism and Thatcherite . . . were the terms and ideas on which the election was fought'.[44] Their potency is suggested by the fact that the Conservatives disproved much conventional wisdom about a government's inability to earn re-election (let alone with a boosted majority, after a full term) under circumstances of record post-war unemployment. The outcome did indicate some change of mood – not least as embodied in a crushing repudiation of Labour. Even so, Mrs Thatcher's landslide majority of seats cannot be taken as any simple token of national conversion to her values. The 'Falklands factor' complicates judgement on that point, as does the surprisingly anodyne nature of the Conservative manifesto.[45] More generally, the familiar distorting elements in the electoral system itself were now compounded by the emergence of the Alliance as a second opposition element already capable of almost matching the 'official' one in its share of the gross vote. In 1979 it was the conduct of the Labour movement which was crucial in putting more than three million extra

votes on the Conservative tally; by 1983 that same movement had scored enough further 'own goals' to condemn itself to still graver defeat in a situation where the Tories were losing 700 000 of their own previous gain. Even allowing for the impact of tactical voting, the fall in Conservative support from 43.9 per cent to the level of 42.4 per cent – much better than 1974, but only 0.5 per cent above the share recorded against the adverse landslide in 1966 – indicated how incomplete the task of conversion yet was.

As another election approaches, the cynic might suggest that a Labour victory would, in the long run, do even more than a Conservative one to consolidate Thatcherism, if only through the paradoxical means of revealing how little by way of effective alternative Neil Kinnock's party has devised for the solution of Britain's problems and how deeply its constituency organization has been penetrated by extremists peddling radical socialist solutions which do not command any great measure of public sympathy.[46] For all the cosmetic unity displayed at its 1986 Party Conference, Labour may well not get the chance even of seeing whether it can cope with that particular risk. In 1983 it performed least badly among groups which do not exactly represent the wave of the future. As Ivor Crewe then commented: 'Council tenants are a slowly diminishing group; blacks are a tiny minority; and those over 65 will rapidly depart from the electorate'.[47] Meanwhile, a second term of Thatcherite rule has further (and quite intentionally) sapped Labour's old bases of power, whether in big-city local government, the municipal estates, nationalized industry, or the union movement. It has also effected shifts in public attitudes towards them, of a kind not easy to reverse. If it is to regain its position as a natural party of government rather than one merely of protest, Labour must rethink its message of collective compassion not in the terms proposed by Militant or Tony Benn but in a manner capable of appealing to an electorate increasingly composed of owner-occupiers earning their livelihoods outside older manufacturing industry and the public sector. To acknowledge this (as Mr Kinnock has at least begun to do) and to recognize that here is the kind of ground upon which the Alliance has staked its own claim for support, is simultaneously to appreciate that the influence of Thatcherism must now be gauged not just by the level of direct backing afforded to the Conservatives but also by the extent to which some of its lessons are becoming assimilated (tacitly or otherwise) into the assumptions of its rivals. The course of nego-tiations about patterns of power-sharing in any hung parliament

would provide a fascinating test as to how much of the old consensus still survives, and how much of a new one is forming around something so self-professedly uncompromising as Thatcherism itself. Another outright Conservative victory in 1987 or 1988 would be, on any reading, a remarkable achievement. Even so, to whatever degree it was again the product more of divided opposition under circumstances of exceptional electoral volatility than the result of any less ambiguous endorsement, it would indicate the incompleteness of conversion. In January 1985 Sir Geoffrey Howe declared: 'We have established a post-nationalization, post-trade union monopoly era, an era in which there is no longer a world-weary acceptance of national decline, and a dependent relationship between the individual and the state'.[48] If that claim is to be fully realized, then what does Thatcherism most need to do during any third term in order to sustain its drive towards completing a revolution in attitudes?

Pre-eminently, a third successive Conservative administration would have to show itself capable of delivering some substantial measure of economic recovery. But, for the purpose of vindicating Thatcherism as such, this cannot be just *any* kind of revival. It has to be undertaken along lines which do not represent some brand of covert retreat towards the former Keynesian consensus, and indeed along ones which remain broadly consistent with Mrs Thatcher's original radical alternative. Moreover, performance would certainly have to be better than that indicated, for example, by the forecasts issued in August and November 1986 from the National Institute for Economic and Social Research (NIESR): a record balance of payments deficit after the falling price and output of North Sea oil; a sharp rise in the PSBR; a slowing of growth; an increase in the rate of inflation and, above all, a failure to effect major reduction in unemployment (possibly down to a figure of 2.94 million by the end of 1987, but still hugely disquieting) will not help to change the minds of the unconverted.[49] It is also clear that Thatcherism needs to be seen as adopting (even beyond the pre-election period when market theory gets most directly applied to vote-buying) a less unsympathetic approach to the funding of those areas where adequate public provision is still generally expected by the nation. Its members have proved readier to tolerate the downgrading of Keynes's economic abstractions than the disfigurement of what they view as the more human face of Beveridge's achievement. Mr Kinnock observes: 'Yes, the political context has changed, and the basic British political context of patience, of tolerance, of compassion, not soft options at

all, in fact very tough virtues in British politics, are now being reasserted because of the shock to the system that came as a consequence of Mrs Thatcher's particular form of brutal approach'.[50] In this area of 'welfare' and related issues, those attitudes which Riddell calls her 'Finchley instincts'[51] (so well demonstrated in the leaked Think Tank papers of 1983) remain significantly at odds with the bulk of opinion. Pollsters record that most people still give higher priority to the maintenance of certain standards in essential public services than to compensatory tax reductions. Moreover, it is here perhaps that Richard Rose's argument about there being apparently 'very little difference between the maximum and the minimum amount of public spending that is politically tolerable' has its greatest cogency.[52] Even in Butt's sympathetic address to the CPS on the merits of Mrs Thatcher's performance, it was on this front that he issued the clearest warning about the temptation for her to make a future misjudgement: 'It must ... surely be a first task in a Conservative third term to establish a scale of priorities for the welfare state which puts real need first in respect of the services which the Government concludes must be kept under State management; and to find ways of hiving off responsibility, where that is feasible, without causing hardship'.[53] The establishment of that balance may prove the severest test as to how far the populist pretensions of Thatcherism eventually ring hollow.

The prime minister's critics believe that, already, such hollowness is plain. Even where they do see her reflecting populist promptings – as in her subtle exploitation of a racial xenophobia still widespread in British society – they tend to stigmatize these as the least defensible and ultimately most divisive form of sympathy with grass-roots opinion. More generally, Mrs Thatcher's opponents view inner-city rioting as the most concentrated distillation of perceived injustice, of violent response to a highly selective and 'de-integrative' application of the sacrifices attendant upon delayed gratification, of the politics of Envy enacting its counter-assault upon the politics of Greed. In Young and Sloman's collection, Roy Hattersley accuses Mrs Thatcher of 'a ruthless electoral strategy' aiming to exploit the material betterment of 55 per cent of the population while 'ignoring the 45 per cent whose conditions have deteriorated'; Peter Shore asserts that she has rendered class struggle more rancorous, having 'distributed opportunities and income without a blush in favour of those who are already on the top' while reducing the benefits available to those at the bottom; and Michael Meacher condemns 'a

system of values in which the rich are cosseted and the poor are penalized, in which competitiveness is exhorted without any regard for the losers'.[54] If they are right, Thatcherism has done little to encourage the ethos for an imaginatively flexible and truly united assault on the problems of a Britain which is now, even in the simple geographic terms of North and South, 'two nations'. More dispassionately, Charlot concludes that Mrs Thatcher – who does pride herself upon making a direct appeal to the whole people over and above conventional class allegiance, even if in terms foreign to the members of that centrist establishment (heirs to Butskellism) whom she so detests – has developed a certain brand of populism 'moulded by traditional bourgeois values, but ones which are no less capable of appealing to the lower middle classes and the elite of the British working class'.[55] Supporters go still further: they hark back to Mrs Thatcher's Grantham roots and, like John Selwyn Gummer, urge the belief that (contrary to what the British obstinately tell the opinion pollsters) she has 'a very natural understanding of what the people, the majority, the good hearted, the people who really care about the country, think'.[56] In bringing St Francis into the Conservative pantheon, she has not sought to displace Benjamin Disraeli. 'What I am desperately trying to do', she told an interviewer in February 1983, 'is create one nation, with everyone being a man of property, or having the opportunity to be a man of property'.[57] Against that we might weigh the judgement of James Prior who (even while acknowledging much of her achievement) doubts the legitimacy of her claim to be leading legatee of the Disraelian tradition: 'I think that the country is more divided now than it was, and I think that there is a penalty to be paid for all that. She isn't a One-Nation Conservative'.[58]

This criticism by a prominent 'wet' highlights one of the main senses in which (as Philip Norton argues more fully elsewhere in this volume, Chapter 2) Mrs Thatcher has still to complete the conversion of the party, alongside that of the nation. In so far as she embodies the 'suburbanization' of Conservatism,[59] it is true that she has a more natural constituency behind her than many predecessors as leader. She has certainly used her growing authority, according to Francis Pym, in such a way 'that all the other views which exist within the Conservative Party tend to be pushed to one side or ignored or turned down';[60] or, as Norman St John Stevas put it back in 1981, he had not expected to see the day 'when economic materialism could deck itself out in Tory colours and claim to be not only the authentic voice of conservatism but its only legitimate manifestation'.[61] How-

ever, despite Mrs Thatcher's qualities of dominance, the capacity for rising damp to endanger the fabric of her enterprise ought not to be underestimated. The alleged impregnability of her personal position after the 1983 election looked very much less convincing amidst the Westland ructions. In that context, it became plain even to her supporters that she was being – in a delicate phrase crafted by one of her closest associates on a still more recently embarrassing occasion – economical with the truth. The option of summoning 'the men in dark suits' to press for her withdrawal after the Heseltine–Brittan row seems to have been widely canvassed among Tory MPs possessed of only marginal (and by the time of the Ryedale by-election, what was *not* marginal?) majorities. Backbenchers and frontbenchers alike were caught in the dilemma of not knowing whether salvation lay in loyalty or in a prompt change of leadership. Whatever other conventions she may have shaken, there is no sign that Mrs Thatcher has prepared the party to be any less unforgiving than usual towards a leader who fails to deliver electoral victory. While she does retain power, there will be no frank acknowledgement of any major reversal of overall policy. But, even after the most ingenious casuistry, the Chancellor of the Exchequer's public spending statement of November 1986 could not be convincingly reconciled with the financial rigour of the once pristine 'dry' orthodoxy. At that date, the Cabinet still possessed (in such figures as Douglas Hurd, Kenneth Baker, Peter Walker and Kenneth Clarke) potentially articulate representatives of a 'balanced ticket'. These are politicians who, while claiming to eschew anything so sharp as a U-turn, might well be inclined to engineer – under opportune circumstances – a gentler but sustained curve towards new middle ground. Most crucial of all is the point that, if the Thatcherite revolution is to be fully sustained on its begetter's own terms, then the leadership must be transferred eventually to a disciple who will not react against her in the way that she 'handbagged' Mr Heath. Since Norman Tebbit has come to look daily less like a *dauphin*, and Sir Geoffrey Howe ever less like a *doctrinaire*, the problem of authentic succession remains both vital and unresolved.

At all events, it is only when the grocer's daughter from Grantham has been transformed into its Countess that we shall begin to get her record into overall focus. On that longer perspective, the exaggerations inherent both in the heroic and in the demonological interpretations of Mrs Thatcher's achievement – which it has been so tempting to endorse *in medias res* – are likely to become plainer than

they are now. Taking this broader view, subsequent chroniclers may come to see her efforts as essentially yet another variation on the longstanding theme of Britain's decline relative to other powers. Having tested these strivings by reference to the criterion most crucial to our present condition, they may thus well refuse to confer upon the outcome of her enterprise any really exceptional, any truly 'historic', status. But, if this does turn out to be the case, those same future commentators are also likely to have to concede, at the very least, that the period of Thatcherism's ascendancy did prove to be a particularly interesting phase in the story.

Notes

1. *The Times*, 'Diary', 31 January 1986; Terry Coleman interview, the *Guardian*, 24 July 1985.
2. Quoted in Peter Riddell, *The Thatcher Government*, revised edn (Oxford: Basil Blackwell, 1985) p. 7.
3. Hugo Young and Anne Sloman, *The Thatcher Phenomenon* (London: BBC, 1986) p. 20.
4. Young and Sloman, *The Thatcher Phenomenon* p. 21. The point about the experience of the 1930s is underlined by Patrick Middleton, 'For "Victorian", Read "Georgian": Mrs Thatcher Corrected', *Encounter*, July–August 1986: 5–9.
5. Interview of May 1981, quoted in Martin Holmes, *The First Thatcher Government, 1979–1983: Contemporary Conservatism and Economic Change* (Brighton, Wheatsheaf, 1985) p. 209.
6. *The Right Approach: A statement of Conservative aims* (London: Conservative Central Office, October 1976) p. 18.
7. *The Right Approach*, p. 18.
8. Keith Joseph and Jonathan Sumption, *Equality* (London: Murray, 1978) p. 61.
9. John Selwyn Gummer, in Young and Sloman, *The Thatcher Phenomenon*, p.83.
10. From the *Journeys to England and Ireland* (1833–5), as quoted in *The Right Approach*, p.12.
11. Monica Charlot, 'Doctrine et image: le thatchérisme est-il un populisme?', in Jacques Leruez (ed.), *Le Thatchérisme: Doctrine et action* (Paris: CNRS, 1985) p. 21.
12. Quoted in Young and Sloman, *The Thatcher Phenomenon*, p. 64, and Riddell, *The Thatcher Government*, p. 9. During the 1986 LSE conference discussion another female comparison was offered by Peter Hennessy, who referred to Mrs Thatcher as belonging to 'the Shirley Conran school of public administration'.
13. Quoted in Riddell, *The Thatcher Government*, p. 9; see also Young

and Sloman, *The Thatcher Phenomenon*, pp. 34, 79, 86–87, for similar comment by Francis Pym, Michael Meacher and David Steel.

14. Joel Krieger, *Reagan, Thatcher, and the Politics of Decline* (Cambridge: Polity, 1986) p. 189.

15. See Ronald Butt, *The Unfinished Task: the Conservative record in perspective* (London: CPS, 1986) pp. 11–13.

16. Peter Jackson, 'Policy Implementation and Monetarism: Two Primers', in Peter Jackson (ed.), *Implementing Government Policy Initiatives: The Thatcher Administration, 1979–83* (London: Royal Institute of Public Administration, 1985) p. 29. The classic (and early) statement of warning by Callaghan as premier can be found in the Labour Party's *Report of the Annual Conference 1976*, p. 188.

17. See Young and Sloman, *The Thatcher Phenomenon*, pp. 17–19.

18. Young and Sloman, *The Thatcher Phenomenon*, p. 59. Alan Walters's own account of the upshot, given from the viewpoint of a close adviser, is contained in his study, *Britain's Economic Renaissance: Margaret Thatcher's Reforms, 1979–1984* (Oxford: Oxford University Press, 1986).

19. 'In Search of the Thatcher Factor', *Times Literary Supplement*, 30 May 1986, p. 580.

20. Quoted in David Butler and Dennis Kavanagh, *The British General Election of 1979* (London: Macmillan, 1980) p. 64n.

21. See Butler and Kavanagh, *The British General Election of 1979*, pp. 62–4, for a succinct and authoritative coverage of the contest.

22. Butler and Kavanagh, *The British General Election of 1979*, p. 64; Riddell, *The Thatcher Government*, p. 21.

23. Quoted in Young and Sloman, *The Thatcher Phenomenon*, p. 33.

24. Butler and Kavanagh, *The British General Election of 1979*, p. 340.

25. Butt, *The Unfinished Task*, p. 13.

26. Rudolf Klein, 'Health Policy, 1979 to 1983: The Retreat from Ideology?', in Jackson, (ed.) *Implementing Government Policy*, p. 189.

27. Riddell, *The Thatcher Government* p. 55; see Jackson (ed.), *Implementing Government Policy* for the problems of 'implementation' in general.

28. Krieger, *Reagan, Thatcher* pp. 33–4.

29. See, for example, Mike Goldsmith, 'The Conservatives and Local Government, 1979 and after', in David S. Bell (ed.), *The Conservative Government, 1979–84: An Interim Report* (London: Croom Helm, 1985) pp. 142–57; Clive Ponting, *The Right to Know: The Inside Story of the Belgrano Affair* (London: Sphere, 1985).

30. Holmes, *The First Thatcher Government*, p. 208; for the issues raised in Heseltine's resignation press conference, see *The Times*, 10 January 1986. Note also, generally, the Defence Select Committee Report, *Westland PLC: The Government's Decision-Making* (London: HMSO, 1986).

31. Quoted in the *Financial Times*, 11 January 1986.

32. See Peter Hennessy, *Cabinet*, (Oxford: Basil Blackwell, 1986) Chapter 3 (note especially the interview with David Howell, pp. 95–8), and the same author's contribution to the present volume, chapter 4.

33.   Young and Sloman, *The Thatcher Phenomenon*, p. 45.
34.   See Riddell, *The Thatcher Government*, Chapter 10. On sanctions against South Africa, note Geoffrey Smith's observation (*The Times*, 5 August 1986): 'She defied not only the other six heads of government but also the spirit of what her Cabinet had decided last week'.
35.   See Hennessy, *Cabinet*, p. 122.
36.   Her words at the Lord Mayor's Banquet of November 1982, quoted in Riddell, *The Thatcher Government*, p. 7.
37.   See Holmes, *The First Thatcher Government*, Chapter 4; and compare Riddell, *The Thatcher Government*, pp. 91–2.
38.   John A. Hall, *Powers and Liberties: The Causes and Consequences of the Rise of the West* (Harmondsworth: Penguin, 1986) pp. 176–7.
39.   See Young and Sloman, *The Thatcher Phenomenon*, pp. 72–3.
40.   David Marquand, '"Fire, fire", be it in Noah's Flood', *Government and Opposition*, 20, (4), Autumn 1985, p. 512; and see, generally, Jean-Pierre Ravier, 'Mme Thatcher et les syndicats', in Leruez (ed.), *Le Thatchérisme* pp. 57–68.
41.   See Riddell, *The Thatcher Government*, pp. 263–15 for a brief and sensible overall assessment of its significance. Note also Ian Mac-Gregor (with Rodney Tyler), *The Enemies Within: The Story of the Miners' Strike, 1984–5* (London: Collins, 1986).
42.   Ralf Dahrendorf, *On Britain* (London: BBC, 1982) p. 165.
43.   Quoted in Young and Sloman, *The Thatcher Phenomenon*, p. 136.
44.   David Butler and Dennis Kavanagh, *The British General Election of 1983* (London: Macmillan, 1984) pp. 1–2.
45.   See Butler and Kavanagh, *The British General Election of 1983*, pp. 38–41, 293–4. For a memorable and spirited assault on the tone of all three major Manifestos, see John Carey, 'The Strange Death of Political Language', the *Sunday Times*, 5 June 1983.
46.   See Robert Kilroy-Silk, *Hard Labour* (London: Chatto & Windus, 1986).
47.   Quoted in Krieger, *Reagan, Thatcher* p. 195.
48.   Quoted in Riddell, *The Thatcher Government*, p. 247.
49.   For summary of the NIESR predictions, see *The Times*, 21 August and 27 November 1986.
50.   Quoted in Young and Sloman, *The Thatcher Phenomenon*, p. 138.
51.   Riddell, *The Thatcher Government*, p. 136.
52.   Richard Rose, 'Changing the Prescription', the *Times Higher Educational Supplement*, 6 May 1986.
53.   Butt, *The Unfinished Task*, p. 24. For a stimulating review of the more general issues, see the special issue of *Government and Opposition*, 20, (3), Summer 1985, edited by Geraint Parry under the title 'Welfare State and Welfare Society'.
54.   Quoted in Young and Sloman, *The Thatcher Phenomenon*, pp. 85, 89, 133.
55.   'Doctrine et image', in Leruez (ed.), *Le Thatchérisme*, p. 21.
56.   Quoted in Young and Sloman, *The Thatcher Phenomenon*, p. 89.
57.   To Hugo Young, quoted in Holmes, *The First Thatcher Government*, p. 210.

58.   Quoted in Young and Sloman, *The Thatcher Phenomenon*, p. 141; and
      see, generally, James Prior, *A Balance of Power* (London: Hamish
      Hamilton, 1986).
59.   See Krieger, *Reagan, Thatcher*, p. 63.
60.   Quoted in Young and Sloman, *The Thatcher Phenomenon*, p. 55; and
      see, generally, Francis Pym, *The Politics of Consent* (London: Hamish
      Hamilton, 1984).
61.   Quoted in Holmes, *The First Thatcher Government*, p. 79.

2 Mrs Thatcher and the Conservative Party: Another Institution 'Handbagged'?

Philip Norton

One undisputed growth industry under the present government has been the study of the character and ideology of the prime minister. The premiership of James Callaghan provoked one biography, and nothing on 'Callaghanism'.[1] Margaret Thatcher, since becoming leader of the Conservative Party, has provoked several biographies, and her premiership has been the subject of numerous analyses.[2] 'Thatcherism' is regularly agonised about, analysed, criticized and – far less often – defined.

From the burgeoning literature, there appears widespread (if not complete) acceptance of three propositions. First, that Mrs Thatcher has changed significantly the nature of political debate in Britain. Second, that she has dominated the Cabinet and fought to impose her will upon government policy. Third, that she has sought to reform the structures that determine or affect the implementation of policy. Institutions (not least the civil service) are potential obstacles to the realization of her radical vision. As a consequence, declares Julian Critchley, 'she cannot see an institution without hitting it with her handbag'.[3] Though few challenge the extent to which she has changed the nature of debate,[4] there is much confusion as to the extent to which substance has matched the rhetoric. Has the policy of the government been wholly and truly 'Thatcherite'? Has it had the effect desired in terms of the nation's economic performance? Have the processes of government been remodelled in order to allow a radical policy to be implemented with vigour and faith? Ultimately, has Mrs Thatcher moulded a form of politics that will allow her goal of a neo-liberal society to be realized – and to outlive her occupancy of Downing Street?

These are all important questions. But in the rush to answer them, one significant question has gone largely unexplored. What effect has

Mrs Thatcher had upon the Conservative Party itself? If 'Thatcherism' is to outlive the premiership of its eponymous progenitor, then the one essential body which needs to be moulded – in attitude, structure and composition – in the Thatcher image is the Conservative Party. There appears to be a common assumption that the party has been – indeed, must have been – so moulded. Mrs Thatcher has battled to effect changes in the processes and very nature of British government. During the past twelve years, the Conservative Party has undergone significant changes. Is it not therefore plausible to assume that those changes have been the product of Mrs Thatcher's determined leadership, wielding the formidable powers available to her as a leader? In short, has not the party itself been 'handbagged'? So plausible does this line of reasoning appear that no major study has been devoted to testing it.

Such neglect is understandable, but dangerous. For if the Conservative Party has not been crafted into a vehicle that will carry the message of Thatcherism independently of Mrs Thatcher's leadership, then the impact of Mrs Thatcher on the politics of the 1990s will be much less than many analysts assume. The 'Thatcher phenomenon' – to take the title of Young and Sloman's book on the subject – will prove to be precisely that, and no more.

The purpose of this chapter, then, is to explore the relationship between the Conservative Party *qua* political organization and its present leader. The starting point is to question existing assumptions. In terms of the relationship between leader and led, in terms of organizational infrastructure, and in terms of its composition and attitudes, the Conservative Party has undergone some change (though not as much as some writers appear to believe, and not to the extent that it can be described as transformative); but to ascribe the label of 'dependent variable' to Mrs Thatcher's leadership in explaining such change is to misunderstand the pressures at work. Mrs Thatcher has had some effect upon the party (not least its infrastructure at a national level), but the most significant changes have been the product of disparate pressures upon – not from – Mrs Thatcher, some of which have emanated from within, others from outside, the party itself. The relationship is far more complex and subtle than may be inferred from the existing literature.

In order to explicate the relationship between Mrs Thatcher and the party, and to assess the effect which she has had upon it, we must consider the three questions implicit in the preceding paragraph. First, has Mrs Thatcher changed fundamentally (or at least signific-

antly) the traditional *relationship* that exists between leader and led? Second, has Mrs Thatcher changed fundamentally (or at least significantly) the *organization* of the party? Third, has Mrs Thatcher changed fundamentally (or at least significantly) the *nature* of the party in terms of its composition and attitudes? None of these questions prompts a clear, unambiguous positive response.

THE RELATIONSHIP BETWEEN LEADER AND LED

In keeping with its principles and perceptions of society, the Conservative Party is hierarchical. Great power is vested in the leader. The leader is the fount of all policy. All other bodies within the party serve in an advisory capacity. The leader exercises the power of appointment and dismissal of members of the front bench and of Central Office. Such powers are without parallel in other parties. In the exercise of such powers, some detachment between the leader and the party faithful is assumed. Given this, 'monarchical' or 'Hobbesian' models of party leadership appear plausible.[5] The leader exercises great power, largely free of interference from below; only in the event of demonstrable failure is the leader removed. The leadership style of Mrs Thatcher, seemingly dragging the party along in the wake of her dynamic leadership, would seem to reinforce the utility of such models.

However, both models fail to incorporate adequately the extent of the interdependence of leader and led. Each element of the party has particular tasks to fulfil, but each depends on the others in order to carry out its responsibilities. This interdependence within a hierarchical framework is best subsumed within a 'family' model of leadership.[6] Such a model accords more fully than do other models with the basic tenets of Conservative belief. It draws attention to the subtle nature of the party, emphasizing that – analogous to the family – a natural hierarchy exists, in which deference should be accorded to the older, more experienced members of the party (mechanistic head-counting having little relevance in reaching conclusions); that its smooth running depends on the maintenance of both order and social unity; and that the position of head carries with it not only rights but also important responsibilities. The head may possess the right to have the final say, but there exists the responsibility of taking into account the interests of the 'family' as a whole, interests which may be clear or which may be realized by taking the advice of, or

listening to, the other members of the household.

Is not the usefulness of this model challenged by the experience of 'monarchical' leadership under Mrs Thatcher? The answer is: 'No'. For one thing, the question derives from a false premise. Mrs Thatcher's leadership style is born not of strength in relation to her government, but of relative weakness. She enjoys a less compliant Cabinet than did Edward Heath as prime minister; hence her attempts both to by-pass it and to root out dissidents. For another, it ignores the most significant modification in the relationship between the leader and her party – the increased dependence of the leader on the support of her parliamentary party. Far from operating on a plane way above the interests and concerns of her parliamentary troops, Mrs Thatcher has had to busy herself with ensuring their continued goodwill and support. Ironically, the need to do so is a legacy of the Heath period of leadership.

As party leader (and more especially as prime minister) Edward Heath adopted an imperious manner of leadership on a scale not matched either by his immediate predecessors or by his successor. Decisions were taken alone or in conjunction with a few senior colleagues; those decisions were then taken to Cabinet, where they were ratified without demur[7] (only Margaret Thatcher and Geoffrey Rippon raised occasional voices of dissent). Of greater significance, Mr Heath's stance in relation to his back-benchers was even more Olympian. Supporters on the back-benches were taken for granted; dissidents were ignored or frozen out.[8] No attempt was made to garner support either at the intellectual level of explaining the need for particular policies (or the need for policy reversals, as with the U-turns on industrial aid and the economy in 1972) or at the personal level of cultivating friendships. This disseveration of the normal relationship between party leader and parliamentary supporters led, initially, to an upsurge in intraparty dissent in the division lobbies[9] and, eventually, to the removal of the leader being engineered by the parliamentary party; Mr Heath became not only the first leader to be chosen by election rather than 'emergence', but also the first to be removed by vote of the parliamentary party.

The legacy of the Heath leadership for Mrs Thatcher has been twofold. First, as a consequence of the election rules agreed by the parliamentary party in 1975, she is subject to annual re-election as leader, even when the party is in office. Though the chances of a leader's being voted out while in residence at No. 10 are exceedingly remote (almost as remote as being involuntarily forced out under the

old procedure, popular perceptions to the contrary notwithstanding),[10] the threat of a candidate standing against the incumbent can prove damaging to the party's image. It is thus something that party managers seek to avoid. This gives some modest leverage to dissidents within the parliamentary party and was something they were prepared to contemplate in 1981 and 1985.[11] Second (and more pervasively), there is the need to cultivate support among one's natural supporters who, since the Heath era, have maintained their willingness to enter the 'No' lobby when their conscience, ideology, or constituency pressures so dictate.[12] Given Mrs Thatcher's enthusiasm for avoiding the sins of her predecessor (in terms both of policy and leadership style), it is a cultivation which she has been willing to undertake.

Since 1979, she has maintained close contact with back-benchers. In her first term in office, she met regularly on a rota basis with the officers of the party committees. Ministers were encouraged to discuss policy proposals with the relevant committee. Any disquiet on the back-benches was monitored and reported by the Whips and, most notably, by Mrs Thatcher's Parliamentary Private Secretary, Ian Gow: 'If you mentioned anything to him you'd get a letter from the PM a couple of days or so later'.[13] The prime minister took time to be seen in the Commons' tea and dining rooms.[14] Back-benchers have variously attested to the fact that she was – and is – a good listener.[15] Concessions were variously made to dissenters.[16] In the wake of the 1983 election victory, Mrs Thatcher appears not to have maintained such close contact with back-benchers; for one thing, there are far more of them, and for another she now has a PPS with less acute political antennae than Mr Gow. Lack of sensitivity to back-bench feeling on the Shops Bill and on Commons' procedure and research allowances has produced defeats for the government;[17] on other occasions Mrs Thatcher and her business managers have seen the danger looming and made concessions before matters reached the floor of the House. However, despite various ructions, Mrs Thatcher's awareness of her power base has resulted in her working to maintain the loyalty of her back-benchers. As one (far from loyal) back-bencher has conceded: 'she has more support on the back-benches, which is her natural constituency, than any other party leader I have known'.[18]

As for the relationship between the leader and the party outside Parliament, that remains largely unchanged. Party activists defer to the leadership, policy-making being seen as the preserve of the leader

and her advisers. Loyalty flows naturally to the leader. Mr Heath retained the overwhelming support of the constituency parties until the parliamentary party displaced him, loyalty then flowed to the new leader.[19] Such loyalty, however, is contingent, not certain. Local parties serve to provide effective support services to ensure the return of Conservative candidates; in return, they look to the leadership to provide success in office and to be sensitive to the work they do. Mrs Thatcher has proved as sensitive to party needs as her predecessors (indeed, probably more so). Mr Heath began the practice of attending proceedings at the party conference, as opposed to turning up solely to deliver the leader's address at the end; it is a practice which Mrs Thatcher has maintained. As leader, Mrs Thatcher has done little to undermine – rather, has reinforced – the relationship between leader and party faithful. The strength of that relationship is demonstrated clearly each year at the party conference, both in its public manifestation and in the less public arena of the tea rooms and social gatherings where the leader and her lieutenants do the rounds of the party's foot troops. Mrs Thatcher engages the affection of supporters in a way that her cold, aloof predecessor was unable to do.

The advantage of applying the family model of leadership is that, though far from a perfect fit, it allows of some flexibility in the relationship between leader and led. Some change in relationship can occur not only from one leader to another but also during a particular period of leadership. What Malcolm Rutherford has aptly characterized as Mr Heath's stern, puritanical leadership[20] – rather akin to the upright Victorian father – was not unique in the history of the party, but it proved finally inappropriate in the context of a parliamentary party that, in the wake of electoral defeat, was no longer prepared to be taken for granted.[21] Recognizing more clearly the nature of the party, Mrs Thatcher has proved sensitive to the needs of her constituency. Far from striking out to create a new form of leadership, she has proved a responder rather than an initiator and sought to restore rather than remove the traditional harmony and interdependence that characterizes the relationship.

ORGANIZATION

If there has been no fundamental change in the relationship between the leader and the led, has not Mrs Thatcher utilized her powers as leader to restructure the party organization and to create a machine

geared to ensuring a neo-liberal hegemony within the party? The answer to the first part of the question is a qualified 'Yes'; the second half suggests a misreading of the way the party in reality operates.

Following Mrs Thatcher's election to the leadership in 1975, Central Office was reorganized. Senior staff were subject to changed responsibilities and in some cases their services were dispensed with. The motivation for these changes was political. Central Office was seen as an instrument of the outgoing leader. 'Heathite' personnel – notably the Director-General, Michael Woolf – were rooted out.[22] A similar motivation prompted a circumscribing of the role of the Conservative Research Department. Physically, it was moved from Old Queen Street to the confines of Smith Square. In policy formulation, it was accorded a less central role than before; though it remained important,[23] greater reliance was placed by Mrs Thatcher on her own creation, the Centre for Policy Studies (CPS) and similarly sympathetic bodies.

Such changes were neither exceptional nor exhaustive. Given the use made of Central Office by Mr Heath, who not only brought in supportive personnel (as was his prerogative), but also exercised tight control of the Candidates' List,[24] it would have been remarkable if Mrs Thatcher had not made the changes she did. Under her leadership, political control of selection for the Candidates' List appears to have been less rigorous than under Mr Heath (though the process itself has been made more extensive and professional);[25] the Research Department has regained some of its lost status.[26]

To mention only the changes consequent upon political demand would be to present an incomplete picture. Central Office was also slimmed down and has been subject to various administrative reorganizations – the most recent being in 1986 – for reasons of economy and efficiency. Limited financial resources (the two 1974 elections placed a significant burden on the party's finances and in 1984 the deputy chairman described the party's financial position as 'brittle') have provided the principal motivation for a streamlining of the party's central machinery. Within the context of limited resources, efficiency has been the goal in order to achieve the principal purpose of Central Office: that is, to operate as a support and communication unit. It is less concerned with the substance of policy than with its presentation. If the party's message appears not to be getting across, shifts in personnel and responsibility take place (as with the sideways move of Harvey Thomas to be director of presentation in 1986). Recognition of this primary role is essential to

understanding the relations between Central Office and constituency parties.

There is a close interdependence between the party's professional machinery housed in Central Office and the voluntary workers in the constituencies. Central Office looks to the local parties to maintain an effective and efficient electoral machine; local parties look to Central Office for professional support in carrying out that task. Each depends on the other; if one fails to deliver the goods, complaints are heard from the other.

Though the appointment of the party chairman is within the gift of the party leader, the appointee has a responsibility to local parties. They look to the chairman to fulfil two (not always compatible) roles: as a senior spokesman for the party organization within the government's ranks, preferably at Cabinet level; and as an effective organizer and morale booster. The two roles are often accommodated by giving the chairman a Cabinet post without portfolio, such as the Chancellorship of the Duchy of Lancaster (the post presently held by Norman Tebbit). If either role is neglected, criticism emanates from the constituencies. Mrs Thatcher's first two chairmen rated as successes. Lord Thorneycroft was a senior politician who spent much of his time at his Central Office desk. Cecil Parkinson proved good as both organizer and communicator; he was a close confidant of the Prime Minister and was credited with helping mastermind the 1983 election victory. The two most recent chairmen have proved less successful. John Selwyn Gummer was heavily criticized for lacking sufficient political clout to represent the interests of the party organization to the leader; his organizational skills were also not widely appreciated. Norman Tebbit carries political clout, but has not proved an effective morale booster (hence the injection, albeit short-lived, of Jeffrey Archer as deputy chairman); criticism has also been heard of the failure of Central Office effectively to convey the party's message.

Criticism in this relationship has not been one-sided. Constituency parties guard their autonomy jealously. It is not easy for Central Office to impose its will on voluntary local associations. There are times when, clearly, it would like to, not least in order to ensure a better allocation of resources. Well-funded associations in safe seats are often unwilling to release resources (in money or manpower) to assist in constituencies which are marginal and under-resourced. Seats which need them often lack full-time agents. As electoral machines, some local parties have been allowed to atrophy, either

because the seat is considered unwinnable or because it is considered unloseable. Central Office has made a number of attempts to rectify the position, by cajoling local parties or on occasion by seeking to impose greater central direction. In the mid-1970s an attempt was made to have agents employed by Central Office rather than by local parties; the attempt failed ostensibly because of financial constraints. More recently (in the wake of poor local election results and the by-election loss in Portsmouth South), the party chairman instituted an audit of local parties, designed to elicit details of finance and activity.[27] The purpose was primarily to identify areas of weak organization so that central resources could then be directed to those areas. Even so, it was an exercise that invited suspicion within local associations and did little to dent their traditional autonomy. (The problems facing Central Office in such an exercise were summarized by one parliamentary candidate. When asked what local associations did in response to requests for membership figures, he replied, pithily: 'They lie'.)[28] Recent calls for greater political activity and more money-raising[29] have also encountered a less than enthusiastic response from some party activists. Some associations dislike being chivvied by Central Office when, in return, they receive (in their estimation) insufficient back-up services and little information on how their money is being spent.

Both professional and voluntary wings have, however, recognized in recent years the value of new technology. Both have extended their use of computers and word processors, especially useful in undertaking mass mailings and facilitating regular subscription renewals. The use of such technology has been given added urgency as a result of developments external to the party. The rise of the technology-oriented Social Democratic Party provided a spur to making greater use of computers. More recently, awareness that the Labour Party under General Secretary Larry Whitty was making rapid progress in the use of computer technology acted as a further spur. Central Office has made efforts to keep abreast of (if possible, to be ahead of) the other parties in developing computer-generated mailings to targeted audiences. Early in 1986, a new Special Services Department – with particular responsibility for computers and direct mail – was set up under Sir Christopher Lawson. It was expected that in 1986-7 three million voters would have been reached by direct mail. Constituency parties have also sought to make greater use of such techniques. Probably about a quarter of constituency parties now have computer facilities.

The main activity of both Central Office and constituency associations over recent years has thus been geared to maintaining an effective and – with increasingly limited resources – efficient electoral machine. Clearly, maintenance of an effective organization to fight elections is a major concern of the leadership, but it is not something with which Mrs Thatcher has concerned herself in any consistent way. Her concerns as prime minister are with policy, administration and ensuring her support within the party. If there are problems with the party organization (for instance, a chairman unpopular with the party in the country), she can step in (either to remove him, as with Mr Gummer in 1985, or to support him, as with Mr Tebbit in 1986). But her position is essentially a responsive one, analogous to having to make adjustments to a ship's course through the occasional touch on the tiller. She determines the direction in which the ship should be going; the crew is concerned to make sure that the vessel remains seaworthy. Organizationally, Mrs Thatcher has not made any fundamental changes. Such alterations as have occurred, especially those likely to endure (such as the use of computer technology), have been made in response to developments external to the party and motivated by the principal aim of the party organization: electoral success.

THE NATURE OF THE PARTY

If 'Thatcherism' is to survive Mrs Thatcher's incumbency, the main change would need to be in the basic nature of the party – that is, in its attitudes and its composition. Has there been a sea-change in the thinking of party members? Has the type of person that now occupies leadership positions changed?

The answer to both questions is generally assumed to be: 'Yes'. Again, the line of reasoning appears plausible. As leader, Mrs Thatcher determines party policy. She has enunciated a neo-liberal policy. The party clearly supports the leader. Therefore, is not the party wedded to a neo-liberal philosophy? Many, including senior figures within the party, seem to accept this line of argument. According to Francis Pym, 'she's certainly got the Tory Party very much into her way of thinking'.[31] This, however, is to misread the position.

The relationship between leader and led, as already outlined, is one of loyalty to the leader in return for 'successful' leadership and sensitivity to the activists' existence. The philosophy espoused by the

leader, so long as it is within the broad contours of Conservative belief, is essentially of secondary importance; loyalty flows to the leader *qua* leader. Hence the capacity of the party outside Parliament to shift its support to Mrs Thatcher in the wake of Mr Heath's withdrawal from the leadership contest after the first ballot in 1975.

In terms of policy – and particularly in terms of economic policy – the party both in parliament and outside is best described as agnostic. Only a small proportion of the parliamentary party can be labelled as committed 'wets' or 'dries'. In the parliaments of the 1970s, there were probably no more than 30 or so Conservative MPs who were diehard neo-liberals.[32] The general elections of 1979 and 1983 increased their number (though there were losses as well as gains), but left them still a minority of the parliamentary party. Peter Riddell has estimated that, in the Parliament returned in 1983, there are approximately 80 to 100 Members committed to a free market and monetarist position on economic issues (that is, roughly one-quarter or less of the parliamentary party); he adds, significantly: 'one hesitates to describe them as Thatcherites, since Mrs Thatcher herself does not take a clear-cut or consistent view on these matters. There is, however, probably a group of roughly this size which is closely in tune with her broad social outlook and identifies clearly with her and her aspirations'.[33] Even this figure I would treat as a generous estimate. The number of 'wets' is given by Riddell as about 40 to 60, which again may be erring slightly on the side of generosity; about 30 MPs are identified with the Centre Forward group established by Francis Pym.[34] The remainder – the bulk – of the parliamentary party have, as Riddell fairly observes, no such firm commitment. Indeed, even in the Cabinet the largest single group 'can best be described as comprising men of office – loyal but not zealots'.[35] Support within the parliamentary party is dependent less on ideological purity than on a demonstration of competent and successful government. If the government's economic policy starts to falter, the knights of the shire show signs of wavering (as happened in 1981 and, to a lesser extent, in 1985); if its credibility as a competent government is dented, a similar wavering occurs (as happened at the beginning of 1986 at the height of the Westland affair). On these occasions, Mrs Thatcher's leadership became a topic of discussion.

A similar distribution of opinion may be discerned within the party outside parliament, though with the economic agnostics even more to the fore. This is not to say that Mrs Thatcher has failed to strike a chord among the party faithful. She has, but the nature of that appeal

rests little on her economic philosophy. Mrs Thatcher is an economic liberal by intellectual persuasion. She is a Combative Tory at heart.[36] She believes Conservative beliefs are worth fighting for; and many of these beliefs – on law and order for example – are essentially Tory. She elicits a responsive chord from the party faithful at the annual conference not because of any oratory on the money supply but on account of her partisan feistiness; and also through little touches, such as applauding when calls for a restoration of the death penalty are made. It is an approach appreciated by the party activists, who have given their time and commitment to fighting the good fight for the party in the constituencies. As long as Mrs Thatcher continues to deliver success in government she will continue to have standing ovations, which will arise as much from the desire of the participants as from stage management.

Has there, then, been any underlying change in the composition of the party that might suggest a gradual growth of the neo-liberal element? Is the growth of the neo-liberal contingent in the parliamentary party, relative to the situation in the 1970s, likely to continue? The simple answer would appear to be: 'No'. At the extremes, the party has little to fear from 'entryism'. In the late 1960s and early 1970s there was the occasional problem of attempted takeovers of particular constituencies by Monday Clubbers (dubbed by Harold Wilson 'the skinheads of Surbiton'); today, there is the problem of 'libertarians' within the Federation of Conservative Students (FCS) (and, to some extent, within the Young Conservatives). Such activists operate at the periphery of the party and have done little to affect thinking within the party or to occupy positions of much significance: 'The FCS has some outlandish members, a few louts and some thinkers whose thoughts are unlikely to find their way into Conservative party manifestoes'.[37] The committed neo-liberals have sought instead to work through the medium of groups that are in empathy with current government policy but are not themselves allied formally to the Conservative Party, notably the Centre for Policy Studies, the Institute of Economic Affairs, and the Adam Smith Institute. Through such groups they have been able to influence the thinking of the present leader, but (lacking any institutional base within the Conservative Party) they have no assured basis on which to influence her successors. Support for economic liberalism within the parliamentary party is probably now at a peak, thanks to the results of the 1983 general election. That helped swell the ranks of the committed neo-liberals. Even so, neo-

liberals constituted a minority of the new intake; of the 101 Conservatives returned for the first time, only about 20 or so appear to be implacable 'dries' (even two of these allowed other influences to overcome their economic liberalism and vote against the Shops Bill in 1986).[38] A more significant characteristic of the new intake appears to be attachment to the local community. Assuming a loss of seats at the next general election, the number of neo-liberals in the parliamentary party will decline. Of the thirteen Conservative MPs who authored the 1985 pamphlet *No Turning Back*, ten were returned for the first time in 1983; of these, five sit for marginal seats. A survey published in the *Independent* in November 1986 found that only two 'avowed Thatcherites' had been selected as candidates to replace retiring Conservative MPs: 'While the sample was too small to provide conclusive proof about the shape of the Tory party after the General Election, it indicated that apart from a couple of exceptions the next generation of Mrs Thatcher's troops may hold roughly similar views to the old Tory squires they are replacing.' There is thus little empirical evidence to sustain the thesis that there is a long-term growth of the neo-liberal wing of the party.

Is there any long-term change in the socio-economic composition of the party? There is, but it is a change which predates Mrs Thatcher's leadership and, in the context of the present discussion, is largely irrelevant. The parliamentary party is now more markedly middle-class than it was earlier in the century when the landed classes were more strongly represented.[39] There is, however, no obvious correlation between socio-economic background and either ideological leanings or parliamentary behaviour. Independent parliamentary behaviour (or lack of it) would appear to be explained by factors of psychology and ideology rather than sociology. The occupational background of MPs elected in 1979 showed 'no fundamental change compared with the background of those elected earlier in the seventies',[40] and the new intake of 1983 demonstrates little unity in socio-economic terms. As for the party outside Parliament, observation suggests little significant change. Those attending party conferences in the 1980s appear similar to those attending in the 1960s;[41] indeed, they are sometimes precisely the same people.

CONCLUSION

Mrs Thatcher enjoys the loyalty and support of the party which she

leads. However, that support is contingent, not certain. Further-
more, it flows to her by virtue of the position she holds, not because
of the philosophy which she embraces. As leader, she has had a
tremendous impact upon the party and the wider polity; that is
undeniable. What she has not done, however, is to mould the
Conservative Party in such a way that it will carry 'Thatcherism'
independently of her leadership. That she has not done so is not
unduly surprising.

When Mrs Thatcher became leader, she did so 'without any close
knowledge of how the party machine functions'.[42] Her orientation
was essentially parliamentary. Within two years of entering parliament she was a junior minister and has never been off the
Conservative front-bench since then. Like most of her predecessors,
she has never held senior office within the party organization outside
Parliament (indeed, the only 20th-century leader to have held such
office was Neville Chamberlain).[43] Though she is not unfamiliar with
the party infrastructure, concern with party organization has hence
never manifested itself as a primary feature of her political life.

Second, and more important, the nature of her powers as leader
dictate that she cannot definitively bestow her beliefs on her
successors. In terms of policy formation, the leader is the fount of all
policy. This power clearly put Mrs Thatcher in a formidable position;
it is hardly one that she would wish to change. Yet, paradoxically, it is
this very power which limits her capacity to ensure, authoritatively,
that 'Thatcherism' outlives her service as leader. For the very powers
which are vested in her as leader are those which will be vested in her
successor. If Thatcherite policies are pursued by her successor, that
will be by the choice of her successor. If the new leader chooses
otherwise, then – as far as the party is concerned – so be it. The
choice is within the prerogative of the leader. It is a prerogative which
Mrs Thatcher has exercised decisively as leader. Her successor may
do the same; whether or not he (or she) does so will depend very
much upon who that successor is.

Given that Mrs Thatcher has not changed fundamentally the
attitudes, composition or organization of the party, the only avenue
remaining through which she may bequeath her philosophy to her
successor is that of being able to determine who her successor is. And
that will depend upon the variable central to an understanding of
British Conservatism: circumstance.

Notes

1. The biography is P. Kellner and C. Hitchens, *Callaghan: The Road to No. 10* (London: Cassell, 1976).
2. Among such works, in addition to those listed in footnotes below, are B. Arnold, *Margaret Thatcher: A Study in Power* (London: Hamish Hamilton, 1984); D. Bell (ed.), *The Conservative Government 1979–84* (London: Croom Helm, 1985); J. Bruce-Gardyne, *Mrs Thatcher's First Administration* (London: Macmillan, 1984); P. Cosgrave, *Thatcher: The First Term* (London: Bodley Head, 1985); S. Hall and M. Jacques (eds), *The Politics of Thatcherism* (London: Lawrence & Wishart, 1983); J. Ross, *Thatcher and Friends* (London: Pluto Press, 1983); and N. Wapshott and G. Brock, *Thatcher* (London: Macdonald, 1983).
3. J. Critchley, *Westminster Blues* (London: Futura, 1986) p. 126.
4. As Peter Riddell has observed, Mrs Thatcher has changed the question as well as the answer. P. Riddell, *The Thatcher Government*, revised edn (Oxford: Basil Blackwell, 1985) p. 1. See also A. Aughey, 'Mrs Thatcher's Philosophy', *Parliamentary Affairs*, 36 (4), Autumn 1983: 389–98.
5. See P. Norton and A. Aughey, *Conservatives and Conservatism* (London: Temple Smith, 1981) pp. 240–1.
6. Norton and Aughey, *Conservatives* pp. 242–3. This paragraph draws heavily on this source.
7. Confidential source to author.
8. P. Norton, *Conservative Dissidents* (London: Temple Smith, 1978) Chapter 9.
9. Norton, *Conservative Dissidents* chapter 9.
10. See Norton and Aughey, *Conservatives*, pp. 247–8.
11. 'Thatcher's Divided Tories', *Newsweek*, 26 October 1981; London Weekend Television, *Weekend World*, 25 October 1981; *The Times*, 11 May 1985.
12. P. Norton (ed.), *Parliament in the 1980s* (Oxford: Basil Blackwell, 1985) Chapter 3.
13. M. Brown MP, quoted in M. Holmes, *The First Thatcher Government, 1979–83: Contemporary Conservatism and Economic Change* (Brighton: Wheatsheaf, 1985) p. 83.
14. M. Burch, 'Mrs Thatcher's Approach to Leadership in Government', *Parliamentary Affairs*, 36 (4), Autumn 1983: 409. See also H. Stephenson, *Mrs Thatcher's First Year* (London: Jill Norman, 1980) p. 94.
15. Various Conservative MPs to author.
16. Norton (ed.), *Parliament in the 1980s*, pp. 33–6.
17. More serious in terms of party feeling was the split over top peoples' pay in 1985: see M. Rutherford, *Financial Times*, 27 July 1985, and P. Norton, '"Dr Norton's Parliament" – A Response', *Public Administration Bulletin*, 48, 1985: 76.
18. Critchley, *Westminster Blues*, p. 126.
19. See G. Gardiner, *Margaret Thatcher* (London: William Kimber, 1975) pp. 192, 202.

20.   M. Rutherford, 'The Tories: still quite happy?', the *Financial Times*, 27 January 1984.
21.   See, for example, the comments of C. Patten, quoted in H. Young and A. Sloman, *The Thatcher Phenomenon* (London: BBC, 1986) p. 33.
22.   See especially R. Lewis, *Margaret Thatcher: A Personal and Political Biography* (London: Routledge and Kegan Paul, 1975) pp. 140–1.
23.   On its role in policy-making in 1974–9, see C. Patten, 'Policy Making in Opposition', in Z. Layton-Henry (ed.), *Conservative Party Politics* (London: Macmillan, 1980) pp. 17–20.
24.   See R. Behrens, *The Conservative Party from Heath to Thatcher* (Farnborough: Saxon House, 1980) p. 33.
25.   The procedure was overhauled in 1981 and now includes a two-day selection board. See 'Have carpet bag, will travel', *The Economist*, 12 March 1983, and Critchley, *Westminster Blues*, pp. 25–6.
26.   See, e.g, 'New boys in the backroom', *The Economist*, 16 February 1985.
27.   S. Heffer, 'Big Brother tugs at the Tory grass roots', *The Times*, 5 October 1985.
28.   Reported to the author by a Conservative local party officer to whom the remark was made.
29.   In 1984, party deputy chairman Michael Spicer – warning that more cash had to be raised by constituencies – estimated that to raise the central target of £6 million would necessitate the average contribution from local parties rising by almost tenfold: *Conservative Newsline*, March 1984, p. 8.
30.   Heffer, 'Big Brother'.
31.   Quoted in Young and Sloman, *The Thatcher Phenomenon*, p. 55.
32.   This rough estimate derives from my analysis of the Conservative Right – encompassing economic liberals – in the 1970–4 and 1974–9 parliaments, though the nature of cross-voting in the latter parliament made it difficult to assess with any measure of confidence. Norton, *Conservative Dissidents*, pp. 244–54; P. Norton, *Dissension in the House of Commons 1974–1979* (Oxford: Oxford University Press, 1980) pp. 452–3. (Several members identified as right-wingers in the 1970–4 parliament retired or were defeated in 1974.)
33.   Riddell, *The Thatcher Government*, p. 12.
34.   The *Sunday Times*, 12 and 19 May, 1985.
35.   Riddell, *The Thatcher Government*, p. 12.
36.   See Norton and Aughey, *Conservatives*, Chapter 2
37.   'Right Young Things', *The Economist*, 23 August 1986. In November 1986 the disbandment of the Federation of Conservative Students was announced by Conservative Central Office.
38.   Peter Bruinvels and Terry Dicks. Of the 72 Conservatives to vote against the Second Reading of the Bill, 22 were first returned in 1983.
39.   M. Rush, 'The Member of Parliament', in S. A. Walkland (ed.), *The House of Commons in the Twentieth Century* (Oxford: Oxford University Press, 1979) pp. 97–102.
40.   M. Rush, 'The Members of Parliament', in S. A. Walkland and M. Ryle (eds), *The Commons Today* (London: Fontana, 1981) p. 61. The

only marginal change was in the number of members from 'miscellane-
ous' occupations.

41. This is based on the author's observation, reinforced by discussions
with local party officers. Little data is available; for what there is on the
background of constituency officers in the 1960s, see D. Butler and M.
Pinto-Duschinsky, 'The Conservative Elite 1918–78: Does Unrepre-
sentativeness Matter?' in Layton-Henry (ed.), *Conservative Party
Politics*, pp. 193–8.

42. Sir N. Fisher, *The Tory Leaders* (London: Weidenfeld and Nicolson,
1977) p 185.

43. Chamberlain was the founder chairman of Conservative Research
Department (1929–40) and also served as party chairman (1930–1).
Lord Home was President of the National Union in 1963 and, as such,
made the announcement of Macmillan's resignation to the party
conference; such a position, however, does not signify great involvement in the party organization.

3 Thatcherism and British Society
Julius Gould and Digby Anderson

'Thatcherism and British society' is an all-embracing theme. It can relate, *inter alia*, to the social *sources* of Mrs Thatcher's brand of Conservatism; to the social *bases* of her electoral support; to the social *objectives* which underlie her policies; to the social *limitations* (structural or contingent) on the success (short-run or long-run) of those policies; to the social *groupings* whose members (or active spokesmen) have sought to limit that success, or render it impossible. No attempt will be made here to explore such a wide range of questions. Nor, since this is not an exercise in semantics or methodology, will we give space to definitions of 'British' and 'society'.

Some brief, probably familiar, remarks are nonetheless needed about 'British society'. The Scots philosopher wrote that there was much ruin in a nation. We would agree, and would add – what some may think is the same – that there are many cross-cutting bonds in a society. This makes it difficult to accept a one-dimensional view – one that pushes to the limit the force (and symbolism) of class or status. The position that we favour emphasizes the role of interest groups, their impact on each other, and (through their elites) on public policy. The vigour, assiduity and professionalism of such groups have proceeded well beyond the points mapped by Professor Finer in his pioneering *Anonymous Empire* (1958). So too has their symbiosis with central (and, increasingly, with local) government and with the expanded world of higher education. In recent years it has also been stressed (though seldom by bureaucrats themselves) that each segment of a state bureaucracy has a special interest in consolidating its own power (and is supported in this, first, by its client interest groups and, second, by politicians who bid for votes through judiciously directed slices of 'public' expenditure).

From one perspective, of course, many of these are the classical intermediate groups that stand as a two-way barrier between the state and the citizen. But there is no hidden hand that harmonizes their operations. And (most important) they are 'unequal': they have a

differing power of access to help and protection (overt and covert) from Whitehall. The trade unions in the 1970s enjoyed a remarkable primacy through their special relationship with the Labour government, especially with the Department of Employment. Most of them are in collusive competition with state resources in the form of subsidies, grants, and tax concessions. Professional groups are as zealous to safeguard their profitable lines of demarcation as trade unions were in the defence of their peculiar immunities. And, as the tax and benefit system has proliferated, ordinary citizens (such as future pensioners and present-day parents of university students) can easily be rallied to defend ordinary privileges. If there is a *general* long-term interest in removing some concession or benefit, the defenders of a *partial* interest take a short-term view.

Governments, however temporary their tenure, have been known to manipulate the fiscal and monetary system so as to buy off the claims of such groups. In this, they have been aided and abetted by the more permanent 'government' in the civil service. But a reforming government, of whatever political party, is bound to be confronted by the sectional barriers to economic growth. Moving from scrutiny of them to action about removing them is an uphill task under the pressure of a four- to five-year electoral cycle. Mrs Thatcher has certainly been engaged in such a task since 1979. In the words of Anthony King, her intention was 'to bring about, if she could, nothing less than a total reorientation of British public policy and the content of British political debate'.[1] We may have some reservations about the world 'total', but Professor King's formulation vividly recalls the mood of the hour. In the early 1970s most of the concrete policies that are called 'Thatcherite' – selling council houses, privatizing state industries, curbing the immunities of trade unions – would have been 'politically unthinkable'. By moving into (even by talking about) new directions, Margaret Thatcher has changed the climate of debate about public policy. This is no mean achievement. Those politicians (and, still more, those commentators) who now seek to drive her from office are well aware of these changes. Having sought in vain to block them, they now seek an equivocal accommodation.

GRAMSCI VERSUS BURKE

Over the last decade, 'Thatcher' has become an essential part of the

Left's demonology. Marxist intellectuals in Britain seem to have 'Thatcher' on the brain – especially the part colonized by Gramsci. From influential seats in the academy and in journalism, they have picked away at the record of Labour's timidities and electoral failures; they go on to stress that Thatcherism is a new response from 'the Right' – the use of 'the state apparatus' for the expansion of privilege in a new situation. The thrust of Thatcherism, they say, is to exploit popular aspirations for authoritarian ends. They depict it as an ideology that also serves a *mélange* of interests – those of economic liberals, welfare reformers, controllers or servants of 'the state apparatus', advocates of 'racism' and the cold war. Above all, with enviable nerve, they castigate the media (and other cultural agencies) for circulating 'hegemonic' messages that alternatively lull the virtuous masses into accepting their oppression or arouse them to unnatural patriotic fervour. All this analysis and preaching has a very rational, practical purpose – the creation of a new alliance for socialism.

Its exponents are well aware that the contemporary, consumerist Britain is not that of Keir Hardie, let alone that of the oft-invoked Tolpuddle Martyrs. They know, too, that Stalin's record has by now acquired a very bad press in almost every language: forswearing both crude Stalinism and 'labourism' they promote a new coalition between the genuinely unprivileged, inside and outside the Labour movement, and a whole spectrum of other social groups and interests. These are often spoken of as 'minorities', but they include many people who are middle class, well educated and often highly privileged. This approach is admirably tailored for what one may stereotype as '*Guardian* persons', who combine British non-conformity with the secular religion of state-administered compassion. Such people welcome, too, the retreat from 'Victorian' (or, rather, as we suggest below, 'Georgian') values, and either draw or expect to draw professional advantage as well as personal satisfaction from their further erosion.

It is tempting to move in an entirely opposite direction – towards a Burkean reverence for the cool, the unexcited and the contingent. The traditional Conservative, properly enough, does not clog up his brains with Gramsci. Disclaiming all taint of ideology and expressing deep admiration for Mrs Thatcher, he takes her economic liberalism as just one of the ingredients – on a par with corporatism – that have long coexisted with Conservative thought. Mrs Thatcher is praised for upholding the rule of law as a social bond, but there is sometimes

a note of pained regret that, since she is not one of nature's old Etonians – quite the contrary – she does not crusade on behalf of 'traditional' patterns of hierarchy. However, practical people do not complain about this in an ungentlemanly way. Similarly, to describe Mrs Thatcher's sometimes shifting or inconsistent assumptions as an 'ism' or an ideology is to engage in a dubious, un-Conservative, and alien, even 'Continental' activity. This sceptical line also has it practical purpose: it damps down fervour among such Conservatives as are prone to zealotry, and it seeks, above all, not to frighten the voting horses.

For these Conservatives, it is a matter of ideology that Thatcherism cannot be an ideology. But some other commentators have come to a similar view for other reasons. They argue that there is about Thatcherism nothing special, let alone ideological, in that it was a response dictated by the facts, mostly the economic facts. Any government would have pursued Thatcherite policies given the economic conditions of 1979: there was 'no alternative'. These commentators point to the Thatcherite policies pursued by the socialist government in France after its initial bonanza ran out of steam. They point, too, to the austerity programme currently being imposed by socialists in Australia. They argue that Thatcherite policies had already appeared under the Callaghan administration, initiated by Mr Healey, prompted by the International Monetary Fund (IMF), and even invoked by Mr Callaghan in his call for a Great Debate about education. This thinking is part of a more general view which holds that political parties are less different than they pretend to be, and also less in charge of events than they pretend. In the end, whatever the rhetoric, parties have to respond to the same realities, especially economic realities (and even more especially, international economic realities).

But there is no necessity to make a choice between the extreme views that Thatcherism is a full-blown ideology or that it is a contingent assembly of pragmatic reaction, a choice between Gramsci and Burke. There is – here, if not universally – a possible middle way. For of course there is a 'Thatcher phenomenon'. Its flavour can be gauged by a selection (in no special order) of its associated slogans: conviction politics; wealth creation before its distribution; popular capitalism; enterprise culture; cutting public expenditure; keeping more of what you earn; maintaining the medium-term financial strategy (MTFS); reducing public borrowing; giving the unions back to their members; reversing the 'ratchet effect'; pushing

back the 'nanny state'. If – not unreasonably after two summers of inner-city uproar – we add the law and order motifs (such as support for the police), it all suggests a hard-headed, unsentimental, realistic approach. Equally it can be criticized, and caricatured, as hard-hearted, powered by the *wrong* sort of sentiment and addressing only part of the 'reality' – the part, moreover, which Thatcherite policies themselves have created. The critics say that the image is the *real* reality, the 'uncaring and uncompassionate' image. This is a powerful weapon in the hands of all who see a necessary (rather than an unquestionable contingent) connection between practical compassion and state funding.

'GEORGIAN' RATHER THAN 'VICTORIAN' VALUES

Most but not all of the above slogans are 'economic' in their thrust – though in this, as in other contexts, there can be little that is 'economic' *and nothing else besides*. They certainly gained special relevance amid the economic crises of the 1970s. But there is another set of Thatcherite themes which have a *social* relevance: for example, self-respect and self-reliance; family discipline; self-control rather than 'permissive' self-indulgence; a decent patriotism; individual provision, wherever possible, against the uncertainties of the future.

These would be among what Mrs Thatcher was, on a famous occasion, to call 'Victorian values'. But well before that moment her critics had shown unease at her idea that, quite possibly, some (though not all) of Britain's economic problems had a moral dimension, or had their roots in a morality that took socialist and welfarist assumptions for granted. Earlier Conservative prime ministers had not brooded over such matters. Indeed, in the heyday of consensual politics (though it was not so described at the time) one of them (the late Lord Stockton) is alleged to have deemed such moral perplexities to be the reserve of the bishops. By 1979, however, Conservatives (and others) could entertain a reasonable doubt as to whether the National Morality Service was safe in episcopal hands.

Whether (and how far) the values Mrs Thatcher admires were authentically Victorian; whether they were outweighed by other murkier yet equally Victorian values that are even less compatible with modern sensibilities than the better class of Victorian values – all this, by 1983, was to become a matter for solemn as well as frivolous debate. There seems ground for the view (strongly argued by Patrick

Middleton in *Encounter*)[2] that the values she admires were the values
of the inter-war years. That was a period when 'a publicly uncon-
tested value system' allowed 'a measure of deviancy to occur without
creating a sense of moral threat'. Crime rates were, by earlier and
later standards, agreeably low; and despite all the known hypocrisies
and injustices 'Georgian values' cut across and united social classes; it
was 'a period of remarkable, almost unparalleled social adjustment
and also (daring to measure such a thing) of individual contentment'.
An important part in that 'adjustment' was played, according to Mr
Middleton, by the growth and tone of British broadcasting. He,
therefore, has little hope of restoring the '1920s' package in the age
of mass consumption with all the far from 'Georgian' values diffused
by modern television. His doubts would have been strengthened had
he also taken into account the contraceptive pill, and the ramifying
consequences of its invention on perceptions of sexual roles and
family life.

Why was a change of direction called for between 1974 and 1979?
This is not the place for a partial (in either sense of the word) account
of Britain in the Heath–Wilson–Callaghan years. The 'oil shock', in
the years before the North Sea oil came onstream, struck hard at an
economy whose industrial sector was already uncompetitive. There
were two continuing and related problems. First, could there be a
happy ending to the British saga of lost competitiveness and high unit
costs in manufacturing? To this there was no readily available
answer, least of all from those who shrank (either as employers or
workers) from the glare of competition. Most such people preferred a
state-financed postponement of the evil day. Second, what was to be
done about public-sector pay? Labour-intensive public services had
expanded: governments as paymasters confronted a highly unionized
workforce. Even now, few techniques have been devised in this area
for measuring – let alone rewarding – productivity and effectiveness.
So how was the payment for such services to be regulated – with some
sense of fairness towards the lowest-paid personnel, but without
reinforcing inflationary pressures? The 'revisionists' on the Left had
prematurely assumed that, in a nicely 'mixed' economy, there was no
longer a problem of 'production'. But few on the Labour side, by the
time of Callaghan, believed that social programmes (sometimes
called 'income redistribution') could be painlessly financed by
economic growth. 'Labour governments in Britain ... were elected
on egalitarian expenditure programmes but were forced to deal
almost entirely with problems of production'.[3] Moreover, despite

today's laments for a vanished 'consensus', there was never agreement on the pay issue, either among experts or within the alternating parties of government. Instead there were 'social contracts' and other rather contentious temporary expedients.

The non-solution of these problems heightened inter-group rivalries in British society, well before Mrs Thatcher reached No. 10. From 1974 onwards the bills for all this kept coming in. It was, after all, Mr Wilson (following most of his unheeded predecessors) who warned that one person's pay rise could mean another person's job loss – and his warning did not proceed from an 'alien' economic doctrine.[4] Chancellor Healey, from 1975, had talked and acted in a 'monetarist' style, recognizing (to quote Tony Crosland's reminder to local government) that 'the party was over'; Mr Callaghan himself had told the Labour Party conference in 1976 that 'we cannot now, if we ever could, spend our way out of recession'.

The new mood of 'stabilization' in Mr Healey's Treasury led to outrage on the Left:

> In 1974 the Labour Government initially attempted to maintain demand and its own spending to prevent a major deflation and the onset of recession. But after 1976 this attempt was abandoned. Unemployment had doubled to 1.5 million but no further significant attempt was made to reduce it. Acceptance of permanent high unemployment has become a major feature of British economic policy. Since 1975 the control of inflation has been given a greater priority than either employment or growth.[5]

By late 1978, that outrage had been expressed very forcibly on the streets. Those who believe Mrs Thatcher created social divisiveness should be reminded of the 'winter of discontent', that typically English euphemism for trade union bloody-mindedness against a Labour government.

THE THATCHER PROJECT

This was the setting for the Thatcher project, for the 'total reorientation' to which we have referred. The outlines of the project were clear enough: the release of the economic energies held back by state intervention, trade union obstruction, and managerial ineptitude; the shaping of a cultural (and educational) framework that neither devalued nor subtly denigrated the idea of enterprise; the encourage-

ment of a 'moral' shift that could stem (or reverse) the changes
heralded by the 1960s. But simply to state these very general
objectives conjures up the strength of the opposition that would need
to be outfaced or outflanked. We feel that their proponents *underestimated the strength of the 'consensual opposition'*. As they would seek
to implement their project, new problems would inevitably arise, and
new stumbling blocks would be placed in their way. Special difficulties were bound to occur, within the British system of government,
from the ambitions of individual ministers: the most energetic of
prime ministers, with a very small personal staff, would have to fight
every inch of the way – and be described as 'abrasive' for her pains.

The persistence, if not all of the venom, of the 'consensual'
opposition to 'Thatcher' could have been predicted. It is also one-
sided. 'Thatcher' incurs the charge of bossiness and abrasiveness,
qualities seldom attributed by *bien pensant* observers to Mr Heath or
applied (at the time) to Mr Callaghan's control of Cabinet and some
of his blunt, dismissive television performances. 'Finchley' acquires a
pejorative tone never enjoyed by 'Cardiff'. Mrs Thatcher's Labour
predecessors had aroused spasms of distrust but, almost to the end,
they were admired as professional pragmatists, balanced, for years,
on precarious majorities. From the start, however, Mrs Thatcher was
taken to be a more serious proposition.

The Thatcher project – leaving on one side the modes of its
implementation – was bound to cause alarm and despondency within
a wide variety of strata, not least among the beneficiaries of the social
order threatened with 'reorientation'. In a democracy, such opposition does not need to go underground. It finds comfortable niches in
which to bide its time. It receives support from many quarters – from
the egalitarian High Tables of Oxbridge, from 'highly respected and
independent' research centres, from quality journalism, from the
House of Lords, yea, even among the Bench of Bishops. There were
indeed many within the Conservative Party whose hearts and minds
had not been entirely captured for Thatcherite objectives. (This did
not inhibit invitations to them to join the Cabinet, nor their
willingness to accept.) Such Conservatives, at the very hour of
victory, must have longed for a quieter life. Few of them were
devoted to Adam Smith, dazzled by Milton Friedman, or intoxicated
by Friedrich von Hayek. They would have gratefully anticipated Mr
Francis Pym's subsequent rather skittish *aperçu* (after his departure
from the government) that 'Conservatism and radicalism need not be
incompatible, but they sensibly prefer to indulge in brief and

passionate flirtations rather than a permanent relationship'.[6] 'Wetter' circles within that party could accept a renewed stress on monetary prudence, hoping (not without justification) that economic 'doctrine' would be pragmatically tempered by political manoeuvres and electoral anxieties. After all, such prudence was, in principle, quite compatible with Etonian values. 'Monetarism', though currently supported by economists with foreign-sounding names, had a perfectly respectable British (even, it could be suggested, Keynesian) pedigree. A more restrained enthusiasm, however, greeted any serious intrusion of 'market economics', not because it was un-British but because, *inter alia*, it threatened 'the quiet life' so dear to many in the Conservative camp. The idea of 'market forces' was (and is) deeply upsetting to the managers and beneficiaries of public monopolies and private cartels. Non-market practices, under 'normal' conditions, had produced an untidy, multi-layered web of collectivism and corporatism. Those who sought to disentangle that web were bound to run into trouble and abuse, not only from those who profited (financially and psychologically) from existing non-dynamic arrangements, but also from their brothers (and, increasingly, sisters) in the media and educational establishments who shared their preferences and values.

WAS 'THATCHERITE' POLICY IMPLEMENTED?

The three most crucial areas for the introduction of market principles are the labour market, health care, and education. Had Mrs Thatcher possessed a full-blown doctrine, several things might have followed. We can offer here only the briefest summary.

1. 'Thatcherism' would have united its early preoccupation with 'money supply' to an attack on what Peter Jay has called 'the monopolistic price-setting of labour'.[7]
2. 'Thatcherism' would have pushed market principles, even if only on an experimental basis, into a series of areas. Fuelled by the Radical Right's arguments that genuine public goods are few and far between, it would have set about, for example, making schools responsive to consumer demand either by 'denationalizing' the supply or by empowering the demand for them through a voucher scheme. It would have made teachers' salaries a matter for local negotiation, cut out local education authorities, and

replaced the current state coercion on school attendance with a more proper (according to liberal principles) state insistence on measures and standards of educational attainment.

3. The National Health Service would have been recognized as providing a heterogeneous collection of goods, some properly provided by the minimal state, some not. Certainly it would have acknowledged the possibility of charging for hotel service in hospitals, as well as for actual treatment in hospital and by GPs (with annual ceiling and exemptions), and the case for removing the entrenched privileges of medical professional monopolies. Far from stressing how much it was spending on health services, it would have taken pride in how much it had 'depoliticized' health.

4. It would have chosen from the various policies on cash welfare services that were on offer. It might thus have provided either a basic minimum income guarantee or a negative income tax (removing all other benefits), or adopted stringent means testing. In any case, it would have amalgamated the computations and redistributions of the Inland Revenue and the DHSS.

5. The initial raid on quangos would have become a war. There would no longer have been an expanding Health Educational Council (now to be absorbed into the DHSS) or Central Council for Education and Training in Social Work. Its principles would have led to a dismantling of regulations (for example, the Health and Safety at Work Act), or to curtailment of the activities of the Equal Opportunities Commission and of that for Racial Equality. The victory of the miners' strike would have been followed up by privatization. Such policies would have opened the way for the achievement of another ideological objective – substantially lower taxation.

6. 'Thatcherism' would have united many of these concerns in a manner which discriminated in favour of 'the family' and that morality and charity which provides so much more 'welfare' via relatives, neighbours and friends than politicians and their bureaucratic creatures can ever do. Had it been a genuinely populist ideology, it would have restored the corporal and capital punishments so approved by the people.

We have our own individual preferences and priorities regarding these lines of policy. Many of them might well have been set out as part of a Medium Term Social Strategy (MTSS), comparable (as a set

of markets) with the MTFS in the economic field. It need hardly be underlined that this was 'Thatcherism' as it might have been, not Mrs Thatcher's actual project. It is well to consider the gap between the two and the different explanations and reasons for it. First, some of these policies were never seriously considered anyway. It was not that they formed part of a cohesive ideology that was split up by the vicissitudes of implementation; some were never seriously entertained. Nor is it simply the case that less was done than was wished, than ideology dictated. Some intentions were pursued more vigorously. For example, the first Thatcher administration made economics and the economic ministries a priority. 'Thatcherite' politicians were made ministers in such departments, while the high spending 'social' ministries were left to 'wets'.

In part because of this, the government was much more 'Thatcherite' as a policy-maker than as an employer. It set the conditions, through trade union reform and economic policy, which permitted the private sector to become more competitive, to shed those 'unemployed' whom it had been paying, and the private sector did indeed become more competitive, many companies maintaining or increasing productivity with 30 per cent fewer employees. Having told private employers what to do and helped them to do it, the government (the largest employer) then found it difficult itself to follow through all that its own advice implied. Whatever the redistribution within public spending, the total level remained little changed. Nor is this explained entirely by the costs of unemployment since there, too, ideology would have dictated a cut in rates and restriction on categories recognized as 'unemployed' for the purpose of state benefits.

Let us make one point abundantly clear. The desirability or otherwise of these lines of policy is not at issue here. As we have indicated, we ourselves do not necessarily 'desire' them all, or equally. The point is that, compared to the 'Thatcherism that might have been', the 'Thatcherism that was' is not just less stringent but very different. Certainly the two share some imperatives and much rhetoric, but they are not the same. We doubt whether even the first is coherent enough to be called an ideology; the second surely was not an ideology – even in intention, let alone in implementation.

What inhibited a 'Thatcherism as intended' (quite apart from a 'Thatcherism as might have been') is not definitively known. It clearly fell in part into the area of the 'politically unthinkable': other programmes (including the endless search for a way of controlling

local government's scope for extravagance and subversion) had a stronger claim on parliamentary time. Too little public debate was stirred up over the important legal as well as political difficulties inherent in the peculiarities of British local government (notably in the finance of education). And being a radical Conservative involves outfacing parliamentary colleagues who are nervous about their seats, and very easily unnerved by pressure groups of every kind. It also means accumulating new enemies among the vested interests – professional and charitable bodies which, though not *party* political, wield a hefty political clout – and their ubiquitous stage army of cronies in the press. Think only of the interest groups who would have found that a 'family policy' meant bringing politics into the family. The very idea would have united bishops and lesbians into an unholy alliance; civil servants would have argued that important parts must all await the future installation of their new computer; university departments would have sought (and probably received) public money in order to prove that the idea was absurd; hostile seminars would have been held by 'respected' research centres in order to ensure a future flow of money and respect; and the pages of *New Society* would have filled to overflowing with pithy commina-tions.

It is instructive to pause and consider some elements in these circles who loathe current Thatcherism, and would have found fuller Thatcherism even more distasteful. We have argued that Thatcher-ism, though special, is not a full-blown ideology; and we have argued this on the basis of its mixture of *ideas*. But there are some who see ideology not as the body itself but as the scanty (and, for them, transparent) clothing worn by sectional interests or classes. Is Thatcherism the clothing of a class, the ideology of an interest? Pursue the thought. Those who see ideology in this way also see classes as being in conflict. It would be a fascinating exercise to attempt to define Thatcherism in terms of those who have hated it most! What a heterogeneous lot they would be: those Tory grandees and Communist sects, the bishops and proselytizing homosexuals, 1960s corporatist businessmen and the NUM, the IRA and the BBC, the poverty lobby, and, perhaps, some in the circle that surrounds the Royal Family.

It is no simple task to 'situate' Thatcherism within the 'structure' of contemporary British society. We are, in any case, not attracted by the fashionable Marxoid use of these terms! About all the list of loathers tells us is that, while Thatcherism cannot claim to be an

ideology it has some claim to the title 'radical'. The lady and her
policies (even the thought of them) have upset many in the academic,
business, political and church establishments. What may have hurt
most of all is that *she* has earned such a title, one that *they* had
enjoyed wearing on occasions.

MRS THATCHER AND THE TRADE UNIONS

The flavour of what proved possible (because 'politically thinkable')
comes out clearly from a review of the Thatcher government's
handling of the trade unions. The stated aim was to tilt the balance of
power away from union leaders towards (on the one hand) union
members and (on the other) the employers. The macropolitical aim
was to squash that feature of 'corporatism' that had given union top
brass a key place in both formal and informal policy-making. This is
not the place for a full summary of the Thatcher government's three
laws on trade union reform. It sought to curtail ancient immunities;
limit secondary picketing; and promote secret ballots prior to strikes,
as well as the election of certain key trade union officials. At the
Department of Employment Mr Prior and Mr Tebbit followed a
cautious approach (the downfall of Mr Heath in 1974 was an ever-
present warning against 'confrontation'). Such caution did not
exempt them from condemnation (not all of it ritual or synthetic) by
trade union leaders and industrial correspondents. But the reforms
were popular: those on ballots were especially attractive to ordinary
trade union members. Recognizing the change in the climate of
opinion, the Labour Party and the trade unions seem now committed
to an ambiguous promise that, under a Labour regime, the 'virtuous'
penumbra of the hated Prior–Tebbit Acts would be retained. Even
an ambiguous, highly-qualified promise of this kind (with all sorts of
built-in escape clauses) would have been unthinkable before the
Thatcher era.

Confrontation with unions did, of course, develop in Mrs Thatcher's second term. There was the long drawn-out affair of 'banning'
union membership at the Government Communication Headquarters
(GCHQ). (More remarkable than the 'ban' is the fact that GCHQ,
unlike every other branch of the British 'secret world', had become
unionized in the first place.) But the crucial battles came from 1984
onwards, with the miners and the school-teachers. The full story of
the NUM's defeat still remains to be told, but it is clear that, quite

apart from Mr Scargill's own assiduous contributions, the government's nerve held up at crucial times. Moreover its preparations for the strike (and for the attendant breaches of non-Thatcher law) had been carefully thought through. Yet such is the oddity of British public opinion (and still more of those who form it) that neither the Coal Board nor the government received the plaudits of a grateful nation. Only an expert in counter-factuals could say whether another Saltley and another freezing winter would have been more eagerly received.

Few (but we were among them) predicted that the NUT and the other teaching unions would succeed where the NUM had failed. British teachers are employed by local not central government. Sir Keith Joseph, the Secretary of State for Education and Science until the summer of 1985, confronted an entrenched structure of local management, and (with the exception of the ILEA) none of that structure (or its powers) had been affected by the government's protracted reforms of local government. Centralized pay bargaining remains in place. And the teachers' unions proved more subtle and devious than the miners. They avoided even the project of a costly strike and they wooed a significant measure of public (and parental) sympathy. (To use a familiar historical analogy they deployed 'moral' rather than 'physical' force.) Good teachers, in 1986, were sadly underpaid, given their qualifications and their dedication. But so long as the educational establishment affects to believe that judging 'a good teacher' is an arcane mystery, centralized pay deals will benefit the good, the bad, and the worthless.

Kenneth Baker may have better fortune (and a better press) than Sir Keith Joseph in handling the teachers' unions. He has secured more money with which to smooth his path, and the government may win its rational exercise in damage limitation. But the teachers' representatives have tasted blood, and they seem unlikely to show complete and unanimous gratitude for Mr Baker's generosity. On the contrary (in the run-up to a general election) the anti-Thatcher operators in the teachers' unions have every interest in securing further political capital. They may, for example, in due course promise to abide by revised conditions of service, but the central government is ill-equipped (administratively and legally) to secure compliance, school by school. Mr Baker's Bill on Teacher's Pay and Conditions has at the time of writing (autumn 1986) moved to the House of Lords. Its abolition of the Burnham negotiating machinery is a necessary (but, of course, insufficient) condition for educational

advance. This is especially true of areas controlled by hostile local authorities. Union intransigence may, of course, be counter-productive. The government, however, has already been forced to pay a political cost. For the combination of organized disruption and 'moral' force secured a *victorious* quasi-Saltley for the educational unions. The lesson will not be lost on future Secretaries of State for Education and Science. (On the other hand they – and their advisers – may simply turn the screw of a non-Thatcherite *dirigisme*.)

EDUCATION POLICY

The future historian will ask: why did Thatcherism, though it ingeniously diverted some substantial funds for education to the Manpower Services Commission, fail to alter the structure of local authority control over education? Was it because its exponents yielded to the arguments of civil servants and local Conservative worthies that, for example, a market-oriented voucher system, even an experimental one, was impracticable and that local authority control over education was, except at the fringes, inviolate? Could a durable, far from Thatcherite, symbiosis have been sustained between officials at all levels, educational pundits, and union leaders? And, most interesting of all, why did the government wait until the autumn of 1986 before announcing a programme for some twenty urban high-powered science colleges whose finance and control would be outside the local authorities' grasp?

It is interesting to contrast the heavier hand deployed in regard to the universities. These, too, had become over-dependent on state support: self-interest and government pressure have made them much more market-conscious – though some would say not enough, and in the wrong directions. In order to increase an efficiency that was (by British standards) already high, the universities absorbed uneven and not always deleterious 'real' cuts, some of which they may now hope to recoup. Universities are, after all, bodies which are ancient corporations – or, in narrowly legal terms, independently chartered entities. Yet the DES did not shrink from a measure of *dirigisme* and (except on the important issue of tenure) faced them down. Were universities simply a softer touch, or did Whitehall also have the bureaucratic will to cut them down to a smaller size? If even half that bureaucratic zeal had been employed to dislodge an over-mighty local authority educational structure, school systems might

have come to face market pressures. That could have tested the question: is there an alternative way of raising standards and maximizing individual freedom to choose?

CONCLUSIONS

We remarked earlier that actual Thatcherism started at least with a perfectly understandable but rather narrowly based concern for economics. It would also be true to say that its initial agenda was conceived almost entirely in terms of objectives. There was less sustained (or rigorous) interest in the analysis of the social obstacles to its programme – that is, the problems of 'means' rather than 'ends'.[8] This is yet another indication of its piecemeal status. For even before 1979 (and even within the subject matter of economics) there were some ideas available about the problems of implementation – often from the same source as the ideas about goals (one example is the Virginia school of 'public choice' theory). Or, again, American neo-conservatives could have helped to explain the complexities of the relationship between government and private interests which can neutralize policy initiatives. Of course, politicians are often naively or cynically confident about the possibility of achieving goals. Yet politicians whose 'ideology' was deemed to be based on scepticism about ambitious political action should have been more attuned to the problems of means. Despite their generalized distrust of 'social sciences', they could have found British social scientists who sympathized with their goals and who could have illuminated their path.

'Incompetence' associated with political means (as distinct from dispersed market means) is a barrier to dismantling the structures of state intervention – just as, in the past, it has happily impeded their effective expansion. Indeed, some have argued (one of us for almost 40 years) that 'dismantling' may be even more difficult, because vested interests accrete around areas of collectivism and those interests will lose more from the process of dismantling than the wider population may feel it will gain.

The case for 'limited' or 'unavoidable' government (as Ferdinand Mount[9] has reminded us) 'does not imply feeble government'. Within the framework of the national income as it is – not as it might or should be – it implies efficient, firm, often generous expenditure on social as well as military objectives. But it also implies resolute structures for ensuring that what is 'avoidable' is in fact avoided and

for promoting intelligent, even ingenious, modes of deregulation. Not enough 'planning for deregulation' has been so far attempted in the social field. And those groups within British society which benefit from the *status quo* (and they are not always the poor and the disadvantaged) can be relied upon to fight against projects for 'limited' government with all the energy – and public money – they command.

The experience of Thatcherism raises above all the question of how far (and how fast) political reform from the centre can be pushed in British society. The question is bound to be raised, given the disposition of interests, the central and local electoral systems and the mass media, as well as the underlying attitudes towards (for example) security, ambition, charity and, indeed, change itself. If these have anything like the force we think they have, then the often cautious changes wrought by the Thatcher administrations have been remarkable indeed.

Notes

1. Anthony King, 'Mrs Thatcher's First Term', in A. Ranney (ed.), *Britain at the Polls 1983* (Durham, N. Carolina: Duke University Press, 1985) p. 1.
2. *Encounter*, July–August 1986.
3. John Vaizey, *Capitalism and Socialism* (London: Weidenfeld & Nicolson, 1980) p. 268.
4. He had, it is true, a home in Lord North Street, but it was certainly not the Institute of Economic Affairs!
5. Andrew Gamble, 'Economic Policy', in Henry Drucker *et al.* (eds), *Developments in British Politics* (London: Macmillan, 1983) p. 140.
6. Francis Pym, *The Politics of Consent* (London: Hamish Hamilton 1984) p. 179.
7. This occurs in an unfriendly review of Alan Walters's book, *Britain's Economic Renaissance* in the *Times Literary Supplement* (30 May 1986). Since Mr Jay does not have to stand for office he can concede (unlike most politicians of all parties) that it is 'right' to see 'the reduction in real pay ... as the key to higher employment'. It is not, however, clear how an electorate can be led along this path, despite the 'radical structures' mapped by Martin Weitzman and others that Peter Jay clearly finds more attractive than either Alan Walters's book or the policy advice he has provided for Mrs Thatcher.
8. None of this brief discussion should be taken as neglecting the well-known arguments about the inter-relatedness of the ends and means.
9. Ferdinand Mount, *The Practice of Liberty* (London: CPC, 1986) p. 10.

4 The Prime Minister, the Cabinet and the Thatcher Personality
Peter Hennessy

When it comes to the condition of Cabinet government, Lord Hailsham, the Lord Chancellor, is a prime witness. He may find it difficult to remember the names of some of his colleagues around Mrs Thatcher's cabinet table[1] (his dignified bulk rests right opposite the Prime Minister, perfectly placed for catching her eye[2]) but he has sat at it for sixteen and a half years, a post-war record. He has seen in action Sir Anthony Eden in the dreadful months of Suez (Lord Hailsham was First Lord of the Admiralty in 1956 just below Cabinet rank).[3] Harold Macmillan brought him into the Cabinet in January 1957 and there he remained through the Macmillan and Home years till October 1964. He has been on the Woolsack for the duration of the Heath and Thatcher governments. His judgement of the Thatcher style is, therefore, a collector's item.

It is breathtaking. She reminds him of the late Lord Chief Justice, Lord Goddard, according to legend the hardest man to sit on the bench since the war (Lord Hailsham remembers him as 'a sweet man'):[4]

> I don't think the critics have got it quite right when they say that she doesn't like people who differ from her. She reminds me very much of some judges before whom I've appeared who form their own opinion by arguing with counsel. Now Lord Goddard was one such judge. And you would think for a time he was really against you and had made up his mind that you were wrong before you'd had your say. And indeed if you laid down on your back with your paws in the air and wagged your tail, you'd lose your case ... I think the present Prime Minister is somebody who likes to test her steel in real argument and I don't think she holds it against you even if you hit back pretty hard.[5]

Lord Hailsham is but one of many Cabinet ministers to have delivered his verdict on Mrs Thatcher's style in the Cabinet Room

while she is still the occupant of No. 10. It is yet more evidence that
Mrs Thatcher has performed a minor miracle – she has made the
study of government and public administration interesting again.
Before analyzing the insider intelligence this has produced, it is
sensible to begin by taking the material raw. In a now famous
interview with Kenneth Harris of *The Observer* shortly before
becoming Prime Minister, Mrs Thatcher issued a declaration of
intent: 'It must be a conviction government. As Prime Minister I
could not waste time having any internal arguments'.[6] As such
declarations go, it was unusual in its tone and in the fact that it was
made public. Harold Macmillan, by contrast, began his premiership
by pinning to the Cabinet Room door a passage written in his own
hand from Gilbert and Sullivan's *The Gondoliers*:

> Motto for Private Office and Cabinet Room.
> Quiet, calm deliberation
> Disentangles *every* knot.
>
> H.M.[7]

Mrs Thatcher's early Cabinet contained an acknowledged expert on
the subject, Norman St John Stevas, Leader of the House of
Commons and editor of the collected works of Walter Bagehot. For
him, 'There is no doubt that as regards the Cabinet the most
commanding Prime Minister of modern times has been the present
incumbent, Mrs Thatcher. Convinced of both her own rectitude and
ability, she has tended to reduce the Cabinet to subservience'.[8] Other
victims of her Cabinet purges hum a similar theme. One veteran did
it unattributably: 'She was not really running a team. Every time
you have a Prime Minister who wants to take all the decisions, it
mainly leads to bad results. Attlee didn't. That's why he was so damn
good. Macmillan didn't. The nearest parallel to Maggie is Ted'.[9] The
Westland affair brought Sir Ian Gilmour on to the television news
telling the viewers of both major bulletins on 19 January 1986 that
being a good listener was not one of Mrs Thatcher's virtues[10], and
that there had been 'a downgrading of Cabinet government'.[11]
Gilmour, like St John Stevas, had written on the subject in the past,
in *The Body Politic*.[12] A dissenter-in-place, Peter Walker expressed
his feelings through a merry quip at several after-lunch speeches. He
would quote the Duke of Wellington's reaction to his first Cabinet
meeting as Prime Minister: 'An extraordinary affair. I gave them
their orders and they wanted to stay and discuss them.' Then he

would pause and say, 'I'm so glad we don't have Prime Ministers like
that today'.[13] Perhaps the most outspoken Whitehall critic of the
Thatcher style, however, is not a sacked minister but a former
official, Lord Bancroft, Head of the Home Civil Service, who was
despatched into early retirement when she disbanded the Civil
Service Department in November 1981. 'Amongst the Prime Ministers that I have come across', said Ian Bancroft, 'either closely or not
so closely, the two who have inspired more fear have been Mr
Churchill and Mrs Thatcher. As a result the grovel count amongst
ministers, and some officials, has been much higher than normal'.[14]

Of course, Mrs Thatcher's most famous critic is Michael Heseltine.
But his 'grand remonstrance of protest', as *The Observer's* leader
writer called it,[15] was, at least in its public dimension, a dispute about
procedure, not personality. The Westland Affair deserves special,
separate treatment. But the Prime Minister as manager of Cabinet
had her defenders both before and after, before the immortalization
of the small aircraft company in the west of which the political nation,
until December 1985, knew little. Though critical of her lack of
interest in reforming the machinery of government,[16] Sir John
Hoskyns, the head of Mrs Thatcher's Downing Street Policy Unit
from 1979 to 1982, believes her style and temperament have been
crucial to her success as 'a remarkably effective agent of change':[17]

> She's done that for two or three reasons. I think first her
> temperament and background make her impatient with the whole
> sort of Establishment culture and way of thinking, even way of
> talking. And that, I think, is extremely healthy because I happen to
> think that the Establishment ... is absolutely at the heart of the
> British disease ... she's gone further than that because she has
> been prepared to be extremely unreasonable in order to get change
> – impossible on occasions and many people of a more gentlemanly
> and old-fashioned upbringing were rather shocked at the way she
> carry on.[18]

Sir John Nott, who served Mrs Thatcher at Trade and later Defence,
enjoyed what he called 'a process of combat' in the Cabinet Room. 'It
is possible', Sir John said after leaving Whitehall for the City:

> for the critics to say that Mrs Thatcher was not a particularly good
> chairman. I don't think she's a natural chairman, she's more of a
> managing director ... but the fact is that she's perceptibly moved
> the country away from an accelerating decline ... and by being a

very good chairman, as opposed to being a thrusting, aggressive managing director, she would not have been able to do it.[19]

Leon Brittan, who held three Cabinet posts under Mrs Thatcher till Westland brought him down, reacts strongly to the charge that Mrs Thatcher packs the Cabinet room with compliant placemen. The Prime Minister is quite right to turn her back on 'a system of running the Cabinet on a basis of Buggins' turn, and that nobody can get anywhere unless they've been this that or the other for a very long time'.[20] There were some in the 'permanent government', the senior civil service, who relished the Thatcher style. Sir Frank Cooper, Permanent Secretary at the Ministry of Defence until the end of 1982, was happy to speak publicly about it:

> I think she's changed a number of things. She certainly leads from the front. No one would argue about that and she believes it's the duty of any prime minister to lead from the front. And I would have a great deal of sympathy with that view, quite frankly.[21]

Mrs Thatcher is aware of her Cabinet Room personality and the debate it has aroused. In accepting Jim Prior's resignation in 1984 she wrote: 'I take your point about frankness! That's what Cabinets are for, and lively discussions usually lead to good decisions'.[22] And, with the smoke of Westland still swirling round Whitehall, while her Home Secretary (Douglas Hurd) was telling one television audience 'I think it is very important that people should see we are under Cabinet government',[23] the Prime Minister was telling another:

> Some said that I should, in fact, have dealt with it and asked Mr Heseltine to go earlier. I can only tell you that had I done that ... I know exactly what the press would have said: 'There you are, old bossy-boots at it again'.[24]

The political nation probably has a clearer image of Mrs Thatcher's Cabinet Room style than ever emerged when her recent predecessors filled the seat beneath the portrait of Walpole. But for the first two years of her 1979–83 premiership her image was different from the impression now so firmly rooted. Jim Prior noted this in his memoir, *A Balance of Power*:

> In her early years as Prime Minister, Margaret adhered closely to the traditional principles and practice of Cabinet Government. She operated very strictly through the Cabinet Committee system, with the Cabinet Office taking the minutes'.[25]

A crucial exception to this traditional style, as Mr Prior acknowledges, was economic policy. Shortly after the 1979 election, he recalls, 'I realised that Margaret, Geoffrey [Howe], and Keith [Joseph] really had got the bit between their teeth and were not going to pay attention to the rest of us at all if they could possibly help it'.[26] Jim Prior's explanation for Mrs Thatcher's relative punctiliousness as a manager of Cabinet in her early years provides a choice piece of contemporary history from the Heath years of 1970–4 when she had served as Education Secretary:

> She had always been cold-shouldered by Ted; she sat in Cabinet on his right side, carefully hidden by the Secretary of the Cabinet, who was always leaning forward to take notes. It was the most difficult place for anyone to catch the Prime Minister's eye, and I am sure that she was placed there quite deliberately.[27]

Life in Cabinet Committee was no easier for her:

> In Ted's Government, Margaret had been left out from the *ad hoc* committees which were set up. Any Secretary of State for Education is always stuck in a rather isolated department. She had, however, proved herself a disruptive influence on one Cabinet Committee, the Science Committee, where she had complained that Solly Zuckerman [Chief Scientist, Cabinet Office] and Victor Rothschild [Head of the Central Policy Review Staff] were only officials and had no right to speak. They in their turn had complained about her.[28]

Nobody in 1970–4 saw Mrs Thatcher as a future prime minister. But her management of Cabinet is more than a matter of belated revenge, of doing to them what they did unto her. It is a clear reflection of her temperament and her priorities. It could be argued that the prime minister's personal style does not matter. The electorate knew what she was like in 1979 and 1983, and liked what they saw. But style can clash with system in a way that has important implications. As Lord Hailsham put it: 'There are two functions in the prime ministerial duties: one is to be a chairman and the other is to be a leader, and they are not always compatible'.[29] Mrs Thatcher has proved incapable of imitating Attlee and using silence as a weapon. She cannot overawe her Cabinet by a great set-piece *tour d'horizon* in the manner of Churchill. She cannot make them purr with pleasure like Macmillan with his aphorisms, quotations and reminiscences. She cannot hang back and score at the last minute like Jim Callaghan. It is

almost as if she abhors collectivism in any form, including collective discussion as the indispensable prelude to decision. She goes against the grain of traditional Cabinet government. But does it matter? Is it an efficient way of conducting business? Is it unconstitutional? These are the questions that count.

Any systems analyst allowed free access to the Cabinet Secretary's registry (there is no chance of that; the performance of Cabinet government is the one area that will not be the subject of a Rayner efficiency scrutiny)[30] would find the physical manifestations of a decline in collective discussion. Such debate is the essence of Cabinet government if you accept, as I do, the judgement of Lord Hunt of Tanworth, who served as Secretary from 1973–9. He argues 'that Cabinet government must always be a somewhat cumbrous and complicated affair, and that this is a price well worth paying for the advantage of shared discussion and shared decision – provided the system can keep up with the demands made upon it'.[31] The raw statistics of Cabinet business tell part of the story.

It is rare for Mrs Thatcher to have more than one meeting of the Cabinet per week.[32] Allowing for parliamentary recesses that amounts to between 40 and 45 meetings a year – not a particularly significant statistic if more business is being taken in committee (more of that below). Attlee and Churchill logged twice that figure and Macmillan was in the habit of calling two Cabinet meetings a week. The flow of Cabinet Papers is also well down, to between 60 and 70 a year, or about a sixth of the totals accumulated in the late 1940s, and early 1950s. Far from more being taken in Cabinet committee to compensate, workload is down there as well. When I last conducted an unofficial audit late in 1985, Mrs Thatcher's Cabinet engine room consisted of some 160 committees. She accumulated some 35 standing committees and 125 *ad hocs* in six and a half years; in six and a quarter years Attlee totted up 148 and 313. Churchill 137 and 109 in three and a half years; figures for Eden are not available at the time of writing; the Macmillan and Home years remain a mystery as, very largely, do the periods of Wilson I (1964–70) and of Heath. Wilson II between March 1974 and March 1976 ran up a total of somewhere around 120 *ad hoc* groups; Callaghan in the three years between April 1976 and April 1979 commissioned about 160 *ad hoc* committees, a similar growth rate to Attlee's. Without doubt Mrs Thatcher is running the slimmest Cabinet machine since before the Second World War.[33]

Structure is one thing, content another. Our systems analyst, had

he been able to sit in on Cabinet and Cabinet committee meetings at
various moments in the post-war period, would have found the
quality of discussion changing. Mrs Thatcher is as brisk as Attlee in
curbing wafflers but, in the process, appears to some to suck the
collective marrow out of the proceedings. Sir John Nott may have
relished the style, but to other ministers it was like vinegar on an
oyster. David Howell, a Cabinet minister in the first Thatcher
administration at Energy and Transport, was a backroom architect of
Edward Heath's attempt to bring more reason and analysis to
Cabinet business. He did not enjoy his spell with the Thatcher
colours ('Parliament a demanding mistress; the Prime Minister a
demanding mistress. How much fun can you have with so many
demanding mistresses?'[34]). He comments:

> If by 'conviction government' it is meant that certain slogans were
> going to be elevated and written in tablets of stone and used as the
> put-down at the end of every argument, then, of course, that is
> indeed what happened... Of course there is a deterring effect if
> one knows that one's going to go not into a discussion where
> various points of view will be weighed and gradually a view may be
> achieved, but into a huge argument where tremendous battle lines
> will be drawn up and everyone who doesn't fall into line will be hit
> on the head.[35]

This style of discussion may not be the best way of solving problems
of immense complexity which will not yield to sheer ministerial will,
political conviction and what Lord Rothschild once called the
'promises and panaceas that gleam like false teeth in party manifestos'.[36] Mrs Thatcher's abolition in 1983 of the Central Policy
Review Staff (CPRS), the Cabinet's 'think tank' of which Lord
Rothschild was the first head, was taken rightly as further evidence of
the Prime Minister's dislike of traditional policy analysis as a
precursor to decision-taking, a *beau idéal* in Whitehall since the
Haldane Report of 1918.[37] As Professor John Ashworth, a former
Chief Scientist to the CPRS, expressed it: 'Of its very existence it
sort of encapsulated a view about government for which she had not
great sympathy. She was what she called a conviction politician.
There is a difference between being a conviction politician and being
a rationally guided politician'.[38] Sir Frank Cooper, an admirer of Mrs
Thatcher as we have seen, believes conviction politics are fine for
slaughtering sacred cows which genuinely deserve the abbatoir, but
not so good for constructing new policies from the offal.[39] This is

likely to be one area where, once the shot and shell of current controversy are stilled, future historians of government will fault Mrs Thatcher compared to Mr Heath. It is already a conventional wisdom virtually across the political spectrum that some kind of CPRS needs to be restored. In late 1986, all three leaders of the opposition parties were committed to it and the idea[40] finds favour with some members of Mrs Thatcher's own administration, most notably Douglas Hurd.[41]

The throughput of Cabinet and Cabinet committees is down. What does go through is conducted in Cabinet and the committees the Prime Minister chairs in a brisk, no-nonsense, often combative style which will be long remembered in Whitehall. Nobody could say Mrs Thatcher's governments have been passive administrations, so where is the business being done? A fair amount is conducted by ministerial correspondence, a perfectly acceptable method in constitutional terms. The Franks Report on the Falklands gives an indication of just how much this goes on. One reason, for example, why the Falklands issue figured so infrequently on the agenda of the Cabinet's Oversea and Defence Committee before the Argentine invasion of April 1982 is that Lord Carrington, then Foreign and Commonwealth Secretary, disliked bringing FCO business before committee meetings of his colleagues.[42] Another swathe of high-level business is tackled by Mrs Thatcher in *ad hoc* groups which fall outside Sir Robert Armstrong's Cabinet committee book.

The most important of these is her version of Mr Callaghan's 'Economic Seminar', though it no longer has that name.[43] It handles similar subjects – monetary policy, delicate decisions affecting the money markets. Early in her first premiership it caused her a moment of acute embarrassment. One Cabinet minister, a member of the Economic Strategy Committee but not of this most secret inner group which was meeting straight afterwards, was a bit slow to gather his papers. As he was about to leave, Sir Geoffrey Howe, then Chancellor of the Exchequer, launched into his paper on the plan to abolish exchange controls. 'Oh', said the laggardly minister, 'Are we going to do that? How very interesting.' Embarrassed silence. Then Sir Geoffrey said, 'X I'm afraid you should not be here'. X departed Cabinet door left.[44]

Under Mrs Thatcher the 'Economic Seminar' remains highly important. But it is a flexible, amoeba-like group whose composition changes according to circumstances. 'It's a habit of working, not an approach', explained an insider. 'If there is a problem or a proposal, she'll call a meeting involving those immediately concerned. She may

also invite someone who will be important when it comes to selling it in Cabinet – someone like Willie Whitelaw'.[45]

Other *ad hoc* groups beyond the reach of the MISC series (as recognized *ad hoc* groups are known in Cabinet Office nomenclature) can have a considerable impact even though they only meet once or twice. Mrs Thatcher convened a meeting of ministers to consider the now legendary minute entitled 'It Took a Riot'. This had been prepared for her by Michael Heseltine, then Secretary of State for the Environment, based on his experiences in Merseyside following the inner city riots of July 1981. It proposed an ambitious programme of investment and the designation of Cabinet colleagues as ministers for various decaying areas. Mr Heseltine had evangelized Whitehall on behalf of his cause like a latterday John the Baptist. He held a secret dinner at Locket's restaurant in Westminster for several influential permanent secretaries, including Sir Robert Armstrong. They were impressed.

The Prime Minister, however, prevailed. In September 1981 she convened an *ad hoc* group on inner cities and stacked it against Mr Heseltine. It consisted of the two of them, together with Sir Geoffrey Howe, Chancellor of the Exchequer, Sir Keith Joseph, Industry Secretary, and William Whitelaw, Home Secretary. Whitelaw, concerned as ever to be the mediator, strove to find a middle way between Heseltine and those who did not want a penny extra for the cities for fear of being seen to reward rioters. Heseltine was isolated. There was an increase in the urban programme, but on nothing like the scale he had wanted.[46] On this occasion, he succumbed to the verdict of a loaded ministerial group in the full knowledge that if he took the issue to full Cabinet he would be defeated there as well.[47]

Mrs Thatcher conducts a great deal of business in gatherings like that. The pattern varies, but is often along these lines. Mrs Thatcher will ask a particular Cabinet colleague to prepare a paper on a particular issue just for her, not for the Cabinet or a Cabinet committee. This explains why the tally of Cabinet papers is so low. The Minister is summoned to No. 10 with his back-up team. He sits across the table from Mrs Thatcher and her team which can be a blend of people from the Downing Street Private Office, the Policy Unit, the Cabinet Office, and one or two personal advisers. She then, in the words of one insider, proceeds to 'act as judge and jury in her own cause'.[48] It is this practice more than anything else which causes those on the inside to speak of 'a devaluation of Cabinet government' and her 'presidential style'.[49] The build-up of leaks and stories from

such occasions creates a cumulative impression of a truly overmighty premiership.

But is that impression accurate? A case can be made for both its constitutional propriety and its administrative efficiency. Take first Mrs Thatcher's version of the 'Economic Seminar'. David Howell is a critic of the Thatcher style but he sees nothing wrong in it:

Howell: I don't think one would have expected, not being in the Treasury, to be involved. One would have assumed that, indeed I think it was generally known, that the Prime Minister and Treasury Ministers and her Chancellor kept in very close touch with the financial authorities and the central monetary authorities which means the Bank of England among other people and that all that would go on. I don't think one would assume anything else. If it had a name, or a code word, well that sounds like civil servants playing games. Ministers would assume that went on. Occasionally other ministers might be called into those discussions. But of course the nexus of any government in this country is No. 10 and the Treasury and with the Bank of England as the Treasury's appendage which unfortunately it is. I say 'unfortunately' because I would like to see a more detached monetary authority myself. Therefore one assumes they're very hugger-mugger all the time. Under this government and under the regime that emerged after 1979, which wasn't quite the one we planned for before 1979, but after the one did emerge after 1979, the nexus between No.10 and the Treasury is decisive, it overrules, it's everything. The Treasury always knows they can win. That is why they're able to go for these very precise figures of public spending, scientific precision about estimates for the years ahead and then say 'all argument hereafter ceases. Anyone who wants to change anything will have to somehow change it without altering the figures because they're settled and we know that if we ever go back to No. 10 or the Cabinet we'll always get the backing of the Prime Minister and the appellant will always be overturned'.

Hennessy: Going back to the 'Economic Seminar', you seem to accept these things are bound to exist, these small inner groups. Doesn't it rather vitiate the nature of Cabinet government, though, if a decision, like the one to remove all exchange control, a very fundamental one for any economy, is in fact worked up, although it goes to full Cabinet in the end, in such a body? Doesn't it mean that you're presented with a set of *faits accomplis*? You're meant to

be collectively the highest strategic decision-making body in the land and here are all these great slices of crucial economic decisions done in a group in which ministers are outnumbered three or four to one by officials.

Howell: Yes, well, you say 'meant to be' and you're right to say 'meant to be' because, of course, Cabinet government is only a layer of the government and there is a kind of inner Cabinet government, whether it's called that or not, under different prime ministers, it always tends to develop. On top of that there must be an even more inner kind of government concerned with very very sensitive issues of which exchange control is one. It would have been inconceivable for exchange control to be tossed around and knocked around in Cabinet.

Hennesy: Why?

Howell: Because of the numbers of people involved and because of, well, I suppose I have to say it, the inevitability of leaks.[50]

Senior civil servants, the inside connoisseurs of prime ministerial style and procedure, tend not to be purist about the operational implications of Cabinet conventions, apart from their routine deployment in the occasional public lecture. They seem, in practice, to treat Cabinet government as a chunk of modelling clay to be pummelled and fashioned by the prime minister of the hour. This is the kind of reasoning you hear when senior men think aloud in private about the theme of Cabinet government:

The Cabinet system has been different for Heath, Wilson and Mrs Thatcher. There's a reaction, which we can get in our constitution, to suit the PM of the day and his or her working relationships. The decisions get taken in the way in which people want to take them. . . Mrs Thatcher is very clear about her views, very much a leader. Because of that she doesn't need or want to resolve things by collective discussion. She knows what she wants to do about almost everything. But it *is* a collective machine because they all sink or swim with her. She uses the Cabinet as a sort of sounding board. It restrains her when restraint is necessary. She has her own instinct when she cannot carry her colleagues with her. She lets them know what she thinks. Then they try and adapt and mould it. She has very acute antennae. She's very quick to take the signals if she can't carry it.[51]

Mrs Thatcher's method of conducting business is highly efficient in its use of precious ministerial time and nervous energy. She has a bias towards decision. She has found her own highly distinctive solution to the problem of governmental overload identified by Professor Anthony King in 1975[52], and a staple item in political science analyses every since. It is reminiscent of Harold Wilson's well-known line about the Labour Party needing to be driven fast like a stagecoach so that the passengers are too exhilarated or too sick to object.[53] A fast driver like Mrs Thatcher can get away with it as long as her Cabinet colleagues acquiesce or concur. Douglas Hurd, however, speaking in September 1986, still saw 'a government machine clogged with matter', and said: 'it is up to us to find the time and the energy needed for effective collective discussion . . . if collective decisions are to be of the right quality, then collective decision-taking has to be a principal, and not the last, call on the time and energy of ministers'.[54] There is nothing unconstitutional about Mrs Thatcher's approach. The style of conducting Cabinet business is as malleable as putty – much more a matter of personality than convention or tradition. There have been objections; after the 1981 Budget, Mrs Thatcher was obliged to hold periodic economic Cabinets to discuss strategy.[55] But her ministers had proved remarkably acquiescent towards her manner of conducting business until that helicopter crashed, metaphorically speaking, through the skylight in early December 1985.

Westland *did* raise genuine constitutional issues. Each side claimed the other was breaking the rules. Both sides were right.[56] When Michael Heseltine, Secretary of State for Defence, became convinced as December progressed that he was being denied a chance in a deliberate and persistent fashion to put his case for a European rescue of Westland he took that case to the public. He was, he maintained, thwarted at each level of the Cabinet structure – *ad hoc* group, the standing committee on economic strategy, and full Cabinet. By crusading publicly for a European solution he was flouting *Questions of Procedure for Ministers*, the unpublished constitution of Cabinet government if you accept Pickthorn's view that 'procedure is all the Constitution the poor Briton has'.[57] Heseltine drove a tank through its section on collective responsibility which reads:

> Decisions reached by the Cabinet or Cabinet Committees are normally announced and defended by the Minister concerned as his own decisions. There may be rare occasions when it is desirable

to emphasise the importance of some decision by stating specifically that it is the decision of Her Majesty's Government. This, however, should be the exception rather than the rule. The growth of any general practice whereby decisions of the Cabinet or of Cabinet Committees were announced as such would lead to the embarrassing result that some decisions of Government would be regarded as less authoritative than others. Critics of a decision reached by a particular Committee could press for its review by some other Committee or by the Cabinet, and the constitutional right of individual Ministers to speak in the name of the Government as a whole would be impaired.[58]

Heseltine spared no effort in making the government line on Westland appear 'less authoritative than others', and was vigorously pressing for a review.

But the Prime Minister was also sinning against custom and practice in her treatment of Heseltine. There are no written rules covering the right of a dissenting minister to take an issue to full Cabinet. The normal conventions were explained by Lord Hunt of Tanworth, when interviewed for the 1986 television programme *All the Prime Minister's Men*:

Hennessy: How about Cabinet Ministers having a right to put an issue onto the agenda of full Cabinet, that's been controversial in the Westland affair as well, what's your understanding of the constitutional practice there?

Hunt: The constitutional practice is that the agenda is produced by the Secretary of the Cabinet and approved by the Prime Minister. Any minister can ask for an item to go on, in the ordinary way his department will have asked. And if it is the right time for it to come to Cabinet, if there is room on the agenda, it'll be on. But if a minister is unsatisfied and wants an item included which isn't on, he can always ask. And I've known that happen, and in the ordinary way the Prime Minister will agree.

Hennessy: But Prime Ministers have the right to keep things off the agenda if they want to, for whatever reason?

Hunt: I have never known a Prime Minister keep an item off an agenda for what one might call a disreputable or tactical reason. I mean there have been times where I've known a Prime Minister say, we have ten items next week, there simply isn't time, or it is

not the right time to discuss this because . . . But where you've had
a position of a minister who is unhappy and unsatisfied that an issue
is not being given a hearing, I've never known a Prime Minister
refuse to have it on the agenda.[59]

Under the parameters outlined by Lord Hunt, Heseltine should have
had his full Cabinet discussion. He was a political heavyweight and,
with Leon Brittan at Trade and Industry, one of the two lead
ministers on the Westland issue. He had reason to be aggrieved.

The British constitution has no equivalent of the Ordnance Survey;
our system is without maps. But when corners are cut in relation to
what is generally understood to be standard practice a very high
price can be paid. This was the case with the Westland Affair, which
involved two Cabinet resignations, a prolonged diversion of precious
time and energy at the highest level in the land, and a lingering taste
of incompetence and chicanery which found its most trenchant
expression in a subsequent report from the all-party Commons Select
Committee on Defence.[60]

It was generally expected that the trauma of Westland would
squeeze the Thatcher style of Cabinet government into a more
traditional mould, collective rather than presidential in configuration.
The handling of the proposed sale of Land Rover and BL Trucks
division in the early spring of 1986 suggested this had happened when
the planned sale to General Motors was abandoned in the face of
back-bench hostility and Cabinet doubts. But the Prime Minister's
granting of permission for United states F-111's to fly from British
bases in a raid on Libya in April, after minimal ministerial consultation, suggested to her routine critics at least that the Old Adam of an
overmighty premiership still afflicted Mrs Thatcher. The need for
tight security to surround a special operation of this kind can always
be advanced in exoneration, but the first that most of the Cabinet
heard of the raid was when its completion was announced on BBC
radio on the morning of 15 April 1986 as the bombers were returning
to Upper Heyford and Lakenheath. At a Cabinet meeting that
morning, several senior ministers are reported to have cavilled,
including the veteran Lord Hailsham.[61] Though, as he said later, 'I
don't think anyone resigned over it, and I think therefore one must
take it that it is not an affront to Cabinet government.'[62]

That such a negative definition of the meaning of Cabinet government was needed from so seasoned a figure was an eloquent
reflection of the battering the more reassuring notions of collective

responsibility had received in the Thatcher years. But to depict her era in stark colours as an unconstitutional premiership would be wrong. Progress towards a stronger, more assertive premiership 'had its origins in small sparks eating their way through long historical fuses before the detonations began', to borrow a metaphor Professor Jack Gallagher used to describe another process (the decline of the British Empire) in another era.[63] Temperament (and, arguably, necessity) combined to make Mrs Thatcher a managing director rather than a chairman in the Cabinet Room. Whoever succeeds her in that chair is unlikely wholly to reverse that process, though doubtless much political capital will be made in the early broadcasts from No. 10, using a style derived from Stanley Baldwin and James Callaghan with a possible smattering of Harold Macmillan. Just as Baldwin was anxious to be anybody but Lloyd George and Mrs Thatcher was determined to imitate anybody but Ted Heath, her successor – Labour, Alliance or Conservative – will assuredly be (in style at least) anybody but Margaret. In its perverse way, that is a rare compliment and the Prime Minister, when safely in the Lords as Viscountess Grantham, should draw genuine comfort from it.

Notes

1. Graham Turner, 'How Lord Hailsham Judges Himself and His Peers', the *Sunday Telegraph*, 13 April 1986.
2. Private information.
3. See Peter Hennessy, The Secrets That Will Stay Secret Forever', *Listener*, 11 September 1986.
4. Lord Hailsham delivered this opinion after I finished a television interview with him on 14 May 1986.
5. Lord Hailsham interviewed for Brook Productions' Channel 4 television programme *All the Prime Minister's Men*, 14 May 1986. Transcripts of Brook Productions' interviews for this programme can be read in the British Library of Economic and Political Science at the London School of Economics.
6. Interview with Kenneth Harris, *Observer*, 25 February 1979.
7. It is reproduced in Alan Thompson, *The Day Before Yesterday: An Illustrated History of Britain from Attlee to Macmillan*, (London: Sidgwick and Jackson, 1971) p. 163.
8. Norman St John Stevas, 'Prime Ministers Rise and Fall but the Cabinet Abides', *Daily Telegraph*, 7 August 1986.
9. Quoted in Peter Hennessy, 'From Woodshed to Watershed', *The Times*, 5 March 1984.

10.   *Nine O'Clock News*, BBC, 10 January 1986.
11.   *News At Ten*, ITN, 10 January 1986.
12.   Ian Gilmour, *The Body Politic*, (London: Hutchinson, 1969).
13.   'Friday People', *Guardian*, 22 November 1985.
14.   Lord Bancroft, interviewed for *All the Prime Minister's Men*, 10 April 1986.
15.   'At Last Someone Says No, Prime Minister', leading article, *Observer*, 12 January 1986.
16.   See his introduction to *'Re-skilling Government: The Boundaries of the Reform Process'*, a discussion paper prepared for a conference on 8 September 1986. Available from the Institute of Directors.
17.   Sir John Hoskyns, interviewed for *All the Prime Minister's Men*, 26 March 1986.
18.   Sir John Hoskyns interview, 26 March 1986.
19.   Sir John Nott, interviewed for *All the Prime Minister's Men*, 22 April 1986.
20.   Leon Brittan, interviewed for *All the Prime Minister's Men*, 26 March 1986.
21.   Quoted in Peter Hennessy, *Cabinet* (Oxford: Basil Blackwell, 1986) p. 105.
22.   *The Times*, 1 September 1984.
23.   *Weekend World*, London Weekend Television, 26 January 1986.
24.   *Face the Press*, Tyne Tees Television, 26 January 1986.
25.   Jim Prior, *A Balance of Power*, (London: Hamish Hamilton, 1986) p. 133.
26.   Prior, *A Balance of Power*, p. 119.
27.   Prior, *A Balance of Power*, p. 117.
28.   Prior, *A Balance of Power*, p. 133.
29.   Lord Hailsham, interviewed for *All the Prime Minister's Men*, 14 May 1986.
30.   See Peter Hennessy, 'The Quality of Cabinet Government in Britain', *Policy Studies*, 6 (2), October 1985: 16.
31.   Lord Hunt of Tanworth, 'Cabinet Strategy and Management', CIPFA – RIPA Conference, Eastbourne, 9 June 1983.
32.   I have drawn heavily in this section on Chapter 3, 'Conviction Cabinet 1979–86' in Hennessy, *Cabinet*, pp. 99–101 in particular.
33.   The committees of which I have learned are listed in Table 1, 'Mrs Thatcher's engine room', Hennessy, *Cabinet*, pp. 27–30.
34.   Hennessy, *Cabinet*, p. 98.
35.   Hennessy, *Cabinet*, pp. 95–6.
36.   Lord Rothschild, *Meditations of a Broomstick*, (London: Collins, 1977) p. 171.
37.   Haldane's appeal was 'for the systematic application of thought as preliminary to the settlement of policy and its subsequent administration', Ministry of Reconstruction, *Report of the Machinery of Government Committee*, Col. 9230 (London: HMSO, 1918) p. 6.
38.   Quoted in Peter Hennessy, Susan Morrison and Richard Townsend, *Routine Punctuated by Orgies: The Central Policy Review Staff 1970–83*, Strathclyde Papers on Government and Politics 31, 1985, p. 85.

39. Sir Frank Cooper, interviewed for *All the Prime Minister's Men*, 8 April 1986.
40. Hoskyns, *'Reskilling Government'*.
41. Mr Hurd delivered his views on the need for a small new CPRS on *All the Prime Minister's Men: The Shape of Things to Come*, Channel 4 Television, 24 July 1986.
42. Private information.
43. For the genesis and function of Mr Callaghan's 'Economic Seminar' see Hennessy, *Cabinet*, p. 92.
44. Private information.
45. Private information.
46. Private information.
47. Private information.
48. Private information.
49. Private information.
50. Quoted in Hennessy, *Cabinet*, pp. 103–4.
51. Private information.
52. Anthony King, 'Overload: Problems of Governing in the 1970's', *Political Studies*, xxii, (2–3), June–September 1975.
53. Anthony Sampson, *Anatomy of Britain Today*, (London: Hodder & Stoughton, 1965) p. 105.
54. 'Home Secretary's Lecture to the Royal Institute of Public Administration', University of Durham, 19 September 1986.
55. Francis Pym (one of the objectors), interviewed for *All the Prime Minister's Men*, 25 March 1986.
56. I have written at greater length on this theme. See Peter Hennessy, 'Michael Heseltine, Mottram's Law and the Efficiency of Cabinet Government', *The Political Quarterly*, 57 (2), April–June 1986: 137–43 and 'Helicopter Crashes into Cabinet: Prime Minister and Constitution Hurt', in *The Journal of Law and Society*, 13, (2), Winter 1986.
57. House of Commons Debates, 8 February 1960, Col. 70.
58. Hennessy, *Cabinet*, pp. 11–12.
59. Interview with Lord Hunt of Tanworth, for *All the Prime Minister's Men*, 29 May 1986.
60. House of Commons, Fourth Report from the Defence Committee, Session 1985–6, *Westland PLC: The Government's Decision-Making*, (London: HMSO, 1986).
61. Adam Raphael, Simon Hoggart, Peter Pringle and Robin Smyth, 'The Winning of Thatcher', *Observer*, 20 April 1986.
62. Lord Hailsham's judgement was broadcast in *All the Prime Minister's Men: Conviction Cabinet*, Channel 4 Television, 17 July 1986.
63. John Gallagher, *The Decline, Revival and Fall of the British Empire*, (Cambridge: Cambridge University Press, 1982) p. 73. For pre-Thatcher moves towards a more dominant premiership see Hennessy, *Cabinet*, Chapter 2, pp. 34–93.

5 Mrs Thatcher's Economic Legacy

C. F. Pratten

'Let the Government do its job, which includes the provision of a stable monetary and fiscal framework and a competitive environment... The result ... should be reasonable stability without runaway inflation or mass unemployment'.[1] Sam Brittan, one of Mrs Thatcher's most influential supporters, has admitted that this vision of economic policy, which he believes the Conservatives held in 1979, has been shattered by experience. In the eighth year of Mrs Thatcher's economic experiment, Britain has mass unemployment and there is no end in sight to this state of affairs.

Mrs Thatcher's economic experiment has not succeeded. The interesting questions concern the reasons for the failure, the realities of Britain's economy in 1986, and the policies which could improve its performance. However, we must first outline the economic policies of the Conservative governments since 1979, and summarise the economic record.

THE POLICIES

Macroeconomic Policies

In 1977, the Conservative Central Office published *The Right Approach to the Economy*, which described the economic policies a Conservative government would pursue. Earlier post-war Labour and Conservative governments had used macroeconomic policy to regulate aggregate demand and maintain employment; when unemployment threatened to increase they used Keynesian macroeconomic policies, a combination of lower interest rates and taxes, and increased government expenditure to increase demand and employment. The new Conservative policy would be to use macroeconomic policies to control inflation: Keynesian macroeconomic policy would be used in reverse; interest rates and taxes would be raised, and government expenditure would be lowered to deflate

demand and to reduce and hold down inflation. There would be '*strict* control ... of the rate of growth of the money supply [my emphasis]' and 'firm management of government expenditure'. Mr Lawson later encapsulated the new focus of macroeconomic policy in the statement: 'It is the conquest of inflation and not the pursuit of growth and employment, which is ... the objective of macro-economic policy'.[2]

Sir Geoffrey Howe followed the monetarists' macroeconomic brief while he was Chancellor from 1979 until 1983. Interest rates were pushed sky-high to reduce the rate of growth of the money supply, and in his 1981 budget Sir Geoffrey reduced the PSBR, in spite of a massive increase in unemployment. Since 1984, behind a veil of rhetoric, the government has lost any faith it had in technical monetarism. The money supply, as measured by £M_3, has been allowed to grow erratically, while calculation of the PSBR is held down by the ruse of subtracting the proceeds of privatization as well as taxes from government expenditure. The principles of monetarism have been abandoned. Until very recently, there remained an anti-Keynesian bias in favour of holding down demand – a preference for risking recession and more unemployment, rather than using Keynesian policies to increase demand and risking rapid growth of demand and faster inflation.[3]

Microeconomic Policies

In 1979, most economists focused on the Conservatives' macro-economic policies, involving monetarism. But there was another strand, of a microeconomic kind: the government would seek to develop an 'enterprise culture'. Many of the policies intended to achieve this were negative in the sense that they would eliminate government controls, by abolishing pay, price, dividend, foreign exchange and bank lending controls. Tax reductions, privatization, and the breaking up of monopolies and restrictive practices (particularly those exercised by trade unions) were also included in this list of policies. In brief, the Conservatives claimed that freedom works, and that the economy would perform well only if controls were lifted, incentives restored, and the power of trade unions reduced. Mr Lawson claimed in 'The British Experiment' that 'it is the creation of conditions conducive to growth and employment ... which is ... the objective of microeconomic policy'.

Mrs Thatcher's governments have implemented many of the

microeconomic policies which were proposed in 1977. Controls on prices and incomes – apart from the Wages Councils – were soon abolished, the highest rates of taxes were quickly reduced, and trade union legislation was enacted. The privatization programme was developed.

Focus on Monetarism

It was understandable that economists should concentrate on the Conservatives' macroeconomic policies. These were new (at least to economists without direct experience of the 1930s), and the circumstances in 1979 were different from those experienced during that earlier period. Second, the British economy was apparently to be used as a test bed for an experiment with monetarist macroeconomic policies, and it was unusual for politicians to provide such a clear-cut test of economists' theories. There was another reason for the focus on monetarism. By 1979 Keynesian policies were in trouble. Monetarists pinpointed inflation as the problem. The Keynesian remedy for inflation was incomes policy, but in Britain incomes policies had worked for short periods, not over the long term. For Keynesians, the bugbear was the balance of payments; expansionary policies – policies designed to increase aggregate demand – led to balance of payments deficits and self-defeating deflation. Devaluation – the remedy for balance of payments deficits – worked slowly and could be neutralized by faster inflation induced by the devaluation itself. Keynesians had no panacea for Britain's economic problems; the monetarists claimed to have one – technical monetarism.

At the same time, it was natural that economists should pay little attention to the Conservatives' microeconomic policies. As the Conservatives themselves stated in *The Right Approach to the Economy*, they had been tried before in the 1950s. The opening statement of the document was: 'In the 1950s, "Tory freedom" worked'. There were other reasons why economists should ignore the microeconomic policies. By definition microeconomic policies deal with parts of the economy and individually have a small effect on the macroeconomy; the expertise of many economists when advising on microeconomic policies is also limited. They can advocate removal of restrictions on competition and make cost-benefit calculations. But Britain's post-war economic problem has not been a lack of competition, it has been a lack of competitiveness. Table 5.1 shows changes

Table 5.1   UK share of world exports of manufactures

Administration	UK share (%)	Average annual Percentage change (%)	German share (%)	Average annual change (%)
1951	22.0		10.0	
Conservatives		−3.2		+5.4
1964	14.0		19.7	
Labour		−4.5		0.0
1970	10.8		19.8	
Conservatives		−5.0		+2.3
1974	8.8		21.7	
Labour		+2.0		−1.0
1979	9.7		20.7	
Conservatives		−3.5		−1.8
1985	7.8		18.5	

Source: National Institute Economic Review, various issues.

in the UK's share of world trade in manufactures; it has fallen by a half since 1960, from 16.3 per cent in 1960 to 7.8 in 1985. Between 1951 and 1964 when, so the Conservatives claimed, 'Tory Freedom' worked, Britain's share of world trade in manufactures fell by 3.2 per cent per year. The causes of this decline in competitiveness were not macroeconomic policies alone, and they included factors such as the quality of management, industrial relations, and education for which economists could not claim exclusive expertise.

THE ECONOMIC RECORD

Statistical Comparisons

Although there is widespread agreement that Mrs Thatcher's economic policies have not succeeded, it is a statistical conundrum to measure and demonstrate her failure.

One approach in attempting to estimate what would have happened if different economic policies had been pursued is to make statistical comparisons between the performance of the UK economy post- and pre-1979, and with the performance of other economies. If performance has worsened on both these criteria since Mrs Thatcher took over, then her policies have failed. In practice, there are serious qualifications to be made to such conclusions. Other changes

occurred about the same time that Mrs Thatcher became Prime Minister. Output of North Sea oil increased rapidly after 1979, for example, and other countries adopted monetarist policies. Time-lags between the adoption of new economic policies and their effects must also be considered.

The statistical evidence is summarized in Table 5.2, and Figure 5.1. Section (a) of Table 5.2 show the economic record between 1979 and 1985. The growth of output of the economy (GDP) – the principal indicator of economic performance – was slow, 1 per cent per annum, and unemployment rose by 2 million. The main achievement was to reduce the rate of inflation from 13 to 5 per cent.

This 1979–85 period is compared with data for two earlier ones, 1960–73 and 1973–9, shown in sections (b) and (c) of Table 5.2. The period from 1960 until 1973 is taken as the Keynesian period (although it can be argued that the break with Keynesian policies occurred in 1976 rather than 1979).[4] The period 1973–9 was beset by economic crises stemming from the first oil price shock.

Compared with the Keynesian period, Mrs Thatcher's economic record is dismal. Even with the benefit of North Sea oil, output since 1979 has increased by only 1 per cent a year, compared to 3.1 per cent a year between 1960 and 1973. Understandably, Mrs Thatcher's team prefers the comparison with the period 1973–9, when growth was only 1.3 per cent, but that comparison is sensitive to the starting year. Growth between 1972 and 1979 was 2.2. per cent a year – 1973 was a year of very rapid growth. Comparing the period 1979–85 with 1973–9 Mrs Thatcher scores well on inflation, but very badly on unemployment.

The problem with the comparisons for periods post- and pre-1973 is that since the Keynesian period external conditions have changed – the oil price shocks, slower growth of world output and trade, and floating exchange rates. Can international comparisons provide an adequate assessment of Mrs Thatcher's performance? Other countries as well as Britain were affected by the changed international environment. Figure 5.1 compares UK economic performance with that for the OECD and the EEC (including the UK). This casts Mrs Thatcher's performance in a better light. Growth of output slowed over the three periods distinguished. In each of them the growth of output for the UK was slower than for the OECD and the EEC, but between 1979 and 1985 Britain was closer to the EEC average. Worldwide, consumer prices rose faster between 1973 and 1979 than between 1967 and 1973, but the UK's rate of inflation was substant-

Table 5.2   The economic record

(a)	Period of Mrs Thatcher's monetarist experiment		
	1979	*1985*	*Change*
1. Output			
a. Index of GDP (% p.a.)	100	106	+1.0
b. Index of GDP (% p.a.), excluding the extraction of oil and gas (MLH 104)	100	103	+0.5
2. Retail prices (percentage change from previous year)	13	5	−8
3. Unemployment (million)	1.2	3.2	+2

(b)	1973–9		
	1973	*1979*	*Change*
1. Output			
a. Index of GDP (% p.a.)	100	108	+1.3
b. Index of GDP (% p.a), excluding the extraction of oil and gas (MLH 104)	100	103	+0.5
2. Retail prices (percentage change from previous year)	9	13	+4
3. Unemployment (million)	0.6	1.2	+0.6

(c)	Keynesian period 1960–73		
	1960	*1973*	*Change*
1. Output			
a. Index of GDP (% p.a.)	100	148	+3.1
b. Index of GDP (% p.a.), excluding the extraction of oil and gas (MLH 104)	100	148	+3.1
2. Retail prices (percentage change from previous year)	1	9	+8
3. Unemployment (million)	0.3	0.6	+0.3

Sources: Economic Trends Annual Supplement 1986, and issues of *Economic Trends* and *Monthly Digest of Statistics.*

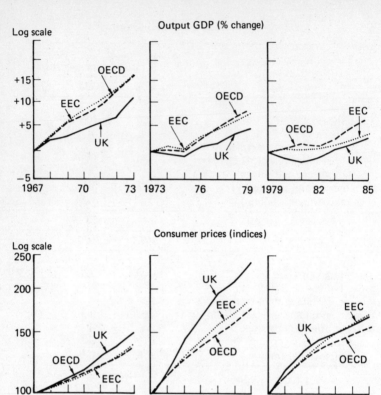

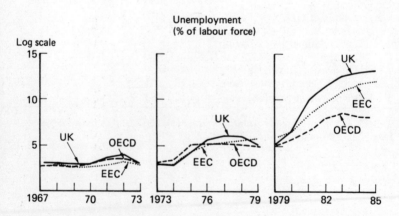

Figure 5.1 International economic comparisons
Sources: Inst. of OECD *Economic Outlook*.

ially above the OECD and EEC averages between 1973 and 1979. From 1979 inflation slowed, and the UK was close to the OECD and EEC averages. Between 1979 and 1985 unemployment has risen more rapidly in the UK than in the OECD, but not much faster than the EEC average.

Necessary Caveats

There are two caveats to these comparisons. One favours Mrs Thatcher, the other does not. Japan and the USA, which carry heavy weighting within the OECD, have had a better economic performance than the UK since 1979, but the EEC may provide a more realistic guide to the economic possibilities for Britain. Japan and the USA are not subject to a balance of payments constraint to the same extent as the UK. The competitiveness of Japanese industry and the political power of the USA enable these countries to have a high level of demand without initiating a balance of payments crisis. On the other side, Britain (alone among the major OECD countries) is self-sufficient for fuel supplies. During the period 1979–85 this gave it a unique chance, a golden opportunity, to outperform those other economies.

In brief, Mrs Thatcher's supporters can argue that many countries had a poor economic record between 1979 and 1985; Britain's failure to manage growth, slow inflation and a high level of unemployment was not unique.

WHY DID MRS THATCHER'S ECONOMIC EXPERIMENT FAIL?

The Labour Market

I started this chapter by outlining Sam Brittan's vision of Mrs Thatcher's economic experiment. The crux of the failure of this vision of price flexibility to achieve full utilization of resources is the labour market.

By way of illustration, plums can be used as an example of market clearing. If there is a glut of plums on the market, the market recipe is to cut the price of plums. Consumers will substitute plums for other fruit. If prices fall far enough, growers will leave their plums to rot on the trees and this provides a floor for the price of plums. Plums will not pile up unsold with wholesalers or retailers. Similarly a fall in wages increases employment, and some people may withdraw from the labour market if wages fall. In the labour market, social security

benefits play the role of the plums left to rot on the trees. They provide a floor for wages.

In practice, the glut of labour which shows up as mass unemployment has not resulted in lower average real wages. Demand for many types of qualified and skilled manpower is buoyant and, understandably, unions representing semi-skilled and unskilled workers resist reductions in relative pay for their members. The pay of many less skilled workers has been protected by Wages Councils. Also many employers are reluctant to reduce the wages of workers who are in easy supply (often unskilled or semi-skilled workers) because they identify with them, in the sense that one of the managers' objectives is to maintain or increase the real wages of their employees; they consider the wages of many unskilled workers already very low and/ or they fear that a reduction in these wages will lead to strikes or low performance. Many managers of firms have used their improved negotiating position to get agreement for improvements in productivity which reduce real wage costs. These concessions affecting productivity are worth more than marginal reductions in pay for unskilled employees. So the relative pay of the glut of unskilled workers falls only very slowly (compared to the price movements for plums).

A theorist would point to a missing link in these simple explanations for the failure of wages to fall. Why do new firms not set up, pay lower wages, and win business by quoting lower prices? In some trades (for example, among scaffolding contractors), this has happened. Large firms have been forced to reduce wages because of price-cutting by small firms, including new small firms entering the trade. In most trades, however, there are steep barriers to entry. New firms cannot set up such things as oil refineries or car factories in industries where there are large economies of scale. A new workforce takes time to learn to produce complex products efficiently, customers are loyal to existing brands, and so on.

Even if relative wages had changed, or real wages generally had fallen since 1981, the effects on the demand for labour would have been muted. It takes time for firms to react to economic incentives, win increased sales because of a reduction in costs, and create jobs in response to a change in wages relative to other costs. Also, if average real wages within the economy had fallen, consumers' expenditure (the largest component of demand) would not have been as buoyant as it has in fact been.

The social consequences of changes in relative wages are clear.

Already the range of income is wide: £2,000 a week for some foreign exchange dealers in the City, £600+ for some professional groups, £150+ for skilled craftsmen with overtime, £70+ for some groups of unskilled workers, and £20+ social security for many unemployed youths. To get substantial reduction in unemployment by changing wages, the pay of the unskilled (and social security benefits) would have had to collapse, perhaps halve.

The problems in the labour market were exacerbated by the history of overmanning in UK industry, and by technical developments which were increasing demand for skilled and qualified manpower and reducing demand for the unskilled.

Although the labour scene provides the clearest evidence of the failure of the price mechanism to clear markets, it is not the only example of market failure. The balance of payments and the exchange rate provide another illustration. Here the price (the exchange rate) is extremely volatile, and this is dangerous. A fall in the exchange rate is self-justifying where devaluation sets off a wage–price spiral. During the years when sterling was a naturally strong currency because of North Sea oil, Mrs Thatcher and Sir Geoffrey Howe applied to the UK the monetarist prescription for inflation, through maintaining interest rates at high levels by international standards and further increasing the exchange rate. With the topping-out of North Sea oil production and the fall in the oil price, the pound is now weak. In order to forestall a sterling crisis, Mrs Thatcher has had to maintain UK interest rates at levels which towered above those of Britains competitors.

It is not difficult to pinpoint the reasons for the failure of Mr Brittan's vision of Mrs Thatcher's economic experiment. However, Mr Brittan's version is that of an eminent economic philosopher. There are other versions, and I shall consider three of them.

Competitiveness

The second version of Mrs Thatcher's experiment focuses on competitiveness. Many influential Conservatives do not share Mr Brittan's vision of the efficiency of a market economy with flexible prices clearing markets. They believe that the solution for Britain's persistent lack of international competitiveness is to remove barriers to competition, to lower restraints (including taxes) on those British firms and individuals who are competitive, and to penalize, and not featherbed, firms and individuals who lack competitiveness. Britain's champions should not be hindered, while the failures should be

given a sharp shock. These beliefs are often combined with a sceptical and pessimistic view of the power of the state to mould (or even influence) the economy.

It is certainly true that a key to sound national economic performance is the international competitiveness of a country's industrial and service sectors. There is also evidence from company histories that shocks can have constructive consequences. Firms facing severe shocks caused by changes in demand, new competitors, or general recession review their operations, appoint new managers not committed to existing policies and personnel, reduce slack, close unpromising lines of business, and look for new avenues for expansion. Has Mrs Thatcher set Britain on a course of increased competitiveness?

One problem for those assessing the effects of Mrs Thatcher's policies here is the difficulty in estimating the long-term effects of the loss of protected Commonwealth and colonial markets, and of Britain's late entry to the EEC. It naturally takes time for firms to adapt to changing market conditions, and to redirect their marketing efforts. Britain's exclusion from the EEC lowered the country's share of world trade, while late entry increased it. If the main effects of switching exports from protected markets to other industrial countries had worked themselves through by about 1979, it was easier for Britain to hold its share of exports under Mrs Thatcher.

One indicator of competitiveness is the change in a country's share of world trade. The continuing slide in Britain's share in *manufactures* since 1979 has been shown in Table 5.1. Britain's lack of competitiveness has persisted; but, again, there is a sense in which the figures are ambiguous. Britain's share of world trade in manufactures fell between 1979 and 1983, but was the same in 1985 as in 1983. However, it fell sharply at the beginning of 1986.

Figures 5.2 and 5.3 summarize two indicators of competitiveness. The indicators are for manufacturing, the sector for which the most reliable data are available; also it is the sector which produced 51 per cent of UK exports of goods and services (excluding profits, dividends and interest received from abroad) in 1985. The oil sector, whose exports were 16 per cent of the total in 1985, is expected to produce a smaller fraction of UK exports in the future, and there is no way the service sector (which accounted for 24 per cent of UK exports in 1985) can fully make up for the declining contribution of oil and a weak performance by manufacturing.

There is no doubt that some aspects of the competitiveness of UK

83

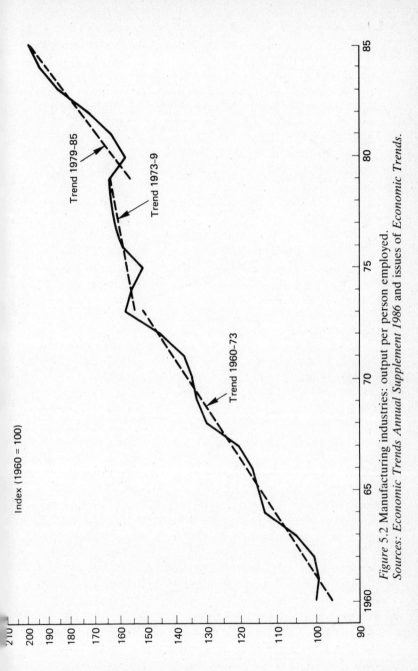

Figure 5.2 Manufacturing industries: output per person employed.
Sources: Economic Trends Annual Supplement 1986 and issues of *Economic Trends.*

84

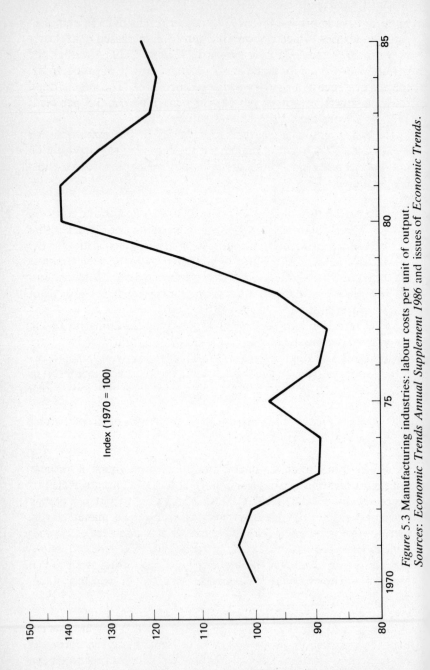

Figure 5.3 Manufacturing industries: labour costs per unit of output.
Sources: *Economic Trends Annual Supplement 1986* and issues of *Economic Trends*.

industry have improved since 1979. Labour productivity in manufacturing industries, which is shown in Figure 5.2, increased much faster between 1979 and 1985 than between 1973 and 1979. Although the period 1973–9 is a poor guide to the potential growth of productivity, there is evidence of a significant change since 1979.[5] The annual trend rates of growth of output per person were 1960–73, 3.5 per cent; 1973–9, 1.0 per cent; 1979–85, 4.2 per cent.

The faster growth of labour productivity in the manufacturing sector since 1979 is not in doubt, but the causes of the acceleration are more controversial. I venture the following as the three principal explanations:

1. The period 1973–9 was exceptional. Growth slowed and firms did not adjust their labour force. Many managements assumed that earlier rates of growth would resume. The intensification of the recession after 1979 led (or forced) them to revise their expectations and rationalize production and employment. With continuing recession (or with a recovery of output) faster growth of labour productivity was inevitable after 1979.
2. The recession and the loss of jobs in manufacturing broke the resistance of many groups of workers to rationalization and more efficient working practices. Workers are now willing to co-operate in such schemes because they expect increases in efficiency to provide greater job security for the jobs which survive.
3. The examples of tough management set in parts of the public and private sector were copied.

I consider trade union legislation and the abandonment of incomes policies as contributory but less important factors. This assessment is supported by the fact that the improvement in output per person employed since 1979 has been concentrated in the manufacturing sector, while trade union legislation and the abandonment of incomes policies have applied throughout the economy. The index of output per person for the economy *excluding* manufacturing is shown in Figure 5.4. The trend rates of increase were 2.2 per cent per annum between 1960 and 1973, 1.5 per cent a year between 1973 and 1979, and 1.6 per cent per annum between 1979 and 1985.[6]

Labour productivity is one of the factors affecting labour costs per unit of output, an important indicator of competitiveness. Increases in productivity reduce labour costs and increase competitiveness.

86

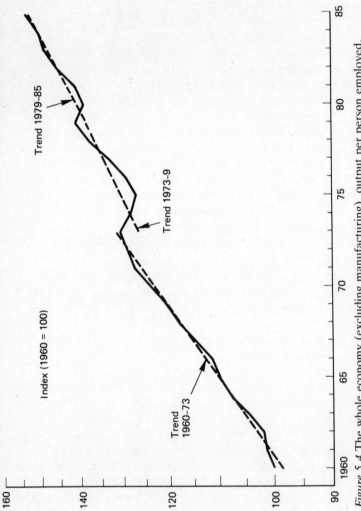

Figure 5.4 The whole economy (excluding manufacturing), output per person employed.
Sources: Economic Trends Annual Supplement 1986 and issues of *Economic Trends.*
Note: The Indices of output per person do not take into account the affect of part-time working on hours of work.

Movements of wages and exchange rates are incorporated into labour costs per unit of output and affect competitiveness. Figure 5.3 shows the movement of labour costs since 1970. The faster growth of labour productivity has reduced labour costs per unit of output, but this reduction has been more than offset since 1979 by the faster increase of wages in the UK than in other industrial countries and by movements of exchange rates. Between 1979 and 1981 Mrs Thatcher's monetarist policies forced up the sterling exchange rate, exacerbating the effects of North Sea oil and the second oil price shock which had also lifted sterling. Since 1981 the sterling rate of exchange has fallen, and labour productivity has increased. These changes have reduced relative labour costs, but not brought them back to their level in the mid-1970s.

Other Aspects of Competitiveness

There is more to competitiveness than increasing output per person and reducing labour costs for a constant product mix, however. I can best illustrate this by using plums again. For many years Czar plums, a smallish purple fruit without distinctive taste and which quickly deteriorate if stored, were grown in Cambridgeshire. Their competitive advantage was to be among the first English plums on the market. Now they are a poor match for peaches and large plums from Italy. However diligently a Czar grower tends his orchard, however ingeniously he markets his crop and however dexterously his workers pick that crop, there is no way he can achieve a good return on his investment and high wages. The answer is to grub up the Czar trees and plant others.

In many trades the substitution of new and improved products which is a vital ingredient of competitiveness requires research and development, new capital equipment and engineers, technicians and craftsmen to set up production. Here the record of Mrs Thatcher's government is bad. She has not provided the conditions for creating new products and investment. The price mechanism has failed to increase the supply of skilled employees. Here one of the problems is that firms provide training but, because the trainees get much of the financial benefit from the process in the form of higher wages when they have acquired skills and experience, firms tend to provide too few training places. Also the state provides most of the resources for education but has had limited control over their use. It is claimed that British financiers (the City) take a short-term view when allocating

finance for research and development (R & D) and investment. In part this reflects the risks involved for firms which have fallen behind in the competitive race when they attempt to catch up by spending more on research and development and new investment. It is often safer to cut production, to cling to market niches (for example, areas where international competition is weak, or where transport costs are proportionately large) and to exploit low costs attributable to the use of written-down plant or low wages.

Table 5.3 tells the story. R & D expenditure has stagnated, investment in UK manufacturing industry has fallen. Already in 1979 it was only half the German level, and Germany is the UK's principal competitor. Mrs Thatcher has failed to exploit the bulge of school leavers to remedy the shortage of qualified and skilled manpower. The number of first-year university students studying science and technology has barely risen, and the number of first-year engineering apprentices has fallen by 60 per cent. There has, however, been an increase in the number of students at polytechnics and in other sectors of further education.

Conclusions on Competitiveness

The Conservatives' harsh remedies for Britain's lack of industrial competitiveness have succeeded in increasing labour productivity; they have failed to lay the foundations for manufacturing industry to provide the growth of exports which will be needed.

I believe the root cause of the failure was that the leaders of the Conservative Party were misinformed about the reality of international industrial competition. They believed (or were advised) that a strong manufacturing industry was not essential for Britain's economic recovery; they were given an exaggerated (even romantic) assessment of the role of new small businesses; and they failed to grasp the role of government in supporting industry, especially in a country with a weak manufacturing sector. Great ingenuity has been displayed by Mrs Thatcher's governments in devising schemes to encourage the formation of new firms. But that was not sufficient; the Department of Industry has been subordinated to the Treasury, and it has had a rapid succession of ministers.

Britain's economic problem – a lack of international competitiveness – could not be solved by macroeconomic policy. The focus of policy should have shifted from the Treasury to the Department of Industry. That is where the problems required genius and a strong

Table 5.3   Some determinants of Competitiveness

Criterion	1978	1983
Expenditure on research and development performed in UK manufacturing industry at 1981 prices[1] (£billion)	3.5	3.3
	1979	*1985*
Investment in UK manufacturing industry at 1981 prices[2] £billion	8.2	6.2
	1979–80	*1984–5*
First-year university under-graduates studying science and technology in the UK[3] (000)	37.3	37.9
	1979	*1985*
Engineering industries, first-year apprentices[4] (000)	22.8	9.3

Sources and Notes:
[1] *Economic Trends*, August 1985. Data for 1984 and 1985 are not available.
[2] *Economic Trends*, July 1986.
[3] *University Statistics 1984*, p. 24.
[4] Number of first-year craft and technician trainees registered with the ETIB.

voice. A powerful minister and a reorganized department could have provided more support for manufacturing industry. As it was, the subsidies provided were late and patchy, and the department has operated without an industrial strategy. It has not built up the knowledge and resources required to provide assistance for industry in a discriminating way.

THE THIRD VERSION

The third version of the Thatcher economic experiment I shall consider is a crude political one. A principal objective of the Conservative Party is to protect and further the interests of the groups or classes in British society which support it. Of course, the party cannot openly set its policies to achieve these objectives, as this would alienate many voters from other groups. But, in practice, behind the veneer of seeking the national interest, the party's aims

are more limited. The bedrock of Tory support is the managerial and professional classes, and to win elections the party requires the support of a majority of qualified and skilled workers.

Britain's lack of competitiveness resulted in the relatively slow growth of the output of the economy; in turn, the slow growth of output meant that it was difficult to reconcile the aspirations of different groups in society. During the 1950s, the problem was not too severe. Although Britain's economy grew relatively slowly, competition from overseas was limited, and economic conditions for most people were much better than in the 1930s and 1940s.

From about 1960 until 1973, while foreign competition intensified, governments found an escape route. They increased government current and investment expenditure which had the advantage of a low import content and a high labour content. International competition would have created unemployment, but the position was camouflaged by increased employment for services and investment which the government paid for out of taxes.

With the further intensification of competition and slowdown in world growth after 1973, this escape route was too expensive for Mrs Thatcher's supporters. With growth down to a snail's pace, increased government expenditure could be paid for only by raising tax rates, by lowering after-tax incomes, and by reducing the international competitiveness of industry. A new way of reconciling the conflicting interests of groups in society was required.

Table 5.4 shows government spending as a percentage of the total expenditure in the economy. Current outlay on goods and services (which includes expenditure on health, education, defence, and police) has continued to rise as a percentage of total expenditure, but the share of investment has been cut back.

Table 5.4 Government expenditure

	Expenditure on goods and services	Investment by the public sector	Total
	(% of GDP at market prices)		
1960	16.4	6.4	22.8
1973	18.2	7.8	26.0
1979	19.8	5.5	25.3
1985	21.1	3.5	24.6

Source: *Economic Trends Annual Supplement* 1986; *Monthly Digest of Statistics*, July 1986.

Mrs Thatcher, perhaps unwittingly, found a solution. If incomes could grow only slowly, then income would have to be transferred to those who supported the Conservative Party. This was achieved by the deflationary macroeconomic policies. Those made unemployed suffered a sharp fall in their income. Total output and income was also reduced by the deflationary policies, but there were four other effects which aided many of Mrs Thatcher's supporters. The increase in productivity meant that output did not fall as much as employment and that left more for profits and for those (the majority) who retained their jobs. Second, mass unemployment weakened the negotiating power of groups of less skilled workers. Their wages may not have fallen as fast as the prices of plums when there is a glut, or as fast as Mr Brittan wishes they would, but they have been falling relative to the pay of other groups. Third, the costs of investments required to provide additional jobs were avoided. The fourth effect was achieved through an improvement in Britain's terms of trade. If more expansionary policies had been adopted, the sterling exchange rate would have been lower, increasing the price of imports relative to the price of exports. In addition, tax revenue from North Sea oil was available to offset the cost of unemployment in terms of outlay on social security.

Another development which has provided a financial bonanza for Mrs Thatcher's supporters is the rise in asset prices. Movements of share prices are shown in Table 5.5. 'I've made more on my house than I've earned during the past ten years' is not an unusual claim for people living in the south of England. Plainly the wealth of many of Mrs Thatcher's supporters has increased during the years of her economic experiment. For Mrs Thatcher, one of the advantages of this increase in wealth is that it results in only a limited increase in consumption. Immediately people feel better off. Their mortgage represents a smaller fraction of the value of their house. They may remortgage their property to finance increased consumption, and spend some of the appreciation on their shares, but initially only a small fraction of the gains is spent. The extra demands placed on the economy are limited but they will continue into the future as people continue to spend more because of past capital gains. This contrasts with the effects of reducing and holding down public sector (and private sector) investment, which has a *small* detrimental impact on welfare at first but with repercussions continuing far into the future.

The gains in share and house prices owe something to Mrs Thatcher's economic policies. Falling inflation and freedom for firms

Table 5.5   Prices of UK equities*

	Average annual percentage change (%)	Average annual change in retail prices (%)	Average annual change in real share prices (%)
1960–73	+ 5.1	+ 5.1	0.0
1973– 9	+ 6.3	+15.6	−8.0
1979–85	+17.2	+ 8.9	+7.6

Financial Times 500 Share Index.
Sources: *British Economy Key Statistics 1900–1970;* issue of *Annual Abstract of Statistics; Economic Trends Annual Supplement 1986.*

to increase prices, profits, and dividends have contributed to the rise in share prices. However the boom in share prices has been worldwide, in part a once-over adjustment. The easing of restrictions on financial institutions, another financial policy pursued by Mrs Thatcher, has increased the flow of funds to mortgages and fuelled the increase in house prices. By and large, therefore, the managerial and professional class and skilled workers have had a good recession. Changes in relative wages and salaries have been to their advantage, and they have gained from the rise in asset prices.

Finally Mrs Thatcher's task in winning support for her economic policies has been simplified by the division of the opposition. Her predecessors had to satisfy a majority of the voters; 40 per cent is now the goal.

MRS THATCHER'S VERSION

I believe that Mrs Thatcher's economic experiment is based on a much less sophisticated analysis of the economy than that held by Sam Brittan. Is it too simplistic to believe her own claims, and to see the basis of her economic policies as the application of the principles of business she observed her father apply and of good domestic housekeeping? Balance the books, work hard, see virtue in saving, be careful and cautious in investment – these are the maxims she has used.

The application of these maxims to the national economy does not, however, work. To take a simple example, if an individual businessman puts off an investment, he can earn interest on the funds

he would have invested, and he has more resources to use later. At a macroeconomic level, if many firms hold back from investment, resources will be left idle and be wasted. In the UK, high interest rates have to be used to prop up sterling; they cannot be reduced to increase industrial investment and to bring idle resources into use, and, for the reasons given earlier, wages do not fall rapidly to clear the labour market.

However, there is one area where the rules of good housekeeping do provide guidance for managing the national economy. Perhaps unfortunately, we live in a world where international institutions have only a weak influence on the economic policies of nation states, and where the creditor countries can dictate to all debtor countries except the USA (and that may be a temporary exception).

Since 1979 the overseas assets and the gold and dollar reserves of the UK have increased from £12 billion to £80 billion, equivalent to £1400 per person in the UK (and this may understate the improvement, because the value of overseas businesses owned by UK companies is underestimated). The overseas investments were not an alternative to investment in the UK. The current account surplus due to oil has been invested overseas. More investment should have been done in the UK, but the negative effect of this on the current account of the balance of payments could have been offset by lowering the exchange rate.

CONCLUSIONS

I have tried to provide a balanced view of the achievements and failures of economic policy during Mrs Thatcher's seven and a half years in power. She has had success in reducing inflation, increasing productivity, and increasing the UK's overseas assets. Britain's principal post-war economic problem has been a lack of international competitiveness. One of Mrs Thatcher's legacies is to have forced a more co-operative and realistic attitude upon some sections of the labour force. This is one determinant of competitiveness.

Mrs Thatcher's macroeconomic policies have shrunk the manufacturing sector unnecessarily, and she has failed to build up or use the potential power of the state to help British industry become more competitive. The critical failures of Mrs Thatcher's governments have been failure to use North Sea oil to expand demand, failure to use the resources which she has allowed to be wasted in mass unemployment,

and failure to provide sound training and higher education for youth. Very late in the day attempts have been made to correct these failures. Her economic legacy is to leave a shrunken manufacturing sector and a labour force whose training has not kept pace with that of our competitors. Finally, her policies have worked to the advantage of the 'top cats' in society and against those of the underdogs.

Notes

1. The *Financial Times*, 31 July 1986
2. N. Lawson 'The British Experiment' in *The Fifth Mais Lecture*, June 1984 (London: City University Business School) p. 2.
3. This preference was manifest in 1985. Forecasts were for moderate growth in 1986. The government chose not to expand demand to ensure a brisk growth of output in 1986, but planned for slow growth or stagnation.
4. Sir Geoffrey Howe accepts this. He has claimed that 'The Healey wing of the Labour government had already started to feel its way towards [monetarism] after 1976', speech made in Cambridge, January 1985.
5. It is important to note that rapid growth facilitates rapid increases in productivity. Since 1979 productivity has increased in spite of declining output of manufactures. Between 1960 and 1973 output of manufacturing industries increased by 3.7 per cent per year. Recent studies which provide estimates of the change in the trend of productivity growth since 1980 are by J. Muellbauer, in *Oxford Review of Economic Policy* (Oxford: Oxford University Press); and by R. Layard and S. Nickell, *The Performance of the British Labour Market* (London: Centre for Labour Economics, LSE, 1986).
6. There are qualifications to the estimates of output per person for the economy excluding manufacturing. The output of some service sector industries is difficult to measure and there has been an increase in part-time employment.

6 The Foreign Policy of the Thatcher Government

Diana Elles

'A strong Britain in a free world' was the headline proclaiming Conservative foreign policy in the 1979 Party Manifesto. On taking office in May 1979, the new Conservative government faced, in particular, four serious challenges. The military threat from the Communist bloc had increased in the years 1974–9, with superiority in conventional arms and parity in nuclear weapons. Within the European Community, the Labour government had succeeded in reducing Britain's bargaining powers in the Council of Ministers, frequently through obstruction and non-co-operation. Labour's economic policies had, in the Manifesto's words 'blunted Britain's competitive edge, making it more difficult for British companies to sell in other Community markets'. Rhodesia was suffering from guerrilla warfare, with an illegal regime in power. These, and many other situations of crisis proportions, had arisen outside the United Kingdom. All required some governmental response.

Considering the measures which have been taken, the questions now posed are, first, whether the two successive Conservative governments under Mrs Thatcher's leadership have made any impact on world affairs through the foreign policy they have pursued since 1979 and, second, what has been Mrs Thatcher's personal role? Indeed, can a country, now assessed as a medium-sized power, influence world events and sustain a foreign policy which other sovereign powers must take into account? Can an individual impose his or her own personality on relations with other states and would any other Conservative leader have followed a different course? In attempting to answer these questions, we should note that it is much more difficult today to disentangle and distinguish foreign affairs from domestic and regional affairs than it was before 1939. The two traditional weapons of foreign policy – diplomacy and the threat of military activity – have both undergone considerable change and restraint. They no longer play the same roles in international politics, or at least not in relations between Western states.

95

CONSTRAINTS ON FOREIGN POLICY FORMULATION

The position of Britain is unique. It is both restrained by its membership of a multiplicity of organizations and yet also enjoys, in consequence of that membership, an increased power to influence events. It is a member of NATO, of the European Community, one of the five permanent members of the United Nations Security Council, a founder member of the Council of Europe and of the OECD, one of the seven members of the world economic summit, a member of the Commonwealth and, through the European Community, a signatory to the Lomé Convention which unites the 12 member states with 66 African, Caribbean and Pacific countries. Britain is also party to numerous bilateral and multilateral treaties which impose their own obligations and responsibilities. Apart from this list of constraints and advantages, there is the 'special relationship' with the United States. From this collectivity of responsibilities it must be judged that Britain has a pivotal role to play in world affairs.

In the formulation of foreign policy, and in the choice of options available at any given time in a democracy, the additional influence of parliamentary and public opinion and the pressures exerted through the mass media must be taken into account. One example of the latter will suffice. During the height of the discussions on whether or not to impose sanctions on South Africa, the media played a crucial role. South African events were invariably shown on the television screen during news time. The majority of ordinary citizens – as far as could be judged from the number of telephone calls to Conservative Central Office and correspondence to Conservative MPs and MEPs – were, rightly or wrongly, not deeply concerned that sanctions should be imposed, although there is no one who does not oppose the system of apartheid. The television news reports, particularly on the BBC, undoubtedly presented a case in favour of sanctions. Every time a news item was shown, it was preceded by a warning that reporters were subject to the state of emergency and control of news; this reminder is not heard regarding news items from the Soviet Union or its satellites. Since economic measures were taken by the European Community, and after the vote in favour of sanctions was adopted by the United States Senate, very little television coverage has been given to events in South Africa. Sanctions having been imposed, South Africa is no longer – for the time being at any rate – newsworthy.

British worldwide trade interests, obligations of assistance in the form of aid (particularly to those countries with whom the UK has historic and traditional ties), residual responsibility for certain British dependent territories, protection of British citizens resident overseas, maintenance of British military bases still remaining, information and cultural policy via the BBC external services and the British Council respectively, all come within the ambit of consideration in the formulation of foreign policy.

Finally, the belief is frequently expressed that there is a long-standing tradition within the Foreign and Commonwealth Office that there should be a continuity of policy in Britain's international relations, on a bipartisan basis, regardless of which political party is in office.

MRS THATCHER'S PRIORITIES

Already in 1976, Mrs Thatcher's priorities were spelt out clearly, in *The Right Approach*: 'The first priority of any government should be to defend its citizens from external threat of actual aggression'. This basic assumption was supported by the firm determination to 'spend what is necessary on our armed forces even while we are cutting public spending on other things'. Defence, as Mrs Thatcher has frequently made clear, is one arm of foreign policy. It was not without reason that Mrs Thatcher came into office with the accolade of 'The Iron Lady'. This has served her in good stead abroad, as indicating someone who makes decisions and who stands by them, and who consequently must be respected; there is no greater strength than for one's opponents to know that you cannot be 'pushed around'. The theme of the importance of defence as an arm of foreign policy recurred in a speech made to Les Grandes Conférences Catholiques in Brussels in June 1978, nearly one year before she took office. Among the principles which would guide her in making foreign policy decisions, the first was (and remains) that: 'as long as we have potential enemies, we must recognize that peace can ... be maintained [only] through strength. Our duty to freedom is to defend our own'. This theme has been repeated with passionate conviction in many of the Prime Minister's major overseas speeches, and is a major plank of her foreign policy. The 1986 Liberal and Labour Party Conferences, at which both parties appeared to support unilateral nuclear disarmament, served to reinforce Mrs Thatcher's policy of

retaining Britain's nuclear deterrent and playing a full role within NATO.

The second principle, or firm conviction, is the moral ascendancy of democracies over other political regimes. Was it not through democratic process that the Western nations, as members of both NATO and of the European Community, renounced war between themselves as an instrument of foreign policy? Third, past commitments 'cannot be made and unmade at will': treaties and other commitments recognized under international law must be renegotiated, if change is needed; this process must be distinguished clearly from evolution of policy in areas not bound by legal instruments.

Foreign policy has to be reactive to events as they occur, but it is also necessary to have a broad picture of Britain and its position in the world at the end of the century. There must be an objective by which foreign policy is to be guided in the intervening years, always accepting that events could force a diversion. It is not sufficient, however, to be reactive; it must be possible for initiatives to be taken in foreign policy as well as in domestic policy. A simple but relevant point is the need for information, and intelligent interpretation of it. Global communication systems open up a wealth of information (and indeed of disinformation); if there is not an accurate and comprehensive analysis of this material, its value could well be negative.

Finally, Mrs Thatcher laid stress on the national character of a people that gives nations historic goals despite changing ideologies. Russian expansionism was an obvious example. Russia was expansionist in the 15th century, and similar policies have been apparent since 1945, with regard to Czechoslovakia, Hungary, and Afghanistan. Mrs Thatcher's deeply held views on her approach to foreign policy were thus stated explicitly, and have guided her through the seven years of her two governments. Her supporters will not have been disappointed.

TRADE AND THE ECONOMY

One of the first major policy decisions, which indicated the close interweaving of domestic and foreign policy, was the lifting of restrictions on exchange control and the removal of the dollar premium. This decision indicated to the international community a complete change in financial policy following a Labour government;

it also served to stimulate overseas commercial opportunities for British business, and released it from one of the most irksome obstacles to successful international trade. Britain as a trading nation with 20 per cent GDP from exports was badly in need of this measure as a step to freer overseas activities. Even the Labour Party now appears to have recognized the value of this decision; Roy Hattersley announced at the beginning of September 1986 that restrictions on exchange control would be part of Labour policy for the economy.

Trading patterns since 1979 have changed, as domestic output has changed from a large manufacturing base to a predominance of invisible exports. Adaptation towards the European markets available within the tariff barrier led to an increased sale of British goods to member states of the Community (from 32 per cent of exports in 1970 to about 50 per cent in 1984). That later figure is obviously a great improvement on the previous one, but there are still many opportunities available to British business in the Community. The general decline in global terms in the trade figures of manufactured goods was criticized by the 1985 House of Lords Report on Overseas Trade,[1] laying some measure of blame on the government for failing to support manufacturing industry. It was easier to blame the government than industrialists, who had failed to study the markets available and who during the years 1964–79 had earned a poor reputation overseas for British goods, in terms of quality, delivery dates and maintenance. The poor export performance was countered by high import penetration, thus causing a sharp fall in the balance of trade in manufactured goods. As we saw in Chapter 5, successful competitiveness of British industry is an essential element in strengthening the position of Britain in the world, both as a means of increasing the prosperity and employment situation of the nation and of opening up and sustaining relations with other countries. A government's task must be to create the climate for investment, both in new industries and in older ones which need to adapt to changing technology and markets. Radical shifts have taken place since 1979, both in industrial relations and the economic situation. British products are beginning to regain their former sound reputation, but there still remains much to be done. With emphasis on small businesses and current high interest rates, more use could be made of European Community funding at special low rates for borrowers. Industry itself must be more aware of the financial benefits of training and retraining personnel, in order to fill the vacancies which exist in so many firms; this is not only a British problem, but a European one.

The one measure which the government has so far failed to introduce, and which without any doubt would be beneficial for trade and industry, is for Britain to join the Exchange Rate Mechanism (ERM) of the European Monetary System (EMS). Whatever the intellectual arguments (and there are at least three different interpretations of the benefits and disadvantages of membership), there is an overwhelming demand for membership from the business community. Stability of the exchange rate is even more important for commerce and trade than the rate itself; the lack of stability and the evident volatility of the pound sterling in relation to both the dollar and other European currencies in our largest export markets, provide good reasons why those who wish to make commercial contracts should make them with industries in countries where the exchange rate remains stable, at least in the short term.

The argument used for so long that sterling was a petrocurrency and was tied to the price of oil has now been disproved since the fall in price to about $10–15 a barrel. It is evident, however, that (writing in October 1986, with the prospect of a general election and the latent possibility of a run on the pound) at present the time may not be 'right', though it should be recognized that the reserves would be boosted by the support of the whole European Monetary Co-operation Fund. Joining the ERM would be good for business, and for Britain, and would also be evidence of the Prime Minister's firm resolve to play a full part in the European Community.

THE EUROPEAN COMMUNITY

Mrs Thatcher's approach to the European Community has often appeared ambivalent to those who would like to see some kind of European federal system, but it is really very clear. Her commitment to Britain's membership of the Community remains firm as ever; she recognizes that both Britain and Europe can benefit from Britain's membership. The 1979 election Manifesto stated unequivocally: 'The next Conservative government will restore Britain's influence by convincing our partners of our commitment to the Community's success'. The Prime Minister's policy towards the European Community is one example of the 'double' element in her reaction to any situation. On one hand, it is an approach that is fundamentally British, certain that 'Britain is best', making decisions which are entirely in the British interest; on the other, it recognizes that in

international relations (both with partners in the Community and with other countries), there is an overriding necessity – perhaps regrettable – to be flexible. This approach is one that reflects the feelings and attitudes of many Conservatives. The period of the British Presidency of the Community (from 1 July–31 December 1986), has also shown that, under Mrs Thatcher's leadership, Britain is becoming an integral part of the 'European scene', and less clearly part of Winston Churchill's 'three-circle concept' which viewed Britain's relationship with the United States, the Commonwealth, and Europe as equal and overlapping; it is through membership of the European Community that Britain has a major role to play in world affairs.

What many Europeans find hard to swallow is the patent honesty and clarity of Mrs Thatcher's observations. 'I must be absolutely clear about this. Britain cannot accept the present situation on the Budget. It is demonstrably unjust. It is politically indefensible.' In the same speech (in Luxembourg in October 1979), Mrs Thatcher continued:

> A longer-term but deeply worrying problem is the cost of the Common Agricultural Policy ... Britain fully accepts the importance of the CAP as one of the Community's central policies. But the CAP cannot go on as it is going on at present. I therefore welcome the growing determination of other Community governments to cut wasteful expenditure on agricultural surpluses ... Wasteful surpluses must disappear ... It is not easy to explain to a housewife why she should help sell butter to Russia at a fraction of the price she pays herself.

In that same speech, Mrs Thatcher attacked the bureaucracy in Brussels, whose activities she said 'have given rise to resentment and irritation'. The style and tone of these observations were of course resented by governments of other member states, particularly those of the original Six and by the newly elected members of the European Parliament. Determination to win the Budget argument, long-drawn out and exhausting for all those involved, had achieved a succession of gains for Mrs Thatcher by 1986, with a net contribution for 1980 and 1981 of less than £200 million. The diplomatic and political skills of Signor Emilio Colombo (the then Italian Foreign Secretary) were of considerable help. In 1984, the Fontainebleau Agreement set out the terms on which Britain's budgetary contribution should be settled and the amounts by which the financial resources of the Community should be increased. It was then considered that the annual haggling

over the British budgetary contribution would be ended.

The first major decision adopted at Fontainebleau and pushed hard by the British government concerned the system of 'budgetary discipline', which had the aim of putting a limit on the growth of agricultural spending and on Community spending as a whole. The second involved the governments of the member states in accepting the need for an abatement system which would provide the mechanism for reducing the British contribution. Further it was agreed that the VAT ceiling should be raised to 1.4 per cent. This figure is frequently misunderstood, since the British contribution for 1986 in fact amounts to 0.68 per cent. The Council's Budgets for 1985 and 1986 have given rise to considerable difference of opinion between the government and the European Parliament, which involved, *inter alia*, the government's taking the Parliament to the European Court of Justice. The case ended in a *de jure* win for the government as the Parliament had exceeded the legally allowed increase in the maximum rate (7.1 per cent). In the end, however, it was the European Parliament which proved to have correctly judged the political situation after the accession of Spain and Portugal; the maximum rate was finalized at 37.5 per cent to cover 1986 expenditure. As Mr Brooke (President-in-Office) stated at the conclusion of the conciliation procedure between the European Parliament and the Council: 'There have been no losers, but Europe has been the winner'.

In the 'Battle of the Budgets', it must be admitted that Mrs Thatcher has won the major arguments on budgetary discipline and has arranged a more equitable contribution to the Community's financial resources; what will not be resolved is the 'budgetary problem' as such. The effect of the devaluation of the dollar and the successful harvest will cause further drains on a limited budget which will not be able to meet obligations either to the agricultural sector or to the rest of the Community in social, industrial and technology policies. The 1.4 per cent VAT ceiling was a calculated risk, but one which – if the Community is to achieve its place in the world of economic prosperity on a level with the United States and Japan – will have to be reviewed. The gradual realization by at least some of the larger member states (certainly Germany, and later France) that they also suffered (or would eventually also suffer) from an unjust imbalance in their financial contributions to the Community's own resources indicated Mrs Thatcher's perseverance and persistence. It must be recognized that Mrs Thatcher is now the only prime minister

remaining from the time that battle was first joined in 1979. If she has won her fight on the Budget in the Community institutions, it is true, too, that she has overwhelmingly won the battle of Europe in the Conservative constituencies at home. There will still be some who do not like 'Europe'; they probably do not like 'abroad'. But membership of the European Community is no longer an electoral issue and even the Labour Party is recognizing (or appears to be recognizing), that membership itself can no longer be questioned, only policies within the Community framework. The 1979 general election showed that the majority of British people neither wanted to leave the Community nor supported unilateral disarmament. In the election campaign of 1983, membership was not even raised as a major issue.

Two other issues show Mrs Thatcher's capacity for combining idealism with pragmatism. Following the proposals contained in Signor Spinelli's Draft Treaty for a European Union (February 1984), Mrs Thatcher stated that she hated the term, and wished it had never been invented. Continental political oratory has a long tradition of elaborate rhetoric, expected by the people, but the age of oratory in Britain is over. Mrs Thatcher is certainly impatient with rhetoric and is willing to call the bluff of those who engage in it. The lengthy arguments about the removal of the Luxembourg Compromise (the veto on Community legislation) during 1985 and the wish of nearly all member states to abolish it were followed first by Germany's application of the veto to defend its farming interests in 1985 and second by total absence of any reference to it in the Single European Act, the draft of which was agreed by the European Council in December 1985. Although the Prime Minister held that it was not necessary to amend the EEC Treaty, and personally opposed the holding of an Intergovernmental Conference in 1985, one of the major elements of the resulting Single European Act was the agreement concerning European political co-operation (EPC). This has formed part of Conservative policy as developed and improved since 1979, particularly when Lord Carrington was Foreign Secretary. One of the overriding arguments for Community membership had been the realization of the need for a strong European voice, to be heard in the councils of the world on global issues which affect the life and prosperity of Europe and its allies. Since 1980, therefore, there has been a gradual development of the process of EPC, recognizing for the first time a need to discuss security matters which had hitherto remained outside Community debate. There was also regular (and effective) co-ordination of foreign policy between the

member states' governments, finalized in the London Report of October 1981. Mrs Thatcher has actively pursued increased co-ordination, convinced of the necessity for close co-operation between the Community's member states in relation to global issues. Benefits flowing from the more effective use of EPC were evidenced by the response of member states at the time of the invasion of the Falklands, when a trade embargo was immediately imposed on Argentina for one month, later extended to three months. The 1985 provisions (mainly drafted by Britain and contained in the Single European Act), considerably strengthened the process of EPC so as to make it more effective, more efficient, and more useful.

This recognition of a need for a European foreign policy instrument has also been reflected in the call for a sound domestic economic base within the Community. The objectives of the Government for the continued development of the Community were set out in the programme for the 1986 United Kingdom Presidency – achievement of a real common market or internal market, the reduction of regulatory burdens on business, and a continued battle for the reform of the CAP. The demarcation line between domestic and foreign policy gets ever thinner as Britain plays an increasingly full role in the Community.

ANGLO-IRISH RELATIONS

The interweaving of domestic and foreign policy has been at its most obvious – and at the same time its most delicate – in the relations between Britain and the Irish Republic. The European Parliament had been used skilfully by John Hume (MEP, Northern Ireland) and Irish MEPs to bring forward the subject of Northern Ireland as a matter for public debate. While drawing £2 billion from community funds for the province since 1973, the Prime Minister properly held that it was totally unacceptable that any political or constitutional aspect should be debated in such a forum; this was a matter for the United Kingdom government. In the event, the European Parliament's report (1984), presented by N. Haagerup excluded such consideration, was balanced and made a useful contribution to the recognition that Northern Ireland needed special assistance from Community funds. Following Mrs Thatcher's adamant refusal to accept the proposals in the New Ireland Forum (contemporaneous

with the Haagerup report), the conclusion of the 1985 Anglo-Irish Accord came as a considerable surprise. It won the admiration and support of many who recognized the immense complexity of the issues involved, and the fact that for the first time since partition the Dáil had voted to recognize the right of the majority of the people of Northern Ireland to decide their own future. Understandably, the Accord has also aroused antagonism from some leading members within the Conservative Party, as well as from the Unionist parties of Northern Ireland. It must be asserted that even if some of these reactions were predictable, the Accord gives major long-term opportunities to the province, provided that Ulster's politicians are prepared to take up the challenge without resorting to violence.

RELATIONS WITH THE UNITED STATES

While progress has been made on the settling of outstanding problems in the Community since 1979, Britain has also had a unique role to play in its relations with the United States. The constant attempts by the Soviet Union to drive a wedge between the United States and the European Community have been resisted firmly by Mrs Thatcher. No government has been more acutely aware of the strength of the United States as a member of the Atlantic Alliance, and its contribution not only to the security but to the very survival of Western Europe. The co-ordinated rise and activities of the peace movements in the early 1980s (before the arrival of the Cruise and Pershing missiles on the European continent) were an obvious example of Soviet-directed policy, strongly resisted by Western governments. Mrs Thatcher has frequently referred to the special nature of the Anglo-American alliance: 'This party is pro-American', she asserted at the Conservative Party Conference in October 1984. This has not prevented her from differing from President Reagan on a number of issues where British interests were involved – the gas pipeline contract with the Soviet Union, to which the United States objected strongly; the landing in October 1983 of American troops on Grenada, a Commonwealth country; and Mrs Thatcher's 1986 statement that she would not write a blank cheque for F-111s to use British bases for further attack on Libya, but would treat any future request on its merits.

THE FALKLANDS

The issues of the Falklands war have been widely debated, and the Franks Report fully analyzed the origins and outcome of the decisions taken by the government at that time. There are, however, two points not always stressed concerning the Argentine attack. First, the subject of the Falklands had been on the regular agenda of the UN Fourth Committee on decolonization some time before 1982, and it was no surprise to the Foreign Office that Argentina had a long-standing interest in possessing the Falklands. Visits had been paid by Mr Edward Rowlands under Labour, and Conservative ministers had also discussed the future of the Islands with the Falklanders. Second (what will probably never be clarified) is the effect of the threatened withdrawal of HMS Endurance from the Islands, set out in the Defence Review of 1981. Lord Carrington had raised strong objections with the Ministry of Defence, assuming that it would wrongly signal to the Argentinians that Britain was unlikely to defend the Islands. This apparent failure to listen to the advice of the then Foreign Secretary, and the general accusation that the Foreign Office was caught napping, are matters for the historian with the necessary documents and information which may eventually become available.

The outcome, of course, is well known. The Argentine forces – in breach of international law and the UN Charter provisions – occupied the Islands on 2 April 1982. Attempts at negotiations for a peaceful outcome and withdrawal of troops failed, as Mrs Thatcher rightly assumed they would. It has been acknowledged by many writers and politicians that the retaking of the Falkland Islands by British forces was an outstanding achievement. The characteristically courageous and determined Prime Minister had led the country to a victory fought in the most extraordinary circumstances by immensely brave members of the armed forces. If Britain had not had a courageous leader, and if the Argentinians had remained in military possession of the Islands, there is absolutely no doubt that Britain's position in the eyes of the international community would have declined, with a consequent loss of negotiating power in any situation where British interests were involved.

Since 1982, many aspects of relations with Argentina remain unresolved. At the time of writing (October 1986), Argentina has still failed to declare an end to hostilities; the question of the fishing limits around the Falklands still needs to be clarified; the costs of maintaining the islands are a heavy burden on the British Budget.

While the military campaign brought a resounding victory, the peace has yet to be firmly established in a form satisfactory to Britain and to the islanders. The 'Fortress Falkland' policy, which in October 1986 still had no clear political alternative, is not one which can be sustained over a long period of time. Probably only Mrs Thatcher is in a position to come to some accommodation with Argentina, looking in the first instance to co-operation over fishing rights in the area.

AREAS OF CONCERN

Britain's changing responsibilities towards her colonies and former colonies are indicated by two landmarks in the history of the Thatcher governments: the first, the remarkably successful settlement of the Rhodesian question under the chairmanship of Lord Carrington, which ended the guerrilla warfare and enabled Zimbabwe to become an independent state; the second, the satisfactory negotiations concerning the future of Hong Kong after the territory's lease from China terminates in 1997.

The issues of foreign policy are not always concerned with reacting to events. Yet crises have been faced not only in the Falklands but also in relation to Poland, the invasion of Afghanistan by the Soviet Union in December 1980, and the taking of 52 American hostages in Iran. All these events called for efficient 'crisis management' in order to provide what might be regarded as damage limitation. East–West relations have for a long time led to a certain ambivalence in Western foreign policies; among the differing opinions, there are those which involve maximum effort to trade with the Eastern bloc, those which aim to discourage trade with the communist world which might improve the economies of potential enemies, and those which note the approach of the Federal Republic of Germany, which is guided by the hope of eventual reunification of East and West Germany and which favours free trade with the GDR.

Mrs Thatcher has taken a wise middle course. While remaining fully aware of the threats and dangers of the power of the Soviet Union, she believes that dialogue must be maintained. She has visited Hungary, and Sir Geoffrey Howe has travelled to Poland and Czechoslovakia. The Prime Minister will be going to Moscow in 1987 to have talks with Mr Gorbachev, implementing her policy of recognizing the essential need to keep open lines of communication.

With no illusions about the Soviet Union's ideological struggle for world supremacy (never denied by the Soviet Union), Mrs Thatcher is able to raise matters which affect both the Eastern bloc and the West. She will undoubtedly be pressing, as Mr Malcolm Rifkind did before her, for the release of dissidents and Soviet Jews.

Trade as an arm of foreign policy has had Mrs Thatcher's full attention, since she never misses an opportunity to help win major contracts for British firms while undertaking official visits to many parts of the world. She introduced her speech to the Diplomatic and Commonwealth Writers Association in April 1981 by listing some forthcoming visits overseas – the Netherlands, Saudi Arabia and the Gulf States (the first time a British prime minister was visiting that area), Ottawa, Melbourne, and Mexico – as well as the forthcoming presidency of the Community for the last six months of that year. As she herself said: 'My 1981 programme may be unusually heavy, but it does bear witness to the degree of involvement of a modern British Prime Minister'. Since that date, of course, thousands of miles have been covered, including important visits to China and to the Far East, where the Prime Minister was able to restore better trade relations with Malaysia, whose policy previously had been 'to buy British last'; opportunities for British firms have now been opened, and there are good prospects for successful marketing.

British aid to Third World countries amounted in 1985 to more than £1 billion. This sum implemented government policy concerning the need to give maximum assistance in this area. But it does raise the question as to the effectiveness of cash aid. The pressure of public opinion, to be seen to be giving, is not always in the best interests of the recipient countries. The emergency programmes obviously need and get maximum support – as was shown, for example, by the loan of RAF aircraft during the 1984–5 Ethiopian famine relief programme. There is still no definitive answer – if such is indeed attainable – as to which methods should and could be used (without infringing national sovereignty) in helping to raise the standard of living of the poorest in the poorest countries. It is not only for Britain but also for other aid donors (especially for the other member states of the European Community) to use most efficiently the financial and technical resources available.

In a different but somewhat similar way, the problems facing the black population of South Africa, suffering under the remaining apparatus of apartheid, must be considered and action implemented at international level, with full participating support of all European

Commmunity member states. Mrs Thatcher has repeatedly stressed her abhorrence of injustice and violence, and has made clear her views on the damage which would be done to those we are seeking to help if sanctions were to be applied. Again, the combination of idealist and pragmatist approaches underlies her reluctance (and, indeed, refusal) to take arbitrary and unilateral action against South Africa, and her wish to act in co-ordination with the whole Community, which can put considerable economic and political pressure on the South African government.

The other single issue facing the whole of the free world is international terrorism. The government has pledged full support to efforts at defeating it; during the 1986 economic summit Mrs Thatcher succeeded in getting agreement on a declaration about joint and concerted effort to this end. There is, however, no easy solution to this latest form of warfare, so long as the festering sores in the Middle East remain unhealed.

CONCLUSIONS

The Prime Minister brings her own style to major foreign policy issues, which receive her personal attention. Examples have been given of events which have engaged her own strong reactions (modified and evolved in the light of external factors), resulting in decisions which were possibly not envisaged *ab initio*. Rhodesia–Zimbabwe, the Single European Act, the Anglo-Irish Accord, and economic measures against South Africa are all issues which serve to show that the image of Mrs Thatcher as inflexible is a fallacious one. Her scepticism about institutions and her dislike of rhetoric reveal her patent honesty and regard for clarity. Together with her own personal courage, these are virtues which are not always evident in political leaders, especially in relation to foreign policy.

One of Mrs Thatcher's less well-known qualities is her deep sense of humanity, and horror at any physical outrage and bloodshed; this quality is masked by the 'Iron Lady' image. Two simple indications of her natural feelings were shown during the Falklands war and her genuine revulsion at the deaths caused by the fighting. In the same way, she expressed openly her 'agonizing' over the use of the British bases for the United States' attack on Libyan installations in April 1986 and the consequent loss of life.

The development of radio and television has enabled political

personalities to make an impression far beyond national frontiers. Mrs Thatcher must have become one of the best known (if not *the* best known) of political leaders in the world since 1979. Both her personality and her policies may arouse controversy, opposition and even anger, but no one doubts her determination to stand up for what she believes to be right and to ensure that Britain's interests are protected. Mrs Thatcher's foreign policy has resulted in the strengthening of the position of Britain in world affairs. Some may disagree on individual aspects of policy, but no one can deny that between 1979 and 1986 Britain became a country which could no longer be disregarded. Much of the credit must be ascribed to the personal leadership of the Prime Minister.

Note

1.   HL 238, 15 October 1985.

7 The Oppositions under Thatcher: or The Irresistible Force Meets the Movable Object
David Marquand

In the general election of June 1983 the Labour Party won 28 per cent of the popular vote and the newly-formed Liberal – SDP Alliance 26 per cent. It was Labour's worst performance since 1918. The Alliance did better than the Liberal Party had done since 1931. In seats the outcome was, of course, very different. Even in seats, however, the modest Alliance score of 23 outshone any Liberal performance since 1931, while Labour's contingent of 209 was its smallest since 1935.[1] To be sure, the 'mould' of British politics still held: Labour was still the chief opposition party and, once memories of polling night faded, public discussion of politics was still dominated by the familiar two-party jousting in the House of Commons. But the party system of which these jousts were the epiphenomena looked more vulnerable than at any time since it had taken shape in the 1920s, while the Labour Party, whose emergence as a potential party of government had been the chief catalyst of that system, seemed to many (including many Labour supporters) to be in terminal decline.[2]

Three years later, it was clear that rumours of its death had been greatly exaggerated. In late August 1986, the *Guardian*'s running average of the last five opinion polls taken before the end of the month showed Labour at 38 per cent, the Conservatives at 34 per cent and the Alliance at 26 per cent. The comparable figures for the preceding four months had been much the same – Labour varying from 38 to 39 per cent, the Conservatives from 33 to 34 per cent and the Alliance from 25 to 27 per cent. Labour had been ahead of the field throughout the year, while the Alliance had trailed behind it throughout the spring and summer.[3] Of course, none of this proves anything about the next general election. Each of the three groups of party strategists currently reading the psephological tea leaves has legitimate grounds for optimism. In the last general election, the

Alliance put on eight percentage points in the course of the campaign. If it went into the next election at 30 per cent in the polls, and put on 8 per cent before polling day, it might emerge with an absolute majority in the House of Commons. Though the Conservatives have been behind the Labour Party in the *Guardian*'s running averages for the whole of 1986, the gap between their 1986 performances and the 43.5 per cent with which they secured a landslide victory in 1983 is not too wide to close. In any case, they could win the election with significantly less than 43.5 per cent. Though Labour has not managed to break the famous 40 per cent barrier so far, a run of mediocre Alliance ratings might enable it to squeeze the Alliance vote and return it to office with a respectable majority; in any case, it is clearly well placed to emerge as the largest single party in the next House of Commons, even on the figures for the spring and summer of 1986. So far as the next election is concerned, the only safe conclusion is that a volatile and wary electorate has still to make up its mind which way to jump.

Yet that is, in itself, remarkable. However future historians may judge the Thatcher governments, there is no doubt that they have presided over a good deal of pain. Record unemployment for the post-war period; a dramatic shake-out of labour from the old, 'smokestack' industries; severe cuts in certain social programmes; the longest and most bitterly fought industrial dispute since the General Strike – these may or may not have been necessary, but no one can deny that they have happened, or that they have brought much suffering with them. Worse still, the long-term economic improvement of which short-term pain was supposed to be the harbinger does not seem to have transpired. Behind the temporary shield of North Sea oil, the forces responsible for nearly a century of relative economic decline are still at work. Faced with accelerating technological change and intensifying international competition, British industry has continued to move, in the jargon, 'down market' – away from the high skill, high-value-added products in which the pacemakers of the industrial world specialize, and towards comparatively low-added-value products, with a lower skill content.[4] Proficiency in certain sorts of services, combined with temporary self-sufficiency in energy and a highly efficient agricultural sector are not adequate compensations. It is too soon to draw up a balance sheet for Mrs Thatcher's economic policies – and, in any case, this is not the place to try. To put it at its lowest, however, it is not at all certain that the pain has been worthwhile, even in her own terms.

In these circumstances, the surprising thing is not that the government may well lose the next election, but that it still has a fair chance of winning it. Part of the reason, of course, is that the opposition to it is divided. More than 60 per cent of the electorate is hostile to the government; if the whole of that 60 per cent were concentrated behind one of the opposition parties, the party concerned would be on course for one of the greatest landslide victories in British electoral history. But that only pushes the problem one stage further back. Why *is* the opposition to the government divided in this way? Why has neither of the opposition parties established a clear and convincing hegemony over the anti-Thatcher forces? Why has Labour recovered sufficiently to prevent the Alliance from breaking through, but not sufficiently to be confident of victory itself? Why has the Alliance held on to its general-election share of the vote, but failed to build on it sufficiently to overtake Labour? The objects of this chapter are to explore these questions, and to examine their implications for 'Thatcherism' in particular, and for British politics in general.

THE LABOUR PARTY

It is convenient to start with Labour – still, after all, the senior opposition party. On one level, there is not much doubt about what has happened. Simply as a machine – as an instrument dedicated to the business of getting votes and anxious to stay in that business – the Labour party has turned out to be much tougher and more resilient than its propensity for self-mutilation in the 1979 Parliament suggested it would be. The younger generation of telegenic professional politicians which rose to leadership positions in the party after the catastrophe of 1983 – the generation of Neil Kinnock himself, John Cunningham, John Smith and Robin Cook in the House of Commons, and of Ken Livingstone and David Blunkett outside it – seems a little short on ideas, but it is impressively long on that most crucial of political attributes, the will to win. More remarkably still, it is clear that a strong will to win also exists lower down in the party, both in parliament and in the constituencies. To put it at its crudest and simplest, there are still a lot of people in the Labour Party who very much want to be in power – not by any means a self-evident proposition in a party of the Left – and who have the sense to see that

if they are to get into power, the party will have to say the sorts of things the voters want to hear. The Kinnock–Hattersley leadership has thus found it surprisingly easy to isolate the ideological Left and to present a smooth, competent and moderate image to the media and the electorate. Kinnock's vaguely left-wing past has, moreover, been an enormous asset from this point of view. Like Ramsay MacDonald in the 1920s and Harold Wilson in the 1960s, he came to the leadership with a substantial ideological credit balance at his command. He has drawn on it quite heavily since his election, but he does not seem to have exhausted it yet. Like MacDonald in 1922 and 1923 and Wilson in 1963 and 1964, he can speak to the wider, national audience which he has to persuade if he is to reach No. 10 Downing Street, without arousing reflex suspicions of treachery or faint-heartedness in the narrower party audience which he also has to satisfy.

The second obvious reason for Labour's recovery deserves more extended treatment. As everyone knows, tension between the Labour Party and the trade unions is built into the very structure of the British labour movement. The party exists to win and hold power in a complex society, where less than half of the working population belongs to a trade union, and where the unions are frequently unpopular. The unions exist to promote the interests of their own members – interests which they have notoriously seen in a much narrower and less 'encompassing' way than have their counterparts in Scandinavia and Central Europe.[5] This tension has manifested itself in recurrent waves of trade-union exasperation with the inhibitions and constraints of parliamentary politics. At repeated, though irregular, intervals, the unions have come to feel that the politicians have let them down; that they can achieve their purposes only through direct industrial action; and that any damage this does to the party is supportable since they can, at a pinch, do without it. Two obvious examples are the periods of labour unrest immediately before the First World War, when the parliamentary party was helping to prop up a minority Liberal government, and immediately after it, when a handful of Labour MPs ineffectually confronted the massed battalions of the Lloyd George coalition. Another is the swing towards 'Direct Action' which followed the fall of the first Labour government in 1924, and culminated in the General Strike of 1926. A third is the upsurge of militancy which followed the collapse of the National Plan and the abortive 'In Place of Strife' proposals, and a fourth (the 'winter of discontent' of 1978–9) which followed

the expenditure cuts of 1976 and the stringent incomes policy of 1976–8.

Just as disappointment with parliamentary politics has repeatedly driven the pendulum of trade-union opinion to 'Direct Action', however, so industrial defeat has repeatedly driven it back to politics. The defeat of the General Strike and the anti-trade union legislation which followed it convinced the unions that they needed the party as much as it needed them. For the first time since 1945, the political wing of the movement had primacy over the industrial wing – not the least of the reasons for its victory in the 1929 election. And what Baldwin did for Ramsay MacDonald then, Mrs Thatcher has done for Kinnock now. From the defeat of 'In Place of Strife' in 1969 until the defeat of Arthur Scargill in 1985, Labour politics were conducted in the shadow of 'Direct Action'. Even when the leaders of the political wing were in office, primacy in the movement lay with the industrial wing. The Wilson–Callaghan government of the 1970s had been able to take office in the first place only because the National Union of Mineworkers (NUM) had shown that it was determined to smash the previous government's statutory incomes policy, and everyone knew it. Though ministers took strong, courageous and remarkably effective action to cut real wages,[6] they did so only when Jack Jones decided that it was necessary, and by methods that he approved. Even Mrs Thatcher's victory in 1979 did not produce a decisive change in the position. High unemployment weakened the unions' bargaining power, and continuing unpopularity put them on the defensive politically. But it was not until Scargill, the hero of the industrial militants, had led his troops into battle and lost, that everyone could see that 'Direct Action' was no longer a feasible option: that 'Thatcherism' could be defeated only through the ballot box.

The benefits to the party have been twofold. 'Scargillism' has ceased to be a bogey, and primacy has at last gone back to the politicians. To be sure, the built-in structural factors which underlie the tension between the two wings of the movement still remain. If a Kinnock government tried to honour its commitment to economic expansion, it would sooner or later face the familiar choice between an unacceptable rate of wage inflation and an incomes policy. If it chose the former, expansion would sooner or later come to an end. If it chose the latter, all the problems which destroyed successive incomes policies in the 1960s and 1970s would return to the agenda. There is no evidence that the Kinnock–Hattersley leadership has a

better solution to these problems than its predecessors had; on the level of policy and decision, therefore, Scargill's defeat has changed nothing. But this essay is not concerned with what might happen under a Labour government, only with Labour's performance in opposition. What matters from that perspective is that Kinnock is the first Labour leader since the 1960s who can talk to the unions from a position of strength; and that is an important electoral asset.

DOCTRINE AND ETHOS IN THE LABOUR MOVEMENT

The slaying of Arthur Scargill and the glossy, telegenic professionalism of the new Labour leadership could not, however, have brought about Labour's recovery all by themselves. Deeper factors have been at work as well; and these deeper factors bristle with ironies. As Henry Drucker has pointed out, the operative ideology of the British Labour movement has always had two dimensions, not one: the obvious, familiar dimension of 'doctrine', learned analyses of which fill multitudinous library shelves, and the nebulous, impalpable dimension of 'ethos', the subtleties of which are almost impossible to catch on paper.[7] Yet of the two, ethos has always been the better guide to the party's behaviour, particularly at times of crisis. By a paradox of political sociology which must torment its leadership, the enduring strength of that ethos through all the vicissitudes of the recent past is both the chief factor in its partial recovery and the chief obstacle to a more decisive recovery in future.

The best way to appreciate the importance of ethos to the party is to look at what has happened to its doctrine. As everyone knows, the doctrine is 'socialism', however defined. It has always been a fuzzy doctrine, stronger on long-term aspiration than on short-term strategy. But for the first 50 of the 70-odd years since the party committed itself to the socialist project, it was, at least, a plausible doctrine for a would-be party of government. The failures of the minority Labour ministries between the two World Wars were, no doubt, disconcerting, but they could be explained away. In any case, they were overshadowed by the achievements of the great reforming government of 1945–50. By the 1950s, it is true, the kind of socialism which the party had preached between the wars was beginning to look threadbare, but the 'revisionists' around Hugh Gaitskell produced an equally plausible successor. Socialism was no longer about owner-

ship. Instead, it was about equality, to be achieved by redistributing the fiscal dividend of economic growth. There were mutterings from the traditionalists, whose attitudes still prevailed in the constituency parties,[8] but for all practical purposes, 'revisionism' became the working doctrine of the leadership.

In the last 20 years, however, doctrine has disintegrated – and not any particular doctrine, moveover, but doctrine as such. Between 1964 and 1970, Gaitskellite 'revisionism' was tried and found wanting. A government elected on the ticket of faster growth, and stuffed with the flower of the Oxford PPE School, contrived a somewhat lower rate of growth than that of the 1950s. More ominously still, the egalitarianism which lay at the heart of the whole 'revisionist' philosophy turned out to be much too vague to operate in practice. Insofar as it could be made operational, moreover, it ran directly counter to the institutional interest of the craft unions (part of whose *raison d'être* was the protection of traditional differentials), as well as to the personal interests of their members (who lost from the higher taxes which were needed to finance the so-called 'social wage').[9] A philosophy of what Peter Clarke has called 'moral reform' – a philosophy based on the assumption that lasting social changes derive from changes in the motives and purposes of society's members, and that a reforming government must therefore try to change motives and purposes through moral persuasion, instead of relying on structure and law to change outward forms[10] – might conceivably have overcome these difficulties. But 'revisionism' was not a philosophy of moral reform. Its ethics and politics were both, in the last resort, utilitarian. And, for utilitarians, motive and purpose are, in economist's language, 'exogenous'. The 'forum', to use Jon Elster's phrase, is in this sense no different from the 'market':[11] the politician's business is to aggregate and reconcile privately-chosen purposes, not to influence their choice. In practice, of course, 'revisionist' ministers did try to change motives and purposes. To mention only the most obvious examples, that was the point of repeated calls for lower wage settlements and higher investment. But their philosophy gave them no convincing grounds on which to base such appeals, and no language in which to phrase them. It is hardly surprising that, as the economic climate worsened, they found fewer and fewer listeners.

This time, however, no successor was in sight. The old, Bevanite 'Left' of the party had never had a doctrine, only a series of negations. It had been against 'capitalism', and against 'revisionist'

flirtations with 'capitalism', but it had never decided what it was for –
still less, how it proposed to get it. In practice, the former Bevanites
who held office in the Labour Cabinets of the 1960s and 1970s usually
followed the 'revisionist' line. At first, the parliamentary Left of the
1970s was in no better case. It stood, not for socialism in any
recognizable sense, but for what might be called 'workerism': the
proposition that any demand, made by any section of the organized
working class, was *ipso facto* legitimate, no matter what effect it
might have on other sections of the organized working class, or
indeed on society at large.[12] By the end of the decade, it is true, it had
at last acquired a doctrine – the doctrine of what might be called the
'escape of the meso-economy', the chief British proponent of which
was Stuart Holland.[13] Unfortunately, the practical implications of this
doctrine are so bleak that it is hard to see how any party seeking
power through the ballot box could, in practice, face them.

The Holland doctrine holds that the growth of a 'meso-economy' of
giant, multi-product and often multi-national firms has negated the
postulates of both classical and Keynesian economics. Through their
market power, these giants have escaped from the control of the
sovereign consumer. They have also escaped from the control of the
sovereign nation state. They can frustrate its monetary policies
(through their access to credit beyond its boundaries) and its fiscal
policies (through transfer prices which lower their profits in high-tax
countries and raise them in countries where taxes are lower). By the
same means, they can also frustrate its attempts to manage the
exchange rate. Since their investment horizons are longer than those
Keynes presupposed, their investment intentions do not respond to
Keynesian 'pump priming' in the expected way. The levers of
Keynesian demand management thus break on the realities of meso-
economic power; 'revisionism', which presupposed the success of
Keynesian demand management, is therefore obsolete. The only
hope lies in a combination of public ownership, import controls and
industrial democracy. Though this conclusion sounds suitably radical,
it does not, however, address the new realities which the doctrine
purports to have uncovered. The underlying tacit assumption is that it
will be put into practice if a future Labour government wishes to do
so. However, if the doctrine is true – if the new centres of meso-
economic power are strong enough to frustrate the Keynesian state –
the giant firms which wield that power are hardly likely to sit quietly
while their wings are clipped. In one way or another, they will resist,
and the government will have to decide how to deal with their

resistance. There is nothing in the theory to show that it will respond more firmly than previous Labour governments have done in similar circumstances; still less is there anything to show that the prevailing balance of social power will allow it to respond more firmly, should it wish to do so. If the theory is true, in other words, it is not enough to put foward radical policies. It is also necessary to devise a radical political strategy to overcome the opposition which such policies are bound to encounter. About the contents of such a strategy, the Left is silent.

The implications are clear. As Drucker argued, the Labour Party is now, for practical purposes, a party without a doctrine. Gaitskellite 'revisionism' lacks the intellectual and moral resources to resolve the contradictions which stultified previous attempts to put it into practice. Hollandite 'fundamentalism' points logically either to a kind of despairing negativism or to a quasi-Leninist political strategy, for which the Labour Party – despite the Militant infestation in some inner-city areas – is hopelessly unsuitable, and for which there is no mass support. That is only the beginning of the story. Because Labour now has, for practical purposes, no doctrine, it has been unable to offer an intellectually coherent alternative to 'Thatcherism', or even to mount an effective challenge to it. More important still, it can offer no distinctive solutions to the central, overriding problems which baffled it in the 1960s and 1970s and which would face it again if it won the next election – the problem of how to manage a vulnerable, medium-sized economy in a world in which national economic sovereignty is increasingly illusory; and the problem of how to overcome the obstacles to economic adjustment which lie behind Britain's century-long economic decline. As a result, the agenda of British politics is still, in essentials, the 'Thatcherite' agenda of the late 1970s and early 1980s. The question that matters – the question that preoccupies the commentators and sets the tone of political discussion – is not how the Conservatives will react to Labour initiatives, but how Labour will accommodate itself to Conservative achievements. The contrast with the early 1960s, when a confident and aggressive Labour opposition articulated and shaped the public mood, and in doing so defined the terms of the party debate, could hardly be more glaring. Then, the Conservatives danced to Labour tunes. Now Labour is learning to dance, clumsily and unhappily, to the tunes which the Conservatives first started to play ten years ago – rather as the Conservatives learned to dance to the tunes of the welfare state and mixed economy in the late 1940s.

As doctrine has gone down, however, ethos has come up; and I suspect that the real moral of the last three years of British political history is that Labour's ethos now corresponds to the social and emotional context within which its bedrock supporters live their lives, if anything more closely than hitherto. That ethos is, of course, almost indefinable. It is an amalgam of inherited habits, values, assumptions and expectations derived, not from theory, but from experience and memory: the sediment left by nearly 200 years of working-class history. Any attempt to put it into words is bound to be arbitrary, and at the same time misleading. It is, above all, the ethos of the underdog: of life's losers: of the objects of history, on whom the subjects act. Perhaps Richard Hoggart caught it best in his famous evocation of the world of 'them' as seen from the vantage point of 'us':

> 'They' are 'the people at the top', 'the higher-ups', the people who give you your dole, call you up, tell you to go to war, fine you, made you split your family in the 'thirties to avoid a reduction in the Means Test allowance, 'get yer in the end', 'aren't really to be trusted', 'talk posh', 'are all twisters really', 'never tell yer owt' (e.g., of a relative in hospital), 'clap yer in clink', 'will do y' down if they can', 'summons yer', 'are all in a click (clique) together', 'treat y' like muck'.[14]

When Hoggart published that passage 30 years ago, it was beginning to sound out of date. Hoggart's world, good 'revisionists' assured themselves, was dead (or, at any rate, dying). It was a product of the poverty and hardship which a combination of Keynesian economics and revisionist politics would gradually eradicate. Another decade or two of rising living standards, progressive taxation and growing social expenditure, and the whole notion of a powerless 'us', facing an alien and impervious 'them', would lose its resonance. And so, for a time, it seemed. But – fortunately for the Kinnock–Hattersley Labour Party – only for a time. The sunlit uplands of ever-increasing material prosperity, on which the 'revisionists' pinned their hopes, have receded beyond the horizon. The end of 'growthmanship', the collapse of the Keynesian system, the disappearance of large sectors of manufacturing industry, the rise in unemployment and the fall in expectations which all this has brought with it[15] – in the forlorn council estates and bedraggled terraces of Labour's heartlands – these must have given Hoggart's world a new lease of life. In 1983, they were overwhelmed by the backwash of the doctrinal obsessions

of the 1970s. The disintegration of doctrine has given Labour a chance to take advantage of them.

But all this is, of course, a distinctly mixed blessing. As Anthony Heath, Roger Jowell and John Curtice have recently shown, the well-worn notion that class voting has been on the wane and that the secular decline in the Labour vote since the early 1950s is the product of a breakdown in the old association between class and voting, is dangerously over-simplified.[16] If classes are divided, not by income (as in most studies of voting behaviour) but by conditions of employment, a much more complex picture emerges. The association between class and voting has not declined steadily over time. Rather, it has fluctuated: in recent elections, it was at its weakest in 1970, not in 1983. Labour is still the party of the working class, defined as 'rank and file manual employees'. Its problem is not that the working class is less likely to vote for it than it used to be, but that there are fewer workers: not the *embourgoisement* of the proletariat, but its erosion. That, however, is cold comfort for the ambitious young men on the front Opposition bench in the House of Commons. They do not want to be the undisputed chieftains of a shrinking proletarian ghetto. They want to govern the country; and, precisely because 'Thatcherism' has enjoyed such a long period of intellectual and cultural hegemony, the gap between the ghetto and the rest of the country is even wider than it used to be. Ethos enabled them to recapture the parts of the ghetto which the party lost between 1979 and 1983; by the same token, it can only hinder their attempts to break out of it into the wider society around it.

THE ALLIANCE

At which point, enter the Alliance. Its problem is the mirror image of Labour's. The Labour Party does not know how to break out of the working-class ghetto; the Alliance does not know how to break into it. This, of course, has been the problem of the political centre since the 1920s. Because the working class is smaller than it used to be, it is not as serious a problem as it once was – a fact that made the Liberal revival possible. But according to Heath, Jowell and Curtice, even today's shrunken working class still accounts for 34 per cent of the electorate: much too large a proportion for a party aspiring to change the system to write off. Despite intermittent attempts, however, the Liberals never solved the problem. When the SDP was formed, many

believed that it would provide the solution. Some of its founders saw it as a potential successor to Labour as the main left-of-centre party in a still class-based party system; most assumed that it would be more successful in winning over working-class labour voters than the Liberals had been on their own. The same view shaped early conceptions of the Alliance. The Liberals, the assumption went, would peg away at their existing constituency; the SDP would bring, as its dowry, a new, ex-Labour, working-class constituency, which the Liberals could not reach. These hopes perished in the 1983 election. There was no discernible difference between the two parties' capacities to appeal to working-class voters; since the election, moreover, they have been equally unable to prevent Labour's reconquest of its working-class base. From the central fact of electoral sociology follows virtually everything else about the Alliance's position in current British politics.

Broadly speaking, there are three possible approaches to the problem. The first is to tackle it head-on: to accept that class is still a major factor in voting behaviour and to try, by one means or another, to detach Labour's working-class base from its old allegiance. The second is to circumvent it: to try to transcend the class divisions which have held the Liberals back in the past by putting forward a view of society and politics to which class is irrelevant, and to persuade the electorate that that view is correct. The third is to accept that, for the time being at any rate, the problem is insoluble: that Labour remains the party of the working class in a system which is (at least partly) class-based; that the Alliance cannot hope to dislodge it from that position; and that new Alliance voters will therefore have to come, not from the old Labour heartlands, but from the Conservatives.

The first approach provides the rationale for the 'long march through the wards'[17] favoured by the 'community politics' wing of the Liberal Party. This wing has spotted that many of the old Labour heartlands have been ill-served by sclerotic Labour machines, which have come to take their working-class constituents for granted. It concludes that persistent campaigning on the bread-and-butter local issues which concern working-class voters can enable the Liberals first to penetrate and eventually to capture what were originally safe Labour seats. In some places, this strategy has been remarkably successful. It has made the Liberals the main opposition to Labour in Liverpool, and put at least two Liberal MPs into the House of Commons. But it has two disadvantages. It is a strategy for possible

victory in the distant future; it offers only scanty and uncertain dividends in the short (or even the medium) term. Worse still, it is a strategy of the particular, not of the general: of disaggregation, not of aggregation. It focuses on local interests and inflames local grievances; it does not tell its exponents how to knit these interests together and reconcile the inevitable conflicts between them. At its worst, it can degenerate into the politics of NIMBY ('not in my backyard'); and the politics of NIMBY can easily slide into the politics of the pork barrel. Because of all this, it is a strategy for a permanent opposition, not for a party which aspires to a share in government.

The national leadership of the Alliance has therefore oscillated between the second and third approaches – sometimes stressing its commitment to a 'new politics' of electoral and constitutional reform; and sometimes offering a mixture of neo-liberal economics and social concern, which might be described as 'Thatcherism with a human face'. Its attempts to adopt the second approach, however, have been too cautious to attain the object of the exercise, while its attempts to adopt the third have trapped it in a contradiction. To be sure, it is solidly committed to proportional representation and the incorporation of the European Convention of Human Rights into British law – both indispensable to any 'new politics' worth the name. But a convincing 'new politics' would involve far more than these. It would also have to answer the questions of whether (and if so, how) the increasingly obsolescent nation state should share power with subnational and supra-national tiers of government, as well as with organized producer groups. So far, the Alliance has flinched from these questions – understandably, since the answers would be bound to be controversial and might lose votes in the short run instead of gaining them. In flinching, however, it has condemned constitutional reform to the status of a minor theme in a programme focused on the conventional bread-and-butter issues around which British politics have revolved since the war. And in doing that, it has tacitly admitted – no doubt, without realizing it – that it does not have sufficient faith in any 'new politics' to trust its future to it: that, although it hopes to break the famous 'mould' one day, it has not found an alternative to it yet; and that, for the time being, the third approach will therefore continue to take precedence over the second.

This leads on to the confusions which have resulted from its attempts to adopt the third approach. Underpinning – or, at any rate, justifying – these is the notion of the so-called 'Social Market'. At

least in outline, the advocates of the 'Social Market' accept the neo-
liberal diagnosis of Britain's economic failures. At the same time,
they wish to distribute the proceeds of economic success according to
non-market criteria, derived from some principle of equity or
fairness. The notion has obvious political attractions. It goes with the
grain of the new individualism which Mrs Thatcher has tapped so
successfully, while at the same time sounding vaguely idealistic; if
Heath, Jowell and Curtice are right, there is a potential constituency
for it.[18] The trouble is that, just as Gaitskellite 'revisionism' could not
provide convincing grounds from which to appeal for the changes of
purpose and motive which its economic policies required, so the
'Social Market' cannot provide convincing grounds for the redistribution which is supposed to be central to its politics. A redistributionist
must be able to answer the question: 'Why should I make sacrifices
for others?' The answer: 'Because it is in your interests' is unlikely to
carry conviction for long, while the answer: 'Because you are a kindly
altruist, who feels compassion for those less fortunate than yourself',
dodges the problem. However emollient the language in which it is
put, the answer has to be: 'Because it is your duty; because you are
part of a community to the other members of which you have
obligations; because no man is an island unto himself'. Almost by
definition, no individualistic ethic can provide the grounds for such an
answer because no individualistic ethic has room for the notions of
community or fraternity from which it springs. But the doctrine of the
'Social Market' is either individualistic or meaningless. The central
proposition on which the whole market–liberal system rests is that
society is made up of separate, atomistic, sovereign individuals,
determining their preferences by and for themselves. If that premise
goes, the rest of the system goes too. The competitive market is no
longer by definition the most efficient mechanism for allocating
resources; and state intervention or producer-group pressures which
'distort' the market are no longer by definition harmful. But it is on
these assumptions that the market–liberal diagnosis of Britain's
economic predicament rests. If they are false, there is no reason to
believe the diagnosis, or to take the cures it implies. Yet if they are
true – if choices are, after all, made by atomistic, sovereign
individuals, determining their own preferences by and for themselves
– community is a chimera, and there is no basis for redistribution
beyond the spasmodic and uncertain altruism of the atomistic
individual.

     At its philosophical core, in short, 'Thatcherism with a human

face', is still, in essence, 'Thatcherism'. Like Labour, though for different reasons, the Alliance has not yet found the basis for a convincing challenge to it. The opposition parties may or may not do well in the next election. If they do, it will not be because they have devised governing philosophies to replace the strange mixture of market liberalism and traditional Conservatism which has prevailed for most of the last ten years.

Notes

1. Since the House of Commons was smaller in the 1930s than it is today, the Liberal contingent in 1935 was larger, as a proportion of the total, than the Alliance contingent today.
2. For a good example of Labour forebodings see Austin Mitchell, *Four Years in the Death of the Labour Party* (London: Methuen, 1983).
3. The *Guardian*, 29 August 1986.
4. See in particular Margaret Sharp, Geoffrey Shepherd and David Marsden, 'Structural Adjustment in the United Kingdom Manufacturing Industry', World Employment Programme research working paper (Geneva: ILO, December 1983).
5. For 'encompassingness' and the relative 'non-encompassingness' of British trade unions, see Mancur Olson, *The Rise and Decline of Nations* (New Haven: Yale University Press, 1982).
6. R. J. Flanagan, David Soskice and Lloyd Ulman, *Unionism, economic stabilisation and incomes policies: European Experience* (Washington, D.C.: The Brookings Institution, 1983).
7. H. M. Drucker, *Doctrine and Ethos in the Labour Party* (London: George Allen & Unwin, 1979).
8. Lewis Minkin, *The Labour Party Conference*, (London: Allen Lane, 1978).
9. For the effects of these pressures see Dudley Jackson, H. A. Turner and Frank Wilkinson, *Do Trade Unions Cause Inflation?* (Cambridge: Cambridge University Press, 1972).
10. Peter Clarke, *Liberals and Social Democrats* (Cambridge: Cambridge University Press, 1978) especially pp. 4–8.
11. Jon Elster, 'The Market and the Forum: three varieties of political theory', in Jon Elster and Aanund Hylland (eds), *Foundations of Social Choice Theory* (Cambridge: Cambridge University Press, 1986) pp. 103–32.
12. For this phase in the history of the Left see John Mackintosh, 'Socialism or Social Democracy?', in David Marquand (ed.) *John P. Mackintosh on Parliament and Social Democracy* (London: Longmans, 1982) pp. 155–68.
13. Stuart Holland, *The Socialist Challenge* (London: Quartet, 1975).

14. Richard Hoggart, *The Uses of Literacy* (London: Chatto & Windus, 1957).
15. For the fall in expectations, see James Alt, *The Politics of Economic Decline: Economic management and political behaviour in Britain since 1964* (Cambridge: Cambridge University Press, 1979).
16. Anthony Heath, Roger Jowell and John Curtice, *How Britain Votes* (Oxford: Pergamon, 1985).
17. A phrase for which I am indebted to Mr John Roper.
18. Heath, Jowell and Curtice, *How Britain Votes*, especially pp. 113–23.

8 Thatcherism and British Political History

S.E. Finer

'Thatcherism' combines a unique political style and, in some measure, political substance. In this chapter I shall address the questions: Will this 'Thatcher experience' prove to be a turning point in the socio-economic life of Britain or just a hiatus? Will it turn out to be historic or simply historical?

Let me first make some general reservations. To begin with, it is unlikely that any government in any country could over a mere seven or eight years permanently alter the social structure, attitudes, and distribution of power; but especially so in Britain. Here, up to 1979, Labour and Conservatives had alternated in power in equal measure. Each successive administration was therefore able to (and showed itself eager to) cancel the more original and radical legislation of its predecessors. To use a government's success or failure to change the deep values and structure of society as the criterion for judging its historical significance is not a sensible procedure. Next, from the end of the far-reaching reforms of the Attlee administration in 1950 no succeeding government even tried (till 1979) to break out of the triangle it had laid out, composed of the public corporation leviathans on the one side, the great social services structure on the other, and full-employment on the third. Each successive government came in like a lion and went out like a lamb. What, after the Thirty Years' Bore (i.e., the period between 1950 and 1979), ever came of the 'white heat of technology', Heath's vow that 'our purpose is to change the course of history, no less', or the Labour Party's boast that it would effect 'an irreversible shift in the balance of power and wealth in favour of the working people and their families'? Nothing. In every case, by mid-term, governments funked it. Hence the expression 'U-turns'; from 1950 onwards governments were Trimmers all. (In all these years only one major irreversible change of policy took place: the country acceded to the EEC; it did so only after two elections and a referendum, and was not finally secure until the advent of the second Thatcher administration in 1983 ended the Labour Party's still smouldering hopes that it could turn the clock

back: the exception proves the general rule.) Third, even if (as I shall argue) the Thatcher government is the first radical one since Attlee, the first not to have trimmed and the first to have broken new ground, it has pursued more limited objectives than usually supposed. The nationalized dinosaurs live on, and so does the great social services structure. And there are entire tracts of socio-economic policy which the government has shown no desire to remodel. The most notable and scandalous example is the clumsy, archaic and counterproductive tax system, and the divorce that exists between it and the social security structure.

With these qualifications, Thatcherism marks a radical departure from the norms and traditions of British politics since 1950. It would be idle to go into detail. Between 1950 and 1979 elections turned, overwhelmingly, on bread-and-butter issues. The central substance of policy concerned steering the economy and reorganizing and re-reorganizing the details of the tax and the social security packages. The amount of sound and fury expended over these was out of all proportion to the magnitude of changes effected. True, this was not the impression given at the time. Yet simply look again at your faded newspaper clippings and see if they do not induce in you only the sense of 'old unhappy far-off things'/And battles long ago' – a suffocating sense of *déjà vu*. In steering the economy, both parties accepted the Keynesian orthodoxy. The battles that raged were over how much more or less of the agreed 'mixed economy' should be public or private. Hence arose a consistent anti-nationalization stance of the Conservatives and an equal but more successful Labour drive to nationalize more and more enterprises – particularly if they were very ailing. That party was in the business of collecting lame ducks to hang around the necks of its Conservative successors. Though the economy was clearly sinking, the angriest contests arose over distribution of the inadequate tax base. In turn, this raised the issue of unbalanced budgets. According to the vulgarly received version of Keynesianism, these were a sovereign specific against industrial decline. At least this was the way the trade unions interpreted it, seeing it, I suspect, much as their remote ancestors had perceived Thomas Attwood's primitive underconsumptionist notions in the 1820s. But the trade unions and Labour were not alone in taking something like this view; from time to time even the Conservatives inflated to make a 'dash for growth', with the inevitable effect on the balance of payments; hence the sequences of 'stop-go' and wage and price freezes.

Connected with the steering of the economy, but transcending it in social and political significance, lay the seemingly unstoppable rise of organized labour. That the unions should have a special place in Labour governments was inevitable, providing as they did the bulk of the party's finance and controlling the vast majority of its Conference votes. But the Conservative governments, too, felt that they had to make deals with the unions, and it seemed as if the country was moving down a corporatist road, where economic policy was decided by a trinity of government, industrialists, and union leaders. The trouble was that the union leaders could not keep their side of the bargain, even when they wanted to. So both the political parties alternately tried collaboration or confrontation, with an equal lack of success.

The contrast with Thatcherism could not be sharper. Keynesian deficit financing was out, as were physical controls and/or subsidies to ailing industries. In came money-supply economics and financial management of the economy. The unions were cold-shouldered. Public expenditure was restrained as far as the fast rising levels of unemployment benefits permitted. Nationalized industries were told to make profits, come what may. Some were sold off. Exchange controls were abolished. The maximum possible scope was given to market forces and nothing – neither the rising unemployment that had stricken Macmillan and Heath with panic, or waves of strikes such as had paralysed former governments – simply nothing was allowed to stand in the way of these policies. Many of them had been brutally (and unnecessarily) clumsy in execution, but the government rolled on unheeding like some great tank, moving along a fixed path and squashing down everything that stood in its way. In brief, Thatcherism introduced a wholly new economic theory and practice and pursued them with an obduracy and consistency quite unknown during the Thirty Years' Bore. The Labour Party calls this 'breaking the consensus', and one can see why. Many Conservatives admit the impeachment and regret it – Heath, Pym, Gilmour, for instance. Mrs Thatcher admits it too; but she glories in it.

I have already demonstrated that there are wide areas of socio-economic policy which the government has neglected altogether. Additionally, there are a number of important sectors where it has made significant changes of detail and emphasis – but has not altered the basic structures. This is true, for example, of the police, social security arrangements, taxes, industrial subsidies, job creation schemes and the like. These are the kinds of things that

politics was all about in the Great Bore War, the so-called 'consensus years'. These areas could be (and surely would be) changed by an incoming Labour government, but without any appreciable effect on society or the economy. Compared with certain other Thatcherite policies they are inconsiderable. The really big things, the radical departures, lie outside them, and these are the ones that I want to look at. I have four reasons for wanting to do this. In the first place they radically depart from the pre-1979 kind of policies. Second, some of them are critical to the kind of society and economy we are likely to have in the future. Third, they reveal by implication certain values which infuse and (one can presume) motivate or at least serve to rationalize them. And, finally, they are not just socio-economic policies. Most of them have a *Doppelgänger* in the shape of a sharply partisan political motivation. I think that this last point has not often been appreciated.

I start with the values from which, it would seem, these policies arise. I am not going to proceed by analyzing party and ministerial statements, because these are so often dictated by day-to-day preoccupations and bloated with rhetoric. I think one gets a clearer picture by looking at the policies themselves and proceeding by inference. I ask myself: 'Given these policies, what kind of principles would I have to assume to make them intelligible and self-consistent?' I do not claim that they constitute a basic Thatcherite philosophy or motivation, although they very well might – only that to my mind they could constitute a rationale for what has been done.

This rationale consists of three elements. The first is the axiom that '*tutto si paga*': there is no such thing as a free lunch – everything must be paid for. One way of bringing this home is to reduce the non-market sector of public provision – by charging for prescriptions for instance; and it underlies the government's insistence that the proposed 'community charge' which is to replace local rates must be paid by everybody. A corollary of the principle is the search for 'value for money' in the public sector; hence we have, for instance, the Local Government Audit Commission, the installation of managers in NHS hospitals, the setting of financial targets for the nationalized industries. Cash limits and balanced budgets also follow from this principle. The second element is not so much the 'career open to talent' but its obverse, 'talents open for a career'; it underlies an educational philosophy that caters for high-fliers and excellence rather than one which in its more recent excesses even bans competitive sports. And, of course, this is all of a piece with a

business philosophy of competition, small enterprises, and 'start-up' schemes. It reinforces the third element, which is the marked preference – for market over non-market provision – as, for example, in the privatization of ancillary hospital services, the general drive to privatize state industries, and the elimination of controls over industry and finance, as far as is consistent with the prevention of fraud and monopoly abuses.

COUNCIL HOUSE SALES

Although the policy of selling off council houses to sitting tenants was initiated under the Heath government, it made slow progress before being halted by the returning Labour administrations (conforming to the self-cancelling character of politics in the Thirty Years' Bore). Between 1976–9 (Labour years and prior to the Thatcher Housing Acts 1980 and 1984) the total sales amounted to 92 520. In the year 1980 alone, the figure was over 85 000. Between 1980–4 over 652 000 houses were sold, and the process is continuing. The proportion of owner-occupied dwellings which stood at 54 per cent in 1977, had reached 67 per cent in late 1986 (the highest proportion in Europe) and the target set is 72 per cent. Municipal housing estates have been the standard and (comparatively speaking) highly idiosyncratic British response to housing need. The Thatcher breakaway could hardly be more dramatically radical, therefore, especially if we remember that just prior to 1979 Labour was considering the municipalization of private rented accommodation.

WIDER SHARE OWNERSHIP

This is really only now making its debut. Often talked about by the Conservatives, it had never been strongly pushed and the 1974 financial débâcle shook the confidence of small investors. The current revival of wider share ownership is a side blow from privatization of state assets, and its potential seems to have been discovered by chance and not design. At all events it seems that in late 1986 the proportion of adults who own shares is 15 per cent. With further and more massive privatization in view, this figure is likely to rise quite steeply. The point here is not that the current ownership of shares is very widely dispersed, but that for the first time it seems as if a way of making it popular has been discovered.

132   *Thatcherism and British Political History*

DENATIONALIZATION

This represents a most radical departure from the pre-1979 norm, not because Conservatives had never wanted it – they had wanted it consistently and passionately – but because they had never found a safe formula for achieving it. They denationalized road haulage in the early 1950s, but had a very bad experience with it, and they denationalized steel in 1952. That was easier as the Act had not yet come into force, but the way it was done left the industry open to renationalization which Labour carried out in 1966. After that the Conservatives seem to have lost hope of ever reversing Labour's piecemeal nationalizations. I can remember Sir Keith Joseph bemoaning what he called the 'ratchet effect': for how, it was asked, could private individuals be expected to put up the enormous sums needed to repurchase these industries, especially with the threat of renationalization hanging over them? The Thatcher government seems to have stumbled on the answer in denationalizing the National Freight Corporation and then British Aerospace. The former was offered to the corporation's employees, who responded enthusiastically and immediately made the company a great success. In selling off British Aerospace preference was given to the company's employees and, next, to small investors. 90 per cent of the employees bought shares; and the issue was three and half times oversubscribed. *Arcana imperii aperta*: the secret was to 'fatten up' the companies, that is, get them into profitable shape and then give preference to small investors in the sell-off. At a stroke this promoted 'wider share ownership', and it also created a constituency with an economic stake in continuing Conservative rule – at least, as long as the Labour Party threatened to renationalize. However inaccurate my account of the finding of this populist formula may be, the fact is that it exists and has encouraged the government to go much further than had ever previously been conceived possible. British Telecom and British Gas have been sold off, and British Airways is next to follow.

THE TRADE UNIONS

One most striking innovation of Thatcherism, however, is surely its attitude to the trade unions. As I suggested earlier, these had been elevated (even by Heath) to the status of an Estate of the Realm.

They had shown that they could paralyse public services. Their restrictive practices and insistence on over-manning had condemned the nationalized industries to chronic deficits. They had used industrial disputes as a stalking horse for political objects. They had in succession torpedoed the Wilson, the Heath, and the Callaghan governments. They were offered a share in supreme economic planning by Heath in 1973, and they simply took it as their birthright in the Labour years 1974–9. No matter which government was in office, the unions were in power. They were intolerable – but, seemingly, unstoppable.

Thatcherism broke completely every traditional relationship with the unions; they were put into political quarantine. The government loftily dissociated itself from industrial disputes. In a succession of Acts it eroded piecemeal the unions' legal immunities, making secondary strike action – their most potent weapon since it converted any single dispute into almost a general strike – illegal. And – aided here by rising unemployment – it showed no fear of public service strikes, letting them run and run and run until the exhausted unions gave in. Social workers, steel workers, post office workers: it was all one; the government was aloof and unyielding. Scargill's 1984 challenge was of a different order. The premise for its success was the use of strong-arm tactics by flying pickets, the formula Scargill had pioneered in 1973. The Thatcher government regarded it as more a political insurrection than an industrial dispute; picket violence met police force. The miners' sad defeat was emblematic. Another of the *arcana imperii* had been brought into the open: the unions were not unstoppable.

FULL EMPLOYMENT

But the cardinal innovation (unlike any of the previous ones, bitterly unpopular) is the Thatcherite attitude to 'full employment'. I put this expression in inverted commas because, as will be seen, it is a term of art. To maintain 'full employment' (whatever that might be) was the third side of the Attlee triangle. The other two, it will be recalled, were the nationalized industries and the social welfare apparatus. Thatcherism, which had attacked the first and stood pat on the second, positively demolished the third.

The point is that the famous 1944 White Paper on which the entire 'full employment' policy was supposed to rest, did not talk of 'full

employment' at all. It spoke of 'a high and stable level of employment', which its authors seemed to have envisaged as a 5–6 per cent unemployment rate (some 1.3 million people). But every government till 1979 envisaged it as something like a mere 2 per cent. What is more, they all regarded such 'full employment' as an absolute and overriding commitment, whereas in the White Paper it figures as just one responsibility among others. Conservative governments as well as Labour shared this misinterpretation; when unemployment soared to 2.6 per cent in the bitter winter of 1963, the Macmillan government panicked to bring it down again. So did Heath when unemployment started to rise in 1972. It was this that prompted his U-turn towards an inflationary policy held in check by a freeze on prices and incomes.

Such 'full employment' of the years up to Callaghan put strains either on the price and wage level, or on the balance of payments, or (more usually) on both. This is why the management of the economy up to 1979 proceeded as a series of repetitive bumps and grinds: sterling crises and devaluations, stop-goes on investment, and short-lived freezes on prices and incomes.

The 1979 government rejected the entire tradition. During the 1983 election campaign there was a famous television interview where, reproached for having betrayed the 1944 White Paper, the Prime Minister astounded her interviewer by quoting it, chapter and verse, to demonstrate that it was her predecessors who had betrayed it, and that it was in fact, a 'Thatcherite' document! And, in truth, that celebrated Paper does indeed state that to achieve a 'high and stable level of employment' it was a prerequisite that British industry could compete internationally and that prices and wages must be stable. Neither condition had in fact obtained at all. Inflation itself had soared over 20 per cent! Wages chased prices, prices outstripped wages which chased prices. . . . To achieve the 'high and stable level' of employment, you must not start with an overriding commitment to full employment come what may, but with an overriding commitment to reduce inflation to zero. Pointing this out to the thunderstruck interviewer, Mrs Thatcher had stood the entire pre-1979 consensus on its head. She had introduced a totally new paradigm. It was to be called 'monetarism', 'Friedmanism', and all kinds of other things. The point of it was that only when (and if) you made British industry internationally competitive and reduced inflation to zero could you obtain the Holy Grail of full employment!

This policy is the most controversial, the most unpopular but also the most unsuccessful of all the Thatcherite breaks with the 'consen-

sus'. For though inflation has come down to a mere 2.5 per cent and productivity has risen sharply, unemployment has risen to over 3 million persons, over 13 per cent of the labour force.

POLITICAL AIMS AND DURABILITY

The 1983 Conservative Manifesto contained few specific commitments, but one that stood out was the pledge to abolish the GLC and the metropolitan counties. Now whereas all the policies recounted above can plausibly be regarded as socio-economic, it is not so easy to see what socio-economic purposes this commitment was designed to serve. The more one muses upon it, another motivation suggests itself: a party political one. If we now review what has been said about the previous policies, I believe that we can see that, in addition to serving a socio-economic purpose, most also aim at a specific *political* target. That target is the Labour Party. Behind the manifestos there lies a 'Hidden Manifesto': to dismantle, to disperse, if possible to destroy, any citadel of Labour votes, money, patronage, and power. For instance: council housing estates were (and still are) 'stagnant pools' of Labour support. Voters whose social profiles are otherwise identical are 20 per cent more likely to vote Labour if they rent a council house than if they are owner-occupiers. The patronage and influence conferred on councillors by the management of the council estates is also quite immense. The Conservatives have taken the view that to own your own house brings about a corresponding change in political attitude, so that the spread of home-ownership on council estates could be envisaged as political seedcorn.

Denationalization also constituted an assault on the Labour Establishment. The existence of the public corporations gave immense patronage to Labour ministers; it also gave the union leaders who commanded their shock troops in these industries the power to disrupt the economy from these 'commanding heights' even when the Labour Party was out of office. Conversely, denationalization offered golden managerial posts to thrusting entrepreneurs (Conservatives all) and, as I suggested earlier, created a widening circle of small investors with a stake in continued Conservative rule.

The Thatcherite assault on the trade unions so obviously strikes a political target that it seems to need no further elaboration: anything that weakens the unions *pro tanto* weakens the Labour Party. But two items of trade union legislation deserve special attention. The

first circumscribes the dictatorial powers of union officials by requiring a secret ballot before a strike is legal, and by requiring a secret ballot for the election of trade union officers. For how is it that, though a majority of union members vote for parties other than Labour, the executive committees and chief officers of the unions are never Alliance or Conservative but are often to the far left of the Labour Party itself? Clearly, this has everything to do with the method of voting. The Ballot Act 1872 replaced the show of hands by secret ballot for parliamentary elections. Over a century has had to elapse before a similar requirement was introduced for the trade union leaders, and it had to be imposed on them.

The second of these more blatantly political provisions is the one concerning trade union political funds. As everybody knows, the unions that affiliate to the Labour Party use these to finance it, and indeed without this revenue it would perish. The law now required the unions to ballot their membership at least every ten years on whether they wished to maintain a political fund. The hope, buoyed up by the public opinion polls, was that a number of moderate unions (at least) would vote against the political fund and thus deprive the Labour Party of income.

So all these measures, though they have a socioeconomic rationale, have a partisan aspect as well. Now when we inspect the commitment to abolish the GLC and the metropolitan counties, the problem is to find any substantial socioeconomic reasons to justify it. Certainly, local authorities spend one-quarter of the national total expenditure, but one-third of this comes from local rates. It is true that half of this is paid by companies who are subjected to taxation without representation, but if this were the problem there were several ways of handling it. So, if the difficulty is simply the level of local rates to householders, why should the central government be particularly concerned? It is hard to see an economic rationale. As to the administrative one arising from the alleged clumsiness and costliness of the two-tier arrangement, the dissolution of this system into constituent boroughs would seem to raise almost as many questions as it solves. What, however, is not in the least problematical is that the GLC and at least two of the metropolitan counties had fallen into the hands of a new, extreme, quite untraditional type of Labour councillor. The general point is illustrated by the now well-publicized cases of boroughs like Lambeth and Camden, or the Metropolitan County of Merseyside, which became dominated by political cliques in an incestuous relationship with their public service unions, who

dispensed jobs, money and political support to minority groups in return for votes. British central–local government relationships are peculiar in that they are designed to ensure minimum standards but not to bother about maximal ones and, second, that the main sanction is to withdraw government grant – which entails that the authority, if it decides to go it alone, will have to raise its rates yet further. So the Thatcher government was powerless, administratively, to prevent the process whereby these Labour councils spent prodigally on social services, padded jobs, directed labour departments and selected minorities, and thereby alimented the Labour party with votes, finance and jobs. For what I am now about to write I have no evidence at all, mere inference: but it seems to me that the government reacted in a way similar to the Miami Jews in the 1920s. Confronted by a bunch of people who excluded them from the Miami beaches, they simply went out and bought the beaches. I believe that the Thatcher government, having contemplated with increasing distaste and alarm what Burke would have called these 'ripening hothouses of [Labour] influence', decided to do away with them.

In the ultra-Left's demonology, the massive rise in unemployment is also seen as politically motivated: a deliberate plot to weaken Labour's bargaining power. In some highly vulnerable industries it certainly seems to have depressed militancy, but one needs only to observe the government's dismay at the ceaseless rise in unemployment and its frantic efforts to create new jobs to dismiss the ultra-Left charges as fantasy. Far from willing the increasing unemployment, the Thatcher governments hoped for the precise opposite.

Let me now turn to the question I originally set out to answer: will the Thatcher experience, as analysed above, prove durable, a turning-point; or will it prove, in the event of a Labour victory, as ephemeral as all radical departures did during the Great Bore War?

On the strictly political side – what I have described as the assault on the Labour Establishment – the failure is as complete as it is conspicuous. Take the trade unions. Thatcherism has scored two 'own goals'. The first is ascribable to its very success. The government's contemptuous confrontation and defeat of a string of unions, one after the other, culminating with victory over the NUM, has left the unions nowhere to go except back to the only party that gives them political support. Union history in this country has followed a consistent and wholly explicable rhythm. Whenever direct action has failed, the unions turn to constitutional action. This is what happened after the failure of the Grand Consolidated Trunk Trade Union in

1833, for instance, or after Chartism, or after the General Strike of 1926, and it is happening again now. The Labour Party is, for the trade union leadership, the last White Hope. The other failure *vis-à-vis* the unions, however, is due entirely to the Conservative Party's lethargy as a mass. The decision as to whether to retain political funds was a matter for the trade union membership to decide by ballot. The leaders took the initiative. They hired public relations firms and set out to canvass their message through every avenue open to them – and a union has very many, including its own newspaper. The Conservative Party took no steps to counter this propaganda and ensured its opponents (even in the most right-wing unions) convincing victories by default. It was equally supine in the matter of abolishing the GLC. In all, some nine London boroughs agreed with the government over abolishing the GLC; but they disagreed as to what should be put in its place; and in any event their efforts proved feeble in the face of their opponents. Livingstone hired a public relations firm and took the attack to his enemy. The GLC utilized a legal loophole permitting it to spend a considerable sum on what was, effectively, party propaganda. Its advertising campaign was so effective that within a short time it had secured a majority against abolition. That was not all. The Labour-controlled London boroughs also used this legal loophole. As you walk up Tottenham High Road you could meet at almost every block some shop or other that has been converted into a council office for this or that welfare service. From every one of these shop windows stare great black and yellow posters, reading: 'Your social services – threatened by the government'. The government has shot itself in the foot.

But where those socio-economic measures which I outlined above are concerned, I feel confident that nothing, not even in the event of a Labour victory, will ever be the same again. Home ownership on the widest scale is here for ever; whether it breeds a new set of self-reliant attitudes remains to be seen, but it is quite likely. A Labour government might well renationalize British Telecom and British Airways and indeed the structure of these companies, in which government retains a large stake, makes this fairly easy to do; but the old Morrisonian concept of the gigantic 'semi-public' corporation will never be revived. Indeed even before 1979 the Labour Party was more interested in the Italian variant, where corporations are controlled via government majority shareholdings. Again, it would not be surprising to see the Labour Party restoring many of the trade-union immunities, but pre-strike ballots and the secret and decent

election of union officials seem bound to remain (indeed the TUC General Secretary has stated as much) and I doubt whether even the very left-wing parliamentary Labour Party we must expect in the event of a Labour victory will create a rod for its own back by restoring the full ambit of secondary picketing to the unions. But in respect to the trade unions what will certainly endure (and affect the conduct of all later administrations) is the knowledge that, if the government is resolute and has prepared itself in advance, it can face down any strike. The effect this could have on the conduct of government is incalculable, but it will be entirely to the advantage of government.

What of unemployment? The Labour Party states that reducing unemployment is its first priority. It promises to reduce it by 1 million within two years. But who has yet made a specific commitment to return to 'full employment', and if they did how would they define it? Quite certainly, never again as 2 per cent unemployed. The most likely outcome is that the economy will be run on the much slacker rein of a million and a half or more unemployed (i.e., 6 per cent), the original rate envisaged in 1944. This will be justified along implicitly Thatcherite lines, as something necessary for the attainment of stable prices and wages, and international competitiveness.

About the medium-term future for the concept of balanced budgets, 'value for money', and efficiency in the nationalized industries, I am not so sure. We all know now that in the short term, if a Labour government is returned, we shall see Wilsonry writ smaller, and modified to meet new circumstances. The Labour government, we are promised, will spend great sums of borrowed money; it is going to stuff the great public corporations with unwanted staff and pick up the losses out of taxpayers' money, and it will do the same in the social service departments of the local authorities and the NHS. But will the electorate be indifferent to a rise in inflation, a depressed pound sterling and (very likely) another rash of balance of payments crises? There is a lot of evidence that suggests it has been positively influenced by monetarist and market-economy theories, and that the Labour philosophy of: 'Don't worry – come inside and borrow your way out of debt' is very much on the defensive. Nowhere is this more clearly evident than in the extreme caution of Mr Hattersley, who obviously believes – what many of his party do not care to acknowledge – that the general public accepts the Thatcherite view that money does not grow on trees. There could well be a reversion to Thatcherite stringency.

But, if this comes about only after the interposition of a Labour government, it will be a Thatcherism without Thatcher. Is this possible? She has towered over all her contemporaries, inside her party as well as outside. Her courage – intellectual, psychological, and in the face of physical danger – is quite out of the ordinary. It is her unwavering purpose that has kept her governments on their fixed course through the troughs as well as the crests of party and personal popularity. The temptation to take the easier path, to fudge, and to trim, are immense. She herself has never succumbed to it – but I do not see, as yet, any hard-nosed successor who will do likewise. Mrs Thatcher evokes admiration and detestation for one identical reason: she is 'big'. She has impressed herself on government as nobody has done since the war years of Churchill. She falls short of greatness, but she radiates dominance. I do not believe that in our lifetime we shall ever look upon her like again.

Index

114–16, 117, 128–9, 132–3,
135–6, 137–9
Trades Union Congress, *see* trade
unions

unemployment, 9–10, 13, 44, 48, 72,
76–81, 90, 91, 93, 112, 115, 129,
133–5, 137, 139
see also economic policy
United States of America, policy
towards, 96, 101, 105
universities, 39, 49, 52, 88, 89

'Victorian values', 40, 42–3

Walker, Peter, 16, 56–7
Walters, Alan, 6, 18n, 54n
Wass, Douglas, 2

welfare issues, xi, xiii, xvi, 4, 13–14,
42, 47, 119, 128
Westland affair, 8–9, 16, 31, 56, 57,
58, 66–8
Whitelaw, William, 6, 63
Whitty, Larry, 29
Wilson, Harold, 10, 32, 43, 44, 60,
65, 66, 114, 115, 133, 139
'winter of discontent' (1978–9),
xiv–xv, 5, 44, 114
Woolf, Michael, 27

Young Conservatives, 32

Zimbabwe, policy towards, 95, 107,
109
Zuckerman, Solly, 59

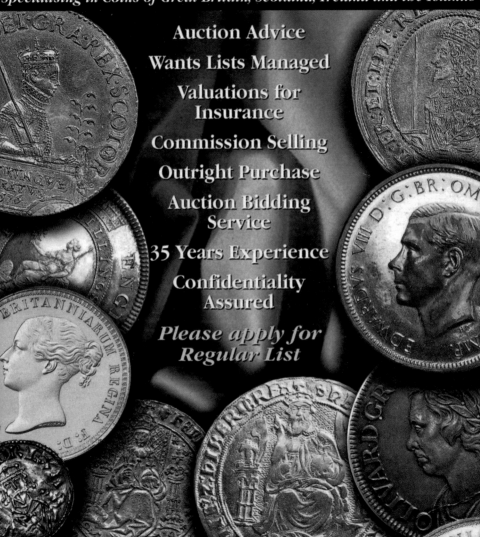

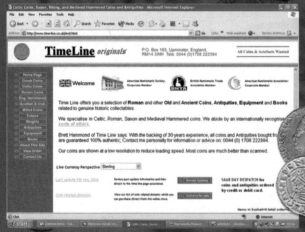

Editor
Deborah Lees

Art Editor
Kate Marsden

Consultant Editors
Steve Fairclough
Mark Rasmussen
Richard West

Advertisement Manager
Jay Jones

Advertising Executive
Neville Dick

Production
Rachel Hearn

Associate Publisher
Ilka Schmitt

An IPC Media annual published by IPC Country & Leisure Media Focus Network (part of the IPC Media Group of Companies) from:
IPC Media,
Focus Network, Leon House, 233 High Street, Croydon CR9 1 HZ.
Tel: 020 8726 8000
Fax: 020 8726 8299

Distributed by
MarketForce,
Kings Reach Tower,
Stamford Street,
London SE9 1LS.
Tel: 020 7633 3300

Pre-press by CTT; printed by Century Web Offset, Penryn, Cornwall.

British COINS
Market Values 2005

CONTENTS

SPECIAL FEATURES

RIGHT:
An extremely fine Charles II, five-guineas, of 1669, fetched £13,800 at the Morton & Eden sale last year

LATEST MARKET PRICES – FULL LISTINGS

British Coin Prices

Designing decisions

Richard West investigates how future British coins are decided upon, from choosing worthy anniversaries and determining the right artist, through to approval from The Queen and the Royal Mint

Commemorative stamps have been with us for many years – the first from the British Post Office was in 1924 – but it has only been in more recent times that commemorative coins have appeared on more of a regular basis. Looking at such coins, some may wonder how the decisions are made as to which events to commemorate, and how the designs are subsequently chosen.

The all-important question of the subject matter is initially decided by the Royal Mint, using researchers to explore potential anniversaries. Every day does provide an anniversary that is worthy of commemoration, although for coins it would generally have to be a significant anniversary, the 25th, 50th, 100th, 200th and so on. Understandably, the anniversary must be of an occurrence, which is of national importance, widely accepted by the public as being significant, and thus totally worthy of the prestigious nature of British coinage. The educational perspective and commercial considerations of any new coin may also be taken into account. In addition to anniversaries, Royal events and other major State occasions will also be considered. There must be a specific reason for each new coin release, albeit the criteria might be different in each case. The 50p coin, designed by the sculptor, James Butler, to mark the 50th anniversary of Roger Bannister running the mile in under four minutes, celebrates more than just the anniversary. Its design epitomises both sporting achievement and human endeavour.

Liaison will take place with Royal Mail to see if the subject matter for new coins and stamps might coincide, but unlike Royal Mail, which receives hundreds of suggestions for new stamps each year, and still gets complaints for missing something that a member of the public feels is vitally important; there is virtually no public lobbying for new coins. Perhaps the public feels it cannot have an input into a matter as momentous as the realm of the coin, or that coin issues are much more sparse than stamps so there is even less chance of their idea making its way onto a coin.

The final list of subjects, possibly with one or two

LEFT: Four Silver £1 coins will be issued separately over four consecutive years, beginning this year with the depiction of the Forth Bridge in Scotland and ending in 2007 with the Millennium Bridge in England

additional ideas, is submitted to the Master of the Mint, who is also the Chancellor of the Exchequer, and to The Queen. All new coin issues are initially announced in Parliament before any work can begin.

LEFT: One of the original drawings submitted by James Butler RA for the commemorative 50 pence piece celebrating Sir Roger Bannister's four-minute mile'

LEFT: One of the original drawings submitted by James Butler RA for the commemorative 50 pence piece celebrating Sir Roger Bannister's four-minute mile'

BOTTOM LEFT: Limited-edition 2004 Roger Bannister Proof 50 Pence in Silver and Gold. The Silver coin is just £25.95 and has an issue limit of 15,000, whereas the 22-carat Gold coin is £265 and there are only 1,250 available

The artists

Having selected the subjects, the next task will be to approach several artists for each to present a number of ideas for one or more of the new coins. The Royal Mint has many artists which it can approach: some have a proven track record of coin and medal design, while others may be trying their hand for the first time. All design disciplines can be involved, whether the artist's particular skills lies as a graphic designer, illustrator, engraver, sculptor or silversmith. Despite having its own list of names, the Mint will also approach others to seek advice as to who might be invited, and it will also always include someone from its own Engraving Department. What is paramount is that those chosen are known for the quality of their work and can produce exceptional designs. An example of a new artist being successful is Edwina Ellis, whose designs of bridges are now being seen on the reverses of £1 coins. She has persuaded the Mint to replace the beading around the edge of each coin with a border that is appropriate for the bridge depicted, such as rail track for the Forth Bridge, and chain links for the Menai Bridge.

An engraver from the Royal Mint, Robert Lowe designed the £2 coin celebrating the 200th anniversary of the first railway locomotive, and his image features a representation of the locomotive that was invented by Richard Trevithick. Beginning work at the Wheal Treasury mine with his father, Trevithick soon revealed an aptitude for engineering. In February 1804, Trevithick's first steam engine, to run on rails, travelled a distance of nine miles, reaching speeds of five miles an hour, carrying 70 passengers, 10 tons of iron and five wagons, from the iron works in Penydarren to the Merthyr–Cardiff Canal.

Design direction

Only rarely is a commission given to just one artist. Competition is seen as the best approach: it allows the brief to be extended to a wide range of artists. In that way, more artists are being added to the list, giving them the experience of coin design, spreading the work around and thus being as fair as possible to all, while at the same time raising the overall standard of the designs. However, not all those invited to submit will be available or will feel it appropriate for them at the time. Normally four to five artists will be invited for each new coin.

All the artists approached will be provided with a thorough written brief, identical for each artist, prepared by the Royal Mint, outlining the ways in which it feels the artists should direct their thinking. The Mint is always keen to discuss ideas with artists, and will hold briefing sessions to which all those who have been asked to submit are invited. These briefing sessions may

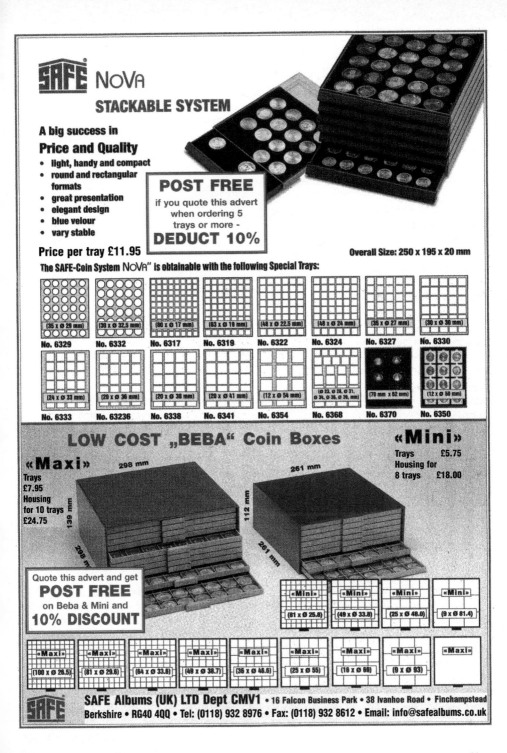

be held in a location appropriate to the theme of the coin, and may be addressed by a noted authority on the subject. The artists will be encouraged to ask any questions that will help in reaching their design solutions: the Royal Mint will also endeavour to provide as much research material as might be applicable for each coin idea or theme.

LEFT: The original drawing submitted by Robert Lowe in the competition to design a £2 coin commemorating Richard Trevithick's steam locomotive

BOTTOM LEFT: The Silver Proof Piedfort £2 coin celebrating Great British Engineering and the impact of the Steam Locomotive

Initially, most artists will submit their ideas as drawings, being asked to submit at least two ideas. While the final adjudication for every new design will be as a plaster model, there will not necessarily be a need for the artist to prepare such a model. There will always be someone from the Engraving Department assigned to each issue, so the preparation of a model can be undertaken by the Mint itself.

Advisory Committee

Once all the ideas have been submitted, the focus now turns on the Royal Mint Advisory Committee. Established in 1922 with the approval of King George V, the Royal Mint Advisory Committee on the Design of Coins, Medals, Seals and Decorations, to give it its full title, operates independently of the Royal Mint, and has as one of its aims to raise the standard of numismatic art. Acting for the Master of the Mint it will

RIGHT: A limited-edition Silver Proof Piedfort Crown coin to commemorate the 100th anniversary of the historic Anglo-French Alliance

adjudicate on the design of all British coins and official medals. From 1953 to 1999 its Chairman was Prince Philip; the current Chairman is Professor Sir Christopher Frayling, with the Chief Executive of the Royal Mint, Gerald Sheehan, as Deputy Chairman. Its members serve for a period of seven years, which can be extended by a further three years.

All the drawings submitted are shown to the Committee – there is no pre-selection on the part of the Royal Mint – but none of the drawings is identified as to its originator. The Committee selects a short list of two or three designs. Plaster models are prepared of these selected designs, which are again viewed by the Committee. At any stage the Committee might suggest amendments to the designs which it feels appropriate for whatever reason. An exception is made when a new Royal portrait is being considered: in such cases drawings are not submitted, and the artists invited have to prepare plaster models. Once the final design has been selected, it has to be approved by both the Chancellor of the Exchequer and The Queen.

For the coin to mark the 70th birthday of The Queen in 1996, the Committee was initially shown over 40 designs, the combined work of 16 artists. For the £2 coin to mark the

Creating Coins

ABOVE: A meeting of the Royal Mint Advisory
Committee in February 2003 at Cutlers' Hall
in the City of London, chaired by Professor
Sir Christopher Frayling

Tercentenary of the Bank of England in 1994, the
nine artists invited submitted 75 ideas.
In the case of official medals, additional approval
will be sought from the Ministry of Defence
and/or the Cabinet Office as appropriate.
Generally speaking about 12 months are allowed
for the preparation of a new coin, the time taken

to prepare the tooling being a major
consideration. However, that time luxury is not
always available. A late decision was made to
mark the 100th anniversary of the Entente
Cordiale, although as usual a number of artists
were approached. The design selected for the
Crown coin was by David Gentleman, his first
British coin design, although an eminent
designer of British stamps since 1962. His
design, combining the two national female
figures of La Semeuse and Britannia, was also
adopted by the French Mint for its coins to mark
the anniversary.

In addition to coins, the past year has seen
the design of a medal awarded to those who
have taken part in the campaign in Iraq. In this
case only one artist was approached, namely
Christopher Lawrence, whose design is of a
Lamassu figure, an Assyrian sculpture of a
winged bull or lion with a human head. It is a
continual process, one that is always forward
looking, to find the subjects and designs, which
are worthy to be British coins for posterity.

The year in coins

If you're wondering whether any of your coin collection could have made you a mint this year, read on as we bring you the latest prices from auction houses and dealer's lists

The British coin market remains a very strong one, though the last year has been one of consolidation in comparison with the huge price advances seen in 2002/3, and general values have advanced by 'only' 10% to 15%. Once again a considerable amount of material has been offered, particularly in the milled gold and silver and the Scottish series, but there have been fewer major auction sales and fewer new records set, simply because fewer really exceptional coins have been available. It is curious that four of the five highest prices during the year 2003/4 were in dealer's fixed price lists.

The major named sale of the year was the Marshall collection, Spink Auction 167, March 31, 2004. Formed during the 1940s with an eye to buying the best, and not known to the current generation of collectors, the Marshall sale was uncannily like the famous Slaney sale of 2003 and caused as great an interest, if on a slightly smaller scale, totalling £626,750. Like Slaney, it produced quite remarkable prices for the best coins, including the year's highest auction price, £34,500 for a magnificent silver Henry VIII portrait testoon (the previous record, in the Shuttlewood sale of 2001, was £8,500), and, possibly more extraordinary still, £21,850 for the finest known Charles II halfcrown of 1681 with elephant and castle below bust (the previous record for the type, set only 18 months before, was a mere £1,525)

On May 31, 2004, Ira & Larry Goldberg Coins & Collectibles Inc., Beverly Hills, offered the

LEFT: In the Anglo-Gallic section, at the Mail sale of the Classical Numismatic Group in May this year, the Gold Florin of Edward III, unwanted in 2002, sold for £9,100

second part of Dr. Jacob Terner's collection, predominantly of high-grade milled coins. Although not as systematic or comprehensive as the first part, sold in 2003, it realized some exceptional prices including £21,750 for an extremely fine George IV sovereign of 1828, an extremely rare date (a very fine example had sold for £5,000 in Triton VII four months before), and totalled almost £500,000. An old collection of milled silver coins also sold well at Dix Noonan Webb (DNW) Sale 59, containing no great rarities, the collection realized a top price of just under £4,500 for a lovely Charles II silver shilling of 1677 with a plume below the bust only, but set many new records for ordinary milled coins with a total realized of £258,000.

In an interesting case of a high-auction price, the Slaney collection went for £138,000 in 2003, for the finest Charles II Petition crown in private hands, drawing out further material, Spink Auction 166, offered four Petition and Reddite crowns in silver and pewter from the LaRiviere collection. Three of the four had imposing provenances going back to the 19th century or earlier and the Jenks/Paget Petition crown, in very fine condition, sold for £33,500. Collectors now put a much higher premium on quality and are prepared to pay substantially more for it.

In another good sale, Morton & Eden, in

association with Sotheby's, offered a lovely small collection of two dozen five-guinea pieces on December 11, 2003. The grade of the group was well above average, for five-guineas are heavy gold coins, which are easily scratched or damaged, and several pieces were almost flawless resulting in a total of £180,200, with a high of £13,800 for a Charles II five-guineas of 1669 with elephant below (Charles II has been one of the strongest reigns this year).

Several other useful offerings included a good compact collection of hammered crowns sold in Spink Auction 169 for a total of £85,000, among them £8,280 for an extremely fine Charles I group 5 Tower under Parliament crown. This piece had realized £700 in 1986, in Spink Auction 50, and £1,700 in 1995 when purchased in Noble Numismatics Sale 48, Melbourne, Australia. In contrast, the UBS sale in Basel, Switzerland on January 27, 2004 contained an extensive group of mixed-grade English hammered and milled gold coins. A Charles I 1643 Oxford triple unite, good very fine and a nice coin but not one of the best, sold for £20,500. Less than a year previously the same coin in the Slaney collection had astonished the market by achieving £25,000.

Celtic Coinage

More Celtic material has been offered at auction over the last year than for some time, including a small but attractive run of high-quality material in Triton VII, New York, January 13, 2004. The highest price for this series of £4,100 was realized in Triton VII for an extremely fine Cunobelin Biga-type gold stater. The Marshall collection provided the runner-up, £2,100 for good very fine Dobunnic BODVOC gold stater, a very rare and desirable

RIGHT: The finest known example of James VI silver, sixteen shilling of 1581 realised £9,200, it maybe would have fetched more in a larger Scottish sale

piece from an old collection. Due to extensive recent finds, the smaller denominations and copper issues are now only in demand in the higher grades and prices continue to be volatile.

English Hammered Gold

Hammered gold has been one of the great market success stories of the last five years. However, even in a very strong market it is doubtful whether anyone could have predicted that a Mary Angel, splendid as it was, would sell for £10,350 in Spink Auction 168, or that an Elizabeth I Half-angel would be fought up to £4,600 in the Marshall sale.

The highest price realized, apart from the UBS triple unite, was for an Elizabeth I ship royal in Morton and Eden's December 2003 sale, £18,400 (up from £5,000 in the Barnes sale in 1974). This may not sound spectacular but the Barnes sale represented the very peak of the great 1970s price boom and, until relatively recently a price was strong if it merely repeated the Barnes level. Now the benchmark is three times that price.

The danger of hammered gold is that it has historically been prone to damage, particularly for use as jewellery, and consequently to repair. This makes a substantial difference to the price, halving it in many cases, and it is always advisable to take advice if in doubt. A characteristic of repaired gold is the rather brassy appearance, which results from the metal being heated up and, while not an infallible indicator, it is always worth looking closely at any coin with this sort of surface.

English Hammered Silver

Although hammered gold is the Rolls Royce of the English series hammered silver has always been the heartland of numismatic collecting, with the greatest diversity and appeal. In 2003/4 it has been somewhat overshadowed by the milled coinage, but the demand for fine quality, silver portrait coins remains unabated. The coins of the Tudors, particularly Henry VIII and Elizabeth I, continue to be extremely popular. The Marshall collection

saw £15,500 for a lovely and extremely rare Elizabeth I pattern shilling – said to be the finest known – and a coin illustrated in the catalogue of the famous Murdoch sale of 1903, and a remarkable £6,900 for a currency milled shilling of the same monarch on an intermediate flan.

The hammered silver field is so large that some areas are always temporarily more popular than others. Hammered crowns were one of the last denominations to join the current boom. Top quality examples are extremely rare and have always been much sought after but, until recently, £500 would have secured a very reasonable Charles I tower crown in very fine condition. The huge crown collection of the late Alan Barr, 800 coins assembled by die-variety, is currently being offered in three parts, at fixed prices, by Mark Rasmussen, and coins purchased by Barr at the famous Selig sale of 1989 for a few hundred pounds.

Charles I provincial material also remains extremely popular and collectors are turning to the common types in the absence of anything rarer being available. Hence the quite extraordinary £2,500 for a type 7 York halfcrown, almost extremely fine, in Spink Auction 168, which until very recently would have sold for well under £1,000. Siege pieces struck during the civil war, possibly the series, which has risen the furthest, and for the longest, continue to set new records. Alan Davisson Auction 21, June 10, 2004, obtained £6,650 for a 1648 Pontefract shilling in almost extremely fine condition, the first time any example has breached the £5,000 level.

Milled Gold

Milled gold, like hammered crowns, has been one of the last sectors of the market to be appreciated by collectors. For many years an excellent five-guinea piece could readily be acquired for around £6,000 and it is probably the example set by one or two exceptional coins at auction, particularly the £35,650 in the 2003

RIGHT: One of the highest prices realised, in English hammered gold, was for this very fine, very rare, Elizabeth I ship royal, which sold for £18,400 at the Morton & Eden sale in December 2003, against an estimate of £12,000-15,000

Slaney sale for a magnificent James II five-guineas of 1687, elephant and castle below bust, which focused attention on the series. As a result a high-grade example is now a solid five-figure coin and recently Spink obtained £22,500 for a sharp Anne five-guineas of 1713, which had only realized £5,000 at auction, in the Graves sale, as recently as October 2001.

Sovereigns, from George III, have also been an exceptionally strong market recently, the demand fuelled in part by internet buying. These coins are struck to a very high standard and look imposing even with a small degree of wear, though generally modern milled gold is desirable only in the highest state of preservation.

Milled Silver

A very great deal of material has been offered during the year and early milled silver up to George II, has been one of the strongest sectors of the market. Demand has been particularly robust for currency coins from sixpences to halfcrowns. Truly extremely fine sixpences of James II (1686, Marshall good EF £1,200) and William and Mary (1694, Dix Noonan Webb 59 £1,850) are selling for comfortably over £1,000 and those of Charles II are hard on their heals. Not so long ago it was quite unusual for a sixpence to realize over £500.

Many new price records have been set for halfcrowns. The Dr Jacob Terner sale saw £8,600 for an FDC 1658 Cromwell halfcrown. This finally broke the 24-year auction record of £3,800 set in the famous Manville sale, Spink Auction 9, in 1980 and broke it in some style. Even the exceptionally common William III 1698 halfcrown has now breached the £1,000 barrier, £1,100 in

DNW Sale 59. In contrast, extremely rare milled silver coins in the lower grades remain unwanted. Baldwin's Auctions 37 could only achieve £1,900 for an honest, good fine Cromwell halfcrown of 1656, very much the rarer date and the only example offered all year. It is probable that a 1658 halfcrown in the same grade would not have fetched much less, and Morton and Eden obtained a staggering £800 for a much worn 1658-shilling, only about fine, though the coin is probably extremely rare in this grade.

Copper and Bronze

Early copper and tin coins are very much in demand; there is such a shortage of good material so the market remains as strong as ever, particularly for those illusive examples in the high grades. These early coins are relatively underrated, for example a tin William and Mary halfpenny recently changed hands at £5500, it was as struck, with full mint lustre and without corrosion (very unusual), exceptional examples are great rarities at least 10 times as rare as a comparable five guinea piece. There have been no significant collections sold through auction during the past year but trading has been strong and demand out ways the supply.

Similarly later copper and bronze coins seem to go from strength to strength and pieces with full mint lustre commanding high premiums.

Scottish Coins

The market has been fortunate that a substantial amount of Scottish material has become available during the year. Much of this was from the collection of the late Dr. James Davidson, parts of whose collection were sold in the 1980s, the balance being offered in DNW sales 59 and 60. The Davidson collection contained a number of gold pieces, generally in average condition, but was very strong in silver and varieties. It is some time since such a good run of the mints of Alexander IIIs first coinage has been available and these were very much sought after. A penny of Renfrew set a new record at £1,150. The

collection also contained some medieval groats of types not often seen, with a James I, second Fleur-de-lis groat of Stirling reaching £1,550 and a James II groat of the same mint £1,450.

The bargain of the Scottish series, ironically, was at the other end of the spectrum. The Marshall collection included a magnificent James VI silver sixteen-shilling piece of 1581, a great rarity and undoubtedly the finest known. It realized £9,200, a handsome price but not out of the way, possibly because the type is a non-portrait one and the Scottish section was only a small element of the total sale.

One of the few British series that still looks on the cheap side is the Scottish gold. Scottish gold fetched enormous prices in the 1970s and early 1980s, and current levels are still around those seen in the famous Horace Hird sale in 1974, in complete contrast to English gold, which sells for about three times the 1974 mark. In part this is because the Scottish gold, which has come onto the market in the last four or five years has come in small parcels, often of only middle grade, accompanying what are essentially collections of silver, and no momentum has built up. It is possible that if a significant Scottish gold collection were offered then prices could rule significantly higher.

Irish Coins

The Irish series has been relatively quiet in 2003/4. Bonhams, February 24, 2004 offered a nice group of Hiberno-Norse pennies, the MacDuinnsleibhe collection. Unfortunately the owner appears to have taken a rather optimistic view when setting the estimates and not many sold. Generally the price levels established by the Millennial sale in Dublin in 2000 are still appropriate, particularly for the late medieval. The exceptions are the irregular coinages of the Great Rebellion, gunmoney and the milled copper in above average condition.

Two important Charles I rebel-money coins, a crown and halfcrown, both from the Millennial

sale reappeared in the May 2004 Goldberg auction. The crown sold for £6,700, up from £3,450 in 2000, and the halfcrown for £4,000, up from £3,650. The latter is much the rarer denomination but does not have the immediate eye appeal of the crown.

Gunmoney, particularly the rarer varieties in good grade, is very sort after. The 1690 gunmoney crown sells for about £150 in good very fine condition, but CNG Auction 64 obtained £400 for an almost extremely fine example. Among the later issues, 20th century Irish coins, like 20th century English, have been boosted by the fact that the century is now closed and very high-grade examples, including the various proof and specimen issues dating from the 1930s to the 1960s now have a devoted following.

Anglo-Gallic Coins

Unusually the year saw the sale of a small but useful collection of Anglo-Gallic coins, DNW Sale 62, which had been assembled largely from American dealers in the 1970s and 1980s. Prices remain stable and quite a number of pieces were purchased by dealers for stock. An exception was an attractive double hardi d'argent of Henry IV, graded very fine but very rare as such, which was fought up to £1,200.

The star Anglo-Gallic coin of 2004 was the gold florin of Edward III, Bordeaux mint, struck around 1352, sold in Classical Numismatic Group Auction 66, May 19, 2004. Extremely rare, and historically important as the only representation known of the pan-European florin design struck in the name of an English monarch, this good very fine piece had not been wanted at £6,500 in 2002 when offered as part of the Ure collection, but now attracted strong demand and the hammer came down at an attractive £9,100.

Keeping your coins

Having begun your coin collection here are some helpful hints, along with the best accessories, which can help you house your collection

ABOVE: Coin cabinets are produced and available from Peter Nichols in St. Leonards-on-Sea

Storage

Careful thought should be given to the storing of coins, for a collection which is carelessly or inadequately housed can suffer irreparable damage. Corrosion depends on the presence of water vapour, and therefore coins should not be stored in damp attics or spare bedrooms but, where possible, in evenly heated warm rooms.

We should also point out, that one must be very careful only to pick up coins by the edges, for sweaty fingerprints contain corrosive salt. The following are suitable methods of storage.

Wooden cabinets

A collection carefully laid out in a wood cabinet is seen at its most impressive. Unfortunately, the modern wooden cabinets, which are custom-built, especially for coins are not cheap. Their main advantages are the choice of tray and hole

sizes, and the fact that because the manufacturer is often himself a collector, he takes care to use only well-matured woods.

Among the makers of wood cabinets are Peter Nichols of St. Leonards, East Sussex (01424 436682), while Safe Albums offers a wooden cabinet with six trays at

ABOVE: Leuchtturm cleaning bath for brass, copper, silver and gold coins is available from the Duncannon Partnership in Reigate

£140, (Tel: 01189 328976).

If one cannot afford a new cabinet, then a secondhand version may be the answer. These can sometimes be purchased at coin auctions, or from dealers, and can be very good value. However, it is not always easy to find one with the tray hole sizes to suit your coins.

Do-it-yourself cabinet makers should also be careful not to use new wood, which will contain corrosive moisture. In this case the best method would be to use wood from an old piece of furniture.

LEFT: Lindner Karat coin album supplied with 10 assorted pages, optional slipcase available. Album price £23.10

Albums, plastic cases, carrying cases and magnifiers

There are many of these on the market, and some of them are both handsome and inexpensive. There are also very attractive Italian and German-made, attaché type carrying cases for collectors, with velvet lining and different sizes of trays, and so on. These can be obtained from a number of dealers, but Collectors' Gallery, 24 The Parade, St. Mary's Place, Shrewsbury SY1 1DL (Tel: 01743 272140) are the UK distributors.

We would also recommend the coin album, which claims to prevent oxidization. The coins are contained in cards with crystal-clear film windows so the collector can see both sides of the coins. The cards then slide into pages in an album, and might be a convenient method of storage, especially for new collectors.

Lindner Publications Ltd., Unit 3A, Hayle Industrial Park, Hayle, Cornwall TR27 5JR (Tel: 01736 751910. Fax: 01736 751911) supplies very useful coin and collecting boxes, as well as albums. To find out more you can also visit the company's website at www.stampaccessories.net

A new extended range of Lighthouse coin accessories, including presentation and attaché carrying cases, are available from the Duncannon Partnership, 4 Beaufort Road, Reigate RH2 9DJ (Tel: 01737 244222). Phone them for a brochure.

ABOVE: Lindner large coin carrying case, supplied with 10 assorted trays. Price £139.50

conjunction with a cardboard box, which makes for simple, unobtrusive storage. This is the most inexpensive method of storing coins.

Still the best article we have seen on the storage of coins and medals, which deals with all the materials which are used, was by Mr L. R. Green, who is Higher Conservation Officer at the Department of Coins and Medals at the British Museum. This appeared in the May 1991 issue of Spink's *Numismatic Circular*.

Cleaning coins

In the course of each week coin dealers examine many coins, which some poor unfortunates have unwittingly ruined by cleaning. They are, therefore, usually the best people to ask about the subject of cleaning coins.

One dealer has told us of a bright-eyed, expectant gentleman who offered his late father's very useful collection of copper coins, which he proudly said he had 'brightened up' the previous day, so as to be certain of a good

ABOVE:
Lindner coin boxes available in standard clear format or smoked-glass format. 130 variations available. Standard clear box £14.95, smoked-glass box £15.50

In Central London, probably the best place to visit is Vera Trinder, 38 Bedford Street, London WC2 E9EU (Tel: 020 7836 2365/6), who does appear to keep a very good stock. Stanley Gibbons, 399 Strand, London WC2 (Tel: 0800 611622) also produces large-size coin albums. Just phone them to get a free brochure.

Lastly, magnifiers can be obtained from the accessory dealers mentioned, as well as W.H. Smith and opticians.

Envelopes

Plastic envelopes, being transparent, are very useful for exhibition, but we never recommend them for long-term storage purposes. They tend to make the coins 'sweat' which, with copper and bronze in particular, can lead to corrosion.

Manilla envelopes are much more suitable since the paper is dry, unlike ordinary paper, and consequently they are ideal for the storage of coins. Most collectors use them in

ABOVE: A variety of attaché cases for keeping your coins are available from the Duncannon Partnership

offer. The dealer did not enjoy his customer's sad disappointment when he found himself unable to make any offers, but then again the coins had been cleaned with harsh metal polish.

We would always advise people never to clean coins unless they are very dirty or corroded. Also do note that by 'dirt' we do not mean oxide which, on silver coins, can give a pleasing bluish tone favoured by many collectors. The following simple instructions may be of some help, but do not, of course, apply to extremely corroded coins, which have been found in the ground, for if important, they are the province of a museum conservationist.

Safe Albums (Tel on: 01189 328976) offers coin cleaning fluid for gold, silver and copper coins from around £7.50 each.

Gold coins

Gold should cause collectors few problems, since it is subject to corrosion only in very extreme conditions. For example, a gold coin

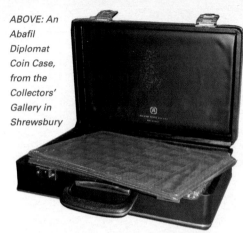

in the sea might have a dull, rusty appearance. However, give it a little bath in methylated spirits and this will usually improve a dirty gold coin. But there's one word of warning here – gold coins should not be rubbed in any way.

Silver coins

Silver coins will discolour easily, and are particularly susceptible to damp or chemicals in the atmosphere. A gentle brushing with a soft, non-nylon, bristle brush will clear loose surface dirt, but if the dirt is deep and greasy, a dip in ammonia and careful drying on cotton wool should do the trick. We should once again stress that there is no need to attempt to clean a coin which simply has a darkish tone.

Copper and bronze coins

There is no safe method of cleaning copper or bronze coins without actually harming them, and we would only recommend the use of a non-nylon, pure bristle brush to deal with dirt.

There is no way of curing the ailments peculiar to these metals, namely verdigris (green spots) or bronze disease (blackish spots) permanently, and we would advise collectors not to buy pieces in such condition, unless they are very inexpensive.

And remember looking after your coins could make you money in the future!

COINS MARKET VALUES

Museum collections

If you're looking for some spectacular coin displays to while away a few hours, look no further than the best museums the UK has to offer...

London, The British Museum

The display ranges over an enormous number of coins and other objects, which have been used as money over the last 4,500 years. The first major British exhibition of British archaeology in over 20 years, 'Buried Treasure: Finding Our Past' – the result of a unique collaboration between The British Museum and four other major UK museums, in Cardiff, Manchester, Newcastle and Norwich – will last until 2006. The exhibition will travel to each venue after London. Currently, there is also an exhibition, 'Status Symbol: identity and beliefs on modern badges.' This runs until January 2005. The Keeper of Coins is: Mr. Joe Cribb, British Museum, Great Russell Street, London WC1B 3DG. Tel: 020 7323 1555. Fax: 020 7323 8171. or E-mail: coins@thebritish-museum.ac.uk or visit www.thebritishmuseum.ac.uk

Edinburgh, National Museums of Scotland

The National Museums house the premier collection of Scottish coins and tokens, but also significant collections of English, British, ancient and foreign material. The Scottish

ABOVE: The HSBC Money Gallery in The British Museum (picture: copyright, British Museum)

coins include the Coats collection, on which Edward Burns based his three-volume standard work, *The Coinage of Scotland*. Many coins of all periods and of types made or used in Scotland are included in the Museum of Scotland. At the adjoining Royal Museum, anyone wishing to view specific coins or series is welcomed by appointment. Curator of Numismatics is: Mr. Nick Holmes, Royal Museum, Chambers Street, Edinburgh EH1 1JF. Tel: 0131 247 4061
E-mail: n.holmes@nms.ac.uk

Glasgow, Hunterian Museum

A new permanent gallery devoted to numismatics has been opened at the Hunterian Museum and features over 2,000 items. The Hunter Coin Cabinet contains the important 18th century collection of the eminent Scot and Royal physician, Dr. William Hunter. The Curator of Coins is: Dr. Donal Bateson, Hunterian Museum, University of Glasgow, Glasgow G12 8QQ. Tel: 0141 339 8855.

Cardiff, National Museum and Gallery

There is an excellent general exhibition of coins and medals including many superb and rare pieces, presented with excellent lighting in good showcases. Two spectacular hoards are currently on show: The Bridgend Hoard (1994) of Roman coins circa AD310. The Tregwynt (Pembs) Civil War hoard of gold and silver coins will now form part of 'Buried Treasure: Finding Our Past' exhibition. The Assistant Keeper in charge of coins is: Mr. E.M. Besly, Department of Archaeology and Numismatics, National Museum and Gallery, Cathays Park, Cardiff CF10 3NP. Tel: 02920 573291. E-mail: Edward.Besly@nmgw.ac.uk

COINS MARKET VALUES

Coin displays

Birmingham, Museum and Art Gallery
Birmingham Museum has one of the largest regional coin collections in England. Although it is very diverse there are important groups of British Celtic, Saxon/Norman and medieval coins. Curator of Antiquities and Numismatics is: David Symons, Birmingham Museum and Art Gallery, Chamberlain Square, Birmingham B3 3DH. Tel: 0121 303 4201 or visit the website at www.bmag.org.uk

Cambridge, The Fitzwilliam Museum
The Department of Coins and Medals at the Fitzwilliam Museum in Cambridge houses one of the greatest collections of Ancient Greek coins in existence, and the famous Grierson collection of European medieval coins, currently being catalogued in a series of 14 volumes. In recent years the Museum has acquired the important collection of Christopher Blunt, and the Dr. William Conte collection of Norman coins (go to www-cm.fitzmuseum.cam.ac.uk/coins/). The Keeper of Coins and Medals is: Dr. Mark Blackburn, Fitzwilliam Museum, Trumpington Street, Cambridge CB2 1RB Tel: 01223 332915.

Oxford, The Ashmolean Museum
The Ashmolean Museum contains the oldest public collection in Great Britain, and is well worth a visit if you are near by. The Curator is Dr. Nick Mayhew, The Ashmolean Museum, Heberden Coin Room, University of Oxford, Oxford OX1 2PH. Tel: 01865 278058.

ABOVE: The British Museum houses these coins from the Hoxne Hoard, buried in the 5th century and found in 1992

York, Yorkshire Museum
The Yorkshire Museum coin collection is particularly strong in the fields of Roman coinage, Northumbrian stycas, English hammered silver and trade tokens. Hoards and single finds from Yorkshire are particularly well represented. Please contact the Yorkshire Museum, Museum Gardens, Curator of Access – Archaeology Andrew Morrison, York YO1 7FR. Tel: 01904 687687. E-mail: andrew.morrison@ymt.org.uk

Belfast, Ulster Museum
The Ulster Museum collection is not on display, sections are occasionally on show as part of historical exhibitions. To view the collection, one needs a prior appointment. The museum acquired many of its important Irish pieces from the Carlyon-Britton collection. Curator of coins is: Mr. Robert Heslip, Ulster Museum, Botanic Gardens, Belfast BT9 5AB. Tel: 02890 383000.

Dublin, National Museum of Ireland
The National Museum has the most important collection of Irish coins and houses the former collection of the Royal Irish Academy. The collection also includes a number of important donations, recent important hoards, and the D.R. Arthur Went collection of medals. The Curator of Coins is: Mr. Michael Kenny, Keeper of the Art & Industrial Division, National Museum of Ireland, Collins Barracks, Benburb Street, Dublin 7, Eire. Tel: 0035 31677 7444.

Other important museums
Other museums in the country with excellent collections of British coins include:–
- Blackburn Museum, Museum Street, Blackburn, Lancashire (01254 667130).
- City Museum, Queen's Road, Bristol BS8 1RL (01179 223571). Good on Bristol mint coins.
- Royal Albert Memorial Museum, Queen Street, Exeter EX4 3RX (01392 665858).
- Manx Museum, Douglas, Isle of Man (01624 675522). Excellent for Viking and Hiberno-Norse.
- The Leeds Museum Resource Centre, Yeadon, Leeds (01132 146526).

• Manchester Museum, The University, Manchester M13 (0161 275 2634).
• Reading Museum, Blagrave Street, Reading, Berkshire (01189 399800).

A useful guide entitled: *Museums and Select Institutions in the UK and Ireland with holdings of numismatic material* has been formulated by Peter Preston-Morley. It's an absolute must at just £5. Many of our museums have co-operated with the British Academy to produce a wonderful series of books under the heading of *Sylloge of Coins of the British Isles*, which now runs to 50 plus volumes. Below we list the ones which deal with coins in these islands (British Isles).

1. Fitzwilliam Museum, Cambridge. *Ancient British and Anglo-Saxon Coins*, by P. Grierson.
2. Hunterian Museum, Glasgow. *Anglo-Saxon Coins*, by A.S. Robertson.
3. *The Coins of the Curitani*, by D. F. Allen.
4. Royal Collection of Coins and Medals, National Museum, Copenhagen. *Part 1, Ancient British and Anglo-Saxon Coins before Aethelred II*, by Georg Galster.
5. Grosvenor Museum, Chester. *Coins with the Chester Mint-Signature*, by E.J.E. Pirie.
6. National Museum of Antiquities of Scotland, Edinburgh. *Anglo-Saxon Coins*, by R.B.K. Stevenson.
7. British Museum. *Hiberno-Norse Coins*, by R.H.M. Dolley.
8. *The Caroligian Coins in the British Museum*, by Michael Dolley and K. F. Morrison.
9. Ashmolean Museum, Oxford. *Part I, Anglo-Irish Coins, John-Edward III*, by M. Dolley and W. Seaby.
10. Ulster Museum. Belfast. *Part I, Anglo-Irish Coins, John Edward III*, by M. Dolley and W. Seaby.
11. Reading University. *Anglo-Saxon and Norman Coins*, by C.E. Blunt and M. Dolley.
12. Ashmolean Museum, Oxford. *Part II, English Coins 1066-1279*, by D.M. Metcalf.
13. Royal Collection of Coins and Medals, National Museum, Copenhagen. *Part 111a, Anglo-Saxon Coins: Cnut, mints Axbridge to Lymne*, by Georg Galster.
14. *Part 111b, Cnut, mints Lincoln and London.*
15. *Part IIIc, mints Lynford to the end.*

16. *Collections of Ancient British, Romano and English Coins formed by Mrs. Emery May Norweb,* by C. E. Blunt, F. Elmore Jones and Commander R. P. Mack.
17. Midland Museums. *Ancient British Coins, and Coins of the British and Gloucestershire Mints,* by L.V. Grinsell, C.E. Blunt and M. Dolley.
18. Royal Collection of Coins and Medals, National Museum, Copenhagen. *Part IV, Anglo-Saxon Coins from Harold and Anglo-Norman Coins,* by Georg Galster.
19. Bristol and Gloucester Museums. *Ancient British Coins and Coins of the British and Gloucestershire Mints,* by L. V. Grinsell, C. E. Blunt and M. Dolley.
20. The R. P. Mack Collection. *Ancient British, Anglo-Saxon and Norman Coins,* by R. P. Mack.
21. Yorkshire Collections. *Coins from Northumbrian Mints c.895-1279; Ancient British and Later Coins from other Mints to 1279,* by E.J.E. Pirie.
23. Ashmolean Museum, Oxford. *Part III, Coins of Henry VII,* by D.M. Metcalf.
24. West Country Museums. *Ancient British, Anglo-Saxon and Anglo-Norman Coins*, by A.J.H. Gunstone.
25. *Anglo-Saxon, Anglo-Norman and Hiberno-Norse Coins in the National Museum, Helsinki and other Public Collections in Finland,* by T. Talvio.
26. Museums in East Anglia. *Morley St. Peter Hoard, and Anglo-Saxon, Norman and Angevin Coins, and Later Coins of the Norwich Mint,* by T.H. McK. Clough.
27. Lincolnshire Collections. *Coins from Lincolnshire Mints and Ancient British and Later Coins to 1272,* by A.J.H. Gunstone.
28. Cumulative Index of Volumes 1-20 of the Sylloge of Coins of the British Isles, by V. Smart.
29. Mersey Country Museums. *Ancient British and Later Coins to 1279,* by M. Warhurst.
30. *Ancient British, Anglo-Saxon and Norman Coins in American Collections,* by J. D. Brady.
31. The Norweb Collection. *Tokens of the British Isles, 1575-1750, Part 1, Bedfordshire to Devon,* by R.H. Thompson.
32. Ulster Museum, Belfast. *Part II. Hiberno-Norse*

Coins, by W. Seaby.

33. *The John G. Brooker Collection Coins of Charles I (1625-1649)*, by J.J. North and P.J. Preston-Mosley.

34. British Museum. *Anglo-Saxon Coins, Part V. Athelstan to Edgar's Reform*, by M.M. Archibald and C.E. Blunt.

35. Ashmolean and Hunterian Museums. *Scottish Coins*, by J.D. Bateson and N.J. Mayhew.

36. State Museum, Berlin Coin Cabinet. *Anglo-Saxon, Anglo-Norman and Hiberno-Norse Coins*, by B. Kluge.

37. Polish Museum. *Anglo-Saxon and later Medieval British Coins*, by A. Mikulakzyk.

38. The Norweb Collection. *Tokens of the British Isles 1575-1750, Part II, Dorset, Durham, Essex and Gloucestershire*, by R.H. Thompson.

39. *Edwardian English Silver Coins*, by J.J. North.

40. Royal Coin Cabinet, Stockholm. *Part IV, Anglo-Saxon Coins. Harold Harthacnut*, by T. Talvin.

41. Cumulative Index to Vols 21-40, by V. Smart.

42. South-Eastern Museums. *Ancient British, Anglo-Saxon and Later Coins to 1279*, by A.J.H. Gunstone, with V. Smart and others.

43. Norweb Collection. *Tokens of the British Isles 1575-1750, Part 3. Hampshire to Lincolnshire*. 1992, by R.H. Thompson and M. Dickinson.

44. *Tokens of the British Isles 1575-1750, Part 4. Norfolk to Somerset*. 1993, by R.H. Thompson and M.J. Dickinson

45. Latvian Collections. *Anglo-Saxon and Later British Coins*, by T. Berga

46. *Tokens 1575-1750. Part V. Staffordshire to Westmorland*, by R.H. Thompson and M.J. Dickinson.

47. Schneider Collection. *Part 1. English Gold Coins 1257-1603*, by Peter Woodhead.

48. Northern Museums – *Ancient British, Anglo-Saxon, Norman and Plantagenet Coins to 1279*, 1997, by J. Booth.

49. Norweb Collection. *Part 6. Wiltshire to Yorkshire, including Ireland, Wales, Isle of Man, Channel Islands and Scotland*, by R.H. Thompson and M.J. Dickinson.

50. Hermitage Museum, St. Petersburg. *Part 1: Anglo-Saxon Coins up to 1016*, by V. M. Potin.

51. Estonian Collections. *Anglo-Saxon, Anglo-Norman and Later British Coins*, by I. Leimus and A. Molvogin.

52. Uppsala University Coin Cabinet. *Anglo-Saxon and Later British Coins*, by E. Lindberger.

53. Scottish Museums. *English Coins, 1066-1279*, by J.D. Bateson.

54. Royal Coin Cabinet Stockholm. *Part V. Anglo-Saxon Coins: Edward the Confessor and Harold II, 1042-1066*, by F. Colman. *Part VI Supplement. Anglo-Norman Pennies*, by M. Blackburn and K. Jonsson. 57 plates forthcoming.

55. Hermitage Museum, St. Petersburg. *Part IV. English, Irish and Scottish Coins, 1066-1485*, by M. Mucha. 22 plates forthcoming.

56. Mass Collection. *English Short Cross Coins, 1180-1247*, 2001, by J.P. Mass. 82 plates.

57. Herbert Schneider Collection. *Part II. English Gold Coins 1603 to the 20th Century*, 2002, by Peter Woodhead. 58 plates.

Reading Material

If you feel you'd like to find out more about what you're collecting, here's a selection of books to add to your numismatic library...

We have included the prices you can expect to pay, but since some of the books are long out of print they can only be obtained second-hand *(indicated in the list by SH in brackets)*.

Allen, Martin. *The Durham Mint*. British Numismatic Society Special Publication No. 4. 2003. 222pp, 12 plates. £45. The first book to be published on the Durham Mint since 1780.

Bateson, J.D. *Coinage in Scotland*. 1997. 175pp, and well illustrated. £20. The most up-to-date narrative account of the coins, and the only currently in print.

Bateson, J.D. *Scottish Coins*. 1987. Shire Publications no.189. 32pp, and illustrated. £2. A useful little 'taster' to the subject. The Shire Publications are always good value.

Besly, E. *Coins and Medals of the English Civil War*. 1990. 121pp, and beautifully illustrated. (SH)

Besly, E. *Loose Change, a Guide to Common Coins and Medals*. Cardiff. 1997. 57pp, £6.95.

Blunt, C.E. Stewart, B.H.I.H., Lyon, C.S.S. *Coinage in 10th Century England*. 1989. 372pp, 27 plates. £60.

Buck, I. *Medieval English Groats*. 2000. 66pp, illustrated in text. £15.

Byatt, D. *Promises to Pay. The First Three Hundred Years of Bank of England Notes*. 1994. 246pp, beautifully illustrated. £35.

British Academy (Publisher) *Sylloge of Coins of the British Isles*. Around 50 volumes, many still in print. (See list under Museums.)

Brooke, G.C. *English Coins*, Reprint Edition. London, 1966. 300pp, 72 plates. (SH). An important one-volume of English coinage.

Challis, C. *A New History of the Royal Mint*. 1992. 806pp, 70 figures and maps. £95. A very substantial volume.

Coincraft's Standard Catalogue of English and UK Coins. 1999. 741pp, 5,000+ photos. £19.50.

Coincraft's Standard Catalogue of the Coins of Scotland, Ireland, Channel Islands and Isle of Man. 1999. 439pp, fully illustrated. A new volume. £34.50.

Cooper, D. *Coins and Minting*. 1996. Shire Publications 106. 32pp, and illustrated. £2.25. An excellent account of minting.

Cooper, D. *The Art and Craft of Coinmaking*. 1988. 264pp, fully illustrated. £2.25. An excellent account of minting.

Dolley, M. *Viking Coins in the Danelaw and Dublin*. 1965. 32pp, 16 plates. (SH). This and the next two are excellent introductory handbooks.

Dolley, M. *Anglo-Saxon Pennies* – Reprint, 1970. 32pp, 16 plates. (SH).

Dolley, M. *The Norman Conquest and English Coinage*. 1966. 40pp, illustrated. (SH).

Dowle, A. and Finn, P. *The Guide Book to the Coinage of Ireland*. 1969. (SH). The first

SMALL SILVER

**HENRY VIII -
THE COMMONWEALTH**

Paul and Bente R Withers

standard catalogue of Irish, useful still for information on patterns and proofs and good bibliography.

Dyer, G.P. (Editor). *Royal Sovereign 1489-1989*. 1989. 99pp, fully illustrated. £30. An attractive book from the Royal Mint to coincide with the Sovereigns 500th anniversary.

Elias, E.R.D. *The Anglo-Gallic Coins*. 1984. 262pp, fully illustrated. £20. Essential for collectors of this series.

Freeman, A. *The Moneyer and Mint in the Reign of Edward the Confessor 1042-1066*. 2 parts, 1985. £40. A complete survey of the coinage of one reign.

Frey, A.R. *Dictionary of Numismatic Names*. Reprinted 1973. 311pp, and an additional 94pp of glossary of numismatic terms. (SH). The best numismatic diary, well worth searching for a second hand copy.

Grinsell, L.V. *The History and Coinage of the Bristol Mint*. Bristol Museum and Art Gallery publication. 1986. 60pp, fully illustrated. £5.

Grueber, H.A. *Handbook of the Coins of Great Britain and Ireland*. Revised edition, London, 1970. 272pp, 64 plates. (SH). A superb book, full of information, and well worth searching for.

Hobbs, Richard. *British Iron Age Coins in the British Museum*. 1996. 246pp, 137 plates. £40. Invaluable. The British Museum Catalogue listing over 4,500 pieces.

Holmes, Richard. *Scottish Coins, a History of Small Change in Scotland*. An invaluable guide to the identification of 'historic' small change.

Edinburgh, 1998. 112pp, illustrated. £5.99.

de Jersey, P. *Celtic Coinage in Britain*. Shire Publications, 1996. 56pp, illustrated. £4.99.

Linecar, H.W.A. *British Coin Designs and Designers*. 1977. 146pp, fully illustrated. (SH).

Linecar, H.W.A. *The Crown Pieces of Great Britain and the Commonwealth of Nations*. 1969. 102pp, fully illustrated. (SH). The only book dealing solely with all British crowns.

Linecar, H.W.A. and Stone, A.G. *English Proof and Pattern Crown-Size Pieces, 1658-1960*. 1968. 116pp, fully illustrated. (SH). An important book.

Manville, H.E. and Robertson, T.J. *Encyclopedia of British Numismatics Vol.1. British Numismatic Auction Catalogues from 1710 to the Present*. 1986. 420pp, illustrated. £25.

Manville, H.E. Vol.2.1. *Numismatic Guide to British and Irish Periodicals 1731-1991*. 1993. 570pp, illustrated £60.

Manville, H.E. Vol.2.2. *Numismatic Guide to British and Irish Periodicals, 1836-1995*. 1997. 634pp, 31 illustrations. £60. A highly important reference work.

Manville, A.E. *Tokens of the Industrial Revolution*, Foreign Silver Coins countermarked for use in Great Britain, c1787-1828. 308pp, 50 plates. £40. A highly important work.

Marsh, M.A. *The Gold Half-Sovereign*, 2nd edition. 2004. 119pp, 54 plates. £18.50.

Mass, J.P. *The J.P. Mass Collection. English Short Cross Coins, 1180-1247*. £50. This outstanding work describes and illustrates 2,200 specimens from the author's collection. 2001.

McCammon, A.L.T. *Currencies of the Anglo-Norman Isles*. 1984. 358pp, 1,000+ illustrations.

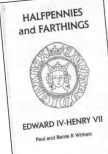

£25. Essential for students and collectors.

North, J.J. *English Hammered Coins. Volume 1. Early Anglo-Saxon to Henry III, c.A.D.600-1272.* 1994. 320pp, 20 plates. £35; Volume 2. *Edward I to Charles II, 1272-1662.* 1993. 224pp, 11 plates. £30. Essential. A great reference for collectors.

North, J.J. and Preston-Morley, P.J. *The John G. Brooker Collection - Coins of Charles 1.* (Sylloge of Coins of the British Isles, Number 33) £19.50.

O'Sullivan, W. *The Earliest Irish Coinage, 1981.* 47pp, 4 plates. (SH) Deals with the Hiberno-Norse Coinage.

O'Sullivan, W. *The Earliest Anglo-Irish Coinage.* 1964. 88pp, 10 plates. (SH). Deals with the coinage from 1185-1216. Reprint available at £5.

Peck, C.W. *English Copper, Tin and Bronze Coins in the British Museum, 1558-1958.* 1960. 648pp, 50 plates. (SH). Essential. The seminal work on the subject.

Rayner, P.A. *English Silver Coins Since 1649.* 254pp, illustrated, 3rd edition. 1992. £19.95. Essential. 3,000 coins listed, 400 illustrated. Deals with varieties, rarities, patterns and proofs and mintage figures.

Robinson, B. *Silver Pennies and Linden Towels: The Story of the Royal Maundy.* 1992. 274pp, 118 illustrations. £29.95. A very important work, entertainingly presented.

Spink. *Standard Catalogue of British Coins.* 40th edition. 2005. Fully illustrated. £20. After half a century still the first point of reference for most collectors of English coins.

Spink and Son (Publishers, but edited by H.A. Linecar). *The Milled Coinage of England 1662-1946.* Reprinted 1976. 146pp, illustrated. (SH). A useful volume dealing with the gold and silver coinage and giving degrees of rarity; superseded on the silver by Rayner, but important for gold.

Spink. *Coins of Scotland, Ireland and the Islands.* 2nd edition. 2003. Fully illustrated. £25. An important addition to one's library.

Stewart, I.H. *The Scottish Coinage.* 2nd edition. 1967. 215pp, 22 plates. (SH). Long out of print, but still essential for the serious collector.

Sutherland, C.H.V. *English Coinage, 600-1900.* 1973. 232pp, 108 plates. (SH). Beautifully written and probably the best narrative account of coinage, worth a search.

Thompson, J.D.A. *Inventory of British Coin Hoards, AD 600-1500.* 1956. 165pp, 24 plates. (SH)

Van Arsdell, R.D. *Celtic Coinage of Britain.* 1989. 584pp, 54 plates, 80 maps. £40. A pioneering work which sparked much debate; important for the number of illustrations alone.

Withers, P. and B. *British Coin Weights.* A corpus of the coin-weights made for use in England, Scotland and Ireland. 1993. 366pp, fully illustrated and with a price guide. £95. An essential volume for the serious student.

Withers, P. and B. *Farthings and Halfpennies, Edward I and II.* 2001. 60pp, illustrated. £10. Very helpful guide to the series. *Farthings and Halfpennies, Edward III and Richard II.* 2002. Illustrated. £10.

Withers, P. and B. R. *Halfpennies and Farthings, Henry IV, V and VI.* 2003. 68pp, illustrated. £12. *Halfpennies and Farthings, Edward IV – Henry VII.* 2004. 56pp, illustrated. £12.

Withers, P. and B. R. *Small Silver, Henry VIII –*

The Commonwealth. 2004. 56pp, illustrated. £12. Irish *Small Silver, John – Edward VI*. 2004. 56pp, illustrated. £12.

Woodhead, P. *The Herbert Schneider Collection of English Gold Coins. Part 1. Henry III-Elizabeth I.* 1996. 466pp, 83 plates each with descriptive text. £60. A wonderful catalogue of the finest collection in private hands. This first volume describes and illustrated 890 coins, most in superb condition.

Woodhead, P. *The Herbert Schneider Collection of English Gold Coins. Volume 2. 1603 to 20th Century.* 58 plates, 2002. Like volume 1 this is a wonderful catalogue of what is probably the

finest collection in private hands, it describes and illustrates 674 coins.

Wren, C.R. *The Voided Long Cross Coinage, 1247-1279.* 1993. 80pp, illustrated. £9.

Wren, C.R. *The Short Cross Coinage 1180-1247.* 1992. 90pp, illustrated. £8.75. Two very good guides to identification with excellent drawings.

Williams, J. *Money, a History.* 1997. 256pp, fully illustrated. £25. A beautiful volume published to accompany the British Museum's HSBC Money Gallery opened in January 1997.

Wilson, A. and Rasmussen, M. *English Pattern Trial and Proof Coins in Gold, 1547-1968.* 2000. 537pp, illustrated. £85. This publication covers a beautiful and fascinating series and is likely to enhance interest in these eminently collectable non-currency gold issues.

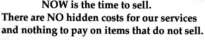

St James's Auctions

Knightsbridge Coins *in association with* Baldwin's Auctions Ltd

Auction 1

Wednesday 13th October 2004

at the De Vere Cavendish Hotel, 81 Jermyn Street, St James's, London SW1

A further selection of items to be offered in the auction

*A fine old collection
of English hammered
and milled coins and
other properties including
Scottish banknote proofs*

For catalogues only:

Baldwin's Auctions Ltd
11 Adelphi Terrace
London WC2N 6BJ
020 7930 9808
auctions@baldwin.sh

For other enquiries and to consign contact:

St James's Auctions
(Knightsbridge Coins)
43 Duke Street, St James's
London SW1Y 6DD
020 7930 7597 / 7888

Collecting Corner

New to the numismatic hobby or just want to find out more about your coin collection? We help you along the way with invaluable advice and suggestions from industry experts

How much is it worth?

There was a time when newcomers to coin collecting would ask the question 'What is it?' Nowadays, certainly the most common question dealers hear is 'What is it worth?' It is a sign of the times that history takes second place to value. The object of COINS MARKET VALUES is to try to place a value on all the coins produced in what is known geographically as the British Isles, in other words England, Wales, Scotland and Ireland, and the Channel Islands, as well as the Anglo-Gallic series.

This is a difficult task because many coins do not turn up in auctions or lists every year, even though they are not really rare. However, we make a stab at a figure so that you, the collector, can at least have an idea of what you will have to pay.

How to sell at auction

In England we are well served with a number of auction houses, giving the potential seller considerable choice. In London alone we have, in alphabetical order, Baldwins, Bonhams, Dix

Noonan Webb, Morton and Eden Ltd. in association with Sotheby's, and Spink. There are also smaller companies up and down the country, such as Croydon Coin Auctions.

The best approach for the seller is first of all to compare all their catalogues and if possible attend the auctions so that you can see how well they are conducted. The type of auctioneer bringing down the gavel may changed your mind. Talk it over with their experts, for you may have special cataloguing requirements and you could find that one of the firms might look after them better than the others.

An obvious coin, like say an 1887 £5, requires little expertise and will probably sell at a certain price in almost any auction. However, if you require expert cataloguing of countermarked coins or early medieval, then you need to know what the company is capable of before you discuss a job rate.

You should remember though that, while it is not complicated to sell by auction, you may have to wait at least three or four months from the time you consign the coins to the auctioneers before

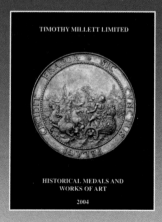

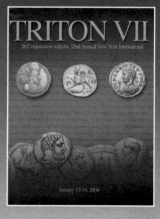

you receive any money. There are times when auctions manage to achieve very high prices, and other times when, for some inexplicable reason, they fail to reach even a modest reserve.

You should also bear in mind that the best deal in the long term is not always the lowest commission rate. Finally, auctioneers will usually charge you at least 10 per cent of the knock-down price, and you should bear in mind that some buyers may also be inhibited from paying a top price by a buyer's premium, generally all charging around 15 per cent.

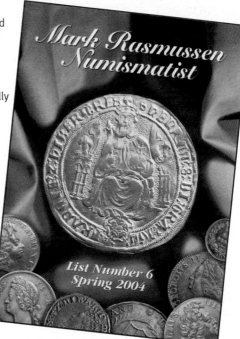

Dealers

The function of a dealer is to have a stock of coins for sale at marked prices. However, they will naturally only wish to buy according to the ebb and flow of their stocks. It is also true to say that dealers infinitely prefer fresh material, and if you strike at the right time it is possible that you could achieve a better price than by waiting for auction, since of course you will receive the money immediately.

Generally speaking, both dealers and auctioneers will not make any charge for a verbal valuation, but you should allow for the dealer to be making a profit of at least 20 per cent.

Bullion coins

Relating to Kruggerands, sovereigns, and so on, most newspapers carry the price of gold, which

is fixed twice daily by a group of leading banks. Anyone can buy sovereigns, and Krugerrands and other bullion coins, and it is better these days now that there is no VAT on top.

Normally, when you sell a bullion coin you expect the coin dealer to make a few pounds profit on each coin, but don't expect a good price

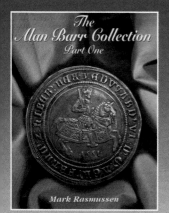

for a mounted coin attached to a watch chain, which will not be worth anything like an undamaged item. Also, read up and learn more about the market.

How to collect coins

You should obviously purchase your coins only from a reputable dealer. How can you decide on a reputable dealer? You can be sure of some protection if you choose one who is a member of the British Numismatic Trade Association or the International Association of Professional Numismatists. Membership lists of these organisations can be obtained from the respective secretaries:
• Mrs. Rosemary Cooke, PO Box 2, Rye, East Sussex TN31 7WE. (Tel/Fax: 01797 229988 or E-mail: bnta@lineone.net
• Jean-Luc Van Der Schueren, 14 Rue de la Bourse, B 1000 Brussels, Belgium (Tel: 0032 2 513 3400; Fax: 0032 2 513 2528).

However, many dealers are not members of either organisation, and it does not mean that they are not honest and professional. The best approach is simply to find one who will unconditionally guarantee that the coins you buy from him are genuine and accurately graded.

As a general rule you should only buy coins in the best condition available, and on this subject you will at first have to rely on the judgement of the dealer you choose. However, remember it will not always be possible to find pieces in 'Extremely Fine' condition, for example, and it can sometimes be worth buying coins which are not quite 'Very Fine'.

In the case of great rarities, of course, you might well have to make do with a coin that is only Fine, or even Poor. If there are only six known specimens of a particular piece, and four are in museums, it seems pointless to wait 20 years for another one to be found in the ground. Over the last few years condition has become too important in many ways, and has driven away collectors, because obviously you cannot buy coins only in top condition, since in certain series that would rule out at least 50 per cent of the available specimens. It very much depends on the type of coin, the reign it comes from and so on, so please be realistic.

It is worth taking out subscriptions with auction houses so that you can receive copies of all their catalogues, because this is an excellent way to keep up with prices as well as the collections that are being offered.

However, one should not overlook the fact that a number of dealers produce price lists, which in many ways are most useful to the collector, because coins can then be chosen at leisure by mail order. It is also easier to work out what one can afford to buy than when in the hot-house atmosphere of the auction room.

The most famous list is Spink's *Numismatic Circular,* first published in 1892 and still going strong with 10 issues a year. It is more than a price list, being an important forum for numismatic debate and the reporting of new finds, etc., (annual subscription £18).

There are also many expert dealers who

  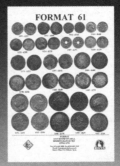 

produce excellent lists; many of them advertise in this publication and obviously we cannot mention them all here, but a good cross section of those who list domestic coins, and not listed in any order of preference, is as follows:–

• A.H. Baldwin and Sons Ltd., 11 Adelphi Terrace, London WC2N 6BJ. Hammered and Milled.
• Lloyd Bennett, PO Box 2, Monmouth, Gwent NP5 3YE. Hammered, Milled, Tokens.
• B.J. Dawson, 52 St. Helens Road, Bolton, Lancashire BL3 3NH. Hammered, Milled, Tokens, Medals.
• Dorset Coin Co. Ltd., 193 Ashley Road, Parkstone, Poole, Dorset BH14 9DL. All Coins and Banknotes.
• Format, 18-19 Bennetts Hill, Birmingham B2 5QJ. All British.
• Grantham Coins, PO Box 60, Grantham, Lincolnshire. Milled, good on Maundy.
• K.B. Coins, 50 Lingfield Road, Martin's Wood, Stevenage, Hertfordshire SG1 5SL. Hammered and Milled.
• C.J. Martin, 85 The Vale, Southgate, London N14 6AT. Celtic and Hammered.
• Peter Morris, PO Box 223, Bromley, Kent BR1 4EQ. Hammered, Milled, Tokens.
• S.R. Porter, 18 Trinity Road, Headington Quarry, Oxford OX3 8QL. Milled and Hammered.
• Mark Rasmussen, PO Box 42, Betchworth, Surrey RH3 7YR. Hammered and Milled.
• Roderick Richardson, The Old Granary Antiques Centre, Kings Staithe Lane, Kings Lynn PE30 1LZ. Hammered and Milled.
• Chris Rudd, PO Box 222, Aylsham, Norfolk

NR11 6TY. Specialist dealer in Celtic Coins.
• Classical Numismatics Group Inc. (Seaby Coins), 14 Old Bond Street, London W1X 4JL. Hammered, some Milled.
• Simmons & Simmons, PO Box 104, Leytonstone, London E11 1ND.

Societies

You should consider joining your local numismatic society, there being quite a number of these throughout the country. At the time of going to press there were over 50 across the UK. To find if there is one near you, get in touch with the British Association of Numismatic Societies: Mr. P.H. Mernick, c/o General Services, 42 Campbell Road, London E8 4DT (Tel: 020 8980 5672; E-mail: bans@mernicks.com; www.coinclubs.freeserve.co.uk).

The BANS organises annual congresses and seminars, and it is a good idea for the serious collector to consider attending one of these. Details are usually well publicised in the numismatic press.

Those collectors who wish to go a little further can apply for membership of the British Numismatic Society, and for their annual membership fee they will receive a copy of the *British Numismatic Journal,* which incorporates details of current research and many important articles, as well as book reviews.

Another useful facet of membership of this society is that you can borrow books from its library in the Warburg Institute.

The Secretary of the British Numismatic Society is Lt. Cdr. C.R.S. Farthing RN, 10

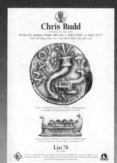

Greenbanks Gardens, Wallington, Fareham, Hants PO16 8SF. (Tel: 01329 284661).

Coin Fairs

Whilst it is always important to visit museums to see coins, it is worth remembering that there is often a fine array on show at coin fairs around the country, and most dealers do not mind showing coins to would-be collectors, even if they cannot afford to buy them on the spot.

The BNTA COINEX show will be held at the London Marriott Hotel on October 9 and 10, 2004 and shouldn't be missed – for details call the BNTA Secretary on 01797 229988. COINEX North, now the Harrogate Coin Fair, is held each Spring (call P. Dawson on 01204 63732).

Howard and Frances Simmons, past organisers of the Cumberland coin shows (no more) have instigated a new event. The London Coin Fairs at the Holiday Inn, Bloomsbury, London (formerly the Post House, Bloomsbury) will take place in February, May and November. Please note that their telephone number has changed to 020 8989 8097.

The Croydon team of Davidson/Monk organise the monthly shows at the Commonwealth Institute, Kensington, London W8. For more details ring 020 8656 4583 or 020 8651 3890.

David Fletcher organises the monthly Midland Coin and Stamp Fair, on the second Sunday of every month. To find out about dates and times just call 024 7671 6587 or visit the website at www.midlandcoinfair.co.uk

There are also fairs held at York racecourse in January and July. For further information on these events ring 01793 513431.

Finally, for details of the very successful Irish coin show in Dublin, in February every year, held in conjunction with the Irish Numismatic Society, contact Michael Kelly (Tel: 00353 1 839 1082).

COINS MARKET VALUES

Coin Grading

IT IS MOST important that newcomers to collecting should get to know the various grades of condition before attempting to buy or sell coins.

The system of grading most commonly used in Britain recognises the following main classes in descending order of quality: Brilliant Uncirculated (B.Unc,BU), Uncirculated (Unc), Extremely Fine (EF), Very Fine (VF), Fine (F), Fair, Poor.

It is not surprising that beginners get confused at their first encounter with these grades. The word 'FINE' implies a coin of high quality, yet this grade turns out to be very near the bottom of the scale and is in fact about the lowest grade acceptable to most collectors of modern coinage in Britain.

American grading

It is not really necessary to go into the details of American grading here, since it is only on a very few occasions that a British collector will order the coins he wants directly from an American dealer. However, across the Atlantic their grading system is quite different from ours, and whilst it purports to be a lot more accurate, it is actually much more prone, in our opinion, to be abused, and we prefer the English dealers' more conservative methods of grading. American dealers use many more terms than we do, ranging from Mint State to About Good. The latter could be described as 'very heavily worn, with portions of lettering, date and legend worn smooth. The date may be partly legible'. In England we would simply say 'Poor'.

Numerical method

The other area which British collectors will find difficult to evaluate is the American numerical method of describing coins as, for example, MS 70, MS 65. The MS simply stands for Mint State and an MS 65 would be described as 'an above average Uncirculated coin which may be brilliant or lightly toned but has some surface marks'. The MS system seemed to be acceptable at first but there now appear to be two schools of thought in America and you will quite frequently see coins graded in the more traditional manner as well as the MS style in sale catalogues. Fortunately American grades have not come into use in this country, although dealers have followed the American manner of embellishing coin descriptions to make them more desirable, which is understandable and in many ways can be an improvement on the old method of saying simply that the coin is 'Fine', which, of course, might not do justice to it.

Full mint lustre

There are two schools of thought on the use of the terms Brilliant Uncirculated and Uncirculated. The former is often considered to be the most useful and descriptive term for coins of copper, bronze, nickel-brass or other base metals, which display what is known as 'full mint lustre'. When this term is being used it is often necessary in the same context to employ the grade Uncirculated to describe coins which have never been in circulation but have lost the original lustre of a newly minted coin. However, some dealers and collectors tend to classify as Uncirculated all coins which have not circulated, whether they are brilliant or toned, and do not use the term Brilliant Uncirculated.

Fleur de coin

Sometimes FDC (fleur de coin) is used to define top grade coins, but this really only applies to pieces in perfect mint state, having no flaws or surface scratches. With modern methods of minting, slight damage to the surface is inevitable, except in the case of proofs, and therefore Brilliant Uncirculated or Uncirculated best describe the highest grade of modern coins.

The word 'proof' should not be used to denote a coin's condition. Proofs are pieces struck on specially prepared blanks from highly polished dies and usually have a mirror-like finish.

Opinions differ

In all this matter of condition it might be said that the grade 'is in the eye of the beholder', and there are always likely to be differences of opinion as to the exact grade of a coin. Some collectors and dealers have tried to make the existing scale of definitions more exact by adding letters such as N (Nearly), G (Good, meaning slightly better than the grade to which the letter is added), A (About or Almost) and so on. To be still more accurate, in cases where a coin wears more on one side than the other, two grades are shown, the first for the obverse, the second for the reverse thus: GVF/EF.

Additional description

Any major faults not apparent from the use of a particular grade are often described separately. These include dents and noticeable scratches, discoloration, areas of corrosion, edge knocks, holes, on otherwise good quality pieces, and the like.

Middle range of grades

One should always look for wear on the highest points of the design, of course, but these vary from coin to coin. To present a comprehensive guide to exact grading one would have to illustrate every grade of every coin type in a given series, on the lines of the famous Guide to the Grading of United States Coins, by Brown and Dunn. This is a complete book in itself (over 200 pages) and obviously such a mammoth task could not be attempted in the space available here. Therefore, on the following page we present representative examples from three different periods in the British series, to illustrate the 'middle' range of coin conditions.

Still in mint state

We have already dealt with the grades BU and Unc; they both describe coins which are still in the state in which they left the Mint, and which have never passed into general circulation. They are likely to show minor scratches and edge knocks due to the mass handling processes of modern minting.

Fair and Poor

At the other end of the scale we have Fair, a grade that is applied to very worn coins which still have the main parts of the design distinguishable, and Poor which denotes a grade in which the design and rim are worn almost flat and few details are discernible.

Here we show (enlarged) examples of the grades EF, VF and F. On the left are hammered long cross pennies of Aethelred II; in the centre, from the later hammered series, are groats of Henry VIII; on the right are shillings of William IV.

Extremely Fine. This describes coins which have been put into circulation, but have received only the minimum of damage since. There may be a few slight marks or minute scratches in the field (flat area around the main design), but otherwise the coin should show very little sign of having been in circulation.

Very Fine. Coins in this condition show some amount of wear on the raised surfaces, but all other detail is still very clear. Here, all three coins have had a little wear as can be seen in the details of the hair and face. However, they are still in attractive condition from the collector's viewpoint.

Fine. In this grade coins show noticeable wear on the raised parts of the design; most other details should still be clear. The penny and the groat show a lot of wear over the whole surface. On the shilling the hair above the ear has worn flat.

Extremely Fine (EF)

Very Fine (VF)

Fine (F)

Abbreviations & Terms

used in the Market Price Guide section

* – Asterisks against some dates indicate that no firm prices were available at the time of going to press.

2mm – P of PENNY is 2mm from trident. On other 1895 pennies the space between is only 1mm.

AE – numismatic symbol for copper or copper alloys.

Arabic 1, Roman I – varieties of the 1 in 1887.

Arcs – decorative border of arcs which vary in number.

B (on William III coins) – minted at Bristol.

1866 shilling lettered BBITANNIAR in error

BBITANNIAR – lettering error.

Bank of England – this issued overstruck Spanish dollars for currency use in Britain 1804-1811.

black – farthings 1897-1918, artificially darkened to avoid confusion with half sovereigns.

briit – lettering error.

B. Unc, BU – Brilliant Uncirculated condition.

C (on milled gold coins) – minted at Ottawa (Canada).

C (on William III coins) – minted at Chester.

close colon – colon close to DEF.

crosslet 4 – having upper and lower serifs to horizontal bar of 4 (see plain 4).

cu-ni – cupro-nickel.

dashes (thus –) following dates in the price list indicate that some particular characteristic of a coin is the same as that last described. Two dashes mean that two characters are repeated, and so on.

debased – in 1920 the silver fineness in British coins was debased from .925 to .500.

diag – diagonal.

'Dorrien and Magens' – issue of shillings by a group of bankers. Suppressed on the day of issue.

DRITANNIAR – lettering error.

E (on William III coins) – minted at Exeter.

E, E* (on Queen Anne coins) – minted at Edinburgh.

Edin – Edinburgh.

EEC – European Economic Community.

EF (over price column) – Extremely Fine condition.

E.I.C. – East India Co (supplier of metal).

Elephant and castle

eleph, eleph & castle – elephant or elephant and castle provenance mark (below the bust) taken from the badge of the African ('Guinea') Company, which imported the metal for the coins.

Eng – English shilling. In 1937, English and Scottish versions of the shilling were introduced. English versions: lion standing on crown (1937-1951); three leopards on a shield (1953-66).

exergue – segment below main design, usually containing the date.

On this penny the exergue is the area containing the date

ext – extremely.

F – face value only.

F (over price column) – Fine condition.

(F) – forgeries exist of these pieces. In some cases the forgeries are complete fakes, in others where the date is rare the date of a common coin has been altered. Collectors are advised to be very cautious when buying any of these coins.

Fair – rather worn condition.

Fantasies – non-currency items, often just produced for the benefit of collectors.

far colon – colon father from DEF than in close colon variety.

FDC – Fleur de coin. A term used to describe coins in perfect mint condition, with no flaws, scratches or other marks.

fig(s) – figure(s).

fillet – hair band.

flan – blank for a coin or medal.

GEOE – lettering error.

Florin of Victoria with the design in the Gothic style

Gothic – Victorian coins featuring Gothic-style portrait and lettering.

guinea-head – die used for obverse of guinea.

H – mintmark of The Mint, Birmingham, Ltd.

hd – head.

hp, harp (early, ord etc.) – varieties of the Irish harp on reverse.

hearts – motif in top RH corner of Hanoverian shield on reverse.

illust – illustration, or illustrated.

im – initial mark.

inc, incuse – incised, sunk in.

inv – inverted.

JH – Jubilee Head.

The Jubilee Head was introduced on the coinage in 1887 to mark Victoria's Golden Jubilee

KN – mintmark of the Kings Norton Metal Co Ltd.

L.C.W. – Initials of Leonard Charles Wyon, engraver.

lge – large.

LIMA – coins bearing this word were struck from bullion captured by British ships from foreign vessels carrying South American treasure, some of which may have come from Peru (capital Lima).

1902 pennies showing the low horizon variety (A) and the normal horizon (B)

low horizon – on normal coins the horizon meets the point where Britannia's left leg crosses behind the right. On this variety the horizon is lower.
LVIII etc – regnal year in Roman numerals on the edge.
matt – type of proof without mirror-like finish.
M (on gold coins) – minted at Melbourne (Australia).
'military' – popular name for the 1813 guinea struck for the payment of troops fighting in the Napoleonic Wars.
mm – mintmark.
Mod eff – modified effigy of George V.
mule – coin struck from wrongly paired dies.
N (on William III coins) – minted at Norwich.

William III shilling with N (for Norwich mint) below the bust

no. – number.
obv – obverse, usually the 'head' side of a coin.
OH – Old Head.
ord – ordinary.
OT – ornamental trident.
P (on gold coins) – minted at Perth (Australia).
pattern – trial piece not issued for currency.

piedfort – a coin which has been specially struck on a thicker than normal blank. In France, whence the term originates, the Kings seem to have issued them as presentation pieces from the 12th century onwards. In Britain medieval and Tudor examples are known, and their issue has now been reintroduced by the Royal Mint, starting with the 20 pence piedfort of 1982.
plain (on silver coins) – no provenance marks in angles between shields on reverse.
plain 4 – with upper serif only to horizontal bar of 4 (see crosslet 4).
pln edge prf – plain edge proof.
plume(s) – symbol denoting Welsh mines as source of metal.
proof, prf – coin specially struck from highly polished dies. Usually has a mirror-like surface.
prov, provenance – a provenance mark on a coin (e.g. rose, plume, elephant) indicates the supplier of the bullion from which the coin was struck.
PT – plain trident.
raised – in relief, not incuse.
RB – round beads in border.
rev – reverse, 'tail' side of coin.
r – right.
r & p – roses and plumes.

Roses and plumes provenance marks

rose – symbol denoting west of England mines as source of metal.
RRITANNIAR – lettering error.
rsd – raised.
S (on gold coins) – minted at Sydney (Australia).
SA (on gold coins) – minted at Pretoria (South Africa).

Scottish shilling 1953-66

Scot – Scottish shilling. Lion seated on crown, holding sword and sceptre (1937-51); lion rampant, on shield (1953-66).
SS C – South Sea Company (source of metal).

1723 shilling bearing the South Sea Company's initials

SEC – SECUNDO, regnal year (on edge).
sh – shield(s).
sm – small.
'spade' – refers to spadelike shape of shield on George III gold coins.

'Spade' guinea, reverse

TB – toothed beads in border.
TER – TERTIO, regnal year (on edge).
trnctn, truncation – base of head or bust where the neck or shoulders terminate.
Unc – Uncirculated condition.
var – variety.
VF – Very Fine condition.
VIGO – struck from bullion captured in Vigo Bay.
VIP – 'very important person'. The so-called VIP crowns were the true proofs for the years of issue. Probably most of the limited number struck would have been presented to high ranking officials.
W.C.C. – Welsh Copper Co (supplier of metal).
wire type – figure of value in thin wire-like script.
W.W. – initials of William Wyon, engraver.
xxri – lettering error.
y, Y (on William III coins) – minted at York.
YH – Young Head.

Victoria Young Head Maundy fourpence

Treasure truths

On September 24, 1997 the Treasure Act 1996 came into being, replacing the old medieval law of treasure trove. This widened the definition of finds that are treasure, and under the new procedures, which are set out in the Code of Practice on the Act, the new Treasure Valuation Committee assists the Secretary of State for Culture to submit an annual report.

In the past, before an object could be declared 'treasure' and therefore be the property of the Crown, it had to pass three tests:– it had to be made substantially of gold or silver; it had to have been deliberately hidden with the intention of recovery; and its owner or the heirs had to be unknown. If then a museum wanted to keep the coins (or artefacts) the lawful finder normally received the full market value; if not the coins were returned to the finder.

The new Act removes the need to establish that objects were hidden with intention of being recovered; it also sets out the precious metal content required for a find to qualify as treasure; and it extends the definition of treasure.

'All coins that contain at least 10 per cent of gold or silver by weight of metal and that come from the same find, provided a find consists of at least two coins with gold or silver content of at least 10 per cent. The coins must be at least 300 years old at the time of discovery. In the case of finds consisting of coins that contain less than 10 per cent gold or silver there must be at least 10 such coins... Single coins will not be treasure, unless they are found in association with objects that are treasure, or unless there is exceptionally strong evidence that they were buried with the intention of recovery (for example, a single coin found in plough soil without any sign of a container would not provide such evidence)'.

As far as the more modern coins are concerned, such as finds of guineas or sovereigns, the Act reads as follows: 'Only objects that are less than 300 years old, that are made substantially of gold or silver, that have been deliberately hidden with the intention of recovery and whose owners or heirs are unknown will come into this category. In practice such finds are rare and the only such discoveries that have been made within recent years have been hoards of gold and silver coins of the eighteenth, nineteenth or twentieth centuries. Single coins found on their own will not qualify under this provision, unless there is exceptionally strong evidence to show that they were buried with the intention of recovery: for

Department for Culture, Media and Sport
Cultural Property Unit

dcms

Treasure Annual Report 2001

Department for Culture, Media and Sport
Cultural Property Unit

dcms

The Treasure Act
Information for finders of Treasure
(England & Wales)

example, a single coin found in plough soil without any sign of a container would provide such. Therefore gold and silver objects that are clearly less than 300 years old need not be reported unless the finder has reason to believe that they may have been deliberately hidden with the intention of recovery'.

All this simplifies the task of coroners in determining whether or not a find is treasure, and it includes a new offence of non-declaration of treasure. It also states that lawful occupiers and landowners will have the right to be informed of finds of treasure from their land and they will be eligible for reward. Finally, following the Government's recent operational review of the Treasure Act. a decision was taken to extend the definition of 'Treasure' to include:–
a) any object (other than a coin), any part of which is base metal which, when found, is one of at least two base metal objects in the same find which are of Prehistoric date.
b) any object (other than a coin), which is of Prehistoric date, and any part of which is gold and silver.

A Treasure (designation) order was debated in parliament on Tuesday July 17, 2002, and came into force on January 1, 2003.

The Committee

The Treasure Trove Reviewing Committee was established in 1977 as an independent body, to advise Ministers on the valuation of treasure trove finds. Under the new Act that body has been replaced by the Treasure Valuation Committee.

Under the new arrangements the national museums will no longer submit valuations to the Treasure Valuation Committee, but instead the committee itself will commission valuation reports from expert advisers. All the interested parties (the finder, the landowner and the museum that intends to acquire the find) will be given the chance to comment on these valuations or indeed commission independent valuations of their own.

These reports are now delivered very quickly and there is no doubt that the new procedures are as transparently fair as it is possible to be. The latest published report, for the period 2001/2, deals with 214 finds and it is attractively illustrated throughout in colour.

At present the committee is chaired by Professor Norman Palmer, a leading authority on the law of treasure trove. The current committee consists of Professor Norman Palmer; Doctor Jack Ogden, National Association of Goldsmiths; Trevor Austin, President of the National Council for Metal Detecting; Doctor Arthur MacGregor, Curator of Antiquities at the Ashmolen Museum; Mrs. Mary Sinclair, a coin dealer – chiefly of the medieval period; and Thomas Curtis, a coin dealer specialising in ancient coins.

Information for finders & metal detectorists:
Copies of *The Treasure Act 1966, Code of Practice (England Wales) 1997*, can be obtained from the Department of National Heritage. This gives much useful information including a current list of coroners in the UK, and a list of coins commonly found that contain less than 10 per cent of gold or silver. It also gives advice on the care of finds, identification and storage, etc.

There is also a very useful leaflet entitled *The Treasure Act, information for finds of treasure*, which deals with everything in a question and answer way, for example:
What should I do if I find something that may be treasure?
How do I report a find of treasure?
What if I do not report a find of treasure?
How do I know that I will receive a fair price for my find?
Note: both these publications can presently be obtained free of charge from:
Department of National Heritage, 2-4 Cockspur Street, London SW1Y 5DH. Tel: 020 7211 6200.

Forgeries

Most collectors know that there have been forgeries since the earliest days of coin production, so it is only to be expected that some new forgeries appear on the scene every year. It seems that there is always someone willing to deceive the collector and the dealer. However, nowadays very few forgers end up making much money. As a result of the actions of the British Numismatic Trade Association, the trade is much more tightly knit than ever before, and anxious to stamp out new forgeries before they have a chance to become a serious menace.

They were last a matter of serious concern in the late 1960s and early 1970s, when an enormous number of 1887 £5 pieces and United States $20 manufactured in Beruit came on to the market. Also in the early 1970s the group of Dennington forgeries could have made a serious impact on the English hammered gold market, but for lucky early detection. (Unfortunately we have noticed a number of these are still in circulation, and so we will deal with them later in this article.) In the late 1970s a crop of forgeries of Ancient British coins came to light causing a panic in

ABOVE: Dennington forgeries: Edward III noble (top) and Mary Fine Sovereign.

academic and trade circles. This caused a lack of confidence in the trade and it has taken a number of years for everyone to feel happy that there was no further problem. The BNTA firmly pursues any mention of forgeries and one hopes that a new spate of copies of Anglo-Saxon coins from the West Country are not allowed to develop. They are being sold as replicas, but they are still deceptive in the wrong hands. Bob Forrest compiled a list of these and it was published by the IAPN *Bulletin of Forgeries* in 1995/6 Vol.20 No.2. He has now done an update of this which will be available at the end of the coming year.

The worrying forgeries

We mentioned earlier the Dennington forgeries. It is now many years since the trial of Anthony Dennington at the Central Criminal Court, where he was found guilty of six charges of 'causing persons to pay money by falsely pretending that they were buying genuine antique coins' *The Times*, July 10, 1969). There are a small number of these pieces still circulating in the trade, and since they have deceived some collectors and dealers, we thought we should record them more fully here. The following is a list of the pieces which appeared in the IBSCC Bulletin in August 1976.

1 Henry III gold penny
2 Edward III Treaty period noble
3 Another, with saltire before King's name
4 Henry IV heavy coinage noble
5 Henry V noble, Class C
(mullet at King's sword arm)
6 Henry VNI mule noble
7 Henry VI noble, annulet issue, London
8 Edward IV ryal, Norwich
9 Another, York
10 Elizabeth I Angel
11 Mary Fine Sovereign 1553

12 James I unite, mintmark mullet
13 James I rose ryal, 3rd coinage, mint mark lis
14 James I 3rd coinage laurel
15 Commonwealth unite 1651
16 Commonwealth half-unite 1651
17 Charles II touch piece

RIGHT: Modern cast copies of Anglo-Saxon pennies: Ceolwulf 1st above and Ceonwulf below.

One can only reiterate that these copies are generally very good and you must beware of them. The following points may be useful.

1 The coins are usually slightly 'shiny' in appearance, and the edges are not good, since they have been filed down and polished.

2 They are usually very 'hard' to touch, whereas there is a certain amount of 'spring' in the genuine articles.

3 They usually feel slightly thick, but not always, not quite like an electrotype but certainly thicker than normal.

4 Although the Mary Fine sovereign reproduction is heavy, at 16.1986 gr, these pieces are usually lighter in weight than the originals.

As far as forgeries of modern coins are concerned, the most worrying aspects has been the enormous increase in well produced forgeries in the last 25 years.

They are so well produced that it is often impossible for the naked eye to detect the difference, and it has therefore become the job of the scientist and metallurgist. Many of these pieces have deceived dealers and collectors, although they do not seem to have caused too great a crisis of confidence. This increase in the number of modern counterfeits has been due to the enormous rise in coin values since the 1960s.

It is well known that the vast majority of these modern forgeries have emanated from the Middle East, as we suggested earlier, where it is not illegal to produce counterfeits of other countries' coins. It has proved to be very good business for a lot of these small forgers in Beruit, and one can only rely on the alertness of the coin trade so that reports are circulated quickly whenever a new forgery is spotted.

Unfortunately, the main problem is still that the forger has every encouragement to continue production of copies, when one thinks of the profit involved. At the time of writing, it only takes about £290 worth of gold to make an 1887-dated five pound piece of correct composition, valued at around £650. We cannot, therefore, be complacent.

There is not enough space here to tell you in detail what to look for, and anyway detecting forgeries requires specialist knowledge, a 508 list of faults would not help. If you turn to the catalogue section of COINS MARKET VALUES you will find that as far as British coins are concerned we have placed (F) beside a number of coins which

we know have been counterfeited, and which frequently turn up. However, you should watch out for sovereigns, in particular, of which there are forgeries of every date from 1900 to 1932 and even recent dates such as 1957 and 1976.

A list follows of the pieces you should be particularly careful about, especially if you notice that they are being offered below the normal catalogue value. Most modern forgeries of, say, Gothic crowns, seem to be offered at prices which are 10 per cent or 20 per cent below the current market price. The moral is, do not automatically think you have a bargain if the price is low – it could be a forgery!

1738, 1739 two guineas
1793, 1798 guineas
(there could also be other dates)
1820 pattern two pounds
1839 five pounds
(in particular the plain edge variety)
1887 five pounds
1887 (two pounds (there seem to be many forgeries of these))
1893 five pounds, two pounds
1902 five pounds, two pounds
1911 five pounds, two pounds
1817, 1819, 1822, 1825, 1827,
1887, 1889, 1892, 1892M,
1908C, 1913C sovereigns; also every date from 1900 to 1932 inclusive, plus 1957,
1959, 1963, 1966, 1967,
1974, 1976 1847 Gothic crowns
1905 halfcrowns

Other safeguards against forgery

(a) The best method of protection against purchasing forgeries is to buy your coins from a reputable dealer who is a member of the British Numismatic Trade Association or the International Association of Professional Numismatists, or one who will unconditionally guarantee that all his coins are genuine.

(b) Legal tender coins, which include five and two pound pieces, sovereigns, half sovereigns and crowns, are protected by the Forgery and Counterfeiting Act, and it is the responsibility of the police to prosecute in cases where this Act has been contravened.

(c) If your dealer is unhelpful over a non-legal tender item, which you have purchased and which you think has been falsely described, you can take legal action under the Trades Description Act 1968. However, we should warn you that it can be a tedious and long-winded business, but if you want to proceed in this you should contact your local Trading Standards Office or Consumer Protection department.

The different types of forgery

There are many different forgeries, but essentially they can be divided into two main groups. First of all there are contemporary forgeries intended to be used as face-value money (as in the cases, some years ago, of the counterfeit 50p pieces, which even worked in slot machines), and secondly forgeries intended to deceive collectors.

Contemporary forgeries, those pieces struck in imitation of currency coins, are obviously not a serious problem to numismatists. The recent ones cause more trouble to bank clerks, anyway, and are not of sufficiently good standard to

deceive numismatic experts. In general, those produced in the Middle Ages were base (which was how the forger made a profit), consisting wholly of base metal or occasionally having a thin coating of the proper metal on the outside. Sometimes they were struck, but more often they were cast.

Whatever the problems they caused at the time of issue, they are now often as interesting as the regular coins of the period.
However, one can be less light-hearted about copies which are made to deceive collectors. The following five methods of reproduction have been used:

1. Electrotyping. These copies would normally deceive an expert.

2. Casting. Old casts are easily recognisable, having marks made by air bubbles on the surface, and showing a generally 'fuzzy' effect. Much more of a problem are the modern cast copies, produced by sophisticated 'pressure-casting', which can be extremely difficult for all but the most expert to distinguish from the originals (more of this later).

3. The fabrication of false dies. With hammered coins counterfeits are not difficult for an expert to detect. However, the sophisticated die-production techniques used in Beirut have resulted in the worrying features of modern gold and silver coins described later.

4. The use of genuine dies put to some illegal use such as re-striking (a mintmaster in West Germany was convicted in 1975 of that very issue).

5 Alteration of a genuine coin. (Ask your dealer how many George V pennies he has seen with the date altered to 1933 – it does happen!)

Counterfeit Coin Club

There is now a Counterfeit Coin Club which produces a small journal four times a year. If you

are interested in joining, write to its President: Ken Peters, 8 Kins Road, Biggin Hill, Kent TN16 3XU (Tel: 01959 573686)

Literature on forgery

The back numbers of Spink's *Numismatic Circulars* and Seaby's *Coin and Medal Bulletins* are useful sources of information on the forgeries that have been recorded over the years.

The ISBCC (set up by an IAPN in 1975 by the late Vincent Newman) also produced a series of important forgery bulletins, mainly on modern coins, and are very useful if you can find them on the second-hand shelves.

The IAPN themselves still produce very good reports on forgeries for their own members.

As far as hammered coins are concerned, still the most useful work is that by L.A. Lawrence in the *British Numismatic Journal* as long ago as 1905! (*Forgery in relation to Numismatics*. BNJ 1905-1907, a series of articles; occasionally it can be found bound as one volume).

British Coin Prices

CELTIC COINAGE

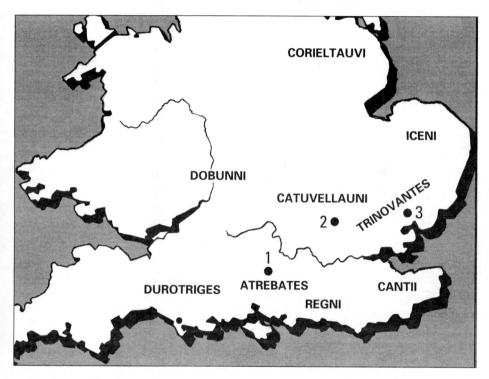

The distribution of the tribes in Britain based on the map in 'The coinage of Ancient Britain', by R.P. Mack, published by Spink and Son Ltd and B.A. Seaby Ltd.

Key to towns:
1. Calleva Atrebatum (Silchester)
2. Verulamium (St Albans)
3. Camulodunum (Colchester)

It is always difficult to produce a priced catalogue of coins, but none is more difficult than the early British series. The market has developed considerably since the publication of R.D. Van Arsdell's *Celtic Coinage of Britain,* which is an essential book for collectors (584 pages, 54 plates and many other illustrations, maps and diagrams).

A word of caution, though; quite a number of forgeries exist, some of relatively recent production, and unfortunately also numerous items from undeclared hoards are on the market, which makes it essential to buy from a reputable dealer.

We are very grateful for the help of Robert Van Arsdell since he produced the synopsis of the material which we have used. We have kept this very basic, and simply linked it up for easy reference with *The Coinage of Ancient Britain* by R. P. Mack, third edition, London 1975 (now out of print), and with the *British Museum Catalogue of British Iron Age Coins* by R. Hobbs, where it is possible. In the following lists Mack types are indicated by 'M' and BMC types by 'B'. The V numbers relate to the Van Arsdell catalogue. The existence of forgeries is indicated by **(F).**

CELTIC COINAGE

Gold staters without legends

AMBIANI

	F	VF
Large flan type M1, 3, V10, 12	**£400**	**£1450**

Ambiani large flan type

	F	VF
Defaced die type M5, 7, V30, 33 ...	**£300**	**£850**
Abstract type M26, 30, V44, 46	**£250**	**£650**
Gallic War type M27, a, V50, 52 **(F)** ...	**£135**	**£300**

Gallic War gold stater

SUESSIONES

	F	VF
Abstract type M34a, V85	**£275**	**£700**

VE MONOGRAM

	F	VF
M82, a, b, V87 **(F)**	**£275**	**£750**

WESTERHAM

	F	VF
M28, 29, V200, 202 , B1-24	**£200**	**£425**

Chute Gold Starter, V1205

CHUTE

	F	VF
M32, V1205, B35-76 **(F)**	**£135**	**£275**

CLACTON

	F	VF
Type I M47, V1458, B137-144	**£300**	**£850**
Type II M46, a, V30, 1455, B145-179	**£325**	**£850**

CORIELTAUVI

	F	VF
Scyphate type M—, V—, B3187-93	**£325**	**£850**

CORIELTAUVI (N.E. COAST TYPE)

	F	VF
Type I M50-51a, V800, B182-191 ...	**£200**	**£450**
Type II M52-57, S27, V804	**£190**	**£425**

Norfolk Wolf stater VA610-3

NORFOLK

	F	VF
Wolf type M49, a, b, V610, B212-278	**£165**	**£400**

CORIELTAUVI

	F	VF
South Ferriby Kite & Domino type, M449-450a, V.811, B3146-3186	**£210**	**£500**

Coritani (South Ferriby)

WHADDON CHASE

	F	VF
M133-138, V1470-1478, B279-350 **(F)**	**£190**	**£475**
Middle , Late Whaddon Chase V1485-1509	**£225**	**£575**

Whaddon Chase stater

WONERSH

	F	VF
M147, 148, V1522, B351-56	**£375**	**£950**

WEALD

	F	VF
M84, 229, V144, 150, B2466-68	**£450**	**£1200**

ICENI

	F	VF
Freckenham Type I M397-399, 403b, V620, B3384-95	**£275**	**£600**
Freckenham Type II M401, 2, 3a, 3c, V626, B3396-3419	**£275**	**£575**
Snettisham Type M—, V—, B3353-83	**£300**	**£700**

Iceni gold stater

ATREBATIC

	F	VF
M58-61, V210-216, B445-76	**£200**	**£425**

Atrebatic stater

SAVERNAKE FOREST
M62, V1526, B359-64 ... ... £225 £500

DOBUNNIC
M374, V1005, B2937-40 ... ... £350 £850

Gold quarter staters without legends

	F	VF
AMBIANI		
Large flan type M2, 4, V15, 20 **(F)**	£225	£600
Defaced die type M6, 8, V35, 37	£200	£500
GEOMETRIC		
M37, 39, 41, 41A, 42, V65, 146, 69, 67	£75	£150
SUSSEX		
M40, 43-45, V143, 1225-1229	£75	£150
VE MONOGRAM		
M83, V87 **(F)**	£140	£350

Atrebatic quarter stater, Bognor Cog Wheel

ATREBATIC
M63-67, 69-75, V220-256, B478-546 £135 £325

Caesar's trophy, quarter stater VA145

KENTISH
Caesar's Trophy type V145 ... ... £110 £275

Gold staters with legends

	F	VF
COMMIUS		
M92, V350, B724-730	£375	£1000
TINCOMARUS		
M93, 93, V362, 363, B761-74	£450	£1200
VERICA		
Equestrian type M121, V500, B1143-58	£225	£550
Vine leaf type M125, V520, B1159-76	£250	£625

Verica gold stater

	F	VF
EPATICCUS		
M262, V575, B2021-23	£800	£2000
DUBNOVELLAUNUS		
In Kent M283, V176, B2492-98	£350	£825
In Essex M275, V1650, B2425-40 ...	£300	£800
EPPILLUS		
In Kent M300-1, V430, B1125-28 ...	£1250	£3750
ADDEDOMAROS (THREE TYPES)		
M266, 7, V1605, B2390-94 **(F)**	£200	£525
TASCIOVANUS		
Bucranium M149, V1680, B1591-1607 **(F)**	£300	£850

VOLISIOS DUMNOCOVEROS

	F	VF
Equestrian M154-7, V1730-1736, B1608-13	£275	£750
TASCIO/RICON M184, V1780, B1625-36	£500	£1250
SEGO		
M194, V1845, B1625-27	£1250	£3500
ANDOCO		
M197, V1860, B2011-14	£550	£1350

Tasciovanus Celtic Warrior

Cunobeline Gold Stater, V1910

CELTIC COINAGE

CUNOBELINE	F	VF
Two horses M201, V1910, B1769-71	£650	£1650
Corn ear M203 etc. V2010,		
B1772-1835 **(F)**	£250	£550

ANDOCO Stater

ANTED of the Dobunni		
M385-6, V1062-1066, B3023-27 **(F)**	£425	£1100
EISU		
M388, V1105, B3039-42 **(F)**	£550	£1250
INAM		
M390, V1140, B3056 **(F)**	extremely rare	
CATTI		
M391, V1130, B3057-60 **(F)**	£375	£900
COMUX		
M392, V1092, B3061-63 **(F)**	£800	£2000
CORIO		
M393, V1035, B3064-3133 ... ... ·	£425	£1000
BODVOC		
M395, V1052, B3135-42 **(F)**	£700	£1750

Bodvoc

VEP CORF		
M459-460, V940, 930, B3296-3300 **(F)**	£425	£950
DUMNOC TIGIR SENO		
M461, V972, B3325-27 **(F)**	£750	£1750
VOLISIOS DUMNOCOVEROS		
M463, V978, B3330-36	£425	£1000

Cunobeline quarter stater V.1913-1

Gold quarter staters with legends

TINCOMARUS

Abstract type M95, V365	£165	£350
Medusa head type M97, V387,		
B811-24	£225	£525
Tablet type M101-4, V387-390,		
B825-79	£125	£275

Tincommius Medusa head gold quarter stater

EPPILLUS	F	VF
CALLEVA M107, V407, B986-1015 ...	£125	£275

Eppillus CALLEVA type

VERICA		
Horse type M111-114, V465-468,		
B1143-46	£110	£225
TASCIOVANUS		
Horse type M152-3, V1690,1692,		
B1641-1650	£120	£250
CUNOBELINE		
Various types, B1836-55 from	£125	£275

Silver coins without legends

DUROTRIGES

Silver stater M317, V1235,		
B2525-2731 **(F)**	£45	£135
Geometric type M319, V1242,		
B2734-79	£35	£100
Starfish type M320, V1270,		
B2780-81	£60	£200

Starfish Unit

DOBUNNIC

Face M374a, b, 5, 6, 8, V1020,		
B2950-3000	£35	£100
Abstract M378a-384d, V1042,		
B3012-22	£30	£90

Corieltauvi, showing boar and horse

CORIELTAUVI

Boar type M405a, V855, B3194-3250	£75	£200
South Ferriby M410 etc, V875	£50	£125

Iceni Unit, V730

ICENI	F	VF
Boar type M407-9, V655-659, B3440-3511 … … … … … … … …	£20	£75
Wreath type M414, 5, 440, V679, 675, B3763-74 … … … … … … …	£25	£80
Face type M412-413e, V665, B3536-55 … … … … … … … …	£85	£225
QUEEN BOUDICA		
Face type M413, 413D, V790, 792, B3556-3759 … … … … … … …	£50	£165

Silver coins of Boudica (left) and Commius (right)

COMMIUS		
Head left M446b, V355, 357, B731-58 … … … … … … … … …	£45	£135

Silver coins with legends

EPPILLUS	F	VF
CALLEVA type M108, V415, B1016-1115	£45	£130
EPATICCUS		
Eagle type M263, V580, B2024-2289	£30	£90
Victory type M263a, V581, B2294-2328	£35	£100

Verica, Lion type unit V505

VERICA		
Lim type M123, V505, B1332-59 …	£40	£135

Silver unit, Epaticcus

CARATACUS		
Eagle Type M265, V593, B2376-2384 (**F**)	£135	£400
TASCIOVANUS		
Equestrian M158, V1745, B1667-68	£85	£275
VER type M161, V1699, B1670-73 …	£85	£275
CUNOBELINE		
Equestrian M216-8, 6, V1951, 1953, 2047, B1862 … … … … …	£110	£325
Bust right M236, VA2055, B1871-73	£85	£275
ANTED of the Dobunni		
M387, V1082, B3032-38 … … … …	£70	£175
EISU		
M389, V1110, B3043-55 … … … …	£55	£150

CELTIC COINAGE

BODVOC
M396, V1057, B3143-45 **(F)** £125   £375

ANTED of the Iceni
M419-421, V710, 711, 715,
B3791-4009 ... ...   £30   £70

ECEN
M424, V730, B4033-4215 ... ...   £25   £65

EDNAM
M423, 425b, V740, 734, B4219-4281   £30   £65

ECE
M425a, 426, 7, 8, V761, 764,
762, 766, B4348-4538 ... ...   £25   £60

AESU
M432, V775, B4558-72 ... ...   £50   £125

PRASUTAGUS
King of the Iceni (husband of Boudica),
B4577-4580 ... ...   £650   £1750

ESUP ASU
M4566, VA924, B3272 ... ...   £85   £275

VEP CORF
M460b, 464, V394, 950, B3277-3382,
B3305-3314 ... ...   £50   £110

DUMNOC TIGIR SENO
M462, V974 B3328-3329 ... ...   £195   £550

VOLISIOS DUMNOCOVEROS
M463a, V978, 980, B3339 ... ...   £165   £450

ALE SCA
M469, V996 ... ...   £165   £450

Bronze, base metal coins without legends

POTIN	F	VF
Experimental type M22a, V104	£45	£100

Potin coin class II

	F	VF
Class I M9-22, V122-131	£30	£80
Class II M23-25, V136-139	£30	£80
Thurrock Types V1402-1442	£40	£125

	F	VF
ARMORICAN		
Billon stater	£30	£100
Billon quarter stater	£50	£135
DUROTRIGES		
Bronze stater M318, V1290	£20	£50
Cast type M332-370, V1322-1370 ...	£35	£110
NORTH THAMES		
M273, 274, 281, V1646 1615, 1669	£35	£110
NORTH KENT		
M295, 296, V154	£70	£275

Bronze coins with legends

	F	VF
DUBNOVELLAUNUS in Essex		
M277, 8, V1665, 1667	£60	£200
TASCIOVANUS		
Head, beard M168, 9, V1707	£50	£200
VERLAMIO M172, V1808	£50	£190
Head, VER M177, V1816	£60	£225
Boar, VER M179, V1713	£60	£210
Equestrian M190, V1892	£95	£375
Centaur M192, V1882	£125	£475
ANDOCO		
M200, V1871	£75	£275
CUNOBELINE		
Victory, TASC M221, V1971	£40	£175
Victory, CUN M22, a, V1973	£45	£190
Winged animal, M225, V2081	£45	£190

Cunobeline bronze with Centaur reverse

	F	VF
Head, beard, M226, 9, V2131, 2085	£40	£165
Panel, sphinx, M230, V1977	£45	£190
Winged beast, M231, V1979	£45	£170
Centaur, M242, V2089	£40	£165
Sow, M243, V2091	£40	£165
Warrior, M244, V2093	£35	£150
Boar, TASC, M245, V1983	£50	£190
Bull, TASC M246, V2095	£40	£150
Metal worker, M248, V2097	£40	£165
Pegasus, M249, V2099	£35	£125
Horse, CAMV, M250, V2101	£45	£190
Jupiter, horse, M251, V2103	£45	£190
Janus head, M252, V2105	£50	£200
Jupiter, lion, M253, V1207	£40	£165
Sphinx, fig, M260, a, V2109	£45	£175

ENGLISH HAMMERED
Gold from 1344 and Silver from *circa* 600

Prices in this section are approximately what collectors can expect to pay for the commonest types of the coins listed; for most other types prices will range upwards from these amounts. Precise valuations cannot be given since they vary from dealer to dealer and, in any case, have to be determined by consideration of a number of factors e.g., the coin's condition (which is of prime importance in deciding its value).

For more detailed information refer to English Hammered Coins, Volumes 1 and 2, by J. J. North and published by Spink and Son Ltd. Any serious collectors should also obtain The Herbert Schneider Collection, Volume One, English Gold Coins 1257-1603, published by Spink and Son, 1996 and Volume Two English Gold Coins 1603 to 20th century, published by Spink and Son, 2002.

GOLD COINS
The Plantagenet Kings

Henry III gold penny

HENRY III 1216-1272
Gold Penny
This specimen sold for £159,500 (including buyers premium) at a Spink auction on 9 July 1996.

F VF
ext. rare

Edward III quarter noble

EDWARD III 1327-77
Third coinage

	F	VF
Florins or Double leopard	ext. rare	
Half florins or leopard...	ext. rare	
Quarter florins or helms	ext. rare	
Nobles ... ... from	£1250	£3000
Half nobles ... ... from	£1000	£3000
Quarter nobles	£375	£900

Fourth coinage
Pre-treaty with France (i.e. before 1315) with French title

	F	VF
Nobles	£500	£1050
Half nobles	£375	£850
Quarter nobles	£200	£400

Transitional treaty period, 1361. Aquitaine title added

	F	VF
Nobles	£525	£1350
Half nobles	£325	£750
Quarter nobles	£185	£400

Edward III 1327-1377, Half noble, Transitional Treaty

Treaty period 1361-9 omit FRANC

	F	VF
Nobles, London	£525	£1200
Nobles, Calais		
(C in centre of rev.)	£550	£1350
Half nobles, London	£350	£800
Half nobles, Calais	£575	£1300
Quarter nobles, London	£200	£425
Quarter nobles, Calais	£225	£500

Post-treaty period 1369-77 French title resumed

	F	VF
Nobles, London	£575	£1350
Nobles, Calais		
(flag at stern or C in centre)	£575	£1350
Half nobles, London	ext. rare	
Half nobles, Calais	£950	£2500

There are many other issues and varieties in this reign. These prices relate to the commoner pieces.

Richard II London half noble

RICHARD II 1377-99

	F	VF
Nobles, London	£700	£1500
Nobles, Calais		
(flag at stern)	£750	£1600
Half nobles, London	£850	£2250

HAMMERED GOLD

	F	VF
Half nobles, Calais		
(flag at stern)	£1250	£3250
Quarter nobles, London	£375	£850

There are many different varieties and different styles of lettering.

HENRY IV 1399-1413
Heavy coinage
Nobles (120grs) London	£4500	£13500
Nobles, Calais (flag at stern)	£5500	£15000
Half nobles, London	£4000	*
Half nobles, Calais	£4500	*
Quarter nobles, London	£1000	£2500
Quarter nobles, Calais.............	£1350	£3250

Light coinage
Nobles (108grs)	£1350	£3500
Half nobles	£2250	£5000
Quarter nobles	£475	£1000

Henry V noble

HENRY V 1413-22
Nobles, many varieties, from	£650	£1350
Half nobles	£600	£1300
Quarter nobles	£300	£650

This reign sees an increase in the use of privy marks to differentiate issues.

Henry VI noble, Annulet issue

HENRY VI 1422-61
Annulet issue (1422-27)
Nobles, London	£575	£1200
Nobles, Calais (flag at stern)	£625	£1500
Nobles, York	£750	£2000
Half nobles, London	£375	£900
Half nobles, Calais	£725	£1800
Half nobles, York	£875	£2500
Quarter nobles, London	£200	£450
Quarter nobles, Calais	£225	£550
Quarter nobles, York	£250	£650

Henry VI, Quarter-Noble, Annulet issue

Rosette-mascle issue 1427-30 ......
	F	VF
Nobles, London	£950	£2250
Nobles, Calais	£1250	£2750
Half nobles, London	£1350	£3250
Half nobles, Calais	£1500	£3500
Quarter nobles, London	£575	£1250
Quarter nobles, Calais	£625	£1500

Pinecone-mascle issue 1430-4
Nobles, London	£850	£2000
Half nobles, London	£1750	£5000
Quarter noble	£750	£1750

Henry VI quarter noble, leaf-mascle

Leaf-mascle issue 1434-5
Nobles	£1850	£4750
Half nobles	£2000	£5000
Quarter nobles	£825	£1850

Leaf-trefoil issue 1435-8
Nobles	£2000	£5000
Quarter noble	£950	£1850

Trefoil issue 1438-43
Nobles	£2250	£6000

Henry VI Gold Noble, Pinecone-mascle, London

Leaf-pellet issue 1445-54
Nobles	£2250	£6000

Cross-pellet issue 1454-60
Nobles	£2500	£6500

EDWARD IV 1st reign 1461-70
Heavy coinage 1461-64/5
Nobles (108grs)	£2500	£6000
Quarter noble		ext. rare

Edward IV noble, heavy coinage

Light coinage 1464-70   F   VF
Ryals or rose nobles (120grs),
  London £575   £1300
  Flemish copy £375   £750

Edward IV Light Coinage 1464-70, Ryal, York

	F	VF
Ryals, Bristol (B in waves)	£625	£1500
Ryals, Coventry (C in waves))	£1250	£2750
Ryals, Norwich (N in waves)	£1350	£3000
Ryals, York (E in waves)	£625	£1500
Half ryals, London	£425	£1000
Half ryals, Bristol (B in waves) ...	£675	£1500
Half ryals, Coventry (C in waves) ...	£2750	£7000
Half ryals Norwich (N in waves) ...	£2350	£6000
Half ryals, York (E in waves)	£425	£1000
Quarter ryals	£300	£625
Angels	£4250	*

Edward IV angel, first reign

	F	VF
HENRY VI (restored) 1470-71		
Angels, London	£1000	£2500
Angels, Bristol (B in waves)	£1350	£4000
Half angels, London	£2000	£5000
Half angels, Bristol (B in waves) ...	£3250	*
EDWARD IV 2nd reign 1471-83		
Angels, London	£475	£950
Angels, Bristol (B in waves)	£1750	£4000
Half angels, some varieties	£425	£900
EDWARD IV or V 1483		
mm halved sun and rose		
Angels	£1250	£5000
Half angels	£2500	*
RICHARD III 1483-85		
Angel, reading **EDWARD**, *mm* boar's		
head on obverse, halved sun and		
rose on reverse	£4250	£10000
Angels, reading **RICHARD or RICAD** ...	£1750	£4000
Half angels	£4000	*

Gold Angel, mm boar's head on obverse, and halved sun and rose on reverse

The Tudor Monarchs

Henry VII sovereign

HENRY VII 1485-1509	F	VF
Sovereigns of 20 shillings (all ext.		
rare) from	£10000	£25000
Ryals	£8500	£22500
Angels, varieties, different *mm* from	£450	£1000
Half angels	£425	£900

HAMMERED GOLD

Henry VII 1485-1509, Angel with Mint Mark pheon

HENRY VIII 1509-47

First coinage 1509-26

	F	VF
Sovereigns of 20 shillings *mm*		
crowned portcullis only	£4750	£13500
Angels (6s 8d) ... ... from	£450	£1000
Half angels	£425	£900

Second coinage 1526-44

Sovereigns of 22s 6d, various *mm* ...	£4500	£12500
Angels (7s 6d)	£575	£1500
Half angels *mm* lis	£750	£1750
George-nobles *mm* rose	£3750	£10000
Half-George noble	£7500	*
Crowns of the rose *mm* rose	£5000	*
Crowns of the double-rose		
HK (Henry and Katherine of Aragon)	£425	£950
HA (Henry and Anne Boleyn) ...	£750	£2000
HI (Henry and Jane Seymour) ...	£475	£1200
HR (HENRICUS REX)	£450	£1000
Halfcrowns of the double-rose		
HK	£400	£900
HI	£525	£1250
HR	£625	£1350

Third coinage 1544-47

Sovereigns of 20s, London ... from	£2750	£7500
Sovereigns of 20s, Southwark	£2650	£7250
Sovereigns of 20s, Bristol	£3750	£10000
Half sovereigns, London	£625	£1500
Half sovereigns, Southwark	£650	£1500
Half sovereigns, Bristol	£825	£2250

Henry VIII Angel, 3rd coinage with mint mark lis (shown slightly enlarged)

Angels	£450	£900
Half angels	£425	£900
Quarter angels	£400	£850
Crowns, HENRIC 8, London	£450	£1000
Crowns, Southwark	£525	£1200
Crowns, Bristol	£450	£1000

	F	VF
Halfcrowns, London	£350	£850
Halfcrowns, Southwark	£375	£900
Halfcrowns, Bristol	£450	£1000

EDWARD VI 1547-53

Posthumous coinage in name of Henry VIII (1547-51)

Sovereigns, London	£4250	£10000
Sovereigns, Bristol	£4750	£12000
Half sovereigns, London	£525	£1500
Half sovereigns, Southwark	£500	£1400
Crowns, London	£475	£1200
Crowns, Southwark	£500	£1250
Halfcrowns, London	£450	£1000
Halfcrowns, Southwark	£425	£900

Coinage in Edward's own name
First period 1547-49

Half sovereigns, Tower, read EDWARD 6	£1350	£3500

Edward VI sovereign, posthumous coinage (not actual size)

Half sovereigns, Southwark	£1250	£3250
Crown	£2500	*
Halfcrowns	£2000	*

Second period 1549-50

Sovereigns	£2750	£8000
Half sovereigns, uncrowned bust		
London	£3000	*
Half sovereigns, SCUTUM on obv. ...	£1000	£2750
Half sovereigns, Durham House		
MDXL VII	£4500	*
Half sovereigns, crowned bust,		
London	£1100	£3000
Half sovereigns, half-length bust,		
Durham House	£4500	*
Crowns, uncrowned bust	£1000	£2750
Crowns, crowned bust	£900	£2350
Halfcrowns, uncrowned bust	£1000	£2500
Halfcrowns, crowned bust	£900	£2250

Edward VI fine sovereign of 30s third period with mint mark ostrich head

*Edward VI Sovereign of
20 Shillings. Third Period*

Third period 1550-53

	F	VF
'Fine' sovereigns of 30s, king enthroned	£12500	£30000
Sovereigns of 20s, half-length figure ...	£2000	£5500
Half sovereigns, similar to last	£1250	£3000
Crowns, similar but SCUTUM on rev ...	£1100	£2750
Halfcrowns, similar	£1350	£3250
Angels	£4750	£15000
Half angel		ext. rare

MARY 1553-4

	F	VF
Sovereigns, different dates, some undated, some *mms*	£2750	£6750
Ryals, dated MDUI (1553)	£8500	£22500
Angels, *mm* pomegranate	£1000	£2500
Half angels	£2750	£6250

Mary Gold Sovereign of 1553

PHILIP AND MARY 1554-8	F	VF
Angels, *mm* lis	£2500	£6500
Half angels	£6000	*

Philip and Mary angel

Elizabeth I 1558-1603
Hammered issues

	F	VF
'Fine' sovereigns of 30s, different issues from	£2500	£6250
Ryals	£5500	£15000
Angels, different issues	£575	£1500
Half angels	£550	£1300
Quarter angels	£525	£1200

Elizabeth I quarter angel

	F	VF
Pounds of 20 shillings, different mint marks from	£1350	£3500
Half pounds, different issues	£950	£2500
Crowns —	£825	£1850
Halfcrowns —	£750	£1750

Elizabeth I hammered halfcrown

Milled issues

	F	VF
Half pounds, one issue but different marks	£1850	£5000
Crowns —	£1500	£4500
Halfcrowns —	£1850	£5500

The Stuart Kings

James I gold Spur-ryal

JAMES I 1603-25

1st coinage 1603-4	F	VF
Sovereigns of 20 shillings two bust	£1250	£3000
Half sovereigns	£2250	£6000
Crowns	£1500	£4000
Halfcrowns	£675	£1500

2nd coinage 1604-19		
Rose-ryals of 30 shillings	£1500	£4000
Spur-ryals of 15 shillings	£2750	£7500
Angels	£750	£1750
Half angels	£2000	£5000
Unites, different busts	£450	£925
Double crowns —	£325	£750
Britain crowns —	£225	£500

James I Rose-ryal of 30 shillings

Halfcrowns —	£175	£375
Thistle crowns, varieties	£225	£550

James I Thistle crown

3rd coinage 1619-25

Rose-ryals, varieties	£2000	£5250
Spur-ryals	£2750	£7500
Angels	£1000	£2500
Laurels, different busts	£425	£900
Half Laurels	£350	£750
Quarter laurels	£200	£475

James I laurel

CHARLES I 1625-49
Tower Mint 1625-42
Initial marks: lis, cross calvary, negro's head, castle, anchor, heart, plume, rose, harp, portcullis, bell, crown, tun, triangle, star, triangle in circle

Charles I Unite, Tower Mint, 1625-43

Angels, varieties	£1750	£4000
Angels, pierced as touchpieces	£725	£1650
Unites –	£475	£1000
Double Crowns –	£375	£800
Crowns –	£200	£400

Charles I Double Crown, Tower Mint with mint mark heart

Tower Mint under Parliament 1642-9 F VF
Initial marks: (P), (R), eye, sun, sceptre

	F	VF
Unites, varieties	£750	£1750
Double crowns –	£575	£1250
Crowns –	£325	£700

Briot's milled issues 1631-2
Initial marks: anemone and **B**, daisy and **B**, **B**

Angels	£3250	£8000
Unites	£1750	£5000
Double crowns	£1350	£3750
Crowns	£2000	*

Coins of provincial mints
Bristol 1645

Unites	£10000	*
Half unites		ext. rare

Chester 1644

Unites	£12500	*

Exeter 1643-44

Unites	£12500	*

Oxford 1642-46

Triple unites, from	£4500	£10000
Unites from	£1250	£3000
Half unites from	£1000	£2750

Truro 1642-43

Half unites		ext. rare

Shrewsbury 1644

Triple unites and unites		ext. rare

Worcester 1643-44

Unites		ext. rare

Charles I Oxford triple unite, 1643

HAMMERED GOLD

Siege pieces 1645-49	F	VF
Pontefract besieged 1648-49		
Unites **(F)**		ext. rare

Commonwealth 1650 gold unite

COMMONWEALTH 1649-60

Unites *im* sun	£900	£2250
– *im* anchor	£2250	£5000
Double crowns *im* sun	£700	£1500
– *im* anchor	£2000	£4500
Crowns *im* sun	£600	£1300
– *im* anchor	£2000	£5000

Commonwealth crown

CHARLES II 1660-85
Hammered Coinage 1660-62

Charles II gold unite

Unites, two issues from	£1100	£2750
Double crowns –	£900	£2250
Crowns –	£950	£2250

SILVER COINS

In this section column headings are mainly F (Fine) and VF (Very Fine), but for pennies of the early Plantagenets - a series in which higher-grade coins are seldom available - prices are shown under the headings Fair and F. Again it should be noted that throughout the section prices are approximate, for the commonest types only, and are the amounts collectors can expect to pay - not dealers' buying prices. Descriptions of some early Anglo-Saxon coins are, of necessity, brief because of pressure on space. Descriptions such as 'cross/moneyer's name' indicate that a cross appears on the obverse and the moneyer's name on the reverse. For more details see Standard Catalogue of British Coins published by Spink and Son Ltd., and English Hammered Coins, Volumes 1 and 2 by J. J. North, published by Spink and Son Ltd.. (A new edition of Volume 2 was published in 1991 and a new edition of Volume 1 was published in 1994).

Anglo-Saxon Sceats and Stycas

Examples of Sceats

	F	VF
EARLY PERIOD c 600-750		
Silver sceats ... ...from	£50	£150

A fascinating series with great variation of styles of early art. Large numbers of types and varieties.

	F	VF
NORTHUMBRIAN KINGS c 737-867		
Silver sceats c 737-796 ...from	£90	£250
Copper stycas c 810-867 ...from	£20	£40

Struck for many kings. Numerous moneyers and different varieties. The copper styca is the commonest coin in the Anglo-Saxon series.

ARCHBISHOPS OF YORK c 732-900		
Silver sceats ... ...from	£75	£185
Copper stycas ... ...from	£20	£50

From here onwards until the reign of Edward I all coins are silver pennies unless otherwise stated

Kings of Kent

	F	VF
HEABERHT c 764		
Monogram/cross		ext. rare

One moneyer (EOBA).

ECGBERHT c 765-780		
Monogram/cross	£950	£2500

Two moneyers (BABBA and UDD)

EADBERHT PRAEN 797-798		
EADBERHT REX/moneyer	£1000	£3500

Three moneyers

Penny of Eadberht Praen

	F	VF
CUTHRED 789-807		
Non-portrait, various designs from	£600	£1500
Bust right	£625	£1600
Different moneyers, varieties etc.		
BALDRED c 825		
Bust right	£900	£3000
Cross/cross	£675	£1750
different types and moneyers		

Baldred penny, bust right

ANONYMOUS c 823		
Bust right	£750	£2250
Different varieties and moneyers.		

Archbishops of Canterbury

	F	VF
JAENBERHT 766-792		
Various types (non-portrait) from	£850	£2500
AETHELHEARD 793-805		
Various types (non-portrait) from	£800	£2000
WULFRED 805-832		
Various groups (portrait types) from	£675	£1850
CEOLNOTH 833-870		
Various groups (portrait types) from	£525	£1250

Ceolnoth penny

AETHERED 870-889
Various types (portrait, non-portrait)

	F	VF
	£1500	£5000

PLEGMUND 890-914
Various types (all non-portrait) from

	F	VF
	£575	£1500

Kings of Mercia

Offa portrait penny

OFFA 757-796

	F	VF
Non-portrait from	£425	£1000
Portrait from	£850	£2500
Many types and varieties		

Cynethryth (wife of Offa) portrait penny

CYNETHRYTH (wife of Offa)

Portraits	£1750	£5500
Non-portrait	£950	£2750

COENWULF 796-821
Various types (portrait, non-portrait) from

	£425	£900

Coenwulf portrait penny

CEOLWULF 1821-823
Various types (portrait) ... ...

	£700	£1750

BEORNWULF 823-825
Various types (portrait) ... ...

	£825	£2250

Beornwulf penny

LUDICA 825-827
Two types (portrait) (F) ... ...

	£2750	£7500

WIGLAF 827-829, 830-840
Two groups (portrait, non-portrait)

	£1850	£5250

BERHTWULF 840-852
Two groups
(portrait, non-portrait) ... ...

	£825	£2500

Berhtwulf penny

BURGRED 852-874
One type (portrait), five variants

	F	VF
	£150	£325

CEOLWULF II 874-c 877
Two types (portrait)) ... ...

	£1750	£5000

Kings of East Anglia

BEONNA c 758
Silver sceat ... ...

	F	VF
	£475	£1000

AETHELBERHT LUL (died 794)
Portrait type (F) ... ...

	ext. rare

Eadwald penny

EADWALD c 796
Non-portrait types ... ...

	F	VF
	£800	£2500

AETHELSTAN I c 850
Various types (portrait, non-portrait) ... ...

	£325	£850

AETHELWEARD c 850
Non-portrait types ... ...

	£450	£1200

EADMUND 855-870
Non-portrait types ... ...

	£250	£600

Viking Invaders 878-954

ALFRED
Imitations of Alfred pennies and halfpennies from
(Many different types, portrait and non portrait)

	F	VF
	£325	£750

ANGLIA
AETHELSTAN II 878-890
Cross/moneyer ... ...

	£1000	£3000

OSWALD (Unknown in history except from coins)
A/cross ... ...

	£1350	£4000

ST EADMUND
Memorial coinage, various legends etc. ... ...

	£100	£250

Many moneyers.
Halfpenny, similar ... ...

	£425	£1000

HAMMERED SILVER

St Eadmund memorial penny

ST MARTIN OF LINCOLN c 925

	F	VF
Sword/cross	£1750	£5000

AETHELRED c 870

Temple/cross	£1500	£4000

YORK
SIEVERT-SIEFRED-CNUT c 897

Crosslet/small cross	£110	£225
Many different groups and varieties		
Halfpenny, similar	£425	£900

EARL SIHTRIC (unknown)

Non-portrait	£1750	£5000

REGNALD c 919-921

Various types, some blundered	£1500	£4250

SIHTRIC I 921-927

Sword/cross	£1750	£5000

ANLAF GUTHFRITHSSON 939-941

Raven/cross	£1750	£5000
Cross/cross	£1650	£4500
Flower/cross	£1850	£5250

ANLAF SIHTRICSSON 941-944, 948-952

Various types	£1450	£4000

SIHTRIC II c 942-943

Shield/standard	£1500	£4500

REGNALD II c 941-943

Cross/cross	£1750	£5000
Shield/standard	£1850	£5250

ERIC BLOODAXE 948, 952-954

Cross/moneyer	£2350	£7000
Sword/cross	£2500	£7500

St Peter of York halfpenny

ST PETER OF YORK c 905-927

Various types ... ...from	£200	£500
Halfpenny, similar	£625	£1500

Kings of Wessex

BEORHTRIC 786-802

	F	VF
Two types (non-portrait)		ext. rare

ECGBERHT 802-839

FOUR GROUPS (portrait, non-portrait)	£875	£2850
Mints of Canterbury, London, Rochester, Winchester		

Aethelwulf Portrait Penny, Canterbury

AETHELWULF 839-858

	F	VF
Four phases (portrait, non-portrait)	£325	£850
from Mints of Canterbury, Rochester (?)		

AETHELBERHT 858-866

Two types (portrait) ... ...from	£325	£850
Many moneyers.		

AETHELRED I 865-871

Portrait types ... ...from	£350	£900
Many moneyers.		

ALFRED THE GREAT 871-899

Portrait in style of Aethelred I ...	£425	£1000
Four other portrait types commonest being those		
with the London monogram reverse	£900	£2350
Halfpennies	£425	£900

Alfred the Great Penny, London monogram on reverse

Non-portrait types ... ...from	£375	£750
Many different styles of lettering etc.		
Halfpennies	£375	£750

EDWARD THE ELDER 899-924
Non-portrait types:

Cross/moneyer's name in two lines	£200	£450
Halfpennies as previous	£750	£1750

Rare penny of Edward the Elder with building on reverse

Portrait types:

Bust/moneyer's name	£625	£1650
Many types, varieties and moneyers.		
Types featuring buildings, floral		
designs, etc	£1250	£4000
Many types, varieties and moneyers.		

Kings of all England

AETHELSTAN 924-39 ... ...   F   VF

Aethelstan 924-939, Penny, building type reverse

Non-portrait types:
Cross/moneyer's name in two lines	£225	£525
Cross/cross	£275	£650

Portrait types:
bust/moneyer's name in two lines	£675	£2000
Bust/small cross	£550	£1400

Many other issues, some featuring buildings as illustrated above. There are also different mints and moneyer's names.

Aethelstan portrait penny with small cross on reverse

EADMUND 939-46
Non-portrait types:
Cross or rosette/moneyer's name in two lines	£225	£600
Silver halfpenny, similar	£700	£1500

Eadmund penny, two-line type

Portrait types:
Crowned bust/small cross	£550	£1400
Helmeted bust/cross crosslet ...	£850	£2500

Many other issues and varieties; also different mint names and moneyers.

EADRED 946-55
Non-portrait types:
Cross/moneyer's name in two lines	£200	£450
Silver halfpenny similar	£600	£1350
Rosette/moneyer's name	£275	£650

HAMMERED SILVER

Eadred penny, portrait type

Portrait types: F   VF
Crowned bust/small cross	£525	£1300

Again many variations and mint names and moneyers.

HOWEL DDA (King of Wales), died c948
Small cross/moneyer's name in two lines (GILLYS)	ext. rare

EADWIG 955-59
Non-portrait types:
Cross/moneyer's name ... from	£300	£700

Many variations, some rare.
Silver halfpennies, similar	£900	£2250

Portrait types:
Bust/cross ... ... from	£2250	£7000

EADGAR 959-75
Non-portrait types:
Cross/moneyer's name ... from	£150	£350
Cross/cross ... ... from	£150	£350
Rosette/rosette ... ... from	£225	£525
Halfpennies ... ... from	£900	£2500

Eadgar, 959-957, Non Portrait Penny, Winchester

Portrait types
Pre-Reform	£675	£1750
Halfpenny, diademed bust/London monogram	£700	£1750
Reform (c.972)	£750	£1750

Many other varieties.

EDWARD THE MARTYR 975-78
Portrait types:
Bust left/small cross	£800	£1850

Many different mints and moneyers.

AETHELRED II 978-1016

Aethelred II 978-1016, Penny, Last small cross type

First small cross ... ... from	£425	£1000
First hand ... ... from	£110	£275
Second hand ... ... from	£100	£250
Benediction hand ... ... from	£675	£1800

HAMMERED SILVER

CRUX ... ... from	F £90	VF £185

Aethelred II CRUX type penny

Aethelred II, Long Cross penny

Long Cross	£100	£200
Helmet	£110	£250
Agnus Dei	£3500	*

Other issues and varieties, many mint names and moneyers.

Aethelred II long cross penny

CNUT 1016-35

Quatrefoil ... ... from	£85	£175

Cnut quatrefoil type penny

Pointed helmet ... ... from	£75	£140

Cnut pointed helmet type penny

Small cross ... ... from	£70	£125
Jewel cross ... ... from	£425	£975

Other types, and many different mint names and moneyers.

HAROLD I 1035-40

Jewel cross ... ... from	£225	£550

	F	VF
Long cross with trefoils ... from	£200	£500
Long cross with fleurs-de-lis from	£200	£500

Many different mint names and moneyers.

HARTHACNUT 1035-42

Jewel cross, bust left	£850	£2500
– bust right	£800	£2250
Arm and sceptre types	£725	£1750
Different mint names and moneyers.		
Scandinavian types struck at Lund	£225	£550

EDWARD THE CONFESSOR 1042-66

PACX type ... ... from	£150	£375
Radiate crown/small cross from	£80	£185
Trefoil quadrilateral	£90	£200
Small flan ... ... from	£70	£160
Expanding cross types ... from	£90	£220

Edward the Confessor Penny, Expanding Cross Type

Helmet types	£100	£235
Sovereign/eagles	£100	£235
Hammer cross	£90	£200

Edward the Confessor Hammer Cross Penny

Bust facing	£85	£185
Cross and piles	£85	£185
Large bust, facing, with sceptre	£975	£3000

Other issues, including a unique gold penny; many different mint names and moneyers.

HAROLD II 1066

Crowned head left with sceptre	£525	£1050

Harold II Penny, bust left with sceptre

Similar but no sceptre	£600	£1350

Harold II, bust left, without sceptre

Crowned head right with sceptre	£1350	£4000

The Norman Kings

WILLIAM I 1066-87

		F	VF
Profile/cross fleury	...from	£250	£600
Bonnet	...from	£200	£400
Canopy	...from	£300	£700
Two sceptres	...from	£225	£525
Two stars	...from	£185	£400
Sword	...from	£300	£700

William I profile/cross fleury penny

		F	VF
Profile/cross and trefoils	...from	£350	£850
PAXS	...from	£185	£400

WILLIAM II 1087-1100

William II, cross voided type penny

		F	VF
Profile	...from	£550	£1250
Cross in quatrefoil	...from	£475	£1000
Cross voided	...from	£475	£1000
Cross pattee over fleury	...from	£525	£1200
Cross fleury and piles	...from	£550	£1350

Henry I penny; small bust/cross and annulets

HENRY I 1100-1135

		F	VF
Annulets	...from	£400	£900
Profile/cross fleury	...from	£275	£700
PAX	...from	£275	£675
Annulets and piles	...from	£325	£800
Voided cross and fleurs	...from	£650	£1650
Pointing bust and stars	...from	£950	£2500
Quatrefoil and piles	...from	£325	£800
Profile/cross and annulets	from	£1350	£3000
Cross in quatrefoil	...from	£625	£1500

Henry I, full face/cross fleury penny

HAMMERED SILVER

	F	VF
Full face/cross fleury	£200	£475
Double inscription	£575	£1350
Small bust/cross and annulets	£425	£1000
Star in lozenge fleury	£400	£900
Pellets in quatrefoil	£200	£500
Quadrilateral on cross fleury	£150	£350
Halfpennies	£1500	£3000

STEPHEN 1135-54

		F	VF
Cross moline (Watford)	...from	£200	£525

Stephen 'Watford' Penny

	F	VF
Cross moline PERERIC	£525	£1350
Voided cross and mullets	£225	£575

Stephen Penny, voided cross pattée with mullets

	F	VF
Profile/cross fleury	£350	£900
Voided cross pommée (Awbridge)	£225	£575

There are also a number of irregular issues produced during the Civil War, all of which are very rare. These include several extremely rare and attractive pieces bearing the names of Empress Matilda and barons, such as Eustace Fitzjohn and Robert de Stuteville.

The Plantagenet Kings

HENRY II 1154-89

	Fair	F

Henry II Cross and Crosslets (Tealby) Penny

	Fair	F
Cross and crosslets ('Tealby' coinage)	£100	£250

The issue is classified by bust variants into six groups, struck at 32 mints.

Henry II Short Cross Penny 1b

HAMMERED SILVER

	F	VF
Short cross pennies	£50	£125

The 'short cross' coinage was introduced in 1180 and continued through successive reigns until Henry III brought about a change in 1247. HENRICVS REX appears on all these coins but they can be classified into reigns by the styles of the busts and lettering. We recommend a copy of C.R. Wren's illustrated guide The Short Cross Coinage 1180-1247, *as the best guide to identification.*

Richard I, 1189-1199, Short Cross Penny

RICHARD I 1189-99		
Short cross pennies	£65	£150
JOHN 1199-1216		
Short cross pennies	£50	£125

John Short Cross Penny

HENRY III 1216-72		
Short cross pennies	£25	£50
Long cross pennies no sceptre	£25	£50
Long cross pennies with sceptre	£20	£45

Henry III, Long Cross Penny, no sceptre

Henry III, Long Cross Penny with sceptre

The 'long cross' pennies, first introduced in 1247, are divided into two groups: those with sceptre and those without. They also fall into five basic classes, with many varieties. We recommend C.R. Wren's, The Voided Long Cross Coinage, 1247-79 *as the best guide to identification.*

Edward I, 1st coinage, Long Cross penny

	F	VF
EDWARD I 1272-1307		
1st coinage 1272-78		
Long cross pennies ... ...from	£25	£65

similar in style to those of Henry III but with more realistic beard.

Edward I Penny, London

New coinage 1278-1307		
Groats	£1500	£5500
Pennies, various classes, mints from	£20	£45
Halfpennies – ... ...from	£25	£60
Farthings – ... ...from	£25	£60

Edward I Farthing, London

Any new collector wishing to become serious about this area should obtain a copy of Edwardian English Silver Coins 1279-1351. Sylloge of coins of the British Isles 39 (The JJ North collection)

EDWARD II 1307-27		
Pennies, various classes, mints from	£25	£60
Halfpennies ... ...from	£50	£125
Farthings ... ...from	£35	£80
EDWARD III 1327-77		
1st and 2nd coinages 1327-43		
Pennies (only 1st coinage) various types and mints	£225	£525
Halfpennies, different types and mints	£20	£50
Farthings	£30	£75
3rd coinage 1344-51 (Florin Coinage)		
Pennies, various types and mints	£25	£75
Halfpennies –	£20	£45
Farthings	£30	£70

Edward III 1327-77, Groat Treaty Period

4th coinage 1351-77

	F	VF
Groats, many types and mints from	£50	£160

Edward III halfgroat Post-Treaty

	F	VF
Halfgroats –	£35	£100
Pennies –	£20	£65
Halfpennies, different types ...	£30	£85
Farthings, a few types	£90	£250

Henry IV halfpenny

RICHARD II 1377-99

	F	VF
Groats, four types from	£350	£1000

Henry VI Annulet issue halfgroat

	F	VF
Halfgroats	£275	£800
Pennies, various types, London	£225	£550
Pennies, various types, York ...	£60	£225
Pennies, Durham	£150	£475
Halfpennies, three main types ...	£30	£85
Farthings, some varieties	£100	£300

HENRY IV 1399-1413

	F	VF
Groats, varieties ... ...from	£1350	£5000
Halfgroats –	£450	£1000
Pennies –	£225	£650
Halfpennies	£175	£450
Farthings –	£650	£1750

Henry V Groat

HAMMERED SILVER

HENRY V 1413-22

	F	VF
Groats, varieties ... ...from	£125	£400
Halfgroats	£100	£300
Pennies	£35	£90
Halfpennies	£25	£80
Farthings	£150	£500

HENRY VI 1422-61
Annulet issue 1422-1427

	F	VF
Groats	£40	£100
Halfgroats	£30	£85
Pennies	£20	£75
Halfpennies	£20	£45
Farthings	£100	£225

Rosette-Mascle issue 1427-1430

	F	VF
Groats	£40	£110
Halfgroats	£35	£90
Pennies	£35	£90
Halfpennies	£20	£50
Farthings	£135	£350

Pinecone-Mascle 1430-1434

	F	VF
Groats	£40	£100
Halfgroats	£35	£90
Pennies	£30	£90
Halfpennies	£20	£50
Farthings	£135	£350

Leaf-Mascle issue 1434-1435

	F	VF
Groats	£110	£300
Halfgroats	£100	£275
Pennies	£65	£150
Halfpennies	£30	£75

Leaf-Trefoil 1435-1438

	F	VF
Groats	£70	£180
Halfgroats	£65	£150
Pennies	£60	£150
Halfpennies	£25	£60
Farthings	£125	£350

Trefoil 1438-1443

	F	VF
Groats	£85	£250
Halfgroats	£150	£350
Halfpennies	£25	£70

Trefoil-Pellet 1443-1445

	F	VF
Groats	£135	£350

Henry VI Groat, Leaf-Pellet issue

Leaf-Pellet 1445-1454

	F	VF
Groats	£65	£175
Halfgroats	£70	£175
Pennies	£40	£100
Halfpennies	£20	£50
Farthings	£150	£375

HAMMERED SILVER

Unmarked 1445-1454	F	VF
Groats	£425	£1000
Halfgroats	£325	£700

Cross-Pellet 1454-1460

Groats	£100	£275
Halfgroats	£275	£650
Pennies	£45	£110
Halfpennies	£30	£80
Farthings	£150	£425

Lis-Pellet 1454-1460

Groats	£225	£625

These are many different varieties, mintmarks and mints in this reign. These prices are for commonest prices in each issue.

EDWARD IV 1st Reign 1461-1470
Heavy coinage 1461-4

Groats, many classes, all London	£150	£350
Halfgroats, many classes, all London	£225	£500
Pennies, different classes. London,		
York and Durham	£135	£350
Halfpennies, different classes,		
all London	£40	£100
Farthings. London	£225	£600

Edward IV Groat. Light Coinage

Light coinage 1464-70

Groats, many different issues, varieties, *mms* and mints from	£45	£135
Halfgroats, ditto	£40	£125
Pennies, ditto	£30	£80
Halfpennies, ditto	£25	£70
Farthings Two issues	£250	£600

Henry VI (restored), Groat, London

HENRY VI (restored) 1470-71

Groats, different mints, *mms* from	£135	£400
Halfgroats – from	£225	£525
Pennies – from	£250	£550
Halfpennies – from	£90	£225

EDWARD IV 2nd reign 1471-83	F	VF
Groats, different varieties, mints etc	£60	£150
Halfgroats	£35	£100
Pennies	£30	£80
Halfpennies	£25	£75

EDWARD IV or V 1483
mm halved sun and rose

Groats	£750	£2250
Pennies	£850	£2750
Halfpennies	£150	£475

RICHARD III 1483-85

Groat, reading **EDWARD,** *mm* boar's head on obverse, halved sun and rose on reverse	£1350	£3250
Groats, reading **RICARD,** London and York mints, various combinations of mms	£425	£1050
Halfgroats	£675	£1500
Pennies, York and Durham (London mint unique)	£150	£400
Halfpennies	£135	£350
Farthing	£850	£2500

PERKIN WARBECK, PRETENDER'

Groat, 1494 [cf. BNJ XXVI, p. 125]	£950	£3000

The Tudor Monarchs

HENRY VII 1485-1509
Facing bust issues:

Henry VII Groat London open crown type

Groats, all London

Open crown without arches ...	£110	£325
Crown with two arches unjewelled	£80	£175
Crown with two jewelled arches	£65	£150
Similar but only one arch jewelled	£55	£140
Similar but tall thin lettering ...	£60	£150
Similar but single arch, tall thin lettering	£70	£175
Halfgroats, London		
Open crown without arches, tressure unbroken	£250	£650
Double arched crown	£40	£110

	F	VF
Unarched crown	£35	£90
Some varieties and different *mms.*		
Halfgroats, Canterbury		
Open crown, without arches ...	£40	£100
Double arched crown	£35	£85
Some varieties and different *mms.*		
Halfgroats, York		
Double arched crown	£40	£110
Unarched crown with tressure		
broken	£40	£100
Double arched crown with keys		
at side of bust	£35	£95
Many varieties and different mms.		
Pennies, facing bust type		
London	£150	£425
Canterbury, open crown	£225	£500
– arched crown	£60	£150
Durham, Bishop Sherwood		
(S on breast)	£60	£150
York	£40	£110
Many varieties and mms.		
Pennies, 'sovereign enthroned' type		
London, many varieties	£40	£110
Durham –	£40	£95
York –	£35	£90
Halfpennies, London		
Open crown	£45	£125
Arched crown	£30	£80
Crown with lower arch	£25	£65
Some varieties and mms.		
Halfpennies, Canterbury		
Open crown	£70	£175
Arched crown	£60	£125
Halfpennies, York		
Arched crown and key below bus	£65	£150
Farthings, all London	£175	£600
Profile issues:		
Testoons im lis, three different		
legends	£5500	£13500

Henry VII profile issue testoon

Groats, all London		
Tentative issue (double band to		
crown)	£175	£525

Henry VII Groat, Tentative issue

HAMMERED SILVER

	F	VF
Regular issue (triple band to		
crown)	£110	£325
Some varieties, and *mms*		
Halfgroats		
London	£90	£275
– no numeral after king's name	£425	£900
Canterbury	£70	£200
York, two keys below shield ...	£65	£180
– XB by shield	£300	£800

HENRY VIII 1509-47
With portrait of Henry VII
1st coinage 1509-26

	F	VF
Groats, London	£110	£325
Groats, Tournai	£450	£1200
Groats, Tournai, without portrait	£1750	*
Halfgroats, London	£100	£275
Halfgroats, Canterbury, varieties	£70	£165
Halfgroats, York, varieties	£65	£160
Halfgroats, Tournai	£700	£2000
Pennies, 'sovereign enthroned'		
type, London	£50	£135
Pennies, Canterbury, varieties ...	£65	£185
Pennies, Durham, varieties ...	£40	£100
Halfpennies, facing bust type,		
London	£25	£70
Canterbury	£70	£175
Farthings, portcullis type, London	£250	£600

Henry VIII second coinage groat,
with Irish title HIB REX

With young portrait of Henry VIII
2nd coinage 1526-44

	F	VF
Groats, London, varieties, *mms*	£85	£250
Groats, Irish title, HIB REX	£300	£800
Groats, York *mms*	£90	£275
Halfgroats, London *mms*	£50	£125
Halfgroats, Canterbury *mms* ...	£45	£125
Halfgroats, York *mms*	£45	£120
Pennies 'sovereign enthroned' type		
London, varieties, *mms*	£35	£120
Canterbury, varieties, *mms* ...	£75	£225
Durham –	£35	£110
York	£175	£525

Henry VIII, Halfpenny, 2nd Coinage, London

	F	VF
Halfpennies, facing bust type		
London, varieties, *mms*	£25	£75
Canterbury	£40	£100
York	£65	£175
Farthings, portcullis type	£300	£700

With old bearded portrait 3rd coinage 1544-47 Posthumous issues 1547-51	F	VF
Testoons (or shillings) London (Tower mint), varieties, *mms*	£675	£2350
Southwark, varieties, *mms* ...	£700	£2500
Bristol, varieties, *mms*	£825	£3000
Groats, six different busts, varieties, *mms*		
London (Tower mint)	£90	£300
Southwark	£90	£300
Bristol	£100	£325
Canterbury	£80	£275
London (Durham House)	£200	£550
York	£75	£225

Henry VIII third coinage groat

Halfgroats, only one style of bust (except York which has two), varieties, mms		
London (Tower mint)	£70	£200
Southwark	£75	£225
Bristol	£75	£250
Canterbury	£50	£150
York	£60	£185
London (Durham House)	£375	£900

Henry VIII Penny, 3rd Coinage Tower

Henry VIII Penny, 3rd Coinage, Bristol

Pennies (facing bust) varieties, mms		
London (Tower mint)	£40	£125
Southwark	£50	£150
London (Durham House)	£450	£1200
Bristol	£60	£165
Canterbury	£40	£110
York	£40	£110
Halfpennies (facing bust) varieties, mms		
London (Tower mint)	£35	£100
Bristol	£75	£225
Canterbury	£45	£125
York	£40	£110

	F	VF
EDWARD VI 1547-53 **1st period 1547-49**		
Shillings, London (Durham House), mm bow, patterns (?)		ext. rare
Groats, London (Tower), mm arrow	£750	£2250
Groats, London (Southwark), mm E, none	£700	£2000
Halfgroats, London (Tower), mm arrow	£425	£1000
Halfgroats, London (Southwark), mm arrow, E	£400	£950
Halfgroats, Canterbury, mm none	£300	£700
Pennies, London (Tower), mm	£350	£1000
Pennies, London (Southwark), mm E	£375	£1100
Pennies, Bristol, mm none	£325	£900
Halfpennies, London (Tower), mm uncertain	£350	£900
Halfpennies, Bristol, mm none	£325	£850

Edward VI 2nd period shilling. Tower mint with mintmark Y.

Edward VI, Shilling, 2nd period Canterbury with mintmark t.

2nd period 1549-50		
Shillings, London (Tower) various mms	£135	£500
Shillings, Bristol, mm TC	£750	£2250
Shillings, Canterbury, mm T or t	£165	£600
Shillings, London (Durham House), mm bow, varieties	£150	£525
3rd period £550-53		
Base silver (similar to issues of 2nd period)		
Shillings, London (Tower), mm lis, lion, rose	£150	£525
Pennies, London (Tower), mm escallop	£65	£175
Pennies, York, mm mullet	£60	£175
Halfpennies, London (Tower) ...	£175	£500

Fine Silver   F   VF

Crown 1551 mm Y, 1551-53

mm tun **£650** **£1650**

Mary Groat

Edward VI Halfcrown 1551, walking horse

Halfcrown, walking horse, 1551,

mm Y **£525** **£1350**

Halfcrowns, galloping horse,

1551-52, mm tun **£525** **£1350**

Edward VI 1552 halfcrown galloping horse

Halfcrowns, walking horse, 1553,

mm tun **£1000** **£3500**

Shillings, mm Y, tun **£110** **£375**

Sixpences, London (Tower),

mm y, tun **£125** **£450**

Sixpences, York, mm mullet ... **£175** **£550**

Threepences, London (Tower),

mm tun **£185** **£600**

Threepences, York mm mullet ... **£400** **£1000**

Pennies, sovereign type **£1000** **£3250**

Farthings, portcullis type ... ... **£1250** *

           F   VF

Mary Portrait Penny

MARY 1553-54

Groats, mm pomegranate **£120** **£400**

Halfgroats, similar **£725** **£2250**

Pennies, rev VERITAS TEMP FILIA ... **£600** **£1750**

Pennies, rev CIVITAS LONDON **£600** **£1750**

PHILIP AND MARY 1554-58

Shillings, full titles, without date **£300** **£1000**

– also without XII **£325** **£1250**

– dated 1554 ... ... **£300** **£1100**

– dated 1554, English titles ... **£325** **£1200**

– dated 1555, English titles only **£300** **£1100**

– dated 1554, English titles only

also without XII **£400** **£1250**

– 1555, as last ... ... **£650** *

– 1554 but date below bust ... **£1350** *

– 1555 but date below bust ... **£1350** *

– 1555 similar to previous but

without ANG ... ... **£2000** *

Sixpences, full titles, 1554 ... ... **£325** **£1100**

– full titles, undated ... ... ext rare

– English titles, 1555 ... ... **£325** **£1200**

– similar but date below bust,

1554 ... ... **£650** *

– English titles, 1557 ... ... **£300** **£1100**

– similar, but date below bust,

1557 ... ... **£1000** *

Groats, *mm* lis **£100** **£400**

Halfgroats, *mm* lis **£375** **£1000**

Philip and Mary Shilling, 1554 and full titles

Pennies, *mm* lis **£375** **£1000**

Base pennies, without portrait **£75** **£225**

HAMMERED SILVER

ELIZABETH I 1558-1603	F	VF
Hammered coinage, 1st issue 1558-61		
Shillings ELIZABETH		
Wire-line circles	£400	£1450
Beaded inner circles	£135	£575
ET for Z	£85	£300

Edward VI shilling greyhound countermark (reign of Elizabeth), and Elizabeth I hammered groat

Groats		
Wire-line inner circles	£150	£550
Beaded inner circles	£70	£235
ET for Z	£50	£200
Halfgroats		
Wire-line inner circles	£150	£550
Beaded inner circles	£40	£125

Elizabeth I Penny, wire-line inner circle

Pennies		
Wire-line inner circles	£200	£700
Beaded inner circles	£30	£80
Countermarked shillings of		
Edward VI, 1560-61		
With portcullis mark		
(Current for 4½d) **(F)**	£1750	*
With greyhound mark		
(current for 2½d) **(F)**	£2250	*

Hammered coinage, 2nd issue 1561-82		
Sixpences, dated 1561-82	£60	£175
Threepences, 1561-82	£40	£125
Halfgroats, undated	£50	£165
Threehalfpences, 1561-62, 1564-70,		
1572-79, 1581-82	£40	£100
Pennies, undated	£25	£80
Threefarthings, 1561-62, 1568,		
1572-78, 1581-82	£75	£175

Elizabeth I Halfcrown, 1601

Hammered coinage, 3rd issue 1583-1603	F	VF
Crowns, im **1**	£1200	£3000
Crowns, im **2**	£1350	£4000
Halfcrowns, im **1**	£700	£1650
Halfcrowns, im **2 (F)**	£1500	£5250
Shillings ELIZAB	£85	£300
Sixpences, 1582-1602	£50	£165
Halfgroats, E D G ROSA etc	£25	£70
Pennies	£20	£70
Halfpennies, portcullis type ...	£25	£75

There are many different mintmarks, such as lis, bell, lion etc., featured on the hammered coins of Elizabeth I, and these marks enable one to date those coins which are not themselves dated. For more details see J.J. North's English Hammered Coinage, Volume 2.

Elizabeth I Miled Coinage, Sixpence, 1562

Milled Coinage		
Shillings		
large size	£325	£1000
Intermediate	£225	£600
Small	£200	£525
Sixpences		
1561	£80	£325
1562	£70	£275
1563-64, 1566	£80	£300
1567-68	£75	£275
1570-71	£275	£850
Groats, undated	£150	£500
Threepences, 1561, 1562-64 ...	£110	£350
Halfgroats	£175	£550
Threefarthings	ext.rare	*

The Stuart Kings

JAMES I 1603-25	F	VF
1st coinage 1603-04		
Crowns, rev EXURGAT etc	£850	£2500
Halfcrowns –	£950	£3250
Shillings, varieties	£85	£325
Sixpences, dated 1603-04,		
varieties	£60	£200
Halfgroats, undated	£25	£75
Pennies –	£20	£60

James I Sixpence, 1603

2nd coinage 1604-19		
Crowns rev QVAE DEVS etc ...	£750	£2250
Halfcrowns –	£1100	£3500

James I 2nd coinage shilling

Shillings, varieties	£75	£250
Sixpences, dated 1604-15,		
varieties etc.	£50	£175
Halfgroats, varieties	£20	£50
Pennies	£20	£50
Halfpennies	£15	£45

James I Shilling, 3rd Coinage

3rd coinage 1619-25		
Crowns	£525	£1250
– Plume over reverse shield ...	£750	£2000
Halfcrowns	£200	£675
– Plume over reverse shield ...	£350	£1000

James I halfcrown with plume over shield on reverse

	F	VF
Shillings	£80	£275
– Plume over reverse shield ...	£125	£650
Sixpences dated 1621-24	£50	£175
Halfgroats	£15	£45
Pennies	£15	£40
Halfpennies	£15	£35

James I sixpence of 1622

CHARLES I 1625-1649
Tower Mint 1625-1643

Crowns		
(Obv. King on horseback. Rev. shield)		
1st horseman/square shield		
im lis, cross calvary	£600	£1500
As last/plume above shield		
im lis, cross calvary, castle ...	£1000	£2750
2nd horseman/oval shield		
im plume, rose harp.		
Some varieties, from	£550	£1350
3rd horseman/round shield		
im bell, crown, tun, anchor,		
triangle, star, portcullis, triangle		
in circle. Some varieties, from	£550	£1350

Halfcrowns
(Obv. King on horseback. Rev. shield)

Charles I
Tower halfcrown:
first horseman

HAMMERED SILVER

	F	VF
1st horseman/square shield		
im lis, cross calvary, negro's head, castle, anchor.		
Many varieties, from	£175	£500
2nd horseman/oval shield		
im plume, rose, harp, portcullis.		
Many varieties, from	£100	£300
3rd horseman/round shield		
im bell, crown, tun, portcullis, anchor, triangle, star		
Many varieties, from	£75	£200
4th horseman/round shield		
im star, triangle in circle	£60	£150

*Charles I
Tower Halfcrown,
mintmark
triangle*

Shillings

	F	VF
1st bust/square shield		
im lis, cross calvary		
Some varieties	£90	£375
2nd bust/square shield		
im cross calvary, negro's head, castle, anchor, heart, plume		
Many varieties, from	£80	£325
3rd bust/oval shield		
im plume, rose	£60	£225
4th bust/oval or round shield		
im harp, portcullis, bell, crown, tun		
Many varieties, from	£50	£175
5th bust/square shield		
im tun, anchor, triangle		
Many varieties, from	£45	£175
6th bust/square shield		
im anchor, triangle, star, triangle in circle		
Some varieties, from	£40	£150

Sixpences
(early ones are dated)

	F	VF
1st bust/square shield, date above		
1625 *im* lis, cross calvary		
1626 *im* cross calvary	£90	£325
2nd bust/square shield, date above		
1625, 1626 *im* cross calvary		
1626, 1627 *im* negro's head		
1626, 1628 *im* castle		
1628, 1629 *im* anchor		
1629 *im* heart		
1630 *im* heart, plume	£100	£375

	F	VF
3rd bust/oval shield		
im plume, rose	£65	£225
4th bust/oval or round shield		
im harp, portcullis, bell, crown, tun	£45	£150

Charles I Tower sixpence mm bell

	F	VF
5th bust/square shield		
im tun, anchor, triangle		
Many varieties, from	£50	£185
6th bust/square shield		
im triangle, star	£45	£165
Halfgroats		
Crowned rose both sides		
im lis, cross calvary, blackamoor's head	£25	£70
2nd bust/oval shield		
im plume, rose	£25	£75
3rd bust/oval shield		
im rose, plume	£25	£75
4th bust/oval or round shield,		
im harp, crown, portcullis, bell, tun, anchor, triangle, star		
Many varieties from	£20	£50
5th bust/round shield		
im anchor	£30	£85
Pennies		
Uncrowned rose both sides		
im one or two pellets, lis, negro's head	£20	£50
2nd bust/oval shield		
im plume	£25	£70
3rd bust/oval shield		
im plume, rose	£20	£50
4th bust/round shield		
im harp, one or two pellets, portcullis, bell, triangle	£15	£45
5th bust/round shield		
im one or two pellets, none	£15	£45
Halfpennies		
Uncrowned rose both sides		
im none	£15	£40

Tower Mint, under Parliament 1643-48

	F	VF
Crowns		
(Obv. King on horseback, Rev. shield)		
4th horseman/round shield		
im (P), (R), eye sun	£650	£1500
5th horseman/round shield		
im sun, sceptre	£675	£1750
Halfcrowns		
(Obv. King on horseback, Rev. shield)		
3rd horseman/round shield		
im (P), (R), eye sun	£50	£200
im (P), foreshortened horse	£175	£525
5th horseman (tall)/round shield		
im sun, sceptre	£75	£225

Charles I Parliament shilling, mm eye

Sixpence of Broit's 2nd milled issue

	F	VF
Briot's hammered issues 1638-39		
im: anchor, triangle over anchor		
Halfcrowns	£750	£1850
Shillings	£350	£900

Shillings (revs. all square shield)
6th bust (crude)

im (**P**), (**R**), eye, sun	£40	£150

7th bust (tall, slim)

im sun, sceptre	£50	£185

8th bust (shorter, older)

im sceptre	£65	£250

Sixpences (revs. all square shield)
6th bust

im (**P**), (**R**), eye sun	£75	£225

7th bust

im (**R**), eye, sun, sceptre ...	£65	£185

8th bust, (crude style)

im eye, sun	£125	£375

Halfgroats
4th bust/round shield

im (**P**), (**R**), eye sceptre ...	£20	£70

7th bust (old/round shield)

im eye, sun, sceptre	£20	£70

Pennies
7th bust/oval shield

im one or two pellets	£25	£75

Charles I
Crown
of Exeter

PROVINCIAL MINTS
York 1642-44
im: lion

Halfcrowns, varieties from	£225	£600
Shillings –	£200	£500
Sixpences –	£225	£650
Threepences	£65	£175

Aberystwyth 1638-42
im: open book

Halfcrowns, varieties from	£860	£2500
Shillings –	£350	£1000
Sixpences –	£275	£750
Groats –	£50	£150

Charles I Briot's crown

Briot's 1st milled issued 1631-32
im: flower and **B**

Crowns	£675	£1650
Halfcrowns...	£400	£1200
Shillings	£300	£700
Sixpences	£100	£350
Halfgroats	£50	£110
Pennies	£60	£150

Briot's 2nd milled issue 1638-39
im: anchor, anchor and B, anchor and mullet

Halfcrowns	£275	£750
Shillings	£135	£425
Sixpences	£75	£185

Aberystwyth groat

Threepences –	£40	£120
Halfgroats –	£50	£150
Pennies –	£70	£200
Halfpennies	£175	£500

Aberystwyth – Furnace 1647-48
im: crown

Halfcrowns from	£1750	£5000
Shillings	£2500	*

HAMMERED SILVER

	F	VF
Sixpences	£1250	£2750
Groats	£225	£525
Threepences	£200	£475
Halfgroats	£275	£750
Pennies	£650	£1800

Shrewsbury 1642
mm: plume without band

	F	VF
Pounds, varieties from	£1850	£4000
Halfpounds –	£800	£2000
Crowns –	£750	£1800
Halfcrowns –	£475	£1200
Shillings –	£875	£2250

Oxford 1642-46
mm: plume with band

	F	VF
Pounds, varieties from	£1750	£4000
Halfpounds –	£750	£1750
Crowns –	£750	£1750
Halfcrowns –	£225	£650
Shillings –	£200	£600
Sixpences –	£225	£625
Groats –	£125	£350
Threepences –	£95	£225
Halfgroats –	£110	£300
Pennies –	£185	£500

Bristol 1643-45
im: Bristol monogram, acorn, plumelet

	F	VF
Halfcrowns, varieties from	£325	£800

Charles I halfcrown of York with mm lion

	F	VF
Shillings –	£300	£700
Sixpences –	£225	£625
Groats –	£175	£450
Threepences –	£175	£475
Halfgroats –	£275	£650
Pennies –	£425	£900

Charles I sixpence, Bristol 1644

A, B, and plumes issues
Associated with Thomas Bushell; previously assigned to Lundy

	F	VF
Halfcrowns, varieties from	£900	£2250

	F	VF
Shillings –	£375	£1000
Sixpences –	£225	£600
Groats –	£200	£500
Threepences –	£175	£450
Halfgroats –	£475	£1000

Truro 1642-43
im: rose, bugle

	F	VF
Crowns, varieties	£350	£850
Halfcrowns –	£750	£2000
Shillings –	£3000	*

Bristol shilling 1644

Exeter 1643-46
im Ex, rose, castle

	F	VF
Halfpounds		ext. rare
Crowns, varieties	£350	£800
Halfcrowns	£275	£650
Shillings	£350	£825
Sixpences	£325	£725
Groats	£110	£300
Threepences	£110	£300
Halfgroats –	£250	£650
Pennies	£350	£900

Worcester 1643-4
im: castle, helmet, leopard's head, lion, two lions, lis, rose, star

	F	VF
Halfcrowns, many varieties ...	£700	£1800

Salopia (Shrewsbury) 1644
im: helmet, lis, rose (in legend)

	F	VF
Halfcrowns, many varieties ...	£850	£2000

Worcester or Salopia (Shrewsbury)
im: bird, boar's head, lis, castle, cross, and annulets, helmet, lion, lis, pear, rose, scroll

	F	VF
Shillings, varieties	£900	£2500
Sixpences	£825	£2250
Groats	£525	£1200
Threepences	£325	£750
Halfgroats	£525	£1250

'HC' mint (probably Hartlebury Castle, Worcester 1646)
im: pear, three pears

	F	VF
Halfcrowns	£1350	£3250

Chester 1644
im: cinquefoil, plume, prostrate gerb, three gerbs

	F	VF
Halfcrowns, varieties	£725	£2000
Shillings	£1200	*
Threepences	£850	£2000

Welsh Marches mint? 1644	F	VF
Halfcrowns...	£650	£1600

Welsh Marches mint, halfcrown

SIEGE PIECES
Carlisle besieged 1644-45

	F	VF
Three shillings	£4250	£10000
Shillings (F)	£3250	£7500

Newark besieged many times
(surrendered May 6, 1646)

Halfcrowns, 1645-46 (F)	£675	£1500

Newark Besieged, Shilling, dated 1645

	F	VF
Shillings, 1645-46, varieties (F)	£475	£1000
Ninepences, 1645-46	£450	£900
Sixpences	£475	£1000

Pontefract besieged 1648-49

Two shillings		ext. rare
Shillings, 1648, varieties	£1250	£3000

Ponefract Besieged 1648, Siege Shilling

Scarborough besieged 1644-45
Many odd values issued here, all of which are
extremely rare. The coin's value was decided by
the intrinsic value of the piece of metal from which
it was made.

HAMMERED SILVER

	F	VF

Examples: 5s 8d, 2s 4d, 1s 9d, 1s 3d, 7d etc. (**F**).
Collectors could expect to pay at least **£5250** or
more in F and **£12000** in VF for any of these.

COMMONWEALTH 1649-60

	F	VF
Crowns, *im* sun 1649,51-54, 56 ...	£650	£1400
Halfcrowns, *im* sun 1649, 1651-6	£225	£500
—*im* anchor 1658-60	£750	£2000

Commonwealth Shilling, 1651

	F	VF
Shillings, *im* sun 1649, 1661-87	£135	£325
—*im* anchor 1658-60	£550	£1200

A superb 1651 sixpence

	F	VF
Sixpences, *im* sun 1649, 1651-7	£110	£300
—*im* anchor 1658-6	£450	£1000
Halfgroats undated	£30	£90
Pennies undated	£25	£70
Halfpennies undated	£25	£70

CHARLES II 1660-85
Hammered coinage 1660-62

	F	VF
Halfcrowns, three issues ... from	£250	£675
Shillings— ... ... from	£150	£475

Charles II hammered issue shilling

	F	VF
Sixpences—	£125	£375
Fourpences, third issue only ...	£30	£80
Threepences— ... ... from	£30	£70
Twopences, three issues ... from	£25	£65
Pennies— ... ... from	£25	£65

'ROYAL' AND 'ROSE' BASE METAL FARTHINGS

Until 1613 English coins were struck only in gold or silver — the monarchy considered that base metal issues would be discreditable to the royal prerogative of coining. However, silver coins had become far too small, farthings so tiny that they had to be discontinued. So to meet demands for small change James I authorised Lord Harington to issue copper farthing tokens. Subsequently this authority passed in turn to the Duke of Lennox, the Duchess of Richmond and Lord Maltravers. It ceased by order of Parliament in 1644.

	Fair	F	VF	EF
JAMES I **Royal farthing tokens**				
Type 1 Harington (circa 1613). Small copper flan with tin-washed surface, mint-mark between sceptres below crown	£10	£30	£75	£125
Type 2 Harington (circa 1613). Larger flan, no tin wash	£15	£15	£40	£80
Type 3 Lennox (1614-25). IACO starts at 1 o'clock position	£3	£10	£25	£60
Type 4 Lennox (1622-25). Oval flan, IACO starts at 7 o'clock	£8	£25	£65	£120
CHARLES I **Royal farthing tokens**				
Type 1 Richmond (1625-34). Single arched crown	£2	£8	£25	£50
Type 2 Transitional (circa 1634). Double arched crown	£6	£20	£50	£100
Type 3 Maltravers (1634-36). Inner circles	£3	£10	£30	£60
Type 4 Richmond (1625-34). As Type 1 but oval	£8	£25	£60	£120
Type 5 Maltravers (1634-36). Double arched crown	£10	£30	£70	*
Rose farthing tokens (rose on reverse)				
Type 1 Small thick flan	£3	£10	£30	*
Type 2 Same, but single arched crown	£2	£7	£25	*
Type 3 Same, but sceptres below crown	£10	£25	£50	*

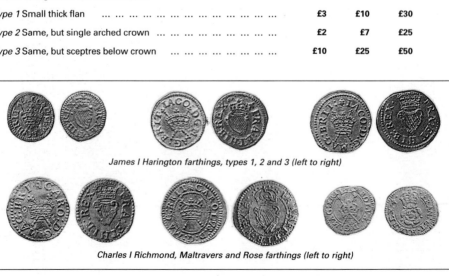

James I Harington farthings, types 1, 2 and 3 (left to right)

Charles I Richmond, Maltravers and Rose farthings (left to right)

MILLED COINAGE from 1656

Again it must be stressed that the prices shown in this guide are the approximate amounts collectors can expect to pay for coins — they are not dealers' buying prices. Information for this guide is drawn from auction results and dealers' lists, with the aim of determining firm valuations. Prices still vary enormously from sale to sale and from one dealer's list to another. Allowance must also be made for the variance in the standards of grading. The prices given here aim at a reasonable assessment of the market at the time of compilation, but they are not the product of computers, which would, in any case, provide only average (not necessarily accurate) prices. It is not possible to forecast such values because of the erratic fluctuations that can occur, not only in boom conditions but also during times of economic uncertainty, and an annual catalogue of this type cannot be up to date on the bullion prices of common sovereigns, for example. If you are buying or selling bullion gold coins, refer to current quotations from bullion dealers.

With some denominations in the silver and copper series, column headings indicating condition change at the beginning of the lists of George III coins. The condition (grade) of a coin is of great importance in determining its market value. Notes on grading and on abbreviations etc. used in these price guides appear elsewhere in this publication.

Cromwell gold patterns

These were struck by order of Cromwell, with the consent of the Council. The dies were made by Thomas Simon, and the coins were struck on Peter Blondeau's machine. The fifty shillings and the broad were struck from the same dies, but the fifty shillings has the edge inscription PROTECTOR LITERIS LITERAE NUMMIS CORONA ER SALUS, while the broad is not so thick and has a grained edge. No original strikings of the half broad are known, but some were struck from dies made by John Tanner in 1738. All three denominations are dated 1656.

Oliver Cromwell gold half broad 1656

	F	VF	EF	Unc
Fifty shillings	*	£13500	£25000	*
Broad	*	£4750	£11000	£16000
Half broad	*	£5500	£9000	*

Five guineas

CHARLES II	F	VF	EF	Unc
1668-78 pointed end to trnctn of bust ...	£1750	£2750	£8000	*
1668, 69, 75—eleph below bust	£1750	£2750	£8000	*
1675-8—eleph & castle below bust	£1750	£2750	£8000	*
1678-84 rounded end to trnctn	£1750	£2250	£7000	*
1680-4—eleph & castle	£1875	£3000	£8000	*
JAMES II				
1686 sceptres in wrong order on rev ...	£1750	£2250	£6500	*
1687-8 sceptres correct	£1750	£2750	£6500	*
1687-8 eleph & castle	£1750	£3000	£6500	*
WILLIAM AND MARY				
1691-4 no prov mark	£1800	£2850	£7500	*
1691-4 eleph & castle	£1950	£3250	£8000	*
WILLIAM III				
1699-1700 no prov mark	£1750	£2500	£7000	*
1699 eleph & castle	£1850	£2900	£7500	*
1701 new bust 'fine work'	£1750	£2500	£7000	£9000

Charles II 1676 five guineas, elephant and castle

FIVE GUINEAS

George II 1729 five guineas

Charles II 1664 two guineas elephant below bust

James II 1687 two guineas

	F	VF	EF	Unc
ANNE				
Pre-Union with Scotland				
1703 VIGO below bust	*	*	£45000	*
1705-6 plain below	£1650	£3000	£7000	*
Post-Union with Scotland				
1706	£1600	£2750	£6250	*
1709 Larger lettering, wider shield and crowns	£1600	£2750	£6250	*
1711, 1713-4 broader bust	£1600	£2750	£6250	£9000

Pre-Union reverses have separate shields (top and right) for England and Scotland. Post-Union reverses have the English and Scottish arms side by side on the top and bottom shields.

	F	VF	EF	Unc
GEORGE I				
1716, 17, 20, 26	£2250	£4000	£9000	*
GEORGE II				
1729, 31, 35, 38, 41 YH	£1700	£2250	£5750	£7500
1729 E,I,C, below head	£1700	£2500	£6250	£8000
1746 OH, lima below	£1700	£2750	£6250	£8500
1748, 53 plain below	£1700	£2750	£6250	£8500
GEORGE III				
1770, 73, 77 patterns only	*	*	£32500	£50000

Two guineas

	F	VF	EF	Unc
CHARLES II				
1664, 5, 9, 71 pointed end to trnctn	£875	£1850	£6500	*
1664 elephant below	£875	£1850	£6500	*
1675-84 rounded end to trnctn	£800	£1750	£5000	*
1676, 78, 82-84 eleph & castle below bust	£900	£2000	£6750	*
1678 elephant below				ext. rare
JAMES II				
1687	£900	£2000	£5250	*
1688/9	£1000	£2250	£6000	*
WILLIAM AND MARY				
1691, 3, 4 eleph & castle	£950	£1850	£5250	*
1693, 4 no prov mark	£850	£1750	£4750	£7000
WILLIAM III				
1701	£1000	£2750	£4750	£6500
ANNE				
(none struck before Union)				
1709, 11, 13, 14	£750	£1500	£3250	£6000
GEORGE I				
1717,20,26	£700	£1500	£3500	£5750
GEORGE II				
1734, 5, 8, 9,YH (F)	£500	£750	£2000	£3500
1739, 40 intermediate head (F)	£550	£800	£2250	£3000
1748, 53 OH	£575	£875	£2500	£3500
GEORGE III				
1768, 73, 77 patterns only	*	*	£14000	£20000

Guineas

	F	VF	EF	Unc
CHARLES II				
1663 pointed trnctn	£625	£1500	£4500	*
1663—eleph	£625	£1500	£4250	*
1664 trnctn indented	£625	£1500	£4000	*
1664—eleph	*	*ext. rare		

GUINEAS

Charles II 1663 guinea elephant below bust

Anne 1713 guinea

George III 1768 guinea

	F	VF	EF	Unc
1664-73 sloping pointed trnctn	£650	£1800	£4000	*
1664, 5, 8 — eleph	£800	£2250	£4750	*
1672-84 rounded trnctn	£525	£1150	£3500	*
1674-84 — eleph & castle	£750	£2250	£5500	*
1677, 8 — eleph				ext. rare

JAMES II
	F	VF	EF	Unc
1685, 6 1st bust	£475	£1200	£3000	£5000
1685 — eleph & castle	£500	£1250	£3750	*
1686-8 2nd bust	£500	£1200	£3000	£5000
1686-8 — eleph & castle	£500	£1250	£3500	*

WILLIAM AND MARY
	F	VF	EF	Unc
1689-94 no prov mark	£500	£1250	£3500	£5500
1689-94 eleph & castle	£525	£1500	£3750	*
1692 eleph	£700	£1750	£4250	*

WILLIAM III
	F	VF	EF	Unc
1695, 6 1st bust	£400	£850	£2500	£3500
1695, 7 — eleph & castle	*	*	*	*
1697-1701 2nd bust	£350	£850	£2500	*
1698-1701 — eleph & castle	£650	£2250	*	*
1701 3rd bust 'fine work'	£500	£1000	£3250	*

ANNE
Pre-Union[1]
	F	VF	EF	Unc
1702, 1705-7 plain below bust	£450	£850	£2750	£4250
1703 VIGO below	£3500	£7500	£16000	*

Post Union[1]
	F	VF	EF	Unc
1707, 8 1st bust	£425	£750	£1650	£2950
1707 — eleph & castle	£650	£1750	£4250	*
1707-9 2nd bust	£425	£850	£1650	£2950
1708-9 — eleph & castle	£700	£1650	£4500	*
1710-1714 3rd bust	£425	£650	£1650	£2500

[1]See note in prices of five guinea pieces for Anne.

GEORGE I
	F	VF	EF	Unc
1714 1st head PR. EL. (Prince Elector) in rev legend	£750	£1500	£2850	£4500
1715 2nd head, tie with two ends	£325	£750	£1750	£3000
1715 3rd head, hair not curling round trnctn	£275	£650	£1800	£2850
1716-23 4th head, tie with loop	£250	£600	£1800	£2850
1721, 2 — eleph & castle	*			ext. rare
1723-7 5th head, smaller, older bust	£275	£650	£1800	£2850
1726 — eleph & castle	£800	£2500	*	*

GEORGE II
	F	VF	EF	Unc
1727 1st YH, small lettering	£700	£1400	£3250	£4500
1727, 8 — larger lettering	£475	£900	£2750	*
1729-32 2nd YH (narrower)	£400	£825	£2750	*
1729, 31, 2 — E.I.C. below	£475	£1250	£3250	£4500
1732-8 — larger lettering	£320	£700	£2250	£3000
1732 — — E.I.C. below	£600	£1250	£3500	*
1739, 40, 43 intermediate head	£300	£625	£1950	£2650
1739 — E.I.C. below	£500	£850	£3250	*
1745, 6 — larger lettering	£285	£625	£2000	*
1745 — LIMA below	£1500	£3000	£6000	*
1747-53, 5, 6, 8, 9, 60, OH	£300	£525	£1500	£2500

GEORGE III
	F	VF	EF	Unc
1761, 1st head	£600	£1500	£3000	£4000
1763, 4, 2nd head	£300	£850	£2250	*
1765-73, 3rd head	£225	£375	£850	£1500
1774-9, 81-6, 4th head	£175	£300	£625	£900
1789-99, 5th head, 'spade' rev (F)	£165	£275	£500	£750
1813, 6th head, rev shield in Garter ('Military guinea')	£350	£600	£1000	£1650

William and Mary 1691 half guinea

William III 1695 half guinea

George I 1719 half guinea

George I half guinea, 1725

George II 1756 half guinea

George III 1788 half guinea with 'spade' type shield on reverse

George I 1718 quarter guinea

Half Guineas

CHARLES II	F	VF	EF	Unc
1669-72 bust with pointed trnctn	£425	£825	£3250	*
1672-84 rounded trnctn...	£425	£825	£3500	*
1676-8, 80, 82-4 — eleph & castle	£475	£1100	£4000	*

JAMES II				
1686-8 no prov mark	£425	£750	£2250	£3500
1686 eleph & castle	£900	*	*	*

WILLIAM AND MARY				
1689 1st busts	£525	£1200	£3000	£4000
1690-4 2nd busts	£500	£950	£3250	*
1691-2 — eleph & castle	£525	£1000	£3500	*
1692 — eleph				ext. rare

WILLIAM III				
1695 no prov mark	£200	£550	£1850	£2500
1695, 6 eleph & castle	£425	£825	£2500	*
1697-1701 larger harp on rev	£250	£600	£2000	*
1698 — eleph & castle	£350	£750	£2500	*

ANNE				
Pre-Union[1]				
1702, 5 plain below bust	£425	£1200	£3250	*
1703 VIGO below	£3250	£7500	£15000	*

Post-Union[1]				
1707-14 plain	£250	£600	£1500	£2250

[1]See note in prices of five guineas for Anne.

GEORGE I				
1715, 17-24, 1st head...................	£200	£450	£1000	£2000
1721 eleph & castle.......................	*	*	*	*
1725-7, smaller older head	£175	£375	£900	£2000

GEORGE II				
1728-39 YH	£300	£550	£1650	*
1729-32, 9 — E.I.C. below	£350	£900	£2500	*
1740, 3, 5, 6, intermediate head	£300	£800	£2250	*
1745 — LIMA below	£700	£2000	£5000	*
1747-53, 5, 6, 58-60 OH	£185	£375	£850	£1650

GEORGE III				
1762, 3, 1st head	£350	£875	£2250	*
1764-6, 8, 9, 72-5, 2nd head	£150	£300	£750	£1250
1774, 5, 3rd head	£600	£1500	£2750	*
1775-9, 81, 83-6, 4th head	£95	£200	£400	£750
1787-91, 93-8, 1800, 5th head	£90	£150	£325	£400
1801-3, 6th head	£70	£110	£250	£350
1804, 6, 8-11, 13, 7th head	£65	£110	£225	£300

Third guineas

GEORGE III	F	VF	EF	Unc
1797-1800 1st head	£60	£85	£200	£300
1801-3 — date close to crown on reverse	£60	£85	£200	£300
1804, 6, 8-11, 2nd head	£60	£80	£200	£300

Quarter guineas

GEORGE I	F	VF	EF	Unc
1718	£70	£150	£275	£425

GEORGE III	F	VF	EF	Unc
1762	£70	£150	£275	£425

NB: *Forgeries exist of pieces marked (F) and if discovered should be reported to the police.*

Britannias
(See under Decimal Coinage)

Five pounds

	F	VF	EF	Unc
GEORGE III				
1820 pattern **(F)**	*	*	*	£45000
GEORGE IV				
1826 proof	*	*	£7000	£10000
VICTORIA				
1839 proof with 'Una and				
the Lion' rev **(F)**	*	*	£16000	£25000
1887 JH **(F)**	£375	£475	£600	£850
1887 proof	*	*	£1450	£2750
1887 proof no B.P.	*	*	£1500	£3000
1893 OH **(F)**	£400	£600	£875	£1500
1893 proof	*	*	£1500	£2850
EDWARD VII				
1902 **(F)**	£350	£450	£550	£750
1902 proof	*	*	£600	£750
GEORGE V				
1911 proof **(F)** ...	*	*	£950	£1500
GEORGE VI				
1937 proof	*	*	*	£725

ELIZABETH II
In 1984 the Royal Mint issued the first of an annual issue of Brilliant Uncirculated £5 coins. These bear the symbol 'U' in a circle to the left of the date on the reverse to indicate the standard of striking.

1981 proof	£400
1984	£400
1985	£425
1986	£425
1987 new effigy	£425
1988	£425
1989 500th anniversary of the sovereign, BU ...	£450
1990 Queen Mother's 90th birthday, proof	£575
1990	£435
1991	£450
1992	£450
1993 Coronation, proof	£700
1993	£475
1994	£500
1995	£535
1996 Queen's 70th Birthday, proof	£645
... ... BU	£575
1997 Golden Wedding, proof	£650
1997	£535
1998 Prince Charles 50th Birthday, proof	£600
1998 New Portrait	£535
1999 Diana Memorial, proof	£600
1999 Millennium, proof	£600
1999	£450
2000 Millennium, proof	£495
2000 Queen Mother Centenary, proof	£495
2000	£450
2001 Victorian Anniversary, proof	£525
2001 as above, reverse frosting, proof	£750
2001	£400
2002 Golden Jubilee, proof	£600
2002 Shield reverse, proof	£600
2002 Queen Mother memorial	£600
2003 Coronation Jubilee, proof	£560
2004 Entente Cordial, proof	£560

Two pounds

	F	VF	EF	Unc
GEORGE III				
1820 pattern **(F)**	*	*	£7500	£13500

George III 1820 pattern two pounds

	F	VF	EF	Unc
GEORGE IV ...				
1823 St George				
on reverse **(F)**	£300	£500	£650	£1200
1826 proof, shield				
reverse	*	*	£2250	£3750

William IV 1831 proof two pounds

	F	VF	EF	Unc
WILLIAM IV				
1831 proof	*	*	£3750	£5500
VICTORIA				
1887 JH **(F)** ...	£185	£220	£300	£375
1887 proof	*	*	£650	£1100
1893 OH **(F)** ...	£220	£300	£425	£700
1893 proof	*	*	£750	£1250
EDWARD VII				
1902 **(F)**	£175	£210	£285	£375
1902 proof	*	*	£275	£375
GEORGE V				
1911 proof **(F)**	*	*	*	£500

1937 proof two pounds

	F	VF	EF	Unc
GEORGE VI				
1937 proof ...	*	*	*	£425

TWO POUNDS

ELIZABETH II	F	VF	EF	Unc
1983 proof				£225
1986 Commonwealth Games, proof				£225
1987 proof				£250
1988 proof				£250
1989 500th anniversary of the sovereign, proof				£275
1990 proof				£250
1991 proof				£250
1993 proof				£250
1994 gold proof				£425
1994 gold proof 'mule'				£750
1995 VE day gold proof				£375
1995 50th Anniversary of UN, proof				£300
1996 European Football Championship				£350
1997 Bimetal gold proof				£350
1998 New portrait, proof				£300
1999 Rugby World Cup...				£300
2000 proof				£275
2001 Marconi, proof...				£295
2002 Shield reverse, proof				£300
2003 DNA bi-colour proof				£295
2004 Locomotive proof				£325

Sovereigns

GEORGE III	F	VF	EF	Unc
1817 (F) £140		£275	£800	£1250
1818 ... ...£140		£300	£900	£1350
1819 ... ...£12500		£25000	£55000	*
1820 ... ...£140		£300	£900	£1250

GEORGE III
Type Laureate head/St George

	F	VF	EF	Unc
1821 ... ...£110		£225	£700	£1200
1822 (F) £110		£225	£700	£1200
1823 ... ...£225		£700	£2500	*
1824 ... ...£110		£225	£700	£1250
1825 ... ...£250		£750	£2000	*

Type bare head/shield

1825 **(F)**	£165	£250	£600	£1100
1826	£165	£250	£600	£1150
1826 proof	*	*	£1200	£2350
1827 **(F)**	£165	£250	£625	£1150
1828 **(F)**	£900	£2000	£6000	*
1829	£165	£250	£600	£1100
1830	£165	£250	£600	£1100

WILLIAM IV

1831	£150	£300	£900	£1500
1831 proof	*	*	£1500	£2750

William IV 1831 proof sovereign

1832 (F)	£165	£265	£650	£1100
1833	£165	£275	£650	£1200
1835	£165	£265	£650	£1100
1836	£165	£265	£650	£1100
1837	£165	£265	£650	£1250

VICTORIA
Type 1, YH obv, shield rev

1838	£75	£200	£675	£1350

Victoria 1839 proof sovereign

	F	VF	EF	Unc
1839	£95	£250	£950	£2000
1839 proof	*	*	£1200	£2750
1841	£600	£1100	£3250	*
1842	*	*	£150	£325
1843	*	*	£150	£300
1843 narrow shield	£1500	£3000	£5500	*
1844	*	*	£150	£300
1845	*	*	£150	£300
1846	*	*	£150	£300
1847	*	*	£150	£300
1848	*	*	£150	£300
1849	*	*	£150	£300
1850	*	*	£150	£300
1851	*	*	£150	£300
1852	*	*	£150	£300
1853	*	*	£120	£275

Victoria 1853 sovereign, shield on reverse

1853 proof	*	*	£4000	£6500
1854	*	*	£135	£275
1855	*	*	£135	£275
1856	*	*	£135	£275
1857	*	*	£135	£275
1858	*	*	£150	£350
1859	*	*	£90	£200
1859 'Ansell' ...	£120	£400	£2000	£3500
1860	*	*	£150	£350
1861	*	*	£110	£225
1862	*	*	£110	£225
1863	*	*	£110	£200
1863 die number below wreath on rev	*	*	£110	£185
1863 '827' on truncation ...	£1500	£2500	£4250	*
1864 die no. ...	*	*	£100	£175
1865 die no. ...	*	*	£100	£175
1866 die no. ...	*	*	£100	£175
1868 die no. ...	*	*	£100	£175
1869 die no. ...	*	*	£100	£175
1870 die no. ...	*	*	£100	£175
1871 die no. ...	*	*	£100	£150
1871 S (Sydney mint) below wreath	*	*	£120	£300
1872	*	*	£90	£125
1872 die no. ...	*	*	£90	£110
1872 M (Melbourne mint) below wreath	*	*	£110	£350
1872 S	*	*	£250	£700
1873 die no. ...	*	*	£90	£150
1873 S	*	*	£110	£300
1874 die no. ...	£300	£850	£3250	*
1874 M	*	*	£150	£375
1875 S	*	*	£125	£350
1877 S	*	*	£100	£275

COINS MARKET VALUES

	F	VF	EF	Unc
1878 S	*	*	£95	£275
1879 S	*	*	£95	£300
1880 M	£200	£850	£1450	£2250
1880 S	*	*	£110	£400
1881 M	*	*	£125	£375
1881 S	*	*	£100	£400
1882 M	*	*	£95	£275
1882 S	*	*	£95	£275
1883 M	*	£150	£450	£1200
1883 S	*	*	£100	£275
1884 M	*	*	£100	£300
1884 S	*	*	£100	£275
1885 M	*	*	£100	£275
1885 S	*	*	£100	£275
1886 M	£400	£1500	£2250	£4500
1886 S	*	*	£100	£275
1887 M	£275	£500	£1750	£3500
1887 S	*	*	£100	£350

Type II. YH obv, St George and Dragon rev

	F	VF	EF	Unc
1871	*	*	£80	£120
1871 S below head	*	£80	£250	£500
1872	*	*	£90	£150
1872 M below head	*	£100	£400	£750
1872 S	*	*	£150	£350
1873	*	*	£80	£125
1873 M	*	*	£125	£250
1873 S	*	*	£150	£350
1874	*	*	£80	£125
1874 M	*	*	£150	£400
1874 S	*	*	£100	£275
1875 M	*	*	£90	£250
1875 S	*	*	£100	£275
1876	*	*	£80	£175
1876 M	*	*	£90	£400
1876 S	*	*	£125	£425
1877 M	*	*	£90	£250
1878	*	*	£80	£125
1878 M	*	*	£90	£250
1879	*	£95	£600	*
1879 M	*	*	£90	£250
1879 S	*	*	£250	£1000
1880	*	*	£80	£125
1880 M	*	*	£90	£250
1880 S	*	*	£100	£250
1881 M	*	*	£175	£500
1881 S	*	*	£90	£250
1882 M	*	*	£90	£200
1882 S	*	*	£80	£160
1883 M	*	*	£80	£180
1883 S	*	*	£80	£250
1884	*	*	£80	£150
1884 M	*	*	£90	£250
1884 S	*	*	£80	£120
1885	*	*	£85	£150
1885 M	*	*	£90	£150
1885 S	*	*	£70	£135
1886 M	*	*	£80	£350
1886 S	*	*	£70	£125
1887 M	*	*	£80	£150
1887 S	*	*	£70	£135

Jubilee head coinage

	F	VF	EF	Unc
1887 (F)	*	*	£60	£90
1887 proof	*	*	£325	£500
1887 M on ground below dragon	*	*	£100	£250
1887 S on ground below dragon	*	*	£325	£525
1888	*	*	*	£80
1888 M	*	*	*	£100
1888 S	*	*	*	£100
1889	*	*	*	£80
1889 M	*	*	*	£100

SOVEREIGNS

	F	VF	EF	Unc
1889 S	*	*	*	£100
1890	*	*	*	£80
1890	*	*	*	£85
1890 S	*	*	*	£100
1891	*	*	*	£80
1891 M	*	*	*	£100
1891 S	*	*	*	£100
1892	*	*	*	£80
1892 M	*	*	*	£100
1892 S	*	*	*	£100
1893	*	*	*	£100
1893 S	*	*	*	£100

Old head coinage

	F	VF	EF	Unc
1893	*	*	*	£75
1893 proof	*	*	£375	£600
1893 M	*	*	*	£80
1893 S	*	*	*	£80
1894	*	*	*	£75
1894 M	*	*	*	£80
1894 S	*	*	*	£80
1895	*	*	*	£75
1895 M	*	*	*	£80
1895 S	*	*	*	£80
1896	*	*	*	£75
1896 M	*	*	*	£80
1896 S	*	*	*	£80
1897 M	*	*	*	£80
1897 S	*	*	*	£80
1898	*	*	*	£75
1898 M	*	*	*	£80
1898 S	*	*	*	£80
1899	*	*	*	£75

1898 Victoria Old Head sovereign

	F	VF	EF	Unc
1899 M	*	*	*	£75
1899 P (Perth mint) on ground below dragon	*	*	*	£650
1899 S	*	*	*	£150
1900	*	*	*	£75
1900 M	*	*	*	£75
1900 P	*	*	*	£110
1900 S	*	*	*	£100
1901	*	*	*	£75
1901 M	*	*	*	£75
1901 P	*	*	*	£110
1901 S	*	*	*	£90

EDWARD VII

	F	VF	EF	Unc
1902	*	*	*	£75
1902 proof	*	*	£100	£150
1902 M	*	*	*	£75
1902 P	*	*	*	£75
1902 S	*	*	*	£75
1903	*	*	*	£75
1903 M	*	*	*	£75
1903 P	*	*	*	£75
1903 S	*	*	*	£75
1904	*	*	*	£75
1904 M	*	*	*	£75
1904 P	*	*	*	£75
1904 S	*	*	*	£75
1905	*	*	*	£75
1905 M	*	*	*	£75
1905 P	*	*	*	£75

SOVEREIGNS

	F	VF	EF	Unc
1905 S	*	*	*	£70
1906	*	*	*	£70
1906 M	*	*	*	£70
1906 P	*	*	*	£70
1906 S	*	*	*	£70
1907	*	*	*	£70
1907 M	*	*	*	£70
1907 P	*	*	*	£70
1907 S	*	*	*	£70
1908	*	*	*	£70
1908 C (Canada, Ottawa mint) on ground below dragon (F)	*	*	£1600	£2700
1908 M	*	*	*	£75
1908 P	*	*	*	£75
1908 S	*	*	*	£75
1909	*	*	*	£75
1909 C	*	*	£100	£300
1909 M	*	*	*	£75
1909 P	*	*	*	£75
1909 S	*	*	*	£75
1910	*	*	*	£75
1910 C	*	*	£100	£300
1910 M	*	*	*	£75
1910 P	*	*	*	£75
1910 S	*	*	*	£75

GEORGE V

	F	VF	EF	Unc
1911	*	*	*	£70
1911 proof	*	*	£150	£250
1911 C	*	*	*	£75
1911 M	*	*	*	£65
1911 P	*	*	*	£65
1911 S	*	*	*	£65
1912	*	*	*	£65
1912 M	*	*	*	£65
1912 P	*	*	*	£65
1912S	*	*	*	£65
1913	*	*	*	£65
1913 C (F)	*	£120	£350	£575
1913 M	*	*	*	£70
1913 P	*	*	*	£70
1913 S	*	*	*	£70
1914	*	*	*	£70
1914 C	*	*	£150	£275
1914 M	*	*	*	£70
1914P	*	*	*	£70
1914 S	*	*	*	£70
1915	*	*	*	£70
1915 M	*	*	*	£70
1915 P	*	*	*	£70
1915 S	*	*	*	£70
1916	*	*	*	£70
1916 C	*	£2750	£5750	*
1916 M	*	*	*	£70
1916 P	*	*	*	£70
1916 S	*	*	*	£70
1917 (F)	*	£2000	£3250	*
1917 C	*	*	£60	£90
1917 M	*	*	*	£70
1917 P	*	*	*	£70
1917 S	*	*	*	£70
1918 C	*	*	£60	£90
1918 I (Indian mint, Bombay), on ground below dragon				£70
1918 M	*	*	*	£70
1918 P	*	*	*	£70
1918 S	*	*	*	£70
1919 C	*	*	£65	£100
1919 M	*	*	*	£70
1919 P	*	*	*	£70
1919 S	*	*	*	£70
1920 M	*	£850	£2500	*
1920 P	*	*	*	£70
1920 S			highest	rarity
1921 M	*	£2750	£4750	£6000
1921 P	*	*	*	£75
1921 S	*	£350	£650	£1000
1922 M	*	£1750	£3500	£6000
1922 P	*	*	*	£75
1922 S	*	£2500	£6000	£8500
1923 M	*	*	*	£75
1923 S	*	£2000	£4000	£6000
1923 SA (South Africa, Pretoria Mint) on ground below dragon	*	£1250	£1750	£2500
1924 M	*	*	£60	£90
1924 P	*	*	*	£75
1924 S	*	£450	£800	£1200
1924 SA	*	*	£2000	£3000
1925	*	*	*	£75
1925 M	*	*	*	£75
1925 P	*	*	£120	£175
1925 S	*	*	*	£75
1925 SA	*	*	*	£70
1926 M	*	*	*	£75
1926 P	*	£100	£200	£1000
1926 S	*	£5000	£8000	£12500
1926 SA	*	*	*	£60
1927 P	*	*	£125	£250
1927 SA	*	*	*	£70
1928 M	*	£800	£1300	£1900
1928 P	*	*	£85	£120
1928 SA	*	*	*	£70
1929 M	*	£400	£750	£1200
1929 P	*	*	*	£70
1929 SA	*	*	*	£70
1930 M	*	*	£100	£175
1930 P	*	*	*	£70
1930 SA	*	*	*	£70
1931 M	*	£100	£175	£300
1931 P	*	*	*	£60
1931 SA	*	*	*	£60
1932 SA	*	*	*	£60

GEORGE VI

	F	VF	EF	Unc
1937 proof only		*	*	£700

ELIZABETH II

	F	VF	EF	Unc
1957	*	*	*	£60
1958	*	*	*	£60
1959	*	*	*	£60
1962	*	*	*	£60
1963	*	*	*	£60
1964	*	*	*	£60
1965	*	*	*	£60
1966	*	*	*	£60
1967	*	*	*	£60
1968	*	*	*	£60
1974	*	*	*	£60
1976	*	*	*	£60
1978	*	*	*	£60
1979	*	*	*	£60
1979 proof	*	*	*	£100
1980	*	*	*	£55
1980 proof	*	*	*	£85
1981	*	*	*	£55
1981 proof	*	*	*	£95
1982	*	*	*	£55
1982 proof	*	*	*	£95
1983 proof	*	*	*	£100
1984 proof	*	*	*	£100
1985 proof	*	*	*	£140
1986 proof	*	*	*	£140
1987 proof	*	*	*	£140
1988 proof	*	*	*	£150
1989 500th anniversary of the sovereign, proof	*	*	*	£250

www.royalmint.com

SOVEREIGNS

	F	VF	EF	Unc
1990 proof ... ...*	*	*	£175
1991 proof ... ...*	*	*	£175
1992 proof ... ...*	*	*	£200
1993 proof ... ...*	*	*	£200
1994 proof ... ...*	*	*	£200
1995 proof ... ...*	*	*	£200
1996 proof ... ...*	*	*	£200
1997 proof ... ...*	*	*	£200
1998 new portrait proof *	*	*	£200
1999 proof ... ...*	*	*	£250
2000 ... ...*	*	*	£85
2000 proof ... ...*	*	*	£150
2001 ... ...*	*	*	£85
2001 proof ... ...*	*	*	£135
2002 Shield reverse *	*	*	£70
2002 Shield reverse, proof*	*	*	£150
2003 Shield reverse, proof*	*	*	£80
2003 proof ... ...*	*	*	£150
2003 Ingot & sovereign ...*	*	*	£135
2004 Forth Rail Bridge, proof	*	*	£345
2004 Forth Rail Bridge proof	*	*	£80
2004 proof Forth Rail Bridge	*	*	£135

Half sovereigns

GEORGE III

	F	VF	EF	Unc
1817 ... ...£70	£100	£275	£425
1818 ... ...£70	£110	£275	£500
1820 ... ...£70	£110	£275	£500

GEORGE IV

Laureate head/ornate shield, date on rev

	F	VF	EF	Unc
1821 ... ...£350	£750	£1500	£2500
1823 plain shield ...£85	£160	£350	£575
1824 ... ...£75	£120	£300	£550
1825 ... ...£75	£120	£300	£550

Bare head, date on obv/shield, full legend rev

	F	VF	EF	Unc
1826 ... ...£85	£120	£300	£600
1827 ... ...£85	£120	£300	£600
1828 ... ...£85	£120	£325	£650

WILLIAM IV

	F	VF	EF	Unc
1834 reduced size ...£110	£200	£575	£850
1835 normal size ...£110	£200	£500	£800
1836 sixpence oberse die			
... ...£750	£1500	£3000	£4000
1836 ... ...£125	£275	£575	£850
1837 ... ...£110	£225	£575	£850

VICTORIA

Young head/shield rev

	F	VF	EF	Unc
1838 ... ...*	£100	£225	£400
1839 proof only ... ...*	*	*	£1250
1841 ... ...*	£100	£225	£400
1842 ... ...*	£90	£175	£350
1843 ... ...*	£100	£225	£475
1844 ... ...*	£100	£225	£425
1845 ... ...£100	£250	£800	*
1846 ... ...*	£100	£225	£475
1847 ... ...*	£100	£225	£425
1848 ... ...*	£125	£275	£500
1849 ... ...*	£100	£200	£375
1850 ... ...£100	£225	£750	£1000
1851 ... ...*	£90	£200	£375
1852 ... ...*	£90	£200	£375
1853 ... ...*	£80	£180	£300
1854		Extremely rare	
1855 ... ...*	£90	£175	£325
1856 ... ...*	£90	£175	£325
1857 ... ...*	£75	£150	£300
1858 ... ...*	£75	£150	£300
1859 ... ...*	£75	£150	£300
1860 ... ...*	£75	£150	£300
1861 ... ...*	£90	£175	£300
1862 ... ...£300	£750	£2000	*
1863 ... ...*	£90	£160	£300
1863 die no ... ...*	£75	£135	£275

	F	VF	EF	Unc
1864 die no.... ...	*	£75	£135	£275
1865 die no.... ...	*	£75	£135	£300
1866 die no.... ...	*	£75	£135	£300
1867 die no.... ...	*	£75	£135	£300
1869 die no.... ...	*	£75	£135	£300
1870 die no.... ...	*	£75	£135	£300
1871 die no. ...	*	£75	£135	£300
1871 S below shield	*	£150	£450	£1200
1872 die no. ...	*	£85	£135	£250
1872 S	*	£190	£550	£1100
1873 die no. ...	*	£75	£150	£250
1873 M below shield	*	£200	£600	£1200
1874 die no. ...	*	*	*	£250
1875 die no. ...	*	*	*	£250
1875 S	*	*	£550	£1200
1876 die no. ...	*	*	£125	£250
1877 die no. ...	*	*	£110	£225
1877 M	£70	£200	£700	£1500
1878 die no. ...	*	*	*	£225
1879 die no. ...	*	*	*	£225
1879 S	£90	£200	£700	£1500
1880	*	*	£110	£225
1880 die no. ...	*	*	£110	£225
1880 S	£80	£175	£650	£1250
1881 S	£80	£175	£650	£1250
1881 M	£80	£175	£650	£1250
1882 S	£200	£600	£2000	£4500
1882 M	*	£120	£500	£2000
1883	*	*	£110	£200
1883 S	*	£90	£450	£950
1884	*	*	£110	£200
1884 M	£80	£200	£1100	£2000
1885	*	*	£100	£200
1885 M	£80	£200	£1100	£2000
1886 S	*	£100	£600	£1100
1886 M	£80	£200	£1100	£2000
1887 S	*	£90	£700	£1750
1887 M	£90	£400	£1750	£3500

Jubilee head/shield rev

	F	VF	EF	Unc
1887	*	*	£60	£80
1887 proof	*	*	£250	£400
1887 M	*	£100	£275	£500
1887 S	*	£100	£375	£500
1889 S	*	£150	£450	*
1890	*	*	£50	£80
1891	*	*	£50	£80
1891 S	*	*	£500	£1000
1892	*	*	£50	£85
1893	*	*	£50	£85
1893 M	*	*	£450	£900

Old head/St George reverse

	F	VF	EF	Unc
1893	*	*	£45	£75
1893 proof	*	*	£225	£450
1893 M	£1500	*	*	*
1893 S	*	£100	£275	£550
1894	*	*	£45	£75
1895	*	*	£45	£75
1896	*	*	£45	£75
1896 M	*	£100	£200	£350
1897	*	*	£40	£80
1897 S	*	£90	£250	£375
1898	*	*	£40	£80
1899	*	*	£40	£80
1899 M	£70	£125	£450	£1500
1899 P Proof only	*	*	*	£10000
1900	*	*	£40	£75
1900 M	£70	£125	£375	*
1900 P	£100	£250	£750	*
1900 S	*	£80	£350	£1000
1901	*	*	£40	£80
1901 P proof only	*	*	*	£7000

EDWARD VII

	F	VF	EF	Unc
1902	*	*	*	£60
1902 proof	*	*	£75	£100

1902
matt
proof
half
sovereign

	F	VF	EF	Unc
1902 S	*	*	£125	£400
1903	*	*	*	£65
1903 S	*	*	£90	£200
1904	*	*	*	£65
1904 P	£100	£200	£500	£1200
1905	*	*	*	£65
1906	*	*	*	£65
1906 M	*	*	£90	£225
1906 S	*	*	£90	£250
1907	*	*	*	£65
1907 M	*	*	£80	£200
1908	*	*	*	£65
1908 M	*	*	£80	£200
1908 P	*	£100	£600	*
1908 S	*	*	£80	£175
1909	*	*	*	£65
1909 M	*	*	£100	£275
1909 P	¦	£150	£400	£1500
1910	*	*	*	£65
1910 S	*	*	£80	£150

GEORGE V

	F	VF	EF	Unc
1911	*	*	*	£50
1911 proof	*	*	£100	£200
1911 P	*	*	£50	£90
1911 S	*	*	*	£80
1912	*	*	*	£45
1912 S	*	*	£50	£80
1913	*	*	*	£40
1914	*	*	*	£40
1914 S	*	*	*	£70
1915	*	*	*	£40
1915 M	*	*	£60	£100
1915 P	*	*	£60	£90
1915 S	*	*	*	£50
1916 S	*	*	*	£50
1918 P	*	£300	£650	£1100
1923 SA proof	*	*	*	£200
1925 SA	*	*	*	£50
1926 SA	*	*	*	£50

GEORGE VI

	F	VF	EF	Unc
1937 proof	*	*	*	£150

ELIZABETH II

	F	VF	EF	Unc
1980 proof	*	*	*	£60
1982	*	*	*	£60
1982 proof	*	*	*	£60
1983 proof	*	*	*	£60
1984 proof	*	*	*	£60
1985 proof	*	*	*	£80
1986 proof	*	*	*	£80
1987 proof	*	*	*	£80
1988 proof	*	*	*	£80
1989 500th anniversary of the sovereign, proof	*	*	*	£100
1990 proof	*	*	*	£80
1991 proof	*	*	*	£80
1992 proof	*	*	*	£90
1993 proof	*	*	*	£85
1994 proof	*	*	*	£85
1995 proof	*	*	*	£85
1996 proof	*	*	*	£85
1997 proof	*	*	*	£85
1998 new portrait proof	*	*	*	£85
1999 proof	*	*	*	£90
2000	*	*	*	£50
2000 proof	*	*	*	£70
2001	*	*	*	£50
2001 proof	*	*	*	£75
2002 shield reverse				£40
2002 shield reverse, proof				£75
2003				£40
2003 proof				£75
2004				£40
2004 proof				£75

Crowns

CROMWELL	F	VF	EF
1658	£1450	£2350	£3500
1658 Dutch copy	£1500	£2500	£4250
1658 Tanner's copy	£1650	£2750	£4500

CHARLES II			
1662 1st bust	£110	£400	£2500
1663 –	£120	£500	£2500
1664 2nd bust	£120	£450	£3000
1665 –	£400	£1000	*
1666 –	£110	£500	£3000
1666 – eleph	£175	£650	£5000
1667 –	£100	£400	£2250
1668 –	£95	£400	£1850
1668/7 –	£100	£450	£2750
1669 –	£200	£750	*
1669/8 –	£200	£750	£2750
1670 –	£100	£400	£2000
1670/69 –	£120	£450	*
1671 –	£100	£450	£2250
1671 3rd bust	£100	£400	£2000
1672 –	£100	£400	£2000
1673 –	£100	£400	£2000
1673/2 –	£110	£350	£2000
1674 –	£4000	*	*
1675 –	£500	£1250	*
1675/4 –	£500	£1250	*
1676 –	£95	£300	£1500
1677 –	£95	£300	£1500
1677/6 –	£95	£300	£1500
1678/7 –	£120	£500	*
1679 –	£95	£300	£1500
1679 4th bust –	£110	£300	£1500
1680 3rd bust –	£140	£500	£1850
1680/79 –	£95	£350	£1750
1680 4th bust –	£95	£300	£1850
1680/79 –	£125	£400	£2000
1681 – elephant & castle	£1100	£2750	*
1681 –	£100	£400	£2000
1682 –	£125	£400	£2000
1682/1 –	£90	£400	£2000
1683 –	£175	£500	£2500
1684 –	£115	£450	£2000

JAMES II			
1686 1st bust	£350	£1000	*
1687 2nd bust	£110	£400	£1750
1688 –	£135	£450	£1750
1688/7 –	£110	£425	£1750

WILLIAM AND MARY			
1691	£300	£700	£2250
1692	£325	£750	£2250
1692/2 inverted QVINTO	£325	£750	£2250
1692/2 inverted QVARTO	£600	£1250	*

WILLIAM III			
1695 1st bust	£95	£300	£1350
1696 –	£95	£300	£1350
1696 – GEI error	£200	£650	*
1696/5 –	£135	£375	£1500
1696 2nd bust		unique	
1696 3rd bust	£95	£300	£1350
1697	£600	£2000	£10000
1700 3rd bust variety	£95	£300	£1350

ANNE			
1703 1st bust VIGO	£200	£500	£2000
1705 –	£450	£1000	£3250
1706 –	£125	£400	£1350
1707 –	£100	£300	£1250
1707 2nd bust	£85	£275	£1000
1707 – E	£85	£275	£1000
1708 –	£85	£300	£1000

	F	VF	EF
1708 – E	£80	£350	*
1708/7 –	£90	£375	*
1708 – plumes	£110	£300	£1100
1713 3rd bust	£110	£300	£1100

GEORGE I			
1716	£200	£450	£2250
1718	£300	£600	£2500
1718/6	£225	£500	£2250
1720	£225	£500	£2250
1720/18	£200	£500	£2250
1723 SS C	£200	£500	£1750
1726 roses & plumes	£250	£800	£3250

GEORGE II			
1732 YH	£225	£425	£1200
1732 – proof	*	*	£3500
1734	£225	£425	£1200
1735	£225	£425	£1000
1736	£225	£425	£1000
1739	£225	£425	£875
1741	£225	£425	£875
1743 OH	£200	£400	£850

1691 William & Mary Crown

1746 – LIMA	£200	£450	£1100
1746 – proof	*	*	£2500
1750	£250	£600	£1500
1751	£275	£625	£1650

GEORGE III	F	VF	EF	Unc
Oval counter-stamp[1]	£150	£225	£425	£600
Octagonal Counterstamp[1]	£350	£500	£1000	*
1804 Bank of England dollar[1]	£100	£150	£375	£575
1818 LVIII	£10	£45	£225	£500
1818 – error edge	£250	*	*	*
1818 LIX	£10	£45	£225	£500

	F	VF	EF	Unc
1819 –	£10	£45	£250	£500
1819 – no edge stops	£50	£140	£375	*
1819/8 LIX	*	£150	£425	*
1819 LIX	£10	£50	£225	£500
1819 – no stop after TUTAMEN	£45	£150	£400	*
1820 LX	*	*	£225	£500
1820/19	£50	£200	£425	*

[1]Beware of contemporary forgeries. The counter-stamps are usually on Spanish-American dollars.

GEORGE IV
	F	VF	EF	Unc
1821 1st hd SEC ...	£35	£150	£600	£1500
1821 – prf	*	*	*	£2250
1821 – TER error edge	*	*	*	£3500
1822 – SEC	£60	£200	£650	£1700
1822 – – prf	*	*	*	*
1822 – TER	£50	£175	£600	£1600
1822 – – prf	*	*	*	£2850
1823 – prf	*	*	*	ext.rare
1826 2nd hd prf	*	*	£1750	£3000

WILLIAM IV
	F	VF	EF	Unc
1831 w.w.	*	*	£4500	£7000
1831 W.WYON	*	*	£5000	£7500
1834 w.w.	*	*	£8000	£12000

VICTORIA
	F	VF	EF	Unc
1839 proof	*	*	£2000	£3750
1844 star stops	£25	£100	£750	£1750
1844 – prf	*	*	*	£9000
1844 cinquefoil stops	£25	£100	£750	£1750
1845	£25	£100	£750	£1750
1845 proof	*	*	*	£8000
1847	£25	£100	£850	£2000

Victoria 1847 Gothic crown

CROWNS

	F	VF	EF	Unc
1847 Gothic	£325	£475	£1000	£2250
1847 – plain edge ...	*	£550	£1100	£2650
1853 SEPTIMO	*	*	£3500	£4500
1853 plain	*	*	£4000	£6250
1887 JH	£12	£20	£50	£100
1887 – proof	*	*	£200	£450
1888 close date	£15	£25	£80	£170
1888 wide date	£25	£100	£300	£400
1889	£15	£25	£65	£140
1890	£15	£25	£65	£165
1891	£15	£25	£80	£190
1892	£15	£25	£95	£200
1893 LVI	£15	£25	£110	£265
1893 – proof	*	*	£225	£500
1893 LVII	£15	£65	£200	£400
1894 LVII	£15	£30	£125	£300
1894 LVIII...	£15	£30	£125	£300
1895 LVIII...	£15	£30	£125	£300
1895 LIX	£15	£30	£125	£300
1896 LIX	£15	£50	£225	£450
1896 LX	£15	£30	£125	£295
1897 LX	£15	£30	£125	£295
1897 LXI	£15	£30	£120	£295
1898 LXI	£15	£30	£165	£400
1898 LXII	£15	£30	£130	£325
1899 LXII	£15	£39	£125	£295
1899 LXIII...	£15	£30	£125	£325
1900 LXIII...	£15	£30	£125	£325
1900 LXIV...	£15	£30	£120	£325

EDWARD VII
	F	VF	EF	Unc
1902	£20	£50	£95	£150
1902 matt proof	*	*	£95	£150

GEORGE V
	F	VF	EF	Unc
1927 proof	£35	£70	£110	£150
1928	£40	£90	£150	£250
1929	£40	£90	£150	£250
1930	£40	£95	£150	£250
1931	£40	£95	£150	£250
1932	£110	£165	£275	£400
1933	£45	£95	£150	£250
1934	£300	£600	£1200	£2000
1935	£5	£7	£10	£20
1935 rsd edge prf ...	*	*	*	£245
1935 gold proof	*	*	*	£11000
1935 prf in good silver (.925)	*	*	£650	£1250
1935 specimen	*	*	*	£40
1936	£65	£90	£225	£350

GEORGE VI
	F	VF	EF	Unc
1937	*	*	£18	£25
1937 proof	*	*	*	£30
1937 'VIP' proof	*	*	*	£600
1951	*	*	*	£5
1951 'VIP' proof	*	*	*	£350

ELIZABETH II
	F	VF	EF	Unc
1953	*	*	*	£5
1953 proof	*	*	*	£15
1953 'VIP' proof	*	*	*	£250
1960	*	*	*	£5
1960 'VIP' proof	*	*	*	£350
1960 polished dies ...	*	*	£4	£10
1965 Churchill	*	*	*	£1.00
1965 – 'satin' finish ...	*	*	*	£750

For issues 1972 onwards see under 25 pence in Decimal Coinage section.

George VI 1937
Crown (reverse)

Cromwell 1658 halfcrown

Double florins

Victoria 1887 halfcrown

VICTORIA	F	VF	EF	Unc
1887 Roman 1	*	£15	£35	£65
1887 – proof	*	*	£125	£275
1887 Arabic 1	*	£15	£35	£70
1887 – proof	*	*	£100	£250
1888	*	£12	£35	£95
1888 inverted 1	£15	£30	£120	£300
1889	*	£10	£35	£85
1889 inverted 1	£15	£35	£120	£300
1890	*	£12	£35	£90

Three shilling bank tokens

Contemporary forgeries of these pieces, as well as of other George III coins, were produced in quite large numbers. Several varieties exist for the pieces dated 1811 and 1812. Prices given here are for the commonest types of these years.

GEORGE III	F	VF	EF	Unc
1811	*	£20	£65	£110
1812 draped bust ...	*	£20	£65	£110
1812 laureate head	*	£20	£65	£110
1813	*	£20	£65	£110
1814	*	£20	£65	£110
1815	*	£20	£65	£110
1816	£100	£250	£600	£1200

Halfcrowns

CROMWELL	F	VF	EF
1656	£1200	£2650	£4500
1658	£800	£1500	£2500

CHARLES II	F	VF	EF
1663 1st bust	£100	£500	£2500
1664 2nd bust	£125	£600	£3000
1666/3 3rd bust	£750	*	*
1666/3 – elephant	£600	£1500	£5500
1667/4 –	ext.rare		
1668/4 –	£175	£600	*
1669 –	£250	£950	*
1669/4 –	£175	£600	*
1670 –	£65	£300	£2500
1671 3rd bust var	£65	£300	£2500
1671/0 –	£75	£375	£2500
1672 –	£80	£375	£2500
1672 4th bust	£100	£400	£2500
1673 –	£65	£300	£2500
1673 – plume below	£1500	*	*
1673 – plume both sides ...	ext. rare		
1674 –	£125	£350	*
1674/3 –	£200	£500	*
1675 –	£80	£350	£1750
1676 –	£80	£350	£1750
1677 –	£80	£350	£1750
1678 –	£175	£550	*
1679 –	£80	£350	£1500
1680 –	£150	£450	*
1681 –	£80	£350	£1750
1681/0 –	£150	£400	£1750
1681 – eleph & castle	£2000	£3250	*
1682 –	£100	£350	*
1682/1 –	£150	£500	*
1682/79 –	ext. rare		
1683 –	£70	£300	£1500
1683 – plume below	ext. rare	*	*
1684/3 –	£150	£600	*

James III 1687 halfcrown

JAMES II	F	VF	EF
1685 1st bust	£100	£400	£2000
1686 –	£100	£400	£1750
1686/5 –	£150	£500	£2250
1687 –	£100	£400	£1750

	F	VF	EF
1687/6 –	£110	£400	£1750
1687 2nd bust	£125	£500	£1750
1688 –	£100	£400	£1750

WILLIAM AND MARY

	F	VF	EF
1689 1st busts 1st shield ...	£60	£275	£1250
1689 – 2nd shield	£60	£275	£1250
1690 – –	£75	£400	£1650
1691 2nd busts 3rd shield ...	£65	£300	£1250
1692 – –	£65	£200	£1250
1693 – –	£60	£275	£1200
1693 – – 3 inverted	£85	£350	£1500
1693 3 over 3 inverted	£80	£275	£1200

William and Mary 1693 Halfcrown

WILLIAM III

	F	VF	EF
1696 large shield early harp	£45	£195	£600
1696 – – B	£50	£190	£650
1696 – – C	£55	£190	£650
1696 – – E	£75	£200	£750
1696 – – N	£100	£300	£1200
1696 – – Y	£50	£190	£700
1696 – – y/E	ext rare	*	*
1696 – ord harp	£75	£350	£950
1696 – – C	£90	£300	£1000
1696 – – E	£95	£300	£950
1696 – – N	£95	£350	£1350
1696 small shield	£35	£165	£525
1696 – B	£50	£200	£700
1696 – C	£95	£275	£825
1696 – E	£200	£400	£1200
1696 – N	£60	£200	£700
1696 – y	£95	£275	£825
1696 2nd bust	unique		
1697 1st bust large shield ...	£35	£125	£500
1697 – – B	£60	£200	£600
1697 – – C	£65	£200	£600
1697 – – E	£50	£165	£575
1697 – – E/C	£100	£300	£900
1697 – – N	£65	£200	£700
1697 – – y	£65	£200	£600

1697 Halfcrown of NORWICH: N below bust

	F	VF	EF
1698 – –	£40	£150	£550
1699 – –	£65	£250	£850

	F	VF	EF
1700 – –	£35	£90	£450
1701 – –	£40	£125	£600
1701 – eleph & castle	£2000	*	*
1701 – plumes	£200	£575	£2500

ANNE

	F	VF	EF
1703 plain	£700	£1750	£9000
1703 VIGO	£110	£250	£750
1704 plumes	£250	£600	£6500
1705 –	£110	£325	£900
1706 r & p	£70	£225	£675
1707 –	£50	£225	£625
1707 plain	£40	£200	£475
1707 E	£40	£200	£525
1708 plain	£30	£200	£500
1708 E	£40	£225	£650
1708 plumes	£95	£300	£800
1709 plain	£30	£200	£500
1709 E	£400	*	*
1710 r & p	£75	£225	£675
1712 –	£45	£200	£600
1713 plain	£75	£300	£750
1713 r & p	£60	£200	£600
1714 –	£50	£200	£600
1714/3	£125	£350	£800

GEORGE I

	F	VF	EF
1715 proof	*	*	£5000
1715 r & p	£110	£300	£1350
1717 –	£125	£350	£1375
1720 –	£225	£400	£1500
1720/17 –	£100	£300	£1350
1723 SS C	£100	£275	£1250
1726 small r & p	£2500	£4000	£10000

Spanish Half Dollar with George III counterstamp (octagonal)

GEORGE II

	F	VF	EF
1731 YH proof	*	£1500	£3000
1731	£85	£250	£850
1732	£85	£250	£900
1734	£85	£250	£850
1735	£85	£250	£950
1736	£85	£250	£850
1739	£70	£200	£675
1741	£90	£275	£800
1741/39	£85	£225	£750
1743 OH	£70	£125	£575
1745	£60	£90	£375
1745 LIMA	£50	£100	£450
1746 -	£50	£100	£450
1746 plain, proof	*	*	£1250
1750	£90	£275	£875
1751	£50	£300	£950

GEORGE III

	F	VF	EF	Unc
Oval counterstamp usually on Spanish half dollar	£125	£250	£400	*

HALFCROWNS

	F	VF	EF	Unc
1816 large head	*	£50	£175	£400
1817 –	*	£50	£175	£400
1817 small head ...	*	£50	£170	£400
1818	*	£50	£185	£425
1819	*	£50	£175	£425
1819/8	*	*	*	*
1820	*	£60	£180	£425

George IV halfcrown of 1821

GEORGE IV

	F	VF	EF	Unc
1820 1st hd 1st rev ...	*	£50	£185	£400
1821 –	*	£50	£185	£400
1821 proof	*	*	£600	£1100
1823	£750	£1750	£5000	*
1823 – 2nd rev	*	£50	£195	£425
1824 – –	£25	£70	£225	£600
1824 2nd hd 3rd rev ...				ext.rare
1825 – –	*	£70	£125	£400
1826 – –	*	£25	£125	£400
1826 – – proof	*	*	£400	£700
1828 – –	*	£35	£225	£600
1829 – –	*	£35	£190	£500

William IV 1831 halfcrown

WILLIAM IV

	F	VF	EF	Unc
1831		Extremely rare		
1831 proof	*	*	£425	£750
1834 ww	£30	£110	£350	£675
1834 ww in script ...	£12	£40	£150	£450
1835	£25	£80	£250	£575
1836	£12	£50	£135	£400
1836/5	£30	£85	£375	*
1837	£35	£90	£275	£625

VICTORIA

From time to time halfcrowns bearing dates ranging from 1861 to 1871 are found, but except for rare proofs: 1853, 1862 and 1864, no halfcrowns were struck between 1850 and 1874, so pieces dated for this period are now considered to be contemporary or later forgeries.

	F	VF	EF	Unc
1839 plain and ornate fillets, ww	*	£975	£3500	*
1839 – plain edge proof	*	*	£500	£850
1839 plain fillets, ww incuse	*	£1250	£3500	*
1840	£15	£75	£275	£500
1841	£75	£225	£1350	£2500
1842	£15	£40	£250	£600
1843	£50	£125	£350	£800
1844	£15	£40	£225	£500
1845	£15	£40	£225	£500
1846	£20	£50	£200	£500
1848	£75	£175	£800	£1650
1848/6	£75	£200	£750	£1500
1849 large date	£25	£75	£300	£750
1849 small date	£50	£175	£375	£900
1850	£25	£85	£300	£750
1853 proof	*	£350	£800	£1500
1862 proof	*	*	£2250	£4000
1864 proof	*	*	£2250	£4000
1874	*	£30	£110	£300
1875	*	£25	£110	£300
1876	*	£35	£120	£350
1876/5	*	£50	£225	£500
1877	*	£25	£110	£275
1878	*	£25	£110	£275
1879	*	£35	£120	£300
1880	*	£25	£120	£250
1881	*	£25	£120	£250
1882	*	£25	£120	£265
1883	*	£25	£110	£250
1884	*	£25	£110	£250
1885	*	£25	£120	£250
1886	*	£25	£110	£250
1887 YH	*	£25	£125	£300
1887 JH	*	£15	£25	£50
1887 – proof	*	*	£70	£150
1888	*	£20	£40	£90
1889	*	£20	£40	£90
1890	*	£25	£45	£100
1891	*	£25	£45	£100
1892	*	£25	£40	£100
1893 OH	*	£20	£30	£100
1893 – proof	*	*	£90	£175
1894	*	£20	£45	£120
1895	*	£20	£40	£110
1896	*	£20	£35	£110
1897	*	£15	£40	£110
1898	*	£20	£40	£110
1899	*	£20	£40	£120
1900	*	£20	£40	£110
1901	*	£20	£35	£110

EDWARD VII

	F	VF	EF	Unc
1902	*	£20	£45	£90
1902 matt proof	*	*	*	£100
1903	£50	£120	£700	£1100
1904	£35	£90	£500	£950
1905 (F)	£150	£500	£1500	£3000
1906	*	£30	£150	£400
1907	*	£40	£150	£425
1908	*	£40	£350	£725
1909	*	£25	£300	£600
1910	*	£20	£110	£300

GEORGE V

	F	VF	EF	Unc
1911	*	£110	£40	£100
1911 proof	*	*	*	£85
1912	*	£14	£60	£150
1913	*	£14	£65	£165
1914	*	*	£20	£60
1915	*	*	£15	£60
1916	*	*	£15	£60

	F	VF	EF	Unc
1917	*	*	£30	£65
1918	*	*	£20	£50
1919	*	*	£20	£50
1920	*	*	£20	£80
1921	*	*	£25	£85
1922	*	*	£20	£85
1923	*	*	£12	£40
1924	*	*	£25	£60
1925	£12	£25	£245	£500

George V 1926 halfcrown

	F	VF	EF	Unc
1926	*	*	£30	£85
1926 mod eff	*	*	£35	£80
1927	*	*	£20	£50
1927 new rev, proof only	*	*	*	£35
1928	*	*	£10	£25
1929	*	*	£10	£20
1930	£7	£35	£125	£300
1931	*	*	£10	£20
1932	*	*	£15	£35
1933	*	*	£9	£20
1934	*	*	£20	£45
1935	*	*	£6	£14
1936	*	*	£6	£12

GEORGE VI

	F	VF	EF	Unc
1937	*	*	*	£12
1937 proof	*	*	*	£18
1938	*	*	£4	£25
1939	*	*	*	£15
1940	*	*	*	£10
1941	*	*	*	£9
1942	*	*	*	£9
1943	*	*	*	£9
1944	*	*	*	£9
1945	*	*	*	£9
1946	*	*	*	£7
1947	*	*	*	£7
1948	*	*	*	£7
1949	*	*	*	£10
1950	*	*	*	£15
1950 proof	*	*	*	£18
1951	*	*	*	£15
1951 proof	*	*	*	£18

ELIZABETH II

	F	VF	EF	Unc
1953	*	*	*	£10
1953 proof	*	*	*	£12
1954	*	*	£3	£25
1955	*	*	*	£7
1956	*	*	*	£7
1957	*	*	*	£4
1958	*	*	£3	£20
1959	*	*	£4	£45
1960	*	*	*	£4
1961	*	*	*	£2
1962	*	*	*	£4
1963	*	*	*	£2
1964	*	*	*	£2
1965	*	*	*	£2
1966	*	*	*	£1
1967	*	*	*	£1

Florins

The first florins produced in the reign of Victoria bore the legend VICTORIA REGINA and the date, omitting DEI GRATIA (By the Grace of God). They are therefore known as 'Godless' florins.

The date of a Victorian Gothic florin is shown in Roman numerals, in Gothic lettering on the obverse for example: mdccclvii (1857). Gothic florins were issued during the period 1851-1887.

VICTORIA	F	VF	EF	Unc
1848 'Godless' proof with milled edge	*	*	*	£1750
1848 'Godless' proof with plain edge	*	*	*	£675

Victoria 1849 'Godless' florin

	F	VF	EF	Unc
1849 – ww obliterated by circle	£25	£50	£100	£325
1849 – ww inside circle	£15	£40	£85	£225
1851 proof only	*	*	*	£6000
1852	*	£15	£40	£95	£250
1853	*	£15	£40	£95	£250
1853 no stop after date	£20	£50	£100	£350
1853 proof	*	*	*	£1450
1854	£250	£600	£2500	*
1855	*	£35	£100	£325
1856	*	£50	£140	£350
1857	*	£40	£125	£295
1858	*	£40	£125	£295
1859	*	£40	£125	£295
1859 no stop after date	*	£50	£130	£295
1860	*	£50	£140	£350
1862	£40	£200	£1500	*
1863	£80	£300	£1750	*
1864	*	£40	£125	£295
1865	*	£40	£125	£375
1865 colon after date	*	£50	£200	*
1866	*	£50	£135	£325
1866 colon after date	*	£55	£160	*
1867	£15	£70	£170	£375
1868	*	£50	£130	£400
1869	*	£45	£125	£375
1870	*	£40	£120	£275
1871	*	£40	£120	£275

Victoria 1859 Gothic florin

FLORINS

	F	VF	EF	Unc
1872	*	£35	£100	£225
1873	*	£35	£100	£225
1874	*	£35	£125	£275
1874 xxiv/iii - (die 29)	£75	£175	£400	*
1875	*	£45	£125	£275
1876	*	£45	£125	£275
1877	*	£45	£125	£275
1877 no ww	*	*	*	*
1877 42 arcs	*	*	*	*
1878	*	£40	£125	£275
1879 ww 48 arcs	*	£40	£125	£275
1879 die no.	*	*	*	*
1879 ww. 42 arcs	£12	£40	£125	£275
1879 no ww, 38 arcs	*	£45	£125	£275
1880	*	£40	£125	£275
1881	*	£40	£125	£275
1881 xxri	*	£40	£125	£275
1883	*	£40	£110	£225
1884	*	£40	£110	£225
1885	*	£40	£110	£225
1886	*	£40	£110	£225
1887 33 arcs	*	*	*	*
1887 46 arcs	*	£40	£150	£325
1887 JH	*	£10	£20	£35
1887 – proof	*	*	*	£90
1888	*	£10	£30	£75
1889	*	£10	£35	£85
1890	£8	£15	£60	£150
1891	£20	£50	£140	£350
1892	£20	£50	£100	£300
1893 OH	*	£12	£30	£80
1893 proof	*	*	*	£120
1894	*	£12	£50	£125
1895	*	£12	£40	£90
1896	*	£12	£35	£90
1897	*	£12	£35	£90
1898	*	£12	£35	£90
1899	*	£12	£35	£90
1900	*	£12	£35	£90
1901	*	£12	£35	£90

Edward VII 1902 florin

EDWARD VII

	F	VF	EF	Unc
1902	*	£12	£40	£75
1902 matt proof	*	*	*	£65
1903	*	£25	£85	£300
1904	*	£32	£125	£325
1905	£35	£125	£475	£900
1906	*	£20	£95	£275
1907	*	£25	£90	£275
1908	*	£30	£170	£475
1909	*	£25	£150	£375
1910	*	£15	£60	£125

GEORGE V

	F	VF	EF	Unc
1911	*	*	£30	£85
1911 proof	*	*	*	£70
1912	*	*	£40	£95

	F	VF	EF	Unc
1913	*	*	£60	£145
1914	*	*	£25	£50
1915	*	*	£30	£55
1916	*	*	£20	£65
1917	*	*	£25	£55
1918	*	*	£20	£50
1919	*	*	£25	£55
1920	*	*	£25	£65
			£20	£60
1921	*	*	£18	£50
1922	*	*	£18	£45
1923	*	*	£18	£40
1924	*	*	£27	£55
1925	£15	£35	£125	£275
1926	*	*	£30	£80
1927 proof only	*	*		£50

George V 1928 florin

	F	VF	EF	Unc
1928	*	*	£7	£17
1929	*	*	£7	£17
1930	*	*	£10	£35
1931	*	*	£8	£20
1932	£15	£60	£150	£300
1933	*	*	£8	£20
1935	*	*	£8	£17
1936	*	*	£5	£15

GEORGE VI

	F	VF	EF	Unc
1937	*	*	*	£7
1937 proof	*	*	*	£15
1938	*	*	£4	£15
1939	*	*	*	£10
1940	*	*	*	£10
1941	*	*	*	£10
1942	*	*	*	£7
1943	*	*	*	£7
1944	*	*	*	£7
1945	*	*	*	£7
1946	*	*	*	£7
1947	*	*	*	£7
1948	*	*	*	£7
1949	*	*	*	£12
1950	*	*	*	£12
1950 proof	*	*	*	£12
1951	*	*	*	£15
1951 proof	*	*	*	£20

George VI 1949 florin

ELIZABETH II	F	VF	EF	Unc
1953	*	*	*	£6
1953 proof	*	*	*	£10
1954	*	*	*	£45
1955	*	*	*	£5
1956	*	*	*	£5
1957	*	*	*	£45
1958	*	*	*	£20
1959	*	*	*	£35
1960	*	*	*	£3
1961	*	*	*	£3
1962	*	*	*	£2
1963	*	*	*	£2
1964	*	*	*	£2
1965	*	*	*	£2
1966	*	*	*	£1
1967	*	*	*	£1

One and sixpence bank tokens

GEORGE III	F	VF	EF	Unc
1811	£9	£20	£60	£100
1812 laureate bust ...	£9	£20	£65	£110
1812 laureate head	£9	£20	£65	£110
1813	£9	£20	£65	£110
1814	£9	£20	£65	£110
1815	£9	£20	£65	£110
1816	£9	£20	£65	£110

Shillings

1658 shilling of Cromwell

CROMWELL	F	VF	EF
1658	£400	£750	£1500
1658 Dutch copy	*	*	*

Charles II 1671 shilling, plumes below bust

CHARLES II			
1663 1st bust	£80	£225	£850
1663 1st bust var	£80	£225	£850
1666 –	*	*	*
1666 – eleph	£350	£900	£3000
1666 guinea hd, eleph ...	£1250	£2750	*

	F	VF	EF
1666 2nd bust	£500	£2500	£5000
1668 1st bust var	£350	£900	*
1668 2nd bust	£50	£200	£650
1668/7 –	£90	£300	£800
1669/6 1st bust var ...ext. rare		*	*
1669 2nd bust ... ...ext. rare		*	*
1670 –	£85	£350	£900
1671 –	£95	£375	£975
1671 – plumes both sides	£400	£800	*
1672 –	£70	£250	£800
1673 –	£70	£350	£900
1673/2 –	£80	£400	£1250
1673 – plumes both sides	£425	£900	£2500
1674 –	£70	£350	£950
1674/3 –	£70	£350	£900
1674 – plumes both sides	£425	£900	£2500
1674 – plumes rev only ...	£425	£900	£2500
1674 3rd bust	£300	£700	£2500
1675 –	£350	£700	£2500
1675/3 –	£350	£700	£2500
1675 2nd bust	£250	£550	*
1675/4 –	£250	£550	*
1675 – plumes both sides	£425	£900	£2500
1676	£65	£250	£700
1676/5 –	£70	£300	£825
1676 – plumes both sides	£425	£900	£2500
1677 –	£60	£290	£750
1677 – plume obv only ...	£500	£1350	£3500
1678 –	£70	£350	£950
1678/7 –	£70	£350	£950
1679 –	£60	£250	£800
1679/7 –	£70	£250	£850
1679 plumes	£425	£900	£2500
1679 plumes obv only ...	£575	£1200	£3500
1680 –	Extremely rare		
1680 plumes	£425	£900	£2650
1680/79 –	£425	£900	£2650
1681 –	£100	£375	£950
1681/0 –	£100	£375	£950
1681/0 – eleph & castle ...	£1350	*	*
1682/1 –	£400	£875	*
1683 – ... ...Ext rare		*	*
1683 4th bust	£110	£350	£1250
1684 –	£100	£300	£1250

James II 1685 shilling

JAMES II			
1685	£100	£325	£1250
1685 no stops on rev	£150	£500	£1450
1685 plume on rev	Extremely Rare		
1686	£100	£325	£1150
1686 V/S	£100	£350	£1250
1687	£100	£325	£1150
1687/6	£100	£300	£1150
1688	£100	£325	£1250
1688/7	£100	£325	£1250
WILLIAM & MARY			
1692	£125	£350	£875
1693	£125	£300	£800

SHILLINGS

WILLIAM III

	F	VF	EF
1695	£20	£70	£400
1696	£20	£50	£275
1696 no stops on rev ...	£50	£150	£500
1669 in error	£750	*	*
1696 1st bust B	£35	£100	£400
1696 – C	£35	£100	£400
1696 – E	£35	£100	£400
1696 – N	£35	£100	£400
1696 – Y	£35	£100	£400
1696 – Y	£40	£110	£450
1696 2nd bust		unique	
1696 3rd bust C	£120	£300	£750
1696 – E		Extremely rare	
1697 1st bust	£15	£45	£250
1697 – no stops on rev ...	£50	£150	£450
1697 – B	£45	£95	£400
1697 – C	£40	£95	£400

1697 Shilling of BRISTOL: B below bust

	F	VF	EF
1697 – E	£40	£95	£400
1697 – N	£40	£95	£400
1697 – y	£40	£95	£400
1697 – Y	£40	£95	£450
1697 3rd bust	£25	£60	£250
1697 – B	£40	£95	£425
1697 – C	£30	£80	£375
1697 – E	£40	£95	£400
1697 – N	£40	£95	£400
1697 – y	£35	£95	£400
1697 3rd bust var	£20	£65	£250
1697 – B	£30	£80	£350
1697 – C	£120	£250	£650
1698	£35	£95	£400
1698 – plumes	£150	£350	£875
1698 4th bust	£85	£250	£800
1699 –	£90	£250	£800
1699 5th bust	£80	£200	£600
1699 – plumes	£120	£350	£1200
1699 – roses	£120	£350	£1200
1700 –	£25	£60	£200
1700 – no stops on rev ...	£40	£150	£300
1700 – plume	£1500	*	*
1701 –	£65	£200	£500
1701 – plumes	£120	£325	£750

Anne 1702 shilling, VIGO below bust

ANNE

	F	VF	EF
1702 – 1st bust	£60	£200	£475

	F	VF	EF
1702 – plumes	£70	£225	£525
1702 – VIGO	£60	£200	£475
1703 2nd bust VIGO	£60	£200	£425
1704 –	£300	£650	£2000
1704 – plumes	£80	£275	£600
1705 –	£80	£250	£550
1705 – plumes	£75	£225	£500
1705 – r&p	£70	£200	£450
1707 – r&p	£70	£200	£450
1707 – E	£60	£125	£400
1707 – E★	£90	£250	£500
1707 3rd bust	£25	£90	£250
1707 – plumes	£40	£145	£400
1707 – E	£30	£85	£325
1707 Edin bust E★	£250	£450	*
1708 2nd bust E	£80	£225	£575
1708 – E★	£70	£165	£475
1708/7 – E★		Extremely rare	
1708 – r&p	£110	£300	£625
1708 3rd bust	£30	£60	£225
1708 – plumes	£50	£150	£400
1708 – r&p	£60	£250	£500
1708 – E	£80	£200	£450
1708 – E	£95	£225	£550
1708 – Edin bust E★	£80	£200	£475
1709 –	£50	£100	£350
1709 - Edin bust E	£200	£650	*
1709 - Edin bust E *... ...	£90	£225	£500
1710 – r&p	£45	£175	£375
1710 4th bust prf		Extremely rare	
1710 – r&p	£50	£150	£475
1711 3rd bust	£175	£425	£900
1711 4th bust	£20	£70	£200
1712 – r&p	£30	£120	£325
1713/2 –	£50	£135	£350
1714 –	£35	£100	£300
1714/3 –		Extremely rare	

George I 1723 SS C shilling

GEORGE I

	F	VF	EF
1715 1st bust r&p	£30	£100	£350
1716 –	£100	£250	£700
1717 –	£30	£100	£350
1718 –	£40	£110	£350
1719 –	£80	£200	£525
1720 –	£35	£100	£350
1720 – plain	£30	£100	£300
1720 – large 0	£30	£110	£350
1721 –	£175	£500	£850
1721 r&p	£30	£100	£375
1721/0 –	£30	£100	£375
1721/19	£35	£135	£425
1721/18 –	£35	£135	£425
1722 –	£30	£120	£425
1723 –	£30	£125	£425
1723 - SS C	£30	£60	£200
1723 - SSC - C/SS	£35	£90	£225
1723 - SSC Fench arms at date...	£125	£400	£1250
1723 2nd bust SS C...	£50	£100	£275
1723 - r&p	£50	£125	£375
1723 - w.c.c...	£375	£750	£2000
1724 - r&p	£50	£125	£375
1724 - w.c.c	£375	£750	£2000

	F	VF	EF
1725 – r & p	£50	£125	£375
1725 – no obv stops	£75	£175	£525
1725 – w.c.c.	£400	£750	£2000
1726 – r & p	£500	*	*
1726 – w.c.c.	£450	£800	£2150
1727 – r & p	£500	*	*
1727 – – no stops on obv	£400	£1100	*

GEORGE II
	F	VF	EF
1727 YH plumes	£60	£250	£675
1727 – r & p	£60	£135	£425
1728 –	£150	£375	£950
1728 – r & p	£70	£150	£500
1729 – –	£80	£150	£500
1731 – –	£60	£135	£425
1731 – plumes	£120	£300	£825
1732 – r & p	£70	£150	£500
1734 – –	£50	£110	£350
1735 – –	£50	£110	£350
1736 – –	£50	£110	£350
1736/5 – –	£70	£150	£500
1737 – –	£50	£110	£350
1739 – roses	£25	£90	£300
1741 – roses	£25	£90	£300

SHILLINGS
	F	VF	EF	Unc
1787 – no stops on obv	£250	£500	*	*
1787 hearts	£10	£20	£50	£100
1798 'Dorrien and Magens'	*	£2850	£4500	£6000
1816	*	£5	£50	£80
1817	*	£5	£50	£80
1817 GEOE	£50	£125	£350	£750
1818	£4	£25	£100	£175
1819	*	£4	£50	£95
1819/8	*	*	£95	£175
1820	*	£4	£40	£100

GEORGE IV
	F	VF	EF	Unc
1820 1st hd 1st rev pattern or prf	*	*	£2000	£3000
1821 1st hd 1st rev	£10	£30	£125	£250
1821 – proof	*	*	£400	£600
1823 – 2nd rev	£20	£50	£225	*
1824 – –	£8	£35	£125	£225
1825 – –	£15	£40	£130	£250
1825 2nd hd	£10	£25	£110	£200
1826 –	*	£25	£100	£185

1763 'Northumberland' Shilling

George IV 1824 shilling

	F	VF	EF
1743 OH roses	£25	£70	£250
1745 –	£30	£80	£275
1745 – LIMA	£20	£60	£250
1746 – – LIMA	£80	£195	£525
1746/5 – LIMA	£110	£200	£575
1746 – proof	*	£500	£800
1747 – roses	£25	£90	£250
1750 –	£40	£110	£325
1750/6 –	£50	£125	£395
1750 – 5 over 4	£50	£125	£395
1751 –	£80	£200	£500
1758 –	£12	£25	£50

	F	VF	EF	Unc
1826 – proof	*	*	£150	£250
1827	£10	£50	£200	£400
1829	*	£40	£125	£325

WILLIAM IV
	F	VF	EF	Unc
1831 proof	*	*	*	£375
1834	£10	£30	£115	£265
1835	£10	£35	£135	£300
1836	£15	£25	£135	£265
1837	£25	£75	£175	£425

William IV 1837 shilling

VICTORIA
	F	VF	EF	Unc
1838	£8	£18	£100	£200
1839	£8	£20	£100	£200
1839 2nd YH	£8	£20	£100	£200
1839 – proof	*	*	*	£400
1840	£12	£35	£135	£250
1841	£12	£35	£135	£250
1842	£10	£20	£80	£175
1843	£12	£30	£125	£225
1844	£8	£20	£80	£175
1845	£8	£20	£85	£195
1846	£8	£20	£80	£175
1848/6	£40	£125	£450	£750
1849	£12	£25	£125	£225

1728 Young Head Shilling

GEORGE III
	F	VF	EF	Unc
1763 'Northumberland'	£200	£350	£550	£750
1786 proof or pattern	*	*	*	£4000
1787 no hearts	£10	£20	£50	£100
1787 – no stop over head	£15	£35	£85	£150
1787 – no stops at date	£15	£40	£120	£200

SHILLINGS

	F	VF	EF	Unc
1850	£200	£800	£1500	*
1850/46	£200	£800	£1500	*
1851	£40	£150	£450	*
1852	£8	£20	£75	£150
1853	£8	£20	£75	£150
1853 proof	*	*	*	£400
1854	£75	£300	£975	*
1855	£8	£20	£60	£150
1856	£8	£20	£60	£150
1857	£8	£20	£60	£150
1857 F:G:	£200	*	*	*
1858	£8	£20	£60	£150
1859	£8	£20	£60	£150
1860	£10	£25	£80	£225
1861	£10	£25	£80	£225
1862	£15	£35	£100	£265

Victoria 1839 shilling

	F	VF	EF	Unc
1863	£15	£50	£300	£650
1863/1	£60	£150	£500	*
1864	£8	£15	£70	£150
1865	£8	£15	£70	£150
1866	£8	£15	£70	£150
1866 BBITANNIAR ...	*	*	£450	*
1867	£8	£15	£80	£165
1867 3rd YH, die no.	£150	£325	*	*
1868	£8	£20	£80	£150
1869	£12	£30	£80	£190
1870	£10	£25	£80	£175
1871	£8	£20	£65	£160
1872	£8	£20	£65	£160
1873	£8	£20	£65	£160
1874	£8	£20	£65	£160
1875	£8	£20	£65	£150
1876	£10	£25	£70	£160
1877 die no.	£8	£20	£65	£150
1877 no die no	*	*	*	*
1878	£8	£20	£65	£150
1879 3rd YH	£45	£100	£250	*
1879 4th YH	£8	£20	£65	£125
1880	£6	£15	£55	£110
1880 longer line below SHILLING	*	*	*	*
1881	£6	£15	£55	£110
1881 longer line below SHILLING	£6	£15	£50	£110
1881 – Large rev lettering	£6	£15	£50	£100
1882	£10	£35	£85	£185
1883	£6	£15	£50	£100
1884	£6	£15	£50	£100
1885	£6	£15	£50	£100
1886	£6	£15	£50	£100
1887	£7	£25	£90	£165
1887 JH	*	*	£12	£25
1887 proof	*	*	*	£80
1888	*	£6	£35	£60
1889	£40	£100	£300	*
1889 large JH	*	*	£35	£60
1890	*	*	£35	£70
1891	*	*	£35	£70
1892	*	*	£35	£70

Victoria Jubilee Head and Old Head shillings

	F	VF	EF	Unc
1893 OH	*	*	£25	£50
1893 – proof	*	*	*	£100
1893 small obv letters	*	*	£30	£65
1894	*	*	£35	£65
1895	*	*	£30	£55
1896	*	*	£30	£55
1897	*	*	£30	£50
1898	*	*	£30	£50
1899	*	*	£30	£50
1900	*	*	£30	£50
1901	*	*	£25	£40

EDWARD VII

	F	VF	EF	Unc
1902	*	*	£40	£60
1902 matt prf	*	*	£40	£60

Edward VII 1905 shilling

	F	VF	EF	Unc
1903	*	£15	£80	£300
1904	*	£12	£70	£250
1905	£40	£120	£400	£1500
1906	*	*	£40	£125
1907	*	*	£45	£150
1908	£8	£20	£100	£250
1909	£8	£20	£110	£275
1910	*	*	£30	£90

GEORGE V

	F	VF	EF	Unc
1911	*	*	£18	£40
1911 proof	*	*	*	£35
1912	*	*	£25	£65
1913	*	*	£40	£80
1914	*	*	£15	£35
1915	*	*	£15	£35
1916	*	*	£15	£35
1917	*	*	£17	£35
1918	*	*	£15	£30
1919	*	*	£20	£45
1920	*	*	£20	£40
1921	*	*	£25	£50

George V nickel trial shilling, 1924

	F	VF	EF	Unc
1922	*	*	£22	£45
1923	*	*	£18	£40
1923 nickel	*	*	£550	£750
1924	*	*	£25	£45
1924 nickel	*	*	£550	£750
1925	*	*	£30	£75
1926	*	*	£18	£50
1926 mod eff	*	*	£18	£40
1927 –	*	*	£18	£40
1927 new type	*	*	£8	£30
1927 – proof	*	*	*	£20
1928	*	*	*	£12
1929	*	*	£7	£15
1930	*	*	£15	£35
1931	*	*	£7	£15
1932	*	*	£7	£15
1933	*	*	£7	£15
1934	*	*	£10	£28
1935	*	*	£3	£12
1936	*	*	£3	£12

GEORGE VI

	F	VF	EF	Unc
1937 Eng	*	*	*	£6
1937 Eng prf	*	*	*	£8
1937 Scot	*	*	*	£4
1937 Scot prf	*	*	*	£7
1938 Eng	*	*	£5	£20
1938 Scot	*	*	£5	£18
1939 Eng	*	*	*	£8
1939 Scot	*	*	*	£8
1940 Eng	*	*	*	£8
1940 Scot	*	*	*	£8
1941 Eng	*	*	*	£7
1941 Scot	*	*	£2	£8
1942 Eng	*	*	*	£7
1942 Scot	*	*	*	£8
1943 Eng	*	*	*	£7
1943 Scot	*	*	*	£8
1944 Eng	*	*	*	£7
1944 Scot	*	*	*	£7
1945 Eng	*	*	*	£7
1945 Scot	*	*	*	£6
1946 Eng	*	*	*	£6
1946 Scot	*	*	*	£6
1947 Eng	*	*	*	£5
1947 Scot	*	*	*	£5

Reverses: English (left), Scottish (right)

	F	VF	EF	Unc
1948 Eng	*	*	*	£7
1948 Scot	*	*	*	£7
1949 Eng	*	*	*	£15
1949 Scot	*	*	*	£15
1950 Eng	*	*	*	£17
1950 Eng prf	*	*	*	£17
1950 Scot	*	*	*	£17
1950 Scot prf	*	*	*	£17
1951 Eng	*	*	*	£17
1951 Eng prf	*	*	*	£17
1951 Scot	*	*	*	£17
1951 Scot prf	*	*	*	£17

ELIZABETH II

	F	VF	EF	Unc
1953 Eng	*	*	*	£4
1953 Eng prf	*	*	*	£8
1953 Scot	*	*	*	£4

	F	VF	EF	Unc
1953 Scot prf	*	*	*	£8
1954 Eng	*	*	*	£4
1954 Scot	*	*	*	£4
1955 Eng	*	*	*	£4
1955 Scot	*	*	*	£4
1956 Eng	*	*	*	£6
1956 Scot	*	*	*	£8
1957 Eng	*	*	*	£3
1957 Scot	*	*	*	£15
1958 Eng	*	*	*	£15
1958 Scot	*	*	*	£3

Reverses: English (left), Scottish (right)

	F	VF	EF	Unc
1959 Eng	*	*	*	£3
1959 Scot	*	*	*	£25
1960 Eng	*	*	*	£2
1960 Scot	*	*	*	£3
1961 Eng	*	*	*	£2
1961 Scot	*	*	*	£10
1962 Eng	*	*	*	£1
1962 Scot	*	*	*	£1
1963 Eng	*	*	*	£1
1963 Scot	*	*	*	£1
1964 Eng	*	*	*	£1
1964 Scot	*	*	*	£1
1965 Eng	*	*	*	£1
1965 Scot	*	*	*	£1
1966 Eng	*	*	*	£1
1966 Scot	*	*	*	£1

Sixpences

	F	VF	EF
CROMWELL			
1658		of the highest rarity	
1658 Dutch copy	*	£1500	£3000
CHARLES II			
1674	£50	£175	£500
1675	£50	£175	£500
1675/4	£50	£175	£525
1676	£50	£175	£525
1676/5	£50	£175	£525
1677	£50	£175	£550
1678/7	£50	£175	£550

Charles II 1678 sixpence

	F	VF	EF
1679	£50	£150	£550
1680	£60	£225	£700

SIXPENCES

	F	VF	EF
1681	£50	£150	£475
1682	£50	£200	£550
1682/1	£50	£150	£475
1683	£50	£150	£425
1684	£50	£180	£525

James II 1688 sixpence

JAMES II

	F	VF	EF
1686 early shields	£75	£285	£700
1687 –	£75	£285	£700
1687/6	£75	£285	£700
1687 later shield	£75	£285	£700
1687/6	£75	£300	£800
1688 –	£75	£300	£750

WILLIAM AND MARY

	F	VF	EF
1693	£75	£275	£675
1693 3 upside down	£85	£285	£675
1694	£90	£285	£700

William and Mary 1694 sixpence

WILLIAM III

	F	VF	EF
1695 1st bust early harp	£35	£70	£300
1696 - -	£20	£50	£150
1696 - - no obv stops	£25	£70	£250
1696/5	£25	£80	£275
1696 - - B	£20	£55	£200
1696 - - C	£30	£70	£250
1696 - - E	£30	£70	£250
1696 - - N	£30	£80	£250
1696 - - y	£25	£65	£225
1696 - - Y	£35	£80	£285
1696 - later harp	£45	£110	£265
1696 - - B	£45	£150	£350
1696 - - C	£50	£200	£375
1696 - - N	£50	£160	£365
1696 2nd bust	£150	£425	£975
1696 - - E, 3rd Bust, early harp	Extremely rare		
1696 - - y, 3rd Bust, early harp	Extremely rare		
1697 1st bust early harp	£15	£40	£140
1697 - - B	£35	£80	£225
1697 - - C	£35	£90	£225
1697 - - E	£35	£90	£225
1697 - - N	£35	£65	£225
1697 - - y	£35	£65	£225
1697 2nd bust	£100	£300	£700
1697 3rd bust later harp	£15	£40	£175
1697 - - B	£35	£80	£275
1697 - - C	£50	£100	£325
1697 - - E	£55	£95	£325
1697 - - Y	£45	£95	£325
1698 - -	£35	£80	£225
1698 - - plumes	£55	£185	£325
1699 - -	£60	£200	£425
1699 - - plumes	£70	£185	£400

William III 1699 sixpence, plumes

	F	VF	EF
1699 - - roses	£70	£175	£500
1700	£20	£50	£180
1700	£1500	*	*
17001	£30	£50	£200

ANNE

	F	VF	EF
1703 VIGO	£30	£80	£200
1705	£50	£165	£350
1705 plumes	£40	£125	£275
1705 roses & plumes	£45	£120	£345
1707 - -	£40	£110	£250
1707 plain	£25	£70	£165
1707 E	£20	£80	£200

Anne 1707 sixpence, E below bust

	F	VF	EF
1707 plumes	£30	£75	£225
1708 plain	£25	£70	£125
1708 E	£30	£70	£250
1708/7 E	£50	£120	£325
1708 E★	£35	£90	£275
1708/7 E★	£50	£120	£300
1708 Edin bust E★	£35	£90	£275
1708 plumes	£35	£100	£265
1710 roses & plumes	£35	£100	£265
1711	£15	£75	£125

George I 1717 sixpence

GEORGE I

	F	VF	EF
1717	£40	£145	£350
1720/17	£40	£145	£350
1723 SS C, Small letters on obv	£20	£60	£150
1723 SS C, large letters on both sides	£20	£60	£150
1726 roses & plumes	£30	£165	£375

GEORGE II

	F	VF	EF
1728 YH	£60	£200	£450
1728 – plumes	£45	£125	£300
1728 – r & p	£25	£85	£275
1731 - -	£25	£85	£275
1732 - -	£25	£85	£275
1734 - -	£30	£85	£285
1735 - -	£30	£90	£275
1736 - -	£30	£85	£275
1739 – roses	£25	£80	£200
1739 – – O/R	£50	£150	£325

	F	VF	EF
1741 – –	£25	£80	£200
1743 OH	£25	£80	£200
1745 – –	£25	£80	£200
1745/3 – –	£30	£85	£250
1745 – LIMA	£20	£65	£135
1746 – LIMA	£20	£65	£135
1746 – plain proof	*	*	£600

George II 1746 sixpence

	F	VF	EF
1750	£35	£110	£250
1751	£35	£125	£325
1757	£5	£12	£40
1757	£5	£12	£40
1758/7	£10	£35	£50

GEORGE III

	F	VF	EF	Unc
1787 hearts	£10	£20	£50	£85
1787 no hearts	£10	£20	£50	£85
1816	£8	£12	£35	£60
1817	£8	£12	£35	£60
1818	£8	£18	£40	£100
1819	£8	£15	£25	£75
1819 small 8	£10	£20	£75	£150
1820	£8	£15	£30	£75
1820 1 inverted	£30	£100	£350	£600

GEORGE IV

	F	VF	EF	Unc
1820 1st hd 1st rev ...	*	*	*	£1,750
(pattern or proof)				
1821 1st hd 1st rev ...	£8	£20	£85	£175
1821 –				
BBITANNIAR	£90	£175	£500	*
1824 1st hd 2nd				
rev	£8	£20	£85	£175
1825 – –	£8	£20	£85	£175
1826 – –	£20	£60	£200	£400
1826 2nd hd 3rd				
rev	£5	£14	£85	£175

George IV 1825 sixpence

	F	VF	EF	Unc
1826 – – proof	*	*	*	£250
1827	£15	£45	£185	£350
1828	£8	£20	£125	£200
1829	£6	£20	£110	£185

WILLIAM IV

	F	VF	EF	Unc
1831	£6	£20	£90	£175
1831 proof	*	*	*	£275
1834	£6	£30	£70	£175
1835	£6	£20	£85	£175
1836	£15	£35	£125	£225
1837	£12	£30	£125	£225

VICTORIA

	F	VF	EF	Unc
1838	£5	£12	£60	£100
1839	£5	£12	£60	£100
1839 proof	*	*	*	£250

	F	VF	EF	Unc
1840	£5	£10	£60	£120
1841	£5	£10	£60	£150
1842	£5	£10	£75	£125
1843	£5	£10	£60	£120
1844	£5	£10	£60	£120
1845	£5	£10	£60	£120
1846	£3	£10	£60	£120
1848	£15	£90	£400	£650
1848/6	£10	£80	£325	£675
1848/7	£10	£80	£325	£675
1850	£5	£18	£70	£150
1850 5 over 3	£15	£45	£250	£450
1851	£4	£12	£60	£120
1852	£4	£12	£60	£120
1853	£5	£15	£60	£115
1853 proof	*	*	*	£325
1854	£40	£125	£500	*
1855	£4	£12	£60	£110
1856	£4	£12	£60	£115
1857	£4	£12	£60	£115
1858	£4	£12	£60	£110
1859	£4	£12	£60	£110
1859/8	£8	£20	£70	£120
1860	£5	£15	£70	£115
1862	£20	£60	£350	£700
1863	£12	£40	£250	£600
1864	£5	£12	£55	£120
1865	£6	£14	£60	£150
1866	£5	£12	£50	£120
1866 no die no. ...	*	*	*	*
1867	£8	£20	£70	£150
1868	£8	£20	£70	£150
1869	£8	£25	£100	£200
1870	£8	£20	£100	£200
1871	£5	£12	£60	£125
1871 no die no. ...	£5	£12	£60	£125
1872	£5	£12	£60	£120
1873	£5	£12	£60	£120
1874	£5	£12	£60	£120
1875	£5	£12	£65	£120
1876	£6	£20	£75	£165
1877	£5	£12	£60	£110
1877 no die no. ...	£5	£12	£60	£110
1878	£5	£10	£55	£95
1878 DRITANNIAR ...	£65	£150	£450	*
1879 die no.	£8	£20	£80	£165
1879 no die no. ...	£5	£10	£55	£110
1880 2nd YH	£7	£15	£50	£95
1880 3rd YH	£3	£8	£35	£75
1881	£4	£10	£35	£75
1882	£8	£20	£70	£150
1883	£4	£10	£30	£60
1884	£4	£10	£30	£60
1885	£4	£10	£30	£60
1886	£4	£10	£30	£60
1887 YH	£4	£10	£30	£60
1887 JH shield rev	£2	£5	£10	£18

1887 Jubilee Head sixpence, withdrawn type

	F	VF	EF	Unc
1887 – proof	*	*	*	£90
1887 – new rev	£2	£5	£10	£20
1888	£3	£5	£15	£40
1889	£3	£7	£15	£40

SIXPENCES

	F	VF	EF	Unc
1890	*	£3	£15	£50
1891	*	£3	£17	£55
1892	*	£3	£17	£55
1893	£250	£650	£1250	*
1893 OH	*	£3	£15	£45
1893 proof	*	*	*	£100
1894	*	£3	£25	£45
1895	*	£3	£25	£45
1896	*	£3	£25	£45
1897	*	£3	£20	£40
1898	*	£3	£20	£40
1899	*	£3	£25	£45
1900	*	£3	£20	£40
1901	*	£3	£20	£40

EDWARD VII

	F	VF	EF	Unc
1902	*	£5	£25	£45
1902 matt proof ...	*	*	*	£40
1903	*	£7	£25	£65
1904	*	£12	£45	£100
1905	*	£8	£30	£80
1906	*	£5	£25	£70
1907	*	£7	£25	£70
1908	*	£8	£35	£85
1909	*	£6	£30	£65
1910	*	£6	£22	£40

GEORGE V

	F	VF	EF	Unc
1911	*	*	£12	£30
1911 proof	*	*	*	£40
1912	*	*	£20	£45
1913	*	*	£30	£45
1914	*	*	£12	£20
1915	*	*	£12	£20
1916	*	*	£12	£20
1917	*	*	£20	£40
1918	*	*	£12	£15
1919	*	*	£12	£20
1920	*	*	£12	£35
1920 debased	*	*	£12	£35
1921	*	*	£10	£30
1922	*	*	£10	£30
1923	*	*	£10	£40
1924	*	*	£10	£30
1925	*	*	£10	£25
1925 new rim	*	*	£12	£20
1926 new rim	*	*	£12	£25
1926 mod effigy ...	*	*	£6	£25
1927	*	*	£4	£25
1927 new rev prf ...	*	*	£4	£25
1928	*	*	£4	£17
1929	*	*	£4	£17
1930	*	*	£4	£17
1931	*	*	£4	£17
1932	*	*	£7	£22
1933	*	*	£4	£15
1934	*	*	£5	£20

George V 1929 sixpence

	F	VF	EF	Unc
1935	*	*	£3	£10
1936	*	*	£3	£10

GEORGE VI

	F	VF	EF	Unc
1937	*	*	£1	£5
1937 proof	*	*	*	£10
1938	*	*	£4	£12
1939	*	*	£2	£7
1940	*	*	£2	£7
1941	*	*	£2	£7
1942	*	*	£1	£6
1943	*	*	£1	£6
1944	*	*	£1	£6
1945	*	*	£1	£6
1946	*	*	£1	£6
1947	*	*	*	£5
1948	*	*	£1	£5
1949	*	*	£1	£7
1950	*	*	£1	£7
1950 proof	*	*	*	£10
1951	*	*	£1	£12
1951 proof	*	*	*	£10
1952	*	£5	£20	£50

ELIZABETH II

	F	VF	EF	Unc
1953	*	*	*	£3
1953 proof	*	*	*	£5
1954	*	*	*	£5
1955	*	*	*	£3
1956	*	*	*	£3
1957	*	*	*	£3
1958	*	*	*	£2
1959	*	*	*	£2
1960	*	*	*	£2
1961	*	*	*	£2
1962	*	*	*	£1
1963	*	*	*	£1
1964	*	*	*	£1
1965	*	*	*	£1
1966	*	*	*	£1
1967	*	*	*	£1

Groats (fourpences)

William IV 1836 groat
Earlier dates are included in Maundy sets

WILLIAM IV

	F	VF	EF	Unc
1836	*	*	£40	£70
1836 proof	*	*	*	£525
1837	*	£12	£50	£85

Victoria 1842 groat

VICTORIA

	F	VF	EF	Unc
1838	*	£5	£20	£65
1838 8 over 8 on side	*	£10	£35	£110
1839	*	£8	£25	£70
1839 proof	*	*	*	£200
1840	£2	£10	£30	£70
1840 narrow 0	*	£12	£50	*
1841	£3	£10	£35	£80
1841 I for last 1	*	*	*	*
1842	*	£8	£30	£80

	F	VF	EF	Unc
1842/1	£4	£15	£70	£100
1843	*	£5	£25	£80
1844	*	£8	£35	£80
1845	*	£8	£35	£80
1846	*	£8	£35	£80
1847/6	£25	£50	£250	*
1848	*	£8	£25	£65
1848/6	£15	£65	£250	*
1848/7	£5	£15	£50	£125
1849	*	£8	£25	£70
1849/8	*	£8	£45	£90
1851	£15	£60	£200	*
1852	£40	£100	£300	*
1853	£35	£90	£400	*
1853 proof	*	*	*	£300
1854	*	£8	£25	£60
1854 5 over 3	£5	£10	£40	*
1855	*	£8	£25	£60
1857 proof	*	*	*	£850
1862 proof	*	*	*	*
1888 JH	£5	£10	£30	£65

Silver threepences

Earlier dates are included in Maundy sets

WILLIAM IV	F	VF	EF	Unc
1834	*	£10	£60	£125
1835	*	£10	£60	£110
1836	*	£10	£60	£125
1837	£10	£20	£75	£150

Victoria threepence of 1848

VICTORIA

		F	VF	EF	Unc
1838		*	£8	£50	£100
1839		*	£10	£70	£150
1840		*	£10	£60	£120
1841		*	£10	£60	£150
1842		*	£10	£60	£150
1843		*	£10	£60	£110
1844		*	£12	£65	£150
1845		*	£5	£40	£85
1846		*	£15	£85	£165
1847		*	*	£400	£800
1848		*	*	£400	£750
1849		*	£12	£60	£150
1850		*	£5	£45	£80
1851		*	£8	£40	£120
1852		£45	£175	£400	*
1853		*	£20	£70	£175
1854		*	£8	£50	£95
1855		*	£12	£65	£150
1856		*	£10	£60	£150
1857		*	£10	£60	£150
1858		*	£8	£45	£90
1858/6		*	£25	£125	*
1859		*	£4	£40	£100
1860		*	£8	£45	£150
1861		*	£4	£40	£100
1862		*	£8	£50	£95
1863		*	£10	£60	£125
1864		*	£8	£50	£95
1865		*	£10	£60	£125
1866		*	£8	£50	£95
1867		*	£8	£50	£95

SILVER THREEPENCES

	F	VF	EF	Unc
1868	*	£8	£50	£95
1868 RRITANNIAR	ext.rare			*
1869	£10	£30	£100	£150
1870	*	£6	£40	£85
1871	*	£7	£50	£100
1872	*	£5	£45	£100
1873	*	£5	£30	£60
1874	*	£5	£30	£55
1875	*	£5	£30	£55
1876	*	£5	£30	£55
1877	*	£5	£30	£55
1878	*	£5	£30	£55
1879	*	£5	£30	£55
1880	*	£6	£35	£60
1881	*	£6	£35	£60
1882	*	£8	£40	£80
1883	*	£5	£30	£55
1884	*	£5	£30	£55
1885	*	£5	£25	£50
1886	*	£5	£25	£50
1887 YH	*	£6	£30	£55
1887 JH	*	£2	£5	£8
1887 proof	*	*	*	£40
1888	*	£2	£7	£25
1889	*	£2	£6	£20
1890	*	£2	£6	£20
1891	*	£2	£6	£20
1892	*	£3	£10	£25
1893	£12	£40	£100	£250
1893 OH	*	*	£4	£20
1893 OH proof	*	*	*	£65
1894	*	£2	£8	£25
1895	*	£2	£8	£25
1896	*	£2	£6	£25
1897	*	*	£5	£25
1898	*	*	£5	£25
1899	*	*	£5	£25
1900	*	*	£5	£25
1901	*	*	£5	£20

EDWARD VII

	F	VF	EF	Unc
1902	*	*	£6	£12
1902 matt proof	*	*	*	£15
1903	*	£1.50	£15	£40
1904	*	£6	£20	£50
1905	*	£6	£20	£40
1906	*	£3	£15	£40
1907	*	£1.50	£12	£40
1908	*	£1.50	£10	£35
1909	*	£2	£15	£40
1910	*	£1.25	£10	£25

George V 1927 threepence, acorns on reverse

GEORGE V

	F	VF	EF	Unc
1911	*	*	£3	£15
1911 proof	*	*	*	£30
1912	*	*	£3	£15
1913	*	*	£3	£15
1914	*	*	£2	£12
1915	*	*	£2	£12
1916	*	*	£1.50	£10
1917	*	*	£1.50	£10
1918	*	*	£2	£10
1919	*	*	£2	£10

SILVER THREEPENCES

	F	VF	EF	Unc
1920	*	*	£2	£15
1920 debased	*	*	£2	£15
1921	*	*	£2	£17
1922	*	*	£2	£17
1925	*	£1	£6	£23
1926	*	£3	£10	£30
1926 mod effigy ...	*	£1	£6	£25
1927 new rev prf ...	*	*	*	£45
1928	*	£2	£6	£25
1930	*	£1.50	£5	£15
1931	*	*	£1	£7
1932	*	*	£1	£7
1933	*	*	£1	£7
1934	*	*	£1	£7
1935	*	*	£1	£7
1936	*	*	£1	£7

GEORGE VI

	F	VF	EF	Unc
1937	*	*	£1	£2
1937 proof	*	*	*	£10
1938	*	*	£1	£6
1939	*	£1	£3	£10
1940	*	*	£1	£8
1941	*	*	£1	£12
1942	£1	£2	£6	£35
1943	£1	£3	£7	£45
1944	£1.50	£5	£12	£60
1945[2]	*	*	*	*

[1]Threepences issued for use in the Colonies.
[2]All specimens of 1945 were thought to have been melted down but it appears that one or two still exist.

Small silver for Colonies

These tiny coins were struck for use in some of the Colonies – they were never issued for circulation in Britain. However, they are often included in collections of British coins and it is for this reason that prices for them are given here.

TWOPENCES

Other dates are included in Maundy sets.

VICTORIA	F	VF	EF	Unc
1838	*	£2	£15	£35
1838 2nd 8 like S ...	*	£6	£25	£75
1848	*	£2	£15	£35

THREEHALFPENCES

WILLIAM IV	F	VF	EF	Unc
1834	*	£5	£30	£60
1835	*	£5	£65	£125
1835/4	*	£10	£35	£95
1836	*	£5	£30	£60
1837	£10	£25	£100	£250

VICTORIA	F	VF	EF	Unc
1838	*	£5	£25	£50
1839	*	£3	£25	£50
1840	*	£7	£65	£110
1841	*	£5	£30	£60
1842	*	£5	£30	£60
1843	*	£5	£15	£50

George V threepence

	F	VF	EF	Unc
1843/34	£5	£20	£65	£135
1860	£4	£15	£45	£100
1862	£4	£15	£45	£100
1870 proof	Extremely rare			

Maundy sets

EF prices are for evenly matched sets

Charles II 1677 Maundy set

CHARLES II	F	VF	EF
1670	£60	£140	£350
1671	£60	£140	£350
1672	£65	£145	£375
1673	£60	£140	£350
1674	£60	£140	£350
1675	£65	£165	£375
1676	£65	£165	£375
1677	£60	£140	£350
1678	£75	£200	£400
1679	£65	£165	£375
1680	£60	£145	£350
1681	£75	£200	£400
1682	£65	£165	£375
1683	£60	£145	£350
1684	£65	£165	£375

JAMES II			
1686	£70	£225	£450
1687	£65	£225	£450
1688	£70	£225	£450

WILLIAM AND MARY			
1689	£250	£450	£875
1691	£90	£200	£450
1692	£100	£200	£575
1693	£100	£200	£575
1694	£90	£150	£500

WILLIAM III			
1698	£75	£185	£450
1699	£85	£225	£500
1700	£85	£225	£500
1701	£75	£185	£475

	F	VF	EF
ANNE			
1703	£70	£135	£400
1705	£70	£135	£400
1706	£60	£125	£375
1708	£75	£150	£400
1709	£65	£135	£350
1710	£75	£150	£400
1713	£65	£125	£385
GEORGE I			
1723	£75	£150	£400
1727	£70	£130	£375
GEORGE II			
1729	£60	£125	£300
1731	£60	£125	£300
1732	£55	£120	£250
1735	£55	£120	£250
1737	£55	£120	£250
1739	£55	£120	£250
1740	£55	£120	£250
1743	£55	£125	£300
1746	£50	£110	£225
1760	£70	£150	£275

	F	VF	EF	Unc
GEORGE III				
1763	*	£75	£175	£250
1766	*	£80	£200	£275
1772	*	£20	£200	£275
1780	*	£80	£200	£275
1784	*	£80	£200	£275
1786	*	£80	£200	£275
1792 wire type	*	£125	£350	£400

William and Mary 1694 Maundy set

	F	VF	EF	Unc
1795	*	£60	£110	£250
1800	*	£60	£110	£250
1817	*	£65	£110	£250
1818	*	£65	£110	£250
1820	*	£65	£110	£250
GEORGE IV				
1822	*	*	£90	£175
1823	*	*	£90	£175
1824	*	*	£90	£175
1825	*	*	£90	£175
1826	*	*	£90	£175
1827	*	*	£90	£175
1828	*	*	£90	£175
1829	*	*	£90	£175
1830	*	*	£90	£175
WILLIAM IV				
1831	*	£65	£100	£200
1831 proof	*	*	*	£400
1832	*	£65	£100	£225
1833	*	£60	£90	£175
1834	*	£60	£90	£175
1835	*	£60	£90	£175

MAUNDY SETS

	F	VF	EF	Unc
1836	*	£65	£110	£250
1837	*	£65	£110	£250
VICTORIA				
1838			£70	£130
1839			£75	£125
1839 proof			*	£250
1840			£75	£125
1841			£75	£135
1842			£80	£145
1843			£80	£125
1844			£80	£125
1845			£70	£120
1846			£80	£150
1847			£80	£140

George IV 1825

	EF	Unc
1848	£75	£150
1849	£80	£165
1850	£65	£110
1851	£65	£110
1852	£70	£125
1853	£70	£125
1853 proof	*	£500
1854	£70	£125
1855	£70	£125
1856	£70	£110
1857	£70	£110
1858	£70	£110
1859	£70	£110
1860	£70	£100
1861	£70	£100
1862	£70	£100
1863	£70	£100
1864	£70	£100
1865	£70	£100
1866	£70	£100
1867	£70	£100
1868	£70	£100
1869	£70	£100
1870	£70	£90
1871	£70	£90
1872	£70	£90
1873	£70	£90
1874	£70	£90
1875	£70	£90
1876	£70	£90
1877	£70	£90
1878	£70	£90
1879	£70	£90
1880	£70	£90
1881	£70	£90
1882	£70	£90
1883	£70	£90
1884	£70	£90
1885	£70	£90
1886	£70	£90
1887	£70	£90
1888 JH	£60	£85

MAUNDY SETS

		EF	Unc
1889	....	£60	£85
1890	....	£60	£85
1891	....	£60	£85
1892	....	£60	£85
1893 OH	....	£50	£70
1894	....	£50	£70
1895	....	£50	£70
1896	....	£50	£70
1897	....	£50	£70
1898	....	£50	£70
1899	....	£50	£70
1900	....	£50	£85
1901	....	£50	£70

EDWARD VII

		EF	Unc
1902	....	£50	£65
1902 matt proof	....	*	£60
1903	....	£45	£60
1904	....	£45	£60
1905	....	£45	£60
1906	....	£45	£60
1907	....	£45	£60
1908	....	£45	£60
1909	....	£55	£85
1910	....	£55	£85

GEORGE V

		EF	Unc
1911	....	£45	£70
1911 proof	....	*	£75
1912	....	£45	£70
1913	....	£45	£70
1914	....	£45	£75
1915	....	£45	£65
1916	....	£45	£65
1917	....	£45	£65
1918	....	£45	£65
1919	....	£45	£65
1920	....	£45	£65
1921	....	£45	£65
1922	....	£45	£65
1923	....	£45	£65
1924	....	£45	£65
1925	....	£45	£65
1926	....	£45	£65
1927	....	£45	£65
1928	....	£45	£65
1929	....	£45	£65
1930	....	£45	£65
1931	....	£45	£65
1932	....	£45	£65
1933	....	£45	£65
1934	....	£45	£65
1935	....	£45	£65
1936	....	£55	£65

GEORGE VI

			Unc
1937	....	*	£55
1938	....	*	£55
1939	....	*	£60
1940	....	*	£60
1941	....	*	£60
1942	....	*	£60
1943	....	*	£60
1944	....	*	£60
1945	....	*	£60
1946	... ...	*	£60
1947	....	*	£65
1948	....	*	£65
1949	....	*	£65
1950	....	*	£65
1951	....	*	£65
1952	....	*	£65

ELIZABETH II		EF	Unc
1953	... ...	£200	£300
1954	... ...	*	£90
1955	... ...	*	£90
1956	... ...	*	£90
1957	... ...	*	£90
1958	... ...	*	£90
1959	... ...	*	£90
1960	... ...	*	£90
1961	... ...	*	£90
1962	... ...	*	£90
1963	... ...	*	£90
1964	... ...	*	£90
1965	... ...	*	£90
1966	... ...	*	£90
1967	... ...	*	£90
1968	... ...	*	£90
1969	... ...	*	£90
1970	... ...	*	£70
1971	... ...	*	£70
1972	... ...	*	£70
1973	... ...	*	£70
1974	... ...	*	£70
1975	... ...	*	£70
1976	... ...	*	£70
1977	... ...	*	£70
1978	... ...	*	£70
1979	... ...	*	£70
1980	... ...	*	£70
1981	... ...	*	£70
1982	... ...	*	£70
1983	... ...	*	£70
1984	... ...	*	£70
1985	... ...	*	£70
1986	... ...	*	£70
1987	... ...	*	£70
1988	... ...	*	£70
1989	... ...	*	£70
1990	... ...	*	£70
1991	... ...	*	£70
1992	... ...	*	£70
1993	... ...	*	£70
1994	... ...	*	£70
1995	... ...	*	£70
1996	... ...	*	£70
1997	... ...	*	£70
1998	... ...	*	£70
1999	... ...	*	£85
2000	... ...	*	£90
2001	... ...	*	£100
2002	... ...	*	£125
2002 m gold (from set		*	£800
2003	... ...	*	£145
2004	... ...	*	£150

1925 Maundy (part set)

Nickel-brass threepences

1937 threepence of Edward VII, extremely rare

1937-dated Edward VIII threepences, struck in 1936 ready for issue, were melted after Edward's abdication. A few, however, escaped into circulation to become highly prized collectors' pieces. George VI 1937 threepences were struck in large numbers.

EDWARD VIII	F	VF	EF	BU
1937	*	*	£25000	*

GEORGE VI				
1937	*	*	£1	£4
1938	*	*	£3	£20
1939	*	*	£6	£40
1940	*	*	£2	£15
1941	*	*	£1	£6
1942	*	*	£1	£6
1943	*	*	£1	£6
1944	*	*	£1	£6
1945	*	*	£1	£6
1946	£2	£10	£70	£225
1948	*	*	£4	£6
1949	£2	£10	£70	£250
1950	*	*	£8	£25
1951	*	*	£8	£25
1952	*	*	*	£10

Elizabeth II 1953 nickel-brass threepence

ELIZABETH II				
1953	*	*	*	£3
1953 proof	*	*	*	£8
1954	*	*	*	£5
1955	*	*	*	£5
1956	*	*	£1	£5
1957	*	*	*	£4
1958	*	*	£2	£6
1959	*	*	*	£3
1960	*	*	*	£3
1961	*	*	*	£1
1962	*	*	*	£1
1963	*	*	*	£1
1964	*	*	*	£1
1965	*	*	*	£1
1966	*	*	*	*
1967	*	*	*	*

Copper twopence

George III 1797 'cartwheel' twopence

GEORGE III	F	VF	EF	BU
1797	£20	£75	£250	*

Copper pennies

GEORGE III	F	VF	EF	BU
1797 10 leaves	£5	£35	£165	*
1797 11 leaves	£8	£45	£145	*

1797 'cartwheel' penny

	F	VF	EF	BU
1806	£3	£8	£70	£200
1806 no incuse curl	£3	£8	£70	£200
1807	£3	£8	£70	£200

1806 penny of George III

GEORGE IV	F	VF	EF	BU
1825	£5	£15	£90	£350
1826	£3	£12	£80	£350
1826 thin line down				
St Andrew's cross	£5	£15	£85	£350
1826 thick line	£5	£15	£85	£350
1827	£200	£550	£1750	*

COPPER PENNIES

William IV 1831 penny

WILLIAM IV

	F	VF	EF	BU
1831	£10	£50	£250	*
1831.w.w incuse ...	£12	£60	£300	*
1831.w.w incuse ...	£15	£75	£350	*
1834	£15	£75	£300	*
1837	£20	£100	£600	*

Victoria 1841 copper penny

VICTORIA

	F	VF	EF	Unc
1839 proof	*	*	*	£500
1841	£12	£30	£75	£200
1841 no colon after REG	£3	£15	£50	£250
1843	£45	£200	£80	£2000
1843 no colon after REG	£30	£125	£700	£1800
1844	£3	£15	£70	£150
1845	£8	£20	£95	£250
1846 DEF far colon	£3	£15	£85	£225
1846 DEF close colon	£3	£15	£85	£265
1847 DEF close colon	£3	£15	£50	£150
1847 DEF far colon	£3	£15	£50	£150

	F	VF	EF	BU
1848	£3	£15	£50	£150
1848/6	£15	£35	£250	*
1848/7	£3	£15	£50	£150
1849	£40	£120	£650	*
1851 DEF far colon	£3	£15	£90	£250
1851 DEF close colon	£4	£15	£90	£200
1853 OT	£2	£10	£40	£110
1853 colon nearer F	£3	£10	£50	£150
1853 PT	£2	£10	£50	£175
1854 PT	£2	£10	£50	£120
1854/3	£15	£50	£85	£225
1854 OT	£2	£10	£50	£120
1855 OT	£2	£10	£50	£120
1855 PT	£2	£10	£50	£120
1856 PT	£50	£200	£350	*
1856 OT	£20	£50	£150	£700
1857 OT	£2	£10	£50	£120
1857 PT	£2	£10	£50	£120
1857 small date ...	£2	£10	£65	£200
1858	£2	£10	£40	£120
1858 small date ...	£3	£10	£45	£175
1858/3 now thought to be 1858 9/8 (see below)				
1858/7	£2	£5	£35	£120
1858/6	£15	£35	£100	*
1858 no ww	£2	£5	£35	£120
1858 no ww (large 1 and 5 small 8s)	£3	£8	£35	£135
1858 9/8?	£12	£25	£50	£160
1858 9/8? large rose	£12	£30	£65	£175
1859	£3	£10	£35	£125
1859 small date ...	£4	£15	£40	£135
1860/59	£200	£600	£1500	*

Bronze pennies

For fuller details of varieties in bronze pennies see English Copper, Tin and Bronze Coins in the British Museum 1558-1958 by C. W. Peck; The Bronze Coinage of Great Britain by M. J. Freeman and The British Bronze Penny 1860-1970 by Michael Gouby.

VICTORIA

	F	VF	EF	BU
1860 RB, shield crossed with incuse treble lines	*	£15	£50	£175
1860 RB, shield crossed with close double raised lines	£8	£20	£60	£200
1860 RB, double lines, but farther apart, rock to left of lighthouse	£10	£50	£150	£500
1860 RB obv/TB rev	£85	£300	£1000	*
1860 TB obv/RB rev	£85	£300	£1000	*

1860 penny, toothed border on obverse

	F	VF	EF	BU
1860 TB, L.C. WYON on truncation, L.C.W. incuse below shield	*	£17	£55	£175

	F	VF	EF	BU
1860 TB, same obv but L.C.W. incuse below foot	£45	£125	£475	£1000
1860 TB, as previous but heavy flan of 170 grains	ext. rare			
1860 TB, LC, WYON below truncation, L.C.W. incuse below shield	*	£17	£50	£175
1860 TB, no signature on obv. L.C.W. incuse below shield	*	£25	£80	£200
1861 L.C. WYON on truncation, L.C.W. incuse below shield	£15	£60	£175	£450
1861 same obv. no signature on rev	*	£15	£50	£250
1861 L.C. WYON below truncation, L.C.W. incuse below shield	*	£10	£50	£200
1861 similar, but heavy flan (170 grains)	*	*	*	£1500
1861 same obv but no signature on rev	*	£15	£50	£200
1861 no signature on obv, L.C.W. incuse below shield	*	£15	£55	£200
1861-6/8	ext.rare			
1861 no signature either side	*	£12	£45	£160
1862	*	£10	£40	£150
1862 sm date figs ...	ext. rare			
1863	*	£10	£50	£175
1863 slender 3	ext. rare			
1863 die no. (2, 3 or 4) below date	ext. rare			
1864 plain 4	£20	£85	£400	£1000
1864 crossiet 4	£25	£85	£500	£1200
1865	*	£25	£80	£350
1865/3	£15	£75	£350	£800
1866	*	£12	£60	£200
1867	*	£20	£75	£325
1868	£6	£40	£110	£500
1869	£50	£200	£1200	£2000
1870	£6	£40	£150	£375
1871	£8	£60	£250	£600
1872	*	£12	£55	£200
1873	*	£12	£55	£200
1874 (1873 type) ...	*	£12	£55	£200
1874 H (1873 type)	*	£12	£60	£225
1874 new rev, lighthouse tall and thin	*	£20	£60	£200
1874 H as previous	£4	£15	£55	£225
1874 new obv/1873 rev	*	£15	£50	£200
1874 H as previous	*	£15	£50	£200
1874 new obv/new rev	*	£15	£50	£200
1874 H as previous	*	£15	£50	£200
1875	*	£15	£50	£200
1875 H	£30	£125	£450	*
1876 H	*	£15	£85	£275
1877	*	£8	£55	£175
1878	*	£15	£60	£325
1879	*	*	£45	£125
1880	*	*	£60	£200
1881 (1880 obv)	*	*	£60	£200
1881 new obv	*	£15	£70	£225
1881 H	*	*	£45	£200
1882 H	*	*	£35	£125
1882 no H	£75	£300	£800	*
1883	*	*	£25	£130
1884	*	*	£25	£125
1885	*	*	£25	£125
1886	*	*	£25	£125
1887	*	*	£25	£125

BRONZE PENNIES

	F	VF	EF	BU
1888	*	*	£20	£120
1889 14 leaves	*	*	£20	£120
1889 15 leaves	*	*	£20	£120
1890	*	*	£20	£110
1891	*	*	£20	£110
1892	*	*	£20	£120
1893	*	*	£20	£120
1894	*	*	£35	£125
1895 2mm	*	£40	£175	£350

Victoria old head penny of 1895

	F	VF	EF	BU
1895	*	*	£10	£45
1896	*	*	£8	£40
1897	*	*	£8	£25
1897 higher horizon	£5	£25	£175	£400
1898	*	*	£12	£45
1899	*	*	£11	£40
1900	*	*	£10	£35
1901	*	*	£8	£20

Edward VII 1902, penny, low horizon

EDWARD VII

	F	VF	EF	BU
1902 low horizon ...	*	£15	£60	£125
1902	*	*	£5	£25
1903	*	*	£12	£40
1904	*	*	£20	£85
1905	*	*	£15	£60
1906	*	*	£12	£45
1907	*	*	£12	£50

BRONZE PENNIES

	F	VF	EF	BU
1908	*	*	£12	£45
1909	*	*	£12	£45
1910	*	*	£12	£40

GEORGE V

	F	VF	EF	BU
1911	*	*	£10	£20
1912	*	*	£10	£30
1912 H	*	*	£45	£150
1913	*	*	£15	£40
1914	*	*	£10	£28
1915	*	*	£10	£28
1916	*	*	£10	£28
1917	*	*	£10	£28
1918	*	*	£10	£28
1918 H	*	£15	£175	£350
1918 KN	*	£20	£250	£700
1919	*	*	£10	£30
1919 H	*	£5	£200	£500
1919 KN	*	£10	£250	£750
1920	*	*	£10	£30
1921	*	*	£10	£30
1922	*	*	£10	£30
1922 rev as 1927 ext. rare		*	*	*
1926	*	*	£15	£50
1926 mod effigy ...	*	£50	£575	£1200
1927	*	*	£5	£20
1928	*	*	£3	£20
1929	*	*	£3	£20
1930	*	*	£5	£25
1931	*	*	£5	£25
1932	*	*	£8	£40
1933			highest rarity	
1934	*	*	£8	£35
1935	*	*	£2	£15
1936	*	*	*	£15

GEORGE VI

	F	VF	EF	BU
1937	*	*	*	£5
1938	*	*	*	£5
1939	*	*	*	£6
1940	*	*	*	£10
1944	*	*	*	£12
1945	*	*	*	£10
1946	*	*	*	£12
1947	*	*	*	£4
1948	*	*	*	£5
1949	*	*	*	£5

George VI 1948 penny

	F	VF	EF	BU
1950	£2	£5	£15	£35
1951	£2	£5	£20	£50

ELIZABETH II

	F	VF	EF	BU
1953	*	£1	£2	£3
1953 proof	*	*	*	£5

	Fair	F	VF	EF
1961	*	*	*	£0.50
1962	*	*	*	*
1963	*	*	*	*
1964	*	*	*	*
1965	*	*	*	*
1966	*	*	*	*
1967	*	*	*	*

Copper halfpennies

All copper unless otherwise stated

Charles II 1675 halfpenny

CHARLES II

	Fair	F	VF	EF
1672	£5	£45	£150	£800
1672 CRAOLVS		Extremely rare *		
1673	£5	£45	£80	£800
1673 CRAOLVS		Extremely rare *		
1673 no stops on reverse	£10	£50	£200	£800
1673 no stops on obverse	£10	£50	£200	£800
1675	£10	£50	£200	£800
1675 no stops on obverse	£10	£60	£200	£800

James II 1685 tin halfpenny

JAMES II

	Fair	F	VF	EF
1685 (tin)	£30	£150	£450	£3000
1686 (tin)	£35	£160	£500	*
1687 (tin)	£30	£150	£450	*
1687 D over D	*	*	*	*

WILLIAM AND MARY

	Fair	F	VF	EF
1689 (tin) ET on right	£450	£900	£1500	*
1689 (tin) ET on left	*	*	*	*
1690 (tin) dated on edge	£30	£120	£400	£2000
1691 (tin) date in exergue and on edge	£30	£120	£450	£2000

116

	Fair	F	VF	EF
1691/2 (tin) 1691 in exergue 1692 on edge	£30	£120	£450	£2000
1692 (tin) date in exergue and on edge	£30	£75	£450	*
1694 ... ... ,..	£5	£25	£150	£800

William and Mary 1694 halfpenny

	Fair	F	VF	EF
1694 GVLIEMVS ...	£150	*	*	*
1694 no stop after MARIA	£15	£45	£200	£825
1694 BRITANNIA with last I over A	£30	£125	*	*
1694 no stop on reverse	£10	£25	£165	£800

WILLIAM III
Type 1 (date in exergue)

1695	£5	£25	£125	£800
1695 thick flan	£25	£75	£185	*
1695 BRITANNIA ...	£5	£25	£125	£800
1695 no stop on reverse	£5	£30	£125	*
1696	£5	£25	£125	£800
1696 GVLIEMVS, no stop on reverse ...	£25	£65	£185	*
1696 TERTVS	£15	£50	£185	*
1696 obv struck from doubled die	£15	£50	£185	*
1697	£5	£25	£80	*
1697 no stops either side	£5	£25	£120	*
1697 I of TERTIVS over E	£15	£50	£185	*
1697 GVLILMVS no stop on reverse ...	£15	£40	£185	*
1697 no stop after TERTIVS	£10	£25	£80	£800
1698	£10	£25	£80	£800

Type 2 (date in legend)

1698	£5	£25	£150	£800
1699	£5	£15	£150	£700
1699 BRITANNIA ...	£5	£15	£150	£700
1699 GVLIEMVS ...	£5	£25	£150	£850

Type 3 (Britannia's hand on knee, date in exergue)

1699	£5	£20	£125	£700
1699 stop after date	£10	£25	£150	£825
1699 BRITANNIA ...	£5	£20	£150	£700
1699 GVILELMVS ...	£10	£25	£150	£800
1699 TERTVS	£20	£50	£200	*
1699 no stop on reverse	£20	£50	£200	*
1699 no stops on obverse	£10	£30	£150	£800

COPPER HALFPENNIES

	FAIR	F	VF	EF
1699 no stops after GVLIELMVS	£5	£20	£150	£750
1700	£5	£15	£150	£750
1700 no stops on obverse	£5	£15	£150	*
1700 no stop after GVLIELMVS	£5	£15	£150	*
1700 BRITANNIA ...	£5	£15	£150	£750
1700 no stops on reverse	£5	£15	£150	*
1700 GVLIELMS ...	£5	£25	£150	*
1700 GVLIEEMVS ...	£5	£25	£150	*
1700 TER TIVS	£5	£15	£150	*
1700 1 of TERTIVS over V	£10	£25	£225	*
1701 BRITANNIA ...	£5	£15	£150	*
1701 no stops on obverse	£5	£15	£150	*
1701 GVLIELMVS TERTIVS	£5	£25	£200	*

GEORGE I
Type 1

1717	£5	£30	£200	£550
1717 no stops on obverse	£10	£40	£250	£600
1718	*	£35	£200	£600
1718 no stop on obverse	£10	£40	£250	£700
1719 on larger flan of type 2	£15	£50	£300	*
1719 – edge grained	£50	£200	*	*

Type 2

1719 both shoulder straps ornate	£5	£20	£100	£525
1719 – edge grained	£10	£40	*	*
1719 bust with left strap plain	£5	£20	£100	£600
1719 – edge grained	£10	£40	*	*
1720	£5	£20	£100	£525
1721	£5	£20	£100	£525
1721/0	£5	£20	£100	*
1721 stop after date	£5	£20	£100	£525
1722	£5	£20	£100	£525
1722 GEORGIVS ...	£5	£20	£100	*
1723	£5	£20	£100	£525
1723 no stop on reverse	£5	£20	£100	£550
1724	£5	£20	£100	£450

George II 1729 halfpenny

GEORGE II
Young Head

1729	£2	£10	£70	£250
1729 no stop on reverse	£2	£10	£60	£225

COPPER HALFPENNIES

	Fair	F	VF	EF
1730	*	£10	£60	£200
1730 GEOGIVS, no stop on reverse ...	£5	£20	£100	£250
1730 stop after date	£5	£20	£75	£250
1730 no stop after REX or on reverse	£5	£20	£100	£300
1731	*	£10	£60	£200
1731 no stop on reverse	*	£20	£90	£250
1732	*	£15	£60	£200
1732 no stop on reverse	*	£20	£90	£250
1733	*	£15	£60	£200
1733 only obverse stop before REX ...	*	£15	£60	£200
1734	*	£10	£60	£200
1734/3	*	£20	£110	*
1734 no stops on obverse	*	£20	£110	*
1735	*	£15	£60	£200
1736	*	£15	£60	£200
1737	*	£15	£60	£200
1738	*	£15	£60	£200
1739	*	£15	£60	£200

Old Head

	Fair	F	VF	EF
1740	*	£7	£50	£175
1742	*	£7	£50	£175
1742/0	*	£10	£70	£200
1743	*	£7	£50	£175
1744	*	£7	£50	£175
1745	*	£7	£50	£175
1746	*	£7	£50	£175
1747	*	£7	£50	£175
1748	*	£7	£50	£175
1749	*	£7	£50	£175
1750	*	£7	£50	£175
1751	*	£7	£50	£175
1752	*	£7	£50	£175
1753	*	£7	£50	£175
1754	*	£7	£50	£175

GEORGE III

	F	VF	EF	BU
1770	£1	£40	£150	£350
1771	£1	£40	£150	£300
1771 no stop on reverse	£2	£40	£150	£300
1771 ball below spear head	£2	£40	£150	£300
1772	£2	£40	£150	£300
1772 GEORIVS	£18	£100	£225	*
1772 ball below spear head	£2	£40	£150	£300
1772 no stop on reverse	£2	£40	£150	£300
1773	£2	£40	£150	£300
1773 no stop after REX	£2	£40	£150	£300
1773 no stop on reverse	£2	£40	£150	*
1774	£2	£40	£150	£300
1775	£3	£40	£150	£300
1799 5 incuse gunports	*	£5	£50	£110
1799 6 relief gunports	*	£5	£50	£110
1799 9 relief gunports	*	*	£50	£140
1799 no gunports ...	*	*	£50	£115
1799 no gunports and raised line along hull	*	£5	£55	£150
1806 no berries on olive branch	*	*	£45	£125

	F	VF	EF	BU
1806 line under SOHO 3 berries	*	*	£45	£110
1807 similar but double-cut border bead between B and R	*	*	£45	£120

GEORGE IV

	F	VF	EF	BU
1825	*	£30	£125	£250

George IV 1826 halfpenny

	F	VF	EF	BU
1826 two incuse lines down cross	*	£15	£75	£175
1826 raised line down centre of cross ...	*	£15	£75	£200
1827	*	£12	£75	£185

WILLIAM IV

	F	VF	EF	BU
1831	*	£5	£45	£175
1834	*	£5	£45	£175
1837	*	£4	£40	£175

VICTORIA

	F	VF	EF	BU
1838	*	£3	£25	£100
1839 proof	*	*	*	£250
1839 proof, rev inv ...	*	*	*	£300
1841	*	£3	£25	£85
1843	£3	£30	£90	£300
1844	*	£5	£40	£100
1845	£18	£40	£450	*
1846	£2	£5	£40	£110
1847	*	£10	£40	£110
1848	*	£5	£40	£110
1848/7	*	£3	£35	£110
1851	*	£3	£25	£100
1851 7 incuse dots on and above shield	*	£3	£25	£100
1852	*	£3	£25	£100
1852 7 incuse dots on and above shield	*	£3	£25	£100
1853	*	£3	£25	£90
1853/2	£10	£25	£85	*
1854	*	£3	£15	£70

Victoria 1853 copper halfpenny

	F	VF	EF	BU
1855	*	£3	£25	£85
1856	*	£3	£35	£100
1857	*	£3	£25	£75

	F	VF	EF	BU
1857 7 incuse dots on and above shield	*	£5	£25	£85
1858	*	£5	£25	£85
1858/6	£2	£10	£35	£85
1858/7	£1	£5	£25	£70
1858 small date	£1	£5	£25	£70
1859	£1	£5	£25	£120
1859/8	£3	£10	£50	*
1860 prog	*	*	*	£6000

Bronze halfpennies

VICTORIA	F	VF	EF	BU
1860	*	£5	£20	£90
1860 TB 7 berries in wreath	*	£5	£25	£110
1860 TB4 berries in wreath	*	£5	£25	£110
1860 TB similar but centres of four of leaves are double incuse lines	*	£10	£45	£150
1861 obv 4 berries, 15 leaves, raised leaf centres, rev L.C.W. on rock	*	£20	£60	£200
1861 same obv, rev no signature			ext. rare	
1861 same but lighthouse has no vertical lines	*	£15	£45	£185
1861 obv 4 berries, 4 double incuse leaf centres, rev L.C.W. on rock ...	*	£5	£40	£125
1861 same obv, rev no signature	*	£8	£35	£145
1861 obv 7 double incuse leaf centres, rev L.C.W on rock	*	£5	£40	£125
1861 same obv, rev no signature	*	£5	£30	£95
1861 obv 16 leaves, rev lighthouse has rounded top	*	£5	£30	£95
1861 same obv, rev lighthouse has pointed top	*	£5	£30	£95
1861 no signature ...	*	£5	£30	£95
1862 L.C.W. on rock	*	£5	£15	£85
1862 letter (A,B or C) left of lighthouse base ...	£75	£200	*	*
1863	*	£5	£40	£110
1864	*	£6	£40	£165
1865	*	£10	£80	£225
1865/3	£10	£50	£250	£600
1866	*	£8	£45	£165
1867	*	£8	£65	£225
1868	*	£8	£45	£190

Victoria 1889 bronze halfpenny

BRONZE HALFPENNIES

	F	VF	EF	BU
1869	*	£25	£160	£400
1870	*	£5	£45	£150
1871	£10	£45	£175	£400
1872	*	£5	£40	£135
1873	*	£7	£50	£165
1874	*	£15	£75	£300
1874H	*	£5	£30	£120
1875	*	£5	£35	£120
1875H	*	£5	£45	£135
1876H	*	£5	£35	£120
1877	*	£5	£35	£120
1878	*	£15	£55	£250
1879	*	£5	£35	£100
1880	*	£4	£35	£120
1881	*	£4	£35	£120
1881H	*	£4	£30	£110
1882H	*	£4	£30	£110
1883	*	£4	£30	£100
1884	*	£2	£25	£90
1885	*	£2	£25	£90
1886	*	*	£25	£90
1887	*	*	£25	£90
1888	*	*	£25	£90
1889	*	*	£25	£90
1889/8	*	£8	£55	£200
1890	*	*	£25	£75
1891	*	*	£25	£75
1892	*	*	£25	£75
1893	*	*	£25	£75
1894	*	£5	£30	£100
1895 OH	*	*	£3	£50
1896	*	*	£3	£30
1897 normal horizon	*	*	£3	£30
1897 higher horizon	*	*	£3	£30
1898	*	*	£6	£30
1899	*	*	£4	£30
1900	*	*	£15	£20
1901	*	*	£12	£15

EDWARD VII	F	VF	EF	BU
1902 low horizon ...	*	£5	£50	£100
1902	*	*	£5	£15
1903	*	*	£8	£25
1904	*	*	£10	£30
1905	*	*	£6	£20
1906	*	*	£6	£20
1907	*	*	£6	£20
1908	*	*	£6	£20
1909	*	*	£8	£25
1910	*	*	£8	£25

GEORGE V	F	VF	EF	BU
1911	*	*	£8	£25
1912	*	*	£8	£25

George V 1912 halfpenny

1913	*	*	£10	£35
1914	*	*	£8	£25
1915	*	*	£8	£25

BRONZE HALFPENNIES

	Fair	F	VF	EF
1916		*	£2	£25
1917	*	*	£2	£25
1918	*	*	£2	£25
1919	*	*	£2	£25
1920	*	*	£2	£25
1921	*	*	£2	£25
1922	*	*	£3	£25
1923	*	*	£2	£25
1924	*	*	£3	£25
1925	*	*	£4	£25
1925 mod effigy ...	*	*	£4	£30
1926	*	*	£4	£25
1927	*	*	£2.50	£20
1928	*	*	£2	£15
1929	*	*	£2	£15
1930	*	*	£2	£15
1931	*	*	£2	£15
1932	*	*	£2	£15
1933	*	*	£2	£15
1934	*	*	£2	£15
1935	*	*	£2	£12
1936	*	*	£2	£10

GEORGE VI

	Fair	F	VF	EF
1937	*	*	*	£4
1938	*	*	*	£6
1939	*	*	*	£8
1940	*	*	*	£9
1941	*	*	*	£5
1942	*	*	*	£4
1943	*	*	*	£4
1944	*	*	*	£5
1945	*	*	*	£4
1946	*	*	*	£8
1947	*	*	*	£6
1948	*	*	*	£6
1949	*	*	*	£8
1950	*	*	*	£8
1951	*	*	*	£15
1952	*	*	*	£5

ELIZABETH II

	Fair	F	VF	EF
1953	*	*	*	£2
1954	*	*	*	£3
1955	*	*	*	£3
1956	*	*	*	£3
1957	*	*	*	£2
1958	*	*	*	£2
1959	*	*	*	£1
1960	*	*	*	£1
1962	*	*	*	*
1963	*	*	*	*
1964	*	*	*	*
1965	*	*	*	*
1966	*	*	*	*
1967	*	*	*	*

Copper farthings

Copper unless otherwise stated

OLIVER CROMWELL

	Fair	F	VF	EF
Patterns only	*	£2000	£4000	£5500

CHARLES II

	Fair	F	VF	EF
1671 patterns only	*	*	£350	£700
1672	£1	£25	£125	£450
1672 no stop on obverse	£2.75	£25	£125	£450
1672 loose drapery at Britannia's elbow	£2	£25	£125	£450
1673	£1	£25	£125	£450

Oliver Cromwell copper farthing

	Fair	F	VF	EF
1673 CAROLA	£30	£50	£250	*
1673 BRITANNIA ...	*	*	*	*
1673 no stops on obverse ... ... **ext rare**	*	*	*	*
1673 no stop on reverse ... ... **ext rare**	*	*	*	*
1674	*	£25	£125	£450
1675	*	£25	£125	£450
1675 no stop after CAROLVS	*	*	*	*
1676	*	*	*	*
1679	*	£25	£125	£450
1679 no stop on reverse	*	*	*	*
1684 (tin) various edge readings	£25	£125	£450	£1500
1685 (tin)	£30	£150	£500	*

JAMES II

	Fair	F	VF	EF
1684 (tin)		**Extremely rare**		*
1685 (tin) various edge readings	:£30	£120	£400	£1500
1686 (tin) various edge readings	:£40	£150	£450	£1750
1687 (tin) draped bust, various readings		**Extremely rare** *		*

WILLIAM AND MARY

	Fair	F	VF	EF
1689 (tin) date in exergue and on edge, many varieties ...	£150	£450	*	*
1689/90 (tin) 1689 in exergue, 1690 on edge	*	*	*	*
1689/90 (tin) 1690 in exergue, 1689 on edge	*	*	*	*
1690 (tin) various types	:£40	£100	£400	£2000
1691 (tin) small and large figures	:£40	£100	£400	£2000
1692 (tin)	:£40	£100	£400	£2000
1694 many varieties	£10	£40	£125	£575

WILLIAM III

Type 1, date in exergue

	Fair	F	VF	EF
1695		£25	£125	£525
1695 M over V				
1696		£25	£125	£525
1697		£25	£125	£525

William III 1697 farthing

	Fair	F	VF	EF
1698	£25	£100	£350	*
1699	£2	£25	£125	£550
1700	£2	£25	£85	£550

Type 2, date in legend	Fair	F	VF	EF
1698	£5	£35	£125	£550
1699	£5	£35	£125	£550

Anne 1714 pattern farthing

ANNE

	Fair	F	VF	EF
1714 patterns (F) ...	£75	£200	£350	£525

George I 'dump' farthing of 1717

GEORGE I

'Dump Type'

	Fair	F	VF	EF
1717	£30	£100	£275	£600
1718 silver proof ...	*	*	*	£1000

Larger flan

	Fair	F	VF	EF
1719 large lettering on obverse	£3	£10	£90	£450
1719 small lettering on obverse	£3	£10	£100	£475
1719 – last A of BRITANNIA over I	*	*	*	*

George I 1719 farthing

	Fair	F	VF	EF
1719 legend continuous over bust	£20	£60	*	*
1720 large lettering on obverse	£3	£20	£95	£425
1720 small lettering on obverse	£2	£15	£95	£425
1721	£2	£15	£95	£425
1721/0	£10	£30	*	*
1722 large lettering on obverse	£4	£20	£95	£425
1722 small lettering on obverse	£3	£20	£95	£425
1723	£2	£15	£95	£450
1723 R of REX over R	£8	*	*	*
1724	£5	£20	£95	£475

George II 1730 farthing

GEORGE II

	Fair	F	VF	EF
1730	*	£10	£45	£175
1731	*	£10	£45	£175
1732	*	£12	£45	£175
1733	*	£10	£40	£175
1734	*	£10	£45	£185
1734 no stops on obverse	*	£10	£50	£225
1735	*	£10	£40	£150
1735 3 over 3	*	£15	£50	£225
1736	*	£10	£40	£150
1736 triple tie-riband	*	£10	£50	£200
1737 sm date	*	£10	£40	£150
1737 lge date	*	£10	£45	£150
1739	*	£10	£40	£125
1739/5	*	*	*	*
1741 Old Head	*	£10	£45	£125
1744	*	£10	£45	£125
1746	*	£10	£45	£100
1746 V over U	*	*	*	*
1749	*	£10	£45	£125
1750	*	£10	£45	£150
1754/0	*	£20	£80	£200
1754	*	£8	£30	£75

GEORGE III

	F	VF	EF	BU
1771	*	£20	£120	£250
1773	*	£5	£80	£200
1774	*	£5	£80	£200
1775	*	£5	£90	£200
1799	*	*	£45	£90
1806	*	£3	£45	£95
1807	*	£4	£45	£90

GEORGE IV

	F	VF	EF	BU
1821	*	£2	£40	£80
1822	*	£2	£40	£80
1823	*	£3	£40	£80
1825	*	£3	£40	£80
1825 D of DEI over U	£2	£7	£65	*
1826 date on rev ...	*	£2	£40	£100
1826 date on obv ...	*	£3	£45	£75
1826 I for 1 in date	*	*	*	*
1827	*	£3	£45	£75
1828	*	£3	£50	£95
1829	*	£5	£50	£120
1830	*	£7	£45	£95

WILLIAM IV

	F	VF	EF	BU
1831	*	£6	£50	£125
1834	*	£6	£50	£125
1835	*	£6	£45	£140
1836	*	£6	£45	£140
1837	*	£6	£50	£140

VICTORIA

	F	VF	EF	BU
1838	*	£3	£30	£75
1839	*	£3	£25	£65

COPPER FARTHINGS

	F	VF	EF	BU
1840	*	£3	£28	£65
1841	*	£3	£25	£65
1842	*	£35	£100	£200
1843	*	£3	£25	£60
1843 I for 1	£40	£200	*	*
1844	£35	£90	£325	*
1845	*	£4	£25	£80
1846	*	£6	£30	£100
1847	*	£3	£25	£80
1848	*	£4	£25	£85
1849	*	£20	£150	£350
1850	*	£3	£30	£80
1851	*	£15	£45	£125
1851 D over D	£10	£50	£250	£650
1852	*	£12	£45	£125
1853 w.w. raised	*	£2	£25	£70
1853 ww inc	*	£5	£65	£80
1854 ww inc	*	£3	£25	£60
1855 ww inc	*	£3	£35	£100
1855 ww raised	*	£6	£35	£85
1856	*	£4	£40	£110
1856 R over E	£10	£50	£150	*
1857	*	£3	£25	£75
1858	*	£3	£25	£70
1859	*	£15	£45	£120
1860 proof	*	*	*	£5500

Bronze farthings

VICTORIA	F	VF	EF	BU
1860 RB	*	£2	£15	£45
1860 TB/RB (mule)	£50	£150	£300	*
1860 TB	*	£1	£15	£45
1861	*	£1	£12	£45
1862 small 8	*	£2	£12	£40
1862 large 8	£30	£50	£250	*
1863	£20	£40	£150	*
1864	*	£3	£20	£60
1865	*	£3	£20	£60
1865–5/2	*	£5	£25	£70
1866	*	£2	£18	£55
1867	*	*	£20	£65
1868	*	£1	£20	£65
1869	*	£8	£40	£75
1872	*	£2	£18	£55
1873	*	£3	£20	£55
1874 H	*	£3	£25	£50
1874 H G's over G's			Extremely rare	
1875 5 berries/large date	*	£10	£25	£85
1875 5 berries/small date	£8	£20	£75	£200
1875 4 berries/small date	*	*	*	*
1875 H	*	£2	£10	£50
1876 H	*	*	£25	£75
1877 proof				£3000
1878	*	£2	£10	£45
1879	*	*	£10	£45
1879 large 9	*	£1	£12	£45
1880 4 berries	*	£2	£15	£45
1880 3 berries	*	£2	£15	£45
1881 4 berries	*	£5	£20	£50
1881 3 berries	*	£5	£20	£50

	F	VF	EF	BU
1881 H 3 berries	*	£2	£12	£45
1882 H	*	£1	£12	£45
1883	*	£3	£28	£80
1884	*	*	£10	£38
1886	*	*	£10	£38
1887	*	*	£18	£40
1890	*	*	£10	£38
1891	*	*	£10	£38
1892	*	£7	£28	£85
1893	*	*	£8	£30
1894	*	*	£12	£40
1895	*	£12	£50	£125
1895 OH	*	*	£3	£12

Victoria 1896, Old Head Farthing

	F	VF	EF	BU
1897 bright finish	*	*	£2	£15
1897 black finish higher horizon	*	*	£1	£12
1898	*	*	£2	£15
1899	*	*	£1	£12
1900	*	*	£1	£12
1901	*	*	£1	£10

Edward VII, 1907 Farthing

EDWARD VII	F	VF	EF	BU
1902	*	*	£3	£12
1903 low horizon	*	*	£4	£15
1904	*	*	£4	£15
1905	*	*	£4	£15
1906	*	*	£4	£15
1907	*	*	£4	£15
1908	*	*	£4	£15
1909	*	*	£4	£15
1910	*	*	£5	£15

GEORGE V	F	VF	EF	BU
1911	*	*	*	£9
1912	*	*	*	£6
1913	*	*	*	£6
1914	*	*	*	£6
1915	*	*	*	£10
1916	*	*	*	£6
1917	*	*	*	£6
1918 black finish	*	*	*	£20
1919 bright finish	*	*	*	£5
1919	*	*	*	£5
1920	*	*	*	£7
1921	*	*	*	£7
1922	*	*	*	£8
1923	*	*	*	£8
1924	*	*	*	£8
1925	*	*	*	£8

	F	VF	EF	BU
1926 modified effigy	*	*	*	£6
1927	*	*	*	£6
1928	*	*	*	£3
1929	*	*	*	£3
1930	*	*	*	£3
1931	*	*	*	£3
1932	*	*	*	£3
1933	*	*	*	£3
1934	*	*	*	£5
1935	*	*	£1.50	£7
1936	*	*	*	£2

George VI 1951 farthing (wren on reverse)

GEORGE VI
	F	VF	EF	BU
1937	*	*	*	£2
1938	*	*	*	£4
1939	*	*	*	£3
1940	*	*	*	£3
1941	*	*	*	£3
1942	*	*	*	£3
1943	*	*	*	£3
1944	*	*	*	£3
1945	*	*	*	£3
1946	*	*	*	£3
1947	*	*	*	£3
1948	*	*	*	£3
1949	*	*	*	£3
1950	*	*	*	£3
1951	*	*	*	£3
1952	*	*	*	£3

ELIZABETH II
	F	VF	EF	BU
1953	*	*	*	£2
1954	*	*	*	£2
1955	*	*	*	£2
1956	*	*	*	£4

Fractions of farthings

COPPER HALF FARTHINGS

GEORGE IV	F	VF	EF	BU
1828 Britannia breaks legend	£5	£20	£75	£200
1828 Britannia below legend	£8	£35	£125	*
1830 lge date	£5	£25	£85	£225
1830 sm date	£6	£30	£100	*

WILLIAM IV	F	VF	EF	BU
1837	£15	£75	£250	*

Victoria 1839 half farthing

BRONZE FARTHINGS

VICTORIA	F	VF	EF	BU
1839	*	£2	£25	£85
1842	*	£2	£25	£85
1843	*	*	£10	£40
1844	*	*	£10	£35
1844 E over N	£3	£12	£75	£250
1847	*	£3	£20	£55
1851	*	£3	£25	£60
1852	*	£3	£25	£60
1853	*	£4	£40	£95
1853 proof				£350
1854	*	£4	£60	£125
1856	*	£5	£50	£110
1856 large date ...	£6	£25	*	*
1868 bronze proof	*			£300
1868 copper-nickel proof	*			£400

COPPER THIRD FARTHINGS

GEORGE IV	F	VF	EF	BU
1827	*	£10	£40	£100

WILLIAM IV				
1835	*	£10	£50	£125

VICTORIA				
1844	*	£15	£50	£150
1844 RE for REG ...	£20	£50	£200	*
1844 large G in REG	*	£15	£50	£150

BRONZE THIRD FARTHINGS

VICTORIA	F	VF	EF	BU
1866	*	*	£15	£40
1868	*	*	£15	£40
1876	*	*	£15	£45
1878	*	*	£15	£40
1881	*	*	£15	£40
1884	*	*	£10	£30
1885	*	*	£10	£30

Edward VII 1902 third farthing

EDWARD VIII				
1902	*	*	£8	£25

GEORGE V				
1913	*	*	£8	£25

COPPER QUARTER FARTHINGS

VICTORIA				
1839	£3	£10	£30	£75

Victoria 1839 quarter farthing

1851	£4	£12	£40	£85
1852	£3	£10	£30	£75
1853	£5	£12	£40	£85
1853 proof	*	*	*	£550
1868 bronze-proof	*	*	*	£300
1868 copper-nickel proof	*	*	*	£425

Decimal coinage

f denotes face value

ELIZABETH II

BRITANNIAS

A United Kingdom gold bullion coin introduced in the autumn of 1987 contains one ounce of 22ct gold and has a face value of £100. There are also half ounce, quarter ounce and one-tenth ounce versions, with face values of £50, £25 and £10 respectively. All are legal tender.

The Britannia coins bear a portrait of The Queen on the obverse and the figure of Britannia on the reverse.

B.V.

1987-2003 1oz, proof ...	*
1987-2003 inclusive ½oz, proof	*
1987-2003 inclusive ¼oz, proof	*
1987-2003 inclusive ⅒oz, proof	*

(½ and ¼ oz issued only in sets)

To commemorate the 10th anniversary of the first Britannia issue, new reverse designs were introduced for the gold coins as well as a series of 4 silver coins with denominations from £2 to 20 pence. The silver coins were issued in Proof condition only for 1997.

1997. 1oz, ¼oz and ⅒oz issued individually (all coins issued in 4-coin sets)

1997. 1oz, ¼oz silver coins issued individually (all coins issued in 4-coin sets)

1998. Gold and silver coins issued with new portrait of HM the Queen and first reverse design.

2001. New reverse designs introduced for gold and silver coins. Four coin sets listed in the appropriate section following.

FIVE POUNDS

1984 gold, BU	£400
1985 – –	£425
1986 – –	£425
1987 – new uncoupled effigy	£425
1988 – –	£425
1989 – BU, 500th anniversary of	
the sovereign	£450
1990 gold, BU	£435
1990 Queen Mother's 90th birthday, gold,	
proof	£600
1990 – silver, proof	£100
1990 – cu-ni, BU	£10
1991 gold, BU	£450
1992 gold, BU	£450
1993 40th Anniversary of The Coronation	
gold, proof	£700
1993 – silver, proof	£32
1993 – cu-ni, BU	£10
1993 gold BU	£475
1994 gold BU	£500
1995 gold BU	£535
1996 Queen's 70th birthday, gold, proof	£645
1996 – silver, proof	£33
1996 – cu-ni, BU	£10
1996 – gold, BU	£575
1997 Golden Wedding, gold, proof	£650
1997 – silver, proof	£32
1997 – cu-ni, BU	£10
1997 – gold, BU	£535

(Gold versions also listed in FIVE POUNDS section of milled gold.) In 1984 the Royal Mint issued the first of an annual issue of Brilliant Uncirculated £5 coins. These bear the letter 'U' in a circle.

1998 Prince Charles 50th Birthday, gold, proof	£600
1998 – silver, proof	£50
1998 – cu-ni, BU	£10
1998 – gold, BU	£500
1999 Diana Memorial, gold, proof	£600
1999 – silver, proof	£45
1999 – cu-ni, BU	£10
1999 Millennium, gold, proof	£600
1999 – silver, proof	£33
1999 cu-ni, BU	£10
1999 gold, BU	£500
2000 Millennium, gold, proof	£495
2000 silver with 22 carat gold, proof	£37
2000 cu-ni, BU	£10
2000 Queen Mother commemorative,	
gold, proof	£495
2000 silver, proof	£35
2000 silver, piedfort	£68
2000 cu-ni, BU	£10
2000 gold, BU	£500
2001 Victorian Era anniversary	
gold, proof	£525
gold proof with reverse frosting	£750
silver, proof	£35
silver, proof with reverse frosting	£70
cu-ni, BU	£10
gold, BU	£400
2002 Golden Jubilee, gold, proof	£600
2002 – Silver, proof	£35
2002 cu-ni BU	£10
2002 Sheild reverse, gold, proof	£600
2002 Queen Mother memorial, gold, proof ...	£600
2002 –, Silver, proof	£35
2002 cu-ni BU	£10
2003 BU	£535
2003 proof	£650

TWO POUNDS

1983 gold, proof	£225
1986 Commonwealth Games (nickel brass)	£4
1986 –, in folder, BU	£6
1986 silver unc	£15
1986 – – proof	£35 *f*
1986 gold, proof	£225
1987 gold, proof	£250
1988 gold, proof	£250
1989 Bill of Rights (nickel brass)	£4
1989 –, in folder, BU	£6
1989 – silver, proof	£30
1989 Claim of Right (nickel brass)	£4
1989 Bill of Rights (nickel brass)	£4
1989 –, in folder, BU	£6
(For 1989 £2 piedforts see sets)	
1989 500th anniversary of the sovereign,	
gold, proof	£275
1990 gold, proof	£250
1991 gold, proof	£250
1993 gold, proof	£250
1994 Bank of England, gold, proof	£425
1994 –, gold 'mule', proof	£800
1994 –, silver, proof	£30
1994 –, silver piedfort, proof	£60
1994 –, in folder, BU	£8
1994	£4
1995 50th Anniverary of end of Second	
World War, silver, proof	£27
1995 ditto, in folder, BU	£8
1995 –, silver, piedfort, proof	£60
1995 –, gold, proof	£375
1995 50th Anniversary of United Nations,	

gold, proof **£300**
1995 –, in folder, BU **£6**
1995 –, silver, piedfort, proof **£60**
1995 –, proof **£30**
1995 ... ... **£4**
1996 European Football, gold, proof **£350**
1996 –, silver, proof **£27**
1996 –, silver, piedfort **£65**
1996 –, in folder, BU **£6**
1996 ... ... **£4**
1997 Bimetal, gold, proof **£350**
1997 –, silver, proof **£29**
1997 –, in folder, BU **£6**
1997 silver, piedfort **£60**
1997 ... ... **£4**
1998 Bimetal, silver, proof **£29**
1998 – silver, piedfort **£50**
1998 – proof **£6**
1998 –, in folder, BU **£6**
1998 ... ... **£4**
1999 Rugby World Cup, gold, proof **£300**
1999 – silver, proof **£30**
1999 – silver, piedfort **£150**
1999 –, in folder, BU **£6**
1999 ... ... **£4**
2001 Marconi commemorative,
    gold, proof **£295**
2001 – silver, proof **£29**
2001 – silver, proof with reverse frosting ... **£29**
2001 – silver, piedfort **... ... ...** **£50**
2001 – in folder, BU **£6**
Four different reverse designs representing England, Northern Ireland, Scotland and Wales were issued in sets
2002 Commonwealth Games, gold,proof ... *****
2002 Commonwealth Games, silver,proof ... *****
2002 Commonwealth Games, piedfort ... ... *****
2002 Commonwealth Games, BU ... ... *****
2002 Shield reverse, gold,proof **£300**
2003 DNA Gold ti-metal proof **£295**
2003 Silver Bullion Britannia **£14**
2003 Silver proof DNA **£30**
2003 DNA in folder **£7**
(2001 Gold versions are also listed in TWO POUNDS section of milled gold.)

ONE POUND

1983 ... ... **£2**
1983 Unc, in folder **£5**
1983 silver, proof **£35**
1983 – – piedfort **£125**
1984 Scottish reverse **£2**
1984 – Unc, in folder **£5**
1984 – silver, proof **£20**
1984 – – piedfort **£55**
1985 New portrait, Welsh reverse **£4**
1985 – – Unc, in folder **£5**
1985 – – silver, proof **£22**
1985 – – piedfort **£55**
1986 Northern Ireland reverse **£5**
1986 – Unc, in folder **£5**
1986 – silver, proof **£25**
1986 – – – piedfort **£60**
1987 English reverse **£4**
1987 – Unc, in folder **£4**
1987 – silver, proof **£30**
1987 – – – piedfort **£55**
1988 Royal Arms reverse **£5**
1988 – Unc, in folder **£5**
1988 – silver, proof **£35**
1988 – – – piedfort **£55**
1989 Scottish rev as 1984,
    silver, proof **£20**

1989 – – – silver, piedfort **£50**
1990 Welsh reverse as 1985 ... ... **£5**
1990 – silver, proof **£30**
1991 Northern Ireland rev as 1986,
    silver proof **£25**
1992 English rev as 1987,
    silver proof **£25**
1993 Royal Coat of Arms (reverse as
    1983), silver, proof **£30**
1993 – – – piedfort **£65**
1994 Scottish Lion, silver, proof **£35**
Ditto, Unc. in folder **£5**
1994 – silver, piedfort **£55**
1995 Welsh dragon, silver, proof **£25**
Ditto, Unc in folder, Welsh version **£5**
1995 – silver, piedfort **£55**
1996 Northern Ireland Celtic Ring
  Unc in folder **£5**
  Silver, proof **£27**
  Silver, piedfort **£55**
1997 English Lions Unc, in folder **£5**
  silver, proof **£30**
  silver, piedfort **£55**
1998 Royal coat of arms/reverse as 1983,
  silver, proof **£25**
  silver, piedfort **£45**
1999 Scottish Lion (reverse as 1984)
  new portrait, silver proof **£25**
  silver proof, reverse testing **£40**
  silver, piedfort **£45**
2000 Welsh Dragon (reverse as 1995)
  new portrait, silver, proof **£25**
  silver proof, reverse testing **£40**
  silver, piedfort **£47**
2001 Northern Ireland (reverse as 1996)
  new portrait, silver, proof **£25**
  silver, piedfort **£45**
-in folder, BU **£4**
2002 English design (reverse as 1997)
  silver, proof **£27**
  silver, piedfort **£49**
  in folder, BU **£5**
2003 Silver proof **27**
2001.Note that the edge inscriptions on £2 and £1 appear either upright or inverted in relation to the obverse.
(Sovereign and half sovereign prices are not listed here but in the main listings under milled gold.)

FIFTY PENCE

1969 ... ... **£1**
1970 ... ... **£1**
1973 EEC **£1**
1973 – proof **£3**
1976-1981 ... ... **f**
1982 rev changed to FIFTY PENCE
  instead of NEW PENCE ... ... **f**
1983, 1985 ... ... **f**
1992 European Community **£5**
1992 – silver, proof **£30**
1992 – silver, proof piedfort **£55**
1992 – gold, proof **£400**
1994 Normandy landing **£2**
1994 – silver, proof **£28**
1994 – silver, piedfort **£50**
1994 – gold, proof **£400**
1997 new size (27.3mm diameter)
  silver, proof **£27**
  silver, piedfort **£46**
1997 old and new size,
  silver proofs **£50**
1998, 1998 ... ... **f**
1998 European Presidency **£2**

1998 – silver, proof	£25	**TEN PENCE**	
1998 – silver, piedfort	£45	1968	£0.25
1998 – gold, proof	£250	1969	£0.25
1998 National Health Service Commemorative	£2	1970	£0.20
1998 – silver, proof	£25	1971	£0.20
1998 – silver, piedfort	£45	1973	£0.20
1998 – gold, proof	£250	1974-1977, 1979-1981	f
1999 Britannia reverse	*	1992 new size (24.5mm diameter)	
2000 Library Commemorative	£2	silver, proof, piedfort	£40
2000 –, in folder, BU	£5	1992 old and new size, silver, proofs	£30
2000 –, silver, proof	£25	1992, 1995, 1997-2003 – cu-ni	f
2000 –, silver, piedfort	£47	**FIVE PENCE**	
2000 –, gold, proof	£250	1968-1971	*
2003 –, Suffragette, presentation	£5	1975, 1977-1980, 1987, 1988, 1989	f
2004 –, Roger Bannister, gold proof	£265	1990 silver, proof, old and new	£26
2004 –, Roger Bannister, silver proof pied fort	£46	1990 silver, piedfort	£30
TWENTY-FIVE PENCE		1990, 1991, 1992, 1994-1999-2003 – cu-ni	f
1972 Silver Wedding	£1	**TWO PENCE**	
1972 – silver, proof	£30	1971	*
1977 Jubilee	£1	1973-1981	f
1977 – silver, proof	£20	1985 new portrait, rev changed to	
1980 Queen Mother's 80th birthday	£1	TWO PENCE instead of NEW PENCE	*
1980 – in blister pack	£3	1986-2003	f
1980 – silver, proof	£50	**ONE PENNY**	
1981 Royal Wedding	£1	1971	*
1981 – in folder	£3	1973-1981	f
1981 – silver, proof	£30	1982 rev changed to ONE PENNY	
Coronation, Anniv. Silver proof	£35	instead of NEW PENNY	f
Coronation, Anniv. folder	£10	1983, 1984	f
Coronation, Anniv	£5	1985 new portrait	f
Coronation, Anniv. Gold proof crown	£555	1986-2003	f
		HALF PENNY	
		1971	*
TWENTY PENCE		1973-81	*
1982	f	1982 rev changed to HALFPENNY	
1982 silver, proof piedfort	£50	instead of 1/2 NEW PENNY	*
1983-5, 1987-2003	f	1983	*

Proof and Specimen Sets

Proof or specimen sets have been issued since 1887 by the Royal Mint in official cases. Prior to that date, sets were issued privately by the engraver. Some sets are of currency coins, easily distinguishable from proofs which have a vastly superior finish. The two 1887 sets frequently come on to the market, hence their place in this list. The 1953 'plastic' set, though made up of currency coins, is official. It was issued in a plastic packet, hence the name. Apart from the seats stated, as being uncirculated, currency or specimen, all those in the following listing are proof sets.

GEORGE IV   **FDC**
New issue, **1826.** Five pounds to farthing (11 coins) **£21000**

WILLIAM IV
Coronation, **1831.** Two pounds to farthing (14 coins) **£18750**

VICTORIA
Young head, **1839.** 'Una and the Lion' five pounds plus sovereign to farthing (15 coins) **£32500**
Young head, **1853.** Sovereign to half farthing, including 'Gothic' crown (16 coins) **£25000**
Jubilee head, Golden Jubilee, **1887.** Five pounds to Threepence ('full set' – 11 coins) **£6250**
As above, currency set (unofficial) **£1500**
Jubilee head, Golden Jubilee, **1887.** Crown to threepence ('short set' – 7 coins) **£1200**
As above, currency set (unofficial) **£250**
Old head, **1893.** Five pounds to threepence ('full set') – 10 coins) ... ... · **£7500**
Old head, **1893.** Crown to threepence ('short set' – 6 coins) **£1500**

EDWARD VII
Coronation, **1902.** Five pounds to Maundy penny – matt proofs (13 coins) **£1650**
Coronation, **1902.** Sovereign to Maundy penny – matt proofs (11 coins) **£625**

GEORGE V
Coronation, **1911.** Five pounds to Maundy penny (12 coins) **£3250**
Coronation, **1911.** Sovereign to Maundy penny (10 coins) **£900**
Coronation, **1911.** Halfcrown to Maundy penny (8 coins) **£400**
New types, **1927.** Crown to threepence (6 coins) **£300**

GEORGE VI
Coronation, **1937.** Gold set, five pounds to half sovereign (4 coins) **£2200**
Coronation, **1937.** Silver and bronze set, crown to farthing including Maundy money (15 coins) ... **£250**
Mid-century, **1950.** Halfcrown to farthing (9 coins) **£90**
Festival of Britain, **1951.** Crown to farthing (10 coins) **£110**

ELIZABETH II
Coronation, **1953.** Crown to farthing (10 coins) **£85**
Coronation, **1953.** Currency ('plastic') set, official, halfcrown to farthing (9 coins) **£15**
Specimen decimal set, **1968.** 10p, 5p; **1971** 2p, 1p, ½p in wallet (5 coins) **£1**
Last £sd coins, **1970.** (sets issued 1971-73). Halfcrown to Halfpenny (8 coins) **£18**
Proof decimal set, **1971.** (issued 1973), 50p, 10p, 5p, 2p, 1p, ½p (6 coins) **£15**
Proof decimal set, **1972.** 50p, Silver Wedding, 25p, 10p, 5p, 2p, 1p, ½p (7 coins) **£20**
Proof decimal sets, **1973, 1974, 1975, 1976.** 50p, to ½p (6 coins) **£12**
Proof decimal set, **1977.** 50p to ½p, plus Jubilee crown (7 coins) **£12**
Proof decimal set, **1978.** 50p to ½p (6 coins) **£12**
Proof decimal set, **1979.** 50p to ½p (6 coins) **£12**
Proof decimal set, **1980.** 50p to ½p (6 coins) **£10**
Proof gold set, **1980.** Five pounds, two pounds, sovereign, half sovereign (4 coins) **£750**
Commemorative proof coin set, **1981.** Five pounds, sovereign, Royal Wedding Silver crown,
  50p to ½p (9 coins) **£600**
Commemorative set, **1981.** Sovereign and Royal Wedding silver crown (2 coins) **£125**
Proof decimal set, **1981.** 50p to ½p (6 coins) **£10**
Proof gold set, **1982.** Five pounds, two pounds, sovereign, half sovereign (4 coins) **£800**
Proof decimal set, **1982.** 50p to ½p including 20p (7 coins) **£12**
Uncirculated decimal set, **1982.** 50p to ½p including 20p (7 coins) **£9**
Proof gold set, **1983.** Two pounds, sovereign, half sovereign (3 coins) **£325**
Proof decimal set, **1983.** £1 to ½p (8 coins) **£18**
Uncirculated decimal set, **1983.** £1 to ½p (8 coins) **£14**
Proof gold set, **1984.** Five pounds, sovereign, half sovereign (3 coins) **£575**
Proof decimal set, **1984.** £1 (Scottish rev) to ½p (8 coins) **£16**
Uncirculated decimal set, **1984.** £1 (Scottish rev) to ½p (8 coins) **£13**
Proof gold set, **1985.** new portrait. Five pounds, two pounds, sovereign, half sovereign (4 coins) **£750**
Proof decimal set, **1985.** new portrait. £1 (Welsh rev) to 1p (7 coins) in de luxe case **£20**
Proof decimal set, **1985.** As above, in standard case **£16**
Uncirculated decimal set, **1985.** £1 (Welsh rev) to 1p (7 coins) **£12**
Proof gold set, **1986.** Commonwealth Games two pounds, sovereign, half sovereign (3 coins) **£350**
Proof decimal set, **1986.** Commonwealth Games £2, Northern Ireland £1.50p to 1p (8 coins),
  de luxe case **£25**
Proof decimal set, **1986.** As above in standard case **£20**
Uncirculated decimal set, **1986.** As above, in folder **£12**
Proof gold Britannia set, **1987.** One ounce, half ounce, quarter ounce tenth ounce (4 coins) **£650**
Proof decimal set, **1987.** Quarter ounce, tenth ounce (2 coins) **£150**

Proof gold set, **1987.** Two pounds, sovereign, half sovereign (3 coins) £325
Proof decimal set, **1987.** £1 (English rev) to 1p (7 coins) in de luxe case £23
Proof decimal set, **1987.** As above, in standing case £18
Uncirculated decimal set, **1987.** As above, in folder £10
Proof gold Britannia set, **1988.** One ounce, half ounce, quarter ounce, tenth ounce (4 coins) £650
Proof gold Britannia set, **1988.** Quarter ounce, tenth ounce (2 coins) £150
Proof gold set, **1988.** Two pounds, sovereign, half sovereign (3 coins) £325
Proof decimal set **1988.** £1 (Royal Arms rev) to 1p (7 coins) in de luxe case £26
Proof decimal set, **1988.** As above, in standard case £19
Uncirculated decimal set, **1988.** As above, in folder £11
Proof gold Britannia set, **1989.** One ounce, half ounce, quarter ounce, tenth ounce (4 coins) £700
Proof gold Britannia set, **1989.** Quarter ounce, tenth ounce (2 coins) £150
Proof gold set, **1989.** 500th anniversary of the sovereign. Five pounds, two pounds, sovereign,
    half sovereign (4 coins) £1100
Proof gold set, **1989.** 500th anniversary of the sovereign. Two pounds, sovereign, half sovereign (3 coins) £550
Proof decimal set, **1989.** Bill of Rights £2. Claim of Right £2,
    £1 (Scottish rev as 1984), 50p to 1p (9 coins) in de luxe case £35
Proof decimal set, **1989.** As above, in standard case £30
Proof silver, Bill of Rights £2. Claim of Right £2. **1989.** (2 coins) £60
Proof silver piedfort, **1989.** £2 as above (2 coins) £80
Uncirculated. **1989.** As above (2 coins) in folder £15
Uncirculated decimal set, **1989.** £1 (Scottish rev as 1984) to 1p (7 coins) £22
Proof gold Britannia set, 1990 ... ...£775
Proof gold set, **1990.** Five pounds, two pounds, sovereign, half-sovereign (4 coins) £750
Proof gold set, **1990.** Two pounds, sovereign, half sovereign (3 coins) £400
Proof silver set, **1990.** Five pence (23.59mm diam) and five pence (18mm diam, new size) £30
Proof decimal set, **1990.** £1 (Welsh rev as 1985) to 1p including large and small 5p (8 coins) in deluxe case £30
Proof decimal set, **1990.** As above, in standard case £25
Uncirculated decimal set, **1990.** £1 (Welsh rev as 1985) to 1p including large and small 5p (8 coins) £20
Proof gold Britannia set, **1991.** £700
Proof gold set, **1991.** Five pounds, two pounds, sovereign, half sovereign (4 coins) £750
Proof gold set, **1991.** Two pounds, sovereign, half sovereign (3 coins) £400
Proof decimal set, **1991.** £1 to 1p (7 coins) in deluxe case £30
Proof decimal set, **1991.** As above, in standard case £25
Uncirculated decimal set, **1991.** (7 coins) £20
Proof gold Britannia set, **1992.** £700
Proof gold set, **1992.** Five pounds, two pounds, sovereign, half sovereign (4 coins) £750
Proof gold set, **1992.** Two pounds, sovereign, half sovereign (3 coins) £400
Proof silver set, **1992.** Ten pence (large and small size) £30
Proof decimal set, **1992.** £1 (English rev as 1987) to 1p (two 50p, new 10p) (9 coins) in deluxe case £32
Proof decimal set, **1992.** As above, in standard case £28
Uncirculated decimal set, **1992.** £20
Proof gold Britannia set, **1993.** £700
Proof gold set, **1993.** Five pounds, two pounds, sovereign, half sovereign (4 coins) £800
Proof gold set, **1993.** Two pounds, sovereign, half sovereign (3 coins) £400
Proof decimal set, **1993.** Coronation Anniversary £5, £1 to 1p (8 coins) in deluxe case £35
Proof decimal set, **1993.** As above, in standard case £30
Uncirculated decimal set, **1993** (with two 50p, no £5) (8 coins) £25
Proof gold Britannia set, **1994.** £775
Proof gold set, **1994.** Five pounds, two pounds Bank of England, sovereign, half sovereign (4 coins) £800
Proof gold set, **1994.** Two pounds Bank of England, sovereign, half sovereign (3 coins) £450
Proof decimal set, **1994.** £2 Bank of England, £1 (Scottish rev), 50p D-Day to 1p (8 coins) in deluxe case £35
Proof decimal set, **1994.** As above, in standard case £30
Uncirculated decimal set, **1994.** £14
Proof gold Britannia set, **1995.** £850
Proof godl set, **1995.** Five pounds, two pounds Peace, sovereign, half sovereign (4 coins) £800
Proof gold set, **1995.** Two pounds Peace, sovereign, half sovereign (3 coins) £450
Proof decimal set, **1995.** Two pounds Peace, £1 (Welsh rev) to 1p (8 coins) in deluxe case £36
Proof decimal set, **1995.** As above, in standard case £29
Uncirculated decimal set, **1995.** £12
Proof gold Britannia set, **1996.** £900
Proof gold set, **1996.** Five pounds, two pounds, sovereign, half sovereign (4 coins) £800
Proof gold set, **1996.** Two pounds, sovereign, half sovereign (3 coins) £400
Proof silver decimal set, **1996.** £1 to 1p (7 coins) £100
Proof decimal set, **1996.** 60th Birthday £5, £2 Football, £1 Northern Irish rev) to 1p (9 coins) in deluxe case £38
Proof decimal set, **1996.** As above, in standard case £32
Proof gold Britannia set, **1997.** £1000
Uncirculated decimal sert, **1996.** £2 to 1p (8 coins) £11
Proof gold set, **1997.** Five pounds, two pounds (bimetal), sovereign, half sovereign (4 coins) £800
Proof gold set, **1997.** Two pounds (bimetal), sovereign, half sovereign £450
Proof silver set, **1997.**Proof silver Britannia set, **1997.** Two pounds to 20p £85
Proof decimal set, **1997.** Fifthy pence (large and small size) £65
Golden Wedding £5, £2 bimetal. £1 (English rev) to 1p, with new 50p in deluxe case £40
Proof decimal set, **1997.** As above, in standard case £35
Uncirculated decimal set, **1997.** As above but no £5 (9 coins) £11
Proof gold Britannia set, **1998.** £1000
Proof gold set, **1998,** £5 to half sovereign £900
Proof gold set, **1998,** £2 to half sovereign £450
Proof silver set, Britannia **1998,** £2 to 20p £100
Proof decimal set, **1998,** Prince Charles, £5 to 1p in deluxe case £40
Proof decimal set, **1998,** as above, in standard case £33
Uncirculated set, **1998,** as above but no £5 (9 coins) £15
Proof silver set, **1998,** 'EU' and 'NHS' 60p (2 coins) £50
Proof gold Britannia set, **1999.** £1000
Proof gold set, **1999,** £5, £2 Rugby World Cup, sovereign, half sovereign £900

Proof gold set, **1999**, £5, £2 Rugby World Cup, sovereign, half sovereign £900
Proof gold set, **1999**, £2 Rugby World Cup, sovereign, half sovereign £450
Proof decimal set, **1999**, Diana £5 to 1p in deluxe case £40
Proof decimal set, **1999**, as above, in standard case £35
Uncirculated set, **1999**, as above but no £5 (8 coins) £15
Proof gold, Britannia set, **2000** £900
Proof gold, **2000**, £5 to half sovereign £1000
Proof gold, **2000**, £2 to half sovereign £500
Proof silver decimal set, **2000**, £5 to 1p plus Maundy coins (13 coins) £245
Proof decimal set, **2000**, Executive (10 coins) £70
Proof decimal set, **2000**, Deluxe (10 coins) £40
Proof decimal set, **2000**, Standard (10 coins) £30
Proof gold Britannia set, **2001**, new reverse designs £890
Proof gold set, **2001**, Five pounds, £2 Marconi commemorative, sovereign, half sovereign £900
Proof gold set, **2001**, £2 Marconi commemorative, sovereign, half sovereign £415
Proof silver Britannia set, **2001,** new reverse designs, Two pounds to 20p £90
Proof decimal set, **2001,** Executive (10) £75
Proof decimal set, **2001,** Deluxe (10) £48
Proof decimal set, **2001,** Gift (10) £43
Proof decimal set, **2001,** Standard (10) £34
Uncirculated set, **2001,** as above but no £5 (9) £14
Proof gold set, **2002**, £5 to half sovereign, new reverse design £1100
Proof gold set, **2002**, £2 to half sovereign, new reverse design £425
Proof gold set, **2002**, Golden Jubilee £5, £2 bimetal, £1 (English rev) to 1p plus maundy coins (13 coins) £2650
Proof gold set, **2002**, Commonwealth Games £2 (England, N. Ireland, Scotland and Wales) £1150
Proof silver set, **2002**, Commonwealth Games £2 (England, N. Ireland, Scotland and Wales) £98
Proof gold Britannia set, **2002** £900
Proof silver piedfort set, **2002**, Commonwealth Games £2 (England, N. Ireland, Scotland and Wales) £195
Proof decimal, **2002**, Executive (9) Golden Jubilee £5, £2 bimetal, £1 (English rev) to 1p £70
Proof decimal, **2002**, Delux (9) £46
Proof decimal, **2002**, Gift (9) £40
Proof decimal, **2002**, Standard (9) £32
Uncirculated set, **2002**, As above but no £5 (8) £14
Uncirculated set, **2002**, Commonwealth Games £2 (England, N. Ireland, Scotland and Wales) £15
Proof gold set, **2003**, £5 to half sovereign £1000
Proof gold set, **2003**, £2 to half sovereign (DNA £2) £425
Proof decimal set, **2003**, Executive (11) £69
Proof decimal set, **2003**, Deluxe (11) £47
Proof decimal set, **2003**, Standard (11) £34
Uncirculated set, **2003**, (10) £14
Proof Gold set, **2004** £2 to half sovereign (3) £425
Proof Gold set, **2004**, Entente Cordial (2) £965
Proof Gold set, **2004**, D-Day Anniversary, Crowns (3) £1875
Proof Gold Britannia set, **2004** (4) £900
Proof Gold Britannia set, **2004** (3) £415
Proof Silver set, **2004**, Entente Cordial (2) £69
Proof Silver set, **2004**, D-Day Anniversary, crowns (3) £250
Uncirculated set, **2004**, 'New coin pack', (10) £9
Proof Decimal, **2004**, Delux (10) £40
Proof Decimal, **2004**, Executive (10) £65
Proof Decimal, **2004**, Standard (10) £29

Scottish Coins

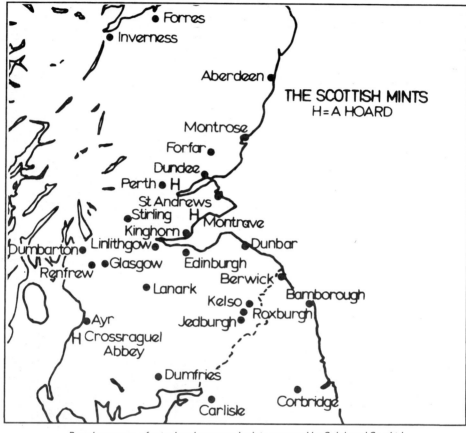

THE SCOTTISH MINTS
H = A HOARD

Based on a map of actual and supposed mints prepared by Spink and Son Ltd.

The number of mints which have been in operation in Scotland can be seen from the map above. The mints of the first coinage of Alexander III are the greatest number ever working together in Scotland, and it is this area that really attracts the collector of the different mint issues. For this reason, when we deal with this reign later on, we give a price for issues of each mint town, but not for any other reign.

MINT TOWN	KING(S)
ABERDEEN	Alexander III, David II Robert III, James I, II, III
AYR	Alexander III
BAMBOROUGH	Henry
BERWICK	David I, Malcom IV, William I, Alexander II, III Robert Bruce, James III
CARLISLE	David I, Henry
CORBRIDGE	Henry
DUMBARTON	Robert III
DUMFRIES	Alexander III
DUNBAR	William I ?, Alexander III
DUNDEE	William I ?, Alexander III
DUNFERMLINE	William I
FORFAR	Alexander III
FORRES	Alexander III
GLASGOW	Alexander III
INVERNESS	Alexander III
JEDBURGH	Malcom IV
KELSO	Alexander II
KINGHORN	Alexander III
LANARK	Alexander III
LINLITHGOW	James I, II
MONTROSE	Alexander III
PERTH	William I, Alexander III, Robert II to James II
RENFREW	Alexander III
ROXBURGH	Alexander III
ST ANDREWS	Alexander III
STIRLING	Alexander III, James I, II Mary Stuart

Prices are for the commonest coins in each case. Collectors should expect to pay these amounts and upwards. For further details see *The Scottish Coinage*, by I. Stewart (Spink, 1967, reprint 1975) and *Coins of Scotland, Ireland and The Islands*, Spink 2003. Gold coins are indicated. All other coins are silver unless another metal is stated.

DAVID I 1124-53	F	VF
Pennies	£525	£1100

Four different groups; struck at the mints of Berwick, Carlisle, Roxburgh and Edinburgh £750 £1750

This superb David I penny of Carlisle realised £1,210 in Spink's Douglas auction in 1997

HENRY 1136-52
(Earl of Huntingdon and Northumberland)
Pennies ... ... £1750 *
Three types; struck at the mints of Corbridge, Carlisle and Barnborough.

MALCOLM IV 1153-65
Pennies ... ... £5000 *
Five types; struck at the mints of Roxburgh and Berwick.

WILLIAM THE LION 1165-1214
Pennies £75 £200
Three issues; struck at the mints of Roxburgh, Berwick, Edinburgh, Dun (Dunfermline?), Perth

ALEXANDER II 1214-49
Pennies £800 £2250
Mints of Berwick and Roxburgh, varieties of bust.

Halfpenny and farthing of Alexander III and penny of Robert Bruce

ALEXANDER III 1249-86
1st coinage pennies 1250-80
Mints

Aberdeen	£100	£225
Ayr	£175	£475
Berwick	£70	£160
'DUN'	£135	£350
Edinburgh	£90	£200
Forfar	£200	£500
Fres	£225	£575
Glasgow	£175	£450
Inverness	£200	£475
Kinghorn	£225	£575
Lanark	£175	£475
Montrose	£450	*
Perth	£85	£185

SCOTTISH COINS

	F	VF
Renfrew	£425	*
Roxburgh	£65	£160
St. Andrews	£135	£350
Stirling	£150	£375
'TERWILANER' (uncertain name)	£450	*

2nd coinage c. 1280 –
Many types and varieties

Pennies	£25	£60
Halfpennies	£75	£250
Farthings	£150	£450

JOHN BALIOL 1292-6
1st coinage (rough surface issue)

Pennies	£100	£275
Halfpennies	£375	£900

2nd coinage (smooth surface issue)	£120	£300
Pennies	£110	£300
Halfpennies	£175	£450

Robert Bruce Penny

ROBERT BRUCE 1306-29

Pennies	£450	£1000
Halfpennies	£575	£1350
Farthings	ext. rare	

Probably all struck at Berwick.

David II Groat, Edinburgh Mint

DAVID II 1329-71

Nobles (gold)	ext. rare	
Groats	£90	£250
Halfgroats	£95	£235
Pennies	£35	£95
Halfpennies	£300	£900
Farthings	£650	*

Three issues, but these denominations were not struck for all issues. Edinburgh and Aberdeen mints.

ROBERT II 1371-90

Groats	£90	£200
Halfgroats	£85	£200
Pennies	£80	£225
Halfpennies	£100	£350

Some varieties. Struck at mints of Dundee, Edinburgh, Perth.

SCOTTISH COINS

ROBERT III 1390-1406

	F	VF
Lion or crowns (gold)	£700	£1800
Demy lions or halfcrowns (gold) ...	£600	£1350
Groats	£85	£200
Halfgroats	£125	£350
Pennies	£300	£725
Halfpennies	£275	£675

Three issues, many varieties. Struck at mints of Edinburgh, Aberdeen, Perth, Dumbarton.

James I Demy or Nine Shilling Piece

JAMES I 1406-37

	F	VF
Demies (gold)	£500	£1100
Half demies (gold)	£675	£1500
Groats	£135	£375
Billon pennies	£150	£400
Billon halfpennies	£375	£1000

Mints, Aberdeen, Edinburgh, Inverness, Linlithgow, Perth, Stirling.

JAMES II 1437-60

	F	VF
Demies (gold) from	£600	£1350
Lions (gold) from	£800	£2000
Half lions (gold) from	Very rare	
Groats	£200	£525
Halfgroats	£525	*
Billon pennies	£200	£550

Two issues, many varieties. Mints: Aberdeen, Edinburgh, Linlithgow, Perth, Roxburgh, Stirling.

ECCLESIASTICAL ISSUES C 1452-80

	F	VF
Bishop Kennedy copper pennies ...	£75	£200
Copper farthings	£175	£500

Different types, varieties

JAMES III 1460-88

	F	VF
Riders (gold) from	£1100	£2750
Half riders (gold)	£1350	£3500
Quarter riders (gold)	£1750	£4500
Unicorns (gold)	£1000	£2250
Groats ... ...from	£200	£450

James III groat and
James V one-third groat

	F	VF
Halfgroats from	£400	£900
Pennies from	£175	£475
Billon placks from	£95	£275
Billon half placks from	£125	£325

	F	VF
Billon pennies from	£125	£325
Copper farthings from	£300	*

Many varieties. Mints: Edinburgh, Berwick, Aberdeen.

James IV Unicorn

JAMES IV 1488-1513

	F	VF
Unicorns (gold)	£950	£2250
Half unicorns (gold)	£750	£1500
Lions or crowns (gold)	£1350	£3500
Half lions (gold)	£1750	£4500
Pattern angel (gold)	unique	
Groats	£325	£800
Halfgroats	£475	£1200
Pennies (light coinage) ... ...ext rare		*
Billon placks	£30	£85
Billon half placks	£125	£425
Billon pennies	£50	£135

Different types, varieties. Mint: Edinburgh only.

James V 'Bonnet' piece of 1540

JAMES V 1513-42

	F	VF
Unicorns (gold)	£1000	£2750
Half unicorns (gold)	£1650	£4250
Crowns (gold)	£675	£1450
'Bonnet' pieces or ducats (gold) ...	£2250	£4750
Two-thirds ducats (gold)	£2000	£4250
One-third ducats (gold)	£3000	£7000
Groats from	£135	£450
One-third groats	£150	£450

James V groat

	F	VF
Billon placks	£30	£90
Billon bawbees	£25	£70
Billon half bawbees	£90	£225
Billon quarter bawbees	unique	

Different issues, varieties. Edinburgh mint.

Note: from here on all Scottish coins were struck at Edinburgh.

MARY 1542-67

1st Period 1542-58

	F	VF
Crown (gold)	£1250	£3000
Twenty shillings (gold)	£2250	*
Lions or forty-four shillings (gold)	£1250	£2750

Extremely rare Francis and Mary ducat which realised £77,000 at a Spink auction in March 1997

	F	VF
Half lions or twenty-two shillings (gold)	£1000	£2500
Ryals or £3 pieces (gold)	£3000	£6500
1555, 1557, 1558	£3750	£7500
Half ryals (gold) 1555,1557,1558 ...	£2000	£5500
Portrait testoons, 1553		

Mary, Queen of Scots Half Testoon, 1560, Francis and Mary

	F	VF
Non-portrait testoons, 1555-8	£185	£500
– half testoons, 1555-8	£225	£600
Billon bawbees	£30	£85
– half bawbees	£80	£200
– pennies (facing bust)	£185	£550
– pennies (no bust) 1556	£150	£500
– lions, 1555, 1558	£30	£90
– placks, 1557	£40	£125

2nd period (Francis and Mary) 1558-60

	F	VF
Ducats or sixty shillings (gold) ...		ext. rare
Non-portrait testoons, 1558-61 ...	£185	£450
– half testoons, 1558-60	£200	£500
Twelvepenny groats (Nonsunt) 1558-9	£85	£185
– lions, 1559-60	£25	£70

3rd period (widowhood) 1560-5

	F	VF
Crown (gold) 1562		ext. rare
Portrait testoons, 1561-2	£1350	£4000
– half testoons, 1561-2	£1650	£5000

4th period (Henry and Mary) 1565-7

	F	VF
Portrait ryals, 1565		ext. rare
Non-portrait ryals, 1565-7	£350	£900

SCOTTISH COINS

Mary and Henry 1565 two thirds ryal

	F	VF
– two thirds ryals, 1565-7	£300	£750
– – undated	£850	£2000
– one-third ryals, 1565-6	£300	£750
– testoons, 1565		ext. rare

5th period (2nd widowhood) 1567

	F	VF
– Non portrait ryals, 1567	£375	£950
– two thirds ryals, 1567	£300	£750
– one third ryals, 1566-7	£400	£950

Mints: Edinburgh, Stirling (but only for some bawbees)

JAMES VI

Before English accession 1567-1603
1st coinage 1567-71

	F	VF
Ryals 1567-71	£300	£750
Two-third ryals –	£250	£650
One-third ryals –	£275	£675

Superb gold £20 piece of 1575 realised £30,800 in Spink auction in March 1997

2nd coinage 1571-80

	F	VF
Twenty pounds (gold)	£17,500	£42,500
Nobles, 1572-7, 1580	£85	£275
Half nobles –	£80	£235
Two merks, 1578-80 –	£1350	£3000
Merks, 1579-80	£1750	£4250

3rd coinage 1580-81

	F	VF
Ducats (gold), 1580	£3000	£6500
Sixteen shillings, 1581	£1650	£4000
Eight shillings, 1581	£1250	£2500
Four shillings, 1581	£1350	£2750
Two shillings, 1581		ext. rare

SCOTTISH COINS

	F	VF
4th coinage 1582-88		
Lion nobles (gold)	£3000	£6750
Two-third lion nobles (gold)	£3250	£7500
One-third lion nobles (gold)	£3750	£8500
Forty shillings, 1582	£3000	£8000
Thirty shillings, 1582-6	£275	£850
Twenty shillings, 1582-5	£250	£750
Ten shillings, 1582-4	£250	£725

James VI twenty shillings, 1582

	F	VF
5th coinage 1588		
Thistle nobles (gold)	£1350	£3250
6th coinage 1591-93		
Hat pieces (gold) 1591-3	£2750	£6000
Balance half merks, 1591-3	£225	£575
Balance quarter merks, 1591	£400	£1000
7th coinage 1594-1601		
Riders (gold)	£675	£1650
Half riders (gold)	£575	£1350
Ten shillings, 1593-5, 1598-1601 ...	£125	£325
Five shillings, 1593-5, 1598-1601 ...	£100	£300
Thirty pennies, 1595-6, 1598-9, 1601	£95	£275
Twelve pennies, 1594-6	£90	£250

James VI Sword and Sceptre piece, 1601

	F	VF
8th coinage 1601-4		
Sword and sceptre pieces (gold) ...	£375	£800
Half sword and sceptre pieces (gold)	£300	£675
Thistle-merks, 1601-4	£90	£225
Half thistle merks –	£65	£185
Quarter thistle-merks –	£45	£150
Eighth thistle-merks, 1601-3	£35	£110
Billon and copper issues		
Billon placks or eight penny groats	£25	£85
Billon half packs	£125	£325
Billon hardheads	£25	£90
Billon saltire placks	£150	£450

	F	VF
Copper twopence 1597	£90	£300
Copper penny 1597	£350	*
After English accession 1603-25		
Units (gold)	£475	£1000
Double crowns (gold)	£625	£1500
Britain crowns (gold)	£425	£950
Halfcrowns (gold)	£400	£900
Thistle crowns (gold)	£350	£750
Sixty shillings	£300	£850
Thirty shillings	£135	£325
Twelve shillings	£135	£325
Six shillings	£375	£900
Two shillings	£40	£100
One shilling	£65	£150

James VI Gold Unit
(after English accession)

	F	VF
Sixpences	*	*
Copper twopences	£20	£50
Copper pennies	£65	£175

Charles I Briot Unit, 3rd coinage

CHARLES 1652-49

	F	VF
1st coinage 1625-36		
Units (gold)	£750	£2000
Double crowns (gold)	£1350	£3250
Britain crowns (gold)	ext. rare	
Sixty shillings	£625	£1650
Thirty shillings	£135	£350
Twelve shillings	£135	£400
Six shillings	£350	£1000
Two shillings	£65	£165
One shilling	£85	£250
2nd coinage 1636		
Half merks	£75	£200
Forty penny pieces	£70	£185
Twenty penny pieces	£70	£175

	F	VF
3rd coinage 1580-81		
Units (gold)	£750	£1650
Half units (gold)	£800	£1850
Britain crowns (gold)	£1000	£2750
Britain half crowns (gold)	£425	£900
Sixty shilling	£350	£1100
Thirty shilling	£125	£300

Charles I Twelve Shillings, 3rd coinage; Falconer's issue.

Charles II, Merk 1669

	F	VF
Twelve shillings	£85	£225
Six shillings	£90	£225
Half Merks	£85	£225
Forty pennies	£35	£90
Twenty pennies	£25	£65
Three shillings	£75	£200
Two shillings	£65	£150
Copper twopences (lion)	£20	£55
– pennies –	£350	*
– twopences (CR crowned)	£15	£40
– twopences (Stirling turners) ...	£15	£35

Merks		
1664	£100	£300
1665	£110	£325
1666	£250	£600
1668	£225	£575
1669	£75	£225
1670	£75	£225
1671	£85	£225
1672	£100	£250
1673	£85	£225
1674	£135	£400
1674 F below bust	£125	£350
1675 F below bust	£125	£350
1675	£175	£550

CHARLES II 1660-85	F	VF
1st coinage		
Four merks		
1664 thistle above bust	£600	£1250
1664 thistle below bust	£675	£1500
1665	£950	*
1670	£850	*
1673	£650	£1350
1674 F below bust	£600	£1200
1675	£625	£1250

Half merks		
1664	£175	£500
1665	£150	£450
1666	£200	£650
1667	£200	£650
1668	£150	£450
1669	£80	£250
1670	£90	£275
1671	£90	£275
1672	£90	£275
1673	£125	£350
1675 F below bust	£125	£350
1675	£125	£350

Two merks		
1664 thistle above bust	£475	£1000

2nd coinage		
Dollars		
1676	£375	£1000
1679	£400	£1100
1680	£525	£1350
1681	£400	£1100
1682	£350	£950

Half dollars		
1675	£375	£900
1676	£550	£1250
1681	£400	£950

Charles II silver two merks 1664

	F	VF
1664 thistle below bust	£325	£850
1670	£575	£1250
1673	£300	£750
1673 F below bust	£425	£950
1674	£350	£850
1674 F below bust	£375	£900
1675	£350	£800

Quarter dollars		
1675	£175	£475
1676	£125	£325
1677	£125	£350
1678	£150	£425
1679	£165	£450
1680	£125	£350
1681	£125	£350
1682	£135	£400

Eighth dollars		
1676	£90	£225
1677	£95	£240
1678/7	£200	£550
1679	£150	£400
1680	£85	£200
1682	£150	£450

Sixteenth dollars

1677	£65	£185
1678/7	£85	£250
1679/7	£125	£400
1680	£80	£225
1681	£75	£200

Charles II 1678 Bawbee

Copper twopence CR" crowned	£20	£60
Copper bawbees, 1677-9	£45	£135
Copper turners, 1677-9	£30	£100

JAMES VII 1685-9

Sixty shillings 1688 proof only[1]	FDC	£1750
– gold proof only[1]		Ext. rare

([1]Struck in 1828, not contemporary)

Forty shillings

1887	£225	£650
1688	£300	£750

James VII 1687 ten shillings

Ten shillings

1687	£135	£450
1688	£225	£600

WILLIAM AND MARY 1689-94

Sixty shillings

1691	£425	£1200
1692	£375	£1000

Forty shillings

1689	£250	£750
1690	£200	£625
1691	£175	£500
1692	£150	£475
1693	£135	£450
1694	£200	£600

Twenty shillings

1693	£325	£900
1694	£475	£1350

Ten shillings

1689	*	*
1690	£200	£575
1691	£125	£375
1692	£135	£400
1694	£250	£675

William and Mary 1694 five shillings

Five shillings	F	VF
1691	£135	£400
1694	£100	£325
Copper bawbee 1691-4	£50	£125
Copper bodle 1691-4	£30	£90

WILLIAM II 1694-1702	F	VF
Pistole (gold) 1701	£2250	£5250
Half pistole (gold) 1701	£2000	£5000

Sixty shillings

1699	*	*

Forty shillings

1695	£175	£500
1696	£200	£525
1697	£225	£550
1698	£250	£625
1699	£250	£625
1700	£675	£1750

Twenty shillings

1695	£150	£475
1696	£125	£375
1697	£275	£750
1698	£125	£375
1699	£375	£900

Ten shillings

1695	£100	£275
1696	£100	£275
1697	£110	£300
1698	£125	£375
1699	£135	£400

Five shillings

1695	£75	£175
1696	£75	£175
1697	£60	£150
1699	£85	£225
1700	£85	£225
1701	£135	£425
1702	£125	£375
Copper bawbee 1695-7	£65	£250
Copper bodle 1695-7	£45	£150

ANNE 1702-14
Pre-Union 1702-7

Ten shillings

1705	£125	£275
1706	£150	£425

Five shillings

1705	£45	£125
1706	£50	£150

Post-Union 1707-14
see under British milled series

JAMES VIII 1688-1766 (The Old Pretender)

Guinea 1716, gold	FDC	£7500
– silver	FDC	£1250
– bronze	FDC	£1500
Crown 1709		unique
Crown 1716, silver	FDC	£1750
– gold		ext. rare
– bronze		ext. rare

NB: All the 1716-dated pieces were struck in 1828 from original dies.

Irish Coins

Hammered Issues 995-1661

Prices are for the commonest coins in each case. It should be remembered taht most of the Irish coins of these times are in fairly poor condition and it is difficult to find specimens in VF condition upwards. For more details see The Guide Book to the Coinage of Ireland AD 995 to the present day, by Anthony Dowle and Patrick Finn (ref. DF in the following lists): Spink's Coins of Scotland, Ireland and the Islands, and also Patrick Finn's Irish Coin Values.

All coins are silver unlesss otherwise stated

HIBERNO-NORSEMEN OF DUBLIN 995-1150

	F	VF
Pennies, imitative of English coins, many types and varieties ...from	£125	£250

Hiberno-Norse penny, c 1015-1035

Hiberno-Norseman of Dublin Penny c1035-1055

JOHN, as Lord of Ireland c 1185-1199

Halfpennies, with profile portrait	£1500	*
Halfpennies, with facing head	£45	£100
Farthings	£250	£650

Different types,varieties, mints, moneyers.

JOHN DE COURCY Lord of Ulster 1177-1205

Halfpenny		unique
Farthings	£525	£1250

Different types,varieties, mints, moneyers.

John as King of England, Rex/Triangle Penny

JOHN as King of England and Lord of Ireland c 1199-1216

	F	VF
Rex/Triangle types		
Pennies ... ...from	£45	£100
Halfpennies	£75	£175
Farthings	£575	£1500

Different types,varieties, mints, moneyers.

HENRY III 1216-1272

Pennies (c 1251-1254) ... ...from	£35	£50

Dublin only, moneyers DAVI and RICHARD. many varieties.

Edward I Waterford penny

EDWARD I 1272-1307

Pennies ... ...from	£25	£60
Halfpennies	£45	£110

Edward I Farthing, Dublin

Farthings	£70	£175

Dublin,Waterford and Cork. Many different issues.

EDWARD III 1327-1377

Halfpennies Dublin mint	ext. rare

There were no Irish coins struck for Edward II, Richard II, Henry IV or Henry V.

HENRY VI 1422-1461

Pennies, Dublin mint	ext. rare

Edward IV untitled crown groats

EDWARD IV 1461-1483

Untitled crown groats ... ...from	£350	£850
– pennies	£900	*
Titled crown groats	£1250	*
– halfgroats	£1500	*
– pennies	£1000	*
Cross on rose/-sun groats	£1650	*

IRISH COINS

	F	VF
Bust/rose-sun double groats	£1350	£4500
– – groats	£1250	*
– – halfgroats	£1250	*
– – pennies	£1000	*
'English style' groats	£85	£225
– halfgroats	£400	£950
– pennies	£45	£110
– halfpennies	£600	*
Bust/rose groats	£300	£750
– – pennies	£90	£250
copper issues		
Crown/cross farthing	£900	*
– – half farthing	£750	*
PATRICIUS/SALVATOR		
Farthing	£650	£1500
3 crowns/sun half-farthing	£800	*

This is, of course, a very abbreviated listing of the issues of Edward IV which are numerous and complicated, and still pose numismatics many problems. There are also many varieties and different mints.

RICHARD III 1483-1485

	F	VF
Bust/rose-cross groats	£750	£2500
— halfgroat		unique
— penny		ext.rare
Cross and Pellet Penny	£1000	*
Three-crown groats	£375	£800
Different mints, varieties, etc.		

HENRY VII 1485-1509
Early issues

	F	VF
Three-crown groats	£85	£225
— halfgroats	£125	£275
— pennies	£375	£950
— halfpennies		ext. rare
Different mints, varieties, etc.		

LAMBERT SIMNEL (pretender) 1487

	F	VF
Three-crown groats	£750	£1750
Different mints, varieties.		

HENRY VII 1485-1509

Henry VII facing bust Groat, Dublin

Later issues

	F	VF
Facing bust groats	~~£90~~	~~£200~~
— halfgroats	£900	*
— pennies	£750	*
Crowned H pennies	£900	*
Many varieties. Mainly Dublin. Waterford is extemely rare.		

HENRY VIII 1509-1547

	F	VF
'Harp' groats	£50	£140
— halfgroat	£300	£850

Henry VIII harp groats (with initials HA and HI)

These harp coins carry crowned initials, e.g., HA (Henry and Anne Boleyn), HI (Henry and Jane Seymour), HK (Henry and Katherine Howard), HR (Henricus Rex).

Henry VIII portrait groat

Posthumous issues	F	VF
Portrait groats current for 6 pence	£90	£250
— halfgroats ...current for 3 pence	£90	£250
— pennies current for 3 halfpence	£250	£750
— halfpennies current for 3 farthings	£450	£1250
Different busts, mintmarks etc.		

EDWARD VI 1547-1553

	F	VF
Base shillings 1552 (MDLII)	£600	£1750
— contemporary copy	£50	£200

Mary 1553 shilling

MARY 1553-1558

	F	VF
Shillings 1553 (MDLIII)	£500	£2000
Shillings 1554 (MDLIIII)		ext. rare
Groats		**ext. rare**
Halfgroats		ext. rare
Pennies		ext. rare
Several varieties of the shillings and groats.		

PHILIP AND MARY 1554-1558

	F	VF
Base shillings	£250	£750
— groats	£65	£225
Several minor varieties.		

ELIZABETH I 1558-1603

	F	VF
Base portrait shillings	£250	£850
— groats	£125	£350

COINS MARKET VALUES

	F	VF

Elizabeth I 1561 portrait shilling

	F	VF
Fine silver portrait shillings 1561	£175	£575
— groats –	£225	£675
Base shillings arms-harp	£135	£500
— sixpences –	£95	£275
— threepences –	£125	£375
— pennies –	£30	£100
— halfpennies –	£65	£175

JAMES I 1603-1625

	F	VF
Shillings	£75	£225
— Sixpences	£60	£175

Different issues, busts and mintmarks.

CHARLES I 1625-1649
Siege money of the Irish Rebellion 1642-1649
Siege coins are rather irregular in size and shape.

Kilkenny Money 1642

	F	VF
Copper halfpennies (F)	£125	£525
Copper farthings (F)	£225	£750

Inchiquin Money 1642-1646
(The only gold coins struck in Ireland)

	F	VF
Gold double pistoles	ext. rare	
Gold pistoles (F)	ext. rare	
Crowns	£1500	£3500

Inchiquin shilling

	F	VF
Halfcrowns	£1250	£2500
Shillings	£1250	£2500
Ninepences	£3250	*
Sixpences	£3000	*
Groats (F)	£2500	*
Threepences ... ... ext. rare		*

Three issues and many varieties.

Ormonde Money 1643

	F	VF
Crowns (F)	£350	£750
Halfcrowns (F)	£275	£625
Shillings	£150	£350

IRISH COINS

	F	VF

Ormonde Money, Halfcrown

Ormonde sixpence

	F	VF
Sixpences (F)	£110	£250
Groats (F)	£90	£225
Threepences	£90	£200
Halfgroats (F)	£300	£675

Many varieties.

Rebel Money 1643

	F	VF
Crowns	£1500	£3500
Halfcrowns	£1500	£3250

Town Pieces 1645-1647
Bandon

	F	VF
Copper farthings (F)	£400	*

Kinsale copper farthing

Kinsale

	F	VF
Copper farthings (F)	£425	*

Youghal

	F	VF
Copper farthings (F)	£450	£1000
Brass twopences	ext. rare	
Pewter threepences	ext. rare	

IRISH COINS

	F	VF
Cork		
Shillings (**F**)	£1250	£3000
Sixpences (**F**)	£575	£1350
Copper halfpennies	£750	*
Copper farthings (**F**)	£450	*
Elizabeth I shillings countermarked		
CORKE (**F**)		ext. rare

Youghal farthing

'Blacksmith's' Money 1649
(Based on English Tower halfcrown)

	F	VF
Halfcrown, varieties	£475	£1250

Dublin Money 1649

	F	VF
Crowns	£2500	£6500
Halfcrowns	£1750	£4500

Charles II Armstrong Issue, Farthing

CHARLES II 1660-1685
Armstrong issues 1660-1661

	F	VF
Copper farthings	£25	£80

Charles II to George IV
This series, of which all the issues except Bank of Ireland tokens were struck in base metal, features a large number of varieties, many of which are unpublished, but there is space here for only the main types and best-known variants. A number of rare proofs have also been omitted.

Except for the 'gunmoney' of James II, Irish copper coins are notably hard to find in the top grades, especially the so-called 'Voce populi' issues and specimens of Wood's coinage (which are reasonably common in the lower grades, apart from the rarities).

We have listed some of the 'gunmoney' of James II in only three grades – Fair, Fine and VF. The majority of these hastily produced coins were not well struck and many pieces with little substantial wear are, arguably, not EF in the strictest sense.

Finally, a note on the dating of gunmoney. In the calendar used up to 1723 the legal or civil year commenced on March 25 in Great Britain and Ireland, so December 1689 came before, not after January, February and March 1689. Coins dated March 1689 and March 1690 were struck in the same month.

CHARLES II	Fair	F	VF	EF
St Patrick's coinage				
Halfpenny	£100	£375	*	*
— star in rev legend	£125	£400	*	*
Farthing	£75	£200	£600	*
— stars in rev legend	£85	£225	£650	*
— cloud around				
St Patrick	*	*	*	*
— martlet below king	£90	£250	£700	*
— annulet below king	£100	£275	£750	*

Charles II St Patrick's Farthing

Regal coinage
Halfpennies

	Fair	F	VF	EF
1680 large letters				
small cross	£12	£50	£150	*
1680 large letters,	£10	£45	£135	£400
pellets	£10	£40	£130	£375
1681 large letters	£10	£40	£130	£400
1681 small letters	*	*	*	*
1682 large letters	£15	£60	£175	*
1682 small letters	£10	£40	£125	£375
1683	£10	£40	£135	£350
1684	£25	£100	£325	*

JAMES II
Regular coinage
Halfpennies

	Fair	F	VF	EF
1685	£10	£45	£135	£375
1686	£10	£40	£125	£350
1687	£50	£300	*	*
1688	£12	£50	£150	*

Emergency coinage
Gunmoney
Crowns

	Fair	F	VF	EF
1690	£15	£50	£135	£300
1690 'chubby'				
horseman, sword				
to E (Sby 6577)	£30	£100	£275	*
1690 similar (DF 373)	£45	£135	£300	*

James II Gunmoney Crown

	Fair	F	VF	EF
Large halfcrowns				
1689 July	£12	£50	£135	*
1689 August	£8	£30	£100	*
1689 September	£8	£30	£100	*
1689 October	£7	£25	£90	*
1689 November	£8	£30	£100	*
1689 December	£8	£30	£100	*
1689 January	£8	£30	£110	*
1689 February	£7	£25	£90	*
1689 March	£7	£25	£90	*
1690 March	£7	£25	£90	*
1690 April	£7	£25	£90	*
1690 May	£9	£35	£110	*
Small halfcrowns				
1690 April	£35	£150	*	*
1690 May	£5	£20	£75	£175
1690 June	£7	£25	£85	£200
1690 July	£8	£30	£100	£250
1690 August	£15	£50	£150	£400
1690 September	*	*	*	*
1690 October	£50	£225	£500	*
Large shillings				
1689 July	£6	£20	£60	£175
1689 August	£6	£18	£50	£150
1689 September	£5	£15	£50	£150
1689 October	£6	£20	£60	£175
1689 November	£6	£18	£50	£150
1689 December	£5	£15	£45	£135
1689 January	£5	£15	£45	£135
1689 February	£5	£15	£45	£135
1689 March	£6	£18	£50	£150
1690 March	£6	£15	£50	£150
1690 April	£6	£20	£60	£175
Small shillings				
1690 April	£7	£25	£80	£225
1690 May	£6	£18	£50	£150
1690 June	£6	£18	£50	£150
1690 July	*	*	*	*
1690 August	*	*	*	*
1690 September	£25	£125	*	*

James II

Gunmoney,
halfcrown, May 1690

Sixpences				
1689 June	£8	£30	£90	£200
1689 July	£7	£25	£85	£185
1689 August	£7	£25	£85	£185
1689 September	£10	£30	£100	£225
1689 October	*	*	*	*
1689 November	£7	£25	£85	£185
1689 December	£7	£25	£85	£185
1689 January	£8	£30	£90	£200
1689 February	£7	£25	£85	£185
1689 March	*	*	*	*
1690 March	*	*	*	*
1690 April	*	*	*	*
1690 May	£15	£50	£150	*
1690 June	*	*	*	*
1690 October	*	*	*	*

Pewter Money				
Crown	£225	£675	£2000	*
Groat	£150	£450	£1350	£2750
Penny large bust	£135	£425	£1000	*
Penny small bust	£110	£325	£750	*

IRISH COINS

	Fair	F	VF	EF

James II Pewter Money, Halfpenny, 1690

	Fair	F	VF	EF
Halfpenny large bust	£65	£200	£575	*
Halfpenny small bust	£50	£175	£425	*

Limerick Money halfpenny

Limerick Money				
Halfpenny	£15	£50	£135	£300
Farthing reversed N	£20	£65	£175	£350
— normal N	£25	£75	£200	*

1693 halfpenny

WILLIAM AND MARY
Halfpennies				
1692	£5	£30	£100	*
1693	£5	£30	£100	*
1694	£6	£35	£125	*

WILLIAM III
1696 Halfpenny draped bust	: £15	£50	£175	*
1696 Halfpenny crude undraped bust	: £50	£250	£575	*

GEORGE I
Wood's coinage
1722 harp left	: £15	£50	£175	*
1722 harp right	£7	£30	£125	£400
1723	£5	£20	£75	£300
1723 obv Rs altered Bs	£6	£25	£100	£325
1723 no stop after date	£5	£25	£80	£300
1723/2	£7	£30	£125	*
1723 star in rev legend	*	*	*	*

IRISH COINS

	Fair	F	VF	EF
1723 no stop before HIBERNIA	£5	£20	£75	£300
1724 head divides rev legend	£7	£30	£125	£375
1724 legend continuous over head	£10	£35	£150	*

George I Wood's farthing, 1723

Farthings

	Fair	F	VF	EF
1722 harp left	£40	£150	£650	*
1723 D: G:	£10	£40	£165	£500
1723 DEI GRATIA ...	£6	£25	£90	£250
1724	£10	£35	£135	£375

GEORGE II
halfpennies

	Fair	F	VF	EF
1736	*	£10	£50	£200
1737	*	£10	£50	£200
1738	£1	£15	£60	£225
1741	*	£10	£50	£200
1742	*	£10	£50	£200
1743	£2	£20	£65	£250
1744	£1	£15	£60	£225
1744/43	£2	£20	£65	£250
1746	£1	£15	£60	£225
1747	*	£10	£50	£200
1748	£2	£15	£75	£275
1749	*	£10	£50	£185
1750	*	£10	£45	£175
1751	*	£10	£45	£175
1752	*	£10	£45	£175
1753	*	£12	£50	£200
1755	*	*	*	*
1760	*	£8	£40	£175

Farthings

	Fair	F	VF	EF
1737	£1	£15	£75	£250
1738	*	£10	£60	£225
1744	*	£10	£50	£200
1760	*	£8	£40	£125

George III, Voce Populi Halfpenny 1760

GEORGE III
Voce populi coinage
Halfpennies (1760)

	Fair	F	VF	EF
Type 1 (DF 565) ...	£45	£135	£400	*

	Fair	F	VF	EF
Type 2(DF 566)	£30	£75	£400	*
Type 3(DF 567)	£40	£110	£375	*
Type 4(DF 569)	£30	£75	£300	*
Type 5(DF 570)	£25	£70	£275	£750
Type 6(DF 571)	£25	£70	£275	£750
Type 7(DF 572)	£30	£75	£325	*
Type 8(DF 573)	£30	£75	£275	£750
Type 9(DF 575)	£40	£110	£375	*
Type 9, P before head (DF 576)	£25	£70	£275	£800
Type 9, P under head (DF 577)	£25	£70	£275	£800

Farthings (1760)

	Fair	F	VF	EF
Type 1 loop to truncation	£65	£225	£1000	£3000
Type 2 no loop ...	*	*	*	*

London coinage
Halfpennies

	F	VF	EF	UNC
1766	*	£8	£60	£250
1769	*	£8	£65	£250
1769 2nd type	*	£15	£90	£300
1775	*	£10	£65	£275
1776	£4	£25	£125	£325
1781	*	£8	£85	£225
1782	*	£8	£85	£225

George III Halfpenny, 1805

Soho coinage

	F	VF	EF	UNC
Penny 1805	£8	£35	£150	£225
Halfpenny 1805 ...	£3	£20	£90	£150
Farthing 1806	£2	£15	£50	£100

Bank of Ireland token coinage

	F	VF	EF	UNC
Six shillings 1804 ...	£50	£85	£250	£600

1804 six shilling Bank of Ireland

IRISH COINS

	F	VF	EF	UNC
Thirty pence 1808	£15	£45	£120	£350
Ten pence 1805 ...	£4	£20	£70	£100
Ten pence 1806 ...	£10	£45	£110	£175
Ten pence 1813 ...	£3	£15	£50	£70
Five pence 1805 ...	£3	£15	£60	£85
Five pence 1806 ...	£5	£25	£75	£100

Bank of Ireland ten pence token, 1813

GEORGE IV

Penny 1822...	£5	£30	£100	£225
Penny 1823...	£5	£35	£110	£235
Halfpenny 1822 ...	£3	£25	£80	£150
Halfpenny 1823 ...	£3	£25	£80	£165

Free State and Republic

Proofs exist for nearly all dates of the modern Irish coinage. However, only a few dates have become available to collectors or dealers and apart from the 1928 proofs, are all very rare. They have therefore been omitted from the list.

TEN SHILLINGS	F	VF	EF	Unc
1966	*	*	£5	£7.50
1966	*	*	*	£15

HALFCROWNS				
1928	£3	£6	£12	£30
1928 proof	*	*	*	£40

Reverse of halfcrown

1930	£3	£10	£90	£325
1931	£6	£20	£125	£350
1933	£3	£15	£100	£300
1934	£5	£20	£60	£200
1937	£30	£75	£450	£1100
1939	£3	£6	£15	£60
1940	£3	£5	£10	£50
1941	£4	£6	£20	£60
1942	£4	£6	£20	£55
1943	£70	£150	£700	£2500
1951	*	£1	£5	£40
1954	*	£1	£5	£40
1955	*	£1	£5	£30
1959	*	£1	£5	£20
1961	*	£1	£5	£25

	F	VF	EF	Unc
1961 mule (normal) obv/pre-1939 rev)	£8	£20	£250	*
1962	*	*	*	£5
1963	*	*	*	£5
1964	*	*	*	£5
1966	*	*	*	£3
1967	*	*	*	£3

1937 florin

FLORINS

1928	£2	£4	£8	£30
1928 proof	*	*	*	£40
1930	£3	£6	£70	£300
1931	£3	£10	£100	£300
1933	£8	£30	£125	£375
1934	£12	£45	£275	£600
1935	£3	£10	£90	£275
1937	£3	£25	£165	£400
1939	£2	£4	£10	£35
1940	£2	£5	£12	£35
1941	£2	£5	£20	£50
1942	£2	£5	£12	£40
1943	£2500	£5000	£8000	£20000
1951	*	*	£3	£20
1954	*	*	£3	£20
1955	*	*	£3	£20
1959	*	*	£3	£20
1961	*	£3	£6	£30
1962	*	*	£3	£18
1963	*	*	£3	£18
1964	*	*	*	£5
1965	*	*	*	£5
1966	*	*	*	£5
1968	*	*	*	£5

SHILLINGS

1928	*	£3	£8	£20
1928 proof	*	*	*	£30
1930	£5	£15	£70	£275
1931	£3	£10	£50	£200
1933	£3	£10	£50	£200
1935	£2	£5	£40	£95
1937	£5	£25	£225	£700
1939	*	£3	£6	£30
1940	*	£3	£8	£30
1941	£2	£5	£8	£30
1942	£2	£5	£8	£28
1951	*	£1	£3	£20
1954	*	*	£3	£15
1955	*	*	£3	£18
1959	*	*	£6	£25
1962	*	*	*	£5
1963	*	*	*	£4
1964	*	*	*	£5
1966	*	*	*	£4
1968	*	*	*	£4

SIXPENCES

1928	*	£1	£3	£15
1928 proof	*	*	*	£25
1934	*	£1	£8	£40
1935	*	£3	£12	£70
1939	*	£1	£5	£30

	F	VF	EF	Unc
1940	*	£1	£5	£25
1942	*	*	£5	£25
1945	£2	£8	£35	£100
1946	£5	£12	£70	£300
1947	£1	£6	£25	£90
1948	*	£2	£8	£30
1949	*	*	£5	£30
1950	£2	£15	£35	£100
1952	*	£1	£4	£18
1953	*	£1	£4	£18
1955	*	£1	£4	£18
1956	*	*	£3	£12
1958	*	£1	£5	£40
1959	*	*	£2	£7
1960	*	*	£2	£7
1961	*	*	£2	£7
1962	*	*	£3	£30
1963	*	*	*	£3
1964	*	*	*	£3
1966	*	*	*	£3
1967	*	*	*	£3

1968 sixpence

1968	*	*	*	£2
1969	*	*	*	£3

THREEPENCES

1928	*	£1	£3	£12
1928 proof	*	£1	£3	£15
1933	£2	£5	£45	£150
1934	*	£3	£15	£50
1935	£2	£5	£25	£85
1939	£1	£5	£50	£165
1940	*	*	£10	£25
1942	*	*	£5	£30
1943	*	*	£8	£60
1946	*	*	£5	£25
1948	*	£2	£15	£70
1949	*	*	£5	£25
1950	*	*	£2	£6
1953	*	*	£2	£5
1956	*	*	£1	£4
1961	*	*	*	£3
1962	*	*	*	£3
1963	*	*	*	£3
1964	*	*	*	£3
1965	*	*	*	£3
1966	*	*	*	£3

1967 threepence

1967	*	*	*	*
1968	*	*	*	*

PENNIES

1928	*	*	£3	£15
1928 proof	*	*	*	£35
1931	*	£2	£10	£45

	F	VF	EF	Unc
1933	*	£3	£15	£75
1935	*	*	£6	£30
1937	*	*	£9	£50
1938 (unique?)	*	*	*	*
1940	£2	£6	£90	£375
1941	*	£1	£6	£30
1942	*	*	£3	£15
1943	*	*	£5	£20
1946	*	*	£3	£15
1948	*	*	£3	£15
1949	*	*	£3	£15
1950	*	*	£3	£15
1952	*	*	£2	£7
1962	*	*	£2	£3
1963	*	*	*	£2
1964	*	*	*	£2
1965	*	*	*	£1
1966	*	*	*	£1
1967	*	*	*	£1
1968	*	*	*	£1

HALFPENNIES

1928	*	£3	£6	£25
1928 proof	*	*	*	£25
1933	£1	£10	£40	£265
1935	*	£5	£25	£150
1937	*	*	£15	£45
1939	£4	£10	£30	£100
1940	*	£10	£35	£125
1941	*	*	£5	£15
1942	*	*	£2	£20
1943	*	*	£3	£15
1946	*	*	£5	£50
1949	*	*	£3	£8
1953	*	*	*	£4
1964	*	*	*	£2
1965	*	*	*	£2
1966	*	*	*	£2
1967	*	*	*	£1.50

FARTHINGS

1928	*	*	£3	£8
1928 proof	*	*	*	£12
1930	*	*	£5	£12
1931	£1	£3	£8	£20
1932	£1	£3	£10	£25
1933	*	£2	£5	£15
1935	*	£5	£12	£35
1936	*	£6	£15	£40
1937	*	£2	£5	£15
1939	*	*	£3	£8
1940	*	£3	£6	£25
1941	*	£1	£3	£6
1943	*	£1	£3	£6
1944	*	£1	£3	£6
1946	*	£1	£3	£5
1949	*	£2	£5	£8
1953	*	*	£3	£5
1959	*	*	£1	£3
1966	*	*	£2	£5

DECIMAL COINAGE
50p, 10p, 5p, 2p, 1p, ½p
All issues face value only.

SETS

1928 (in card case)	*	*	FDC	£165
1928 (in leather case)	*	*	FDC	£250
1966 unc. set	*	*	*	£10
1971 specimen set in folder	*	*	*	£5
1971 proof set	*	*	*	£9

The Anglo-Gallic Series

Chronological table of the Kings of England and France in the period 1154-1453

Henry II 1154-89
He was Duke of Normandy and Count of Anjou, Maine and Touraine. Through his marriage in 1152 with Eleanor of Aquitaine he became Duke of Aquitaine and Count of Poitou. He relinquished both these titles to his son Richard who in 1169 did homage to Louis VII of France. In 1185 he forced Richard to surrender Aquitaine and Poitou to ELEANOR who later – during Richard's absence – actually governed her provinces.

Richard I (Coeur de Lion) 1189-99
After his homage to the French King, he was, in 1172, formally installed as Duke of Aquitaine and Count of Poitou. Although his father forced him in 1185 to surrender Aquitaine and Poitou to his mother he retained actual government. Later Eleanor ruled in his absence.

John 1199-1216
He lost all provinces of the Angevin Empire except Aquitaine and part of Poitou.

Henry III 1216-72
In 1252 he ceded Aquitaine to his son Edward.

Edward I 1272-1307
He governed Aquitaine since 1252. In 1279 he became Count of Ponthieu in the right of his wife, Eleanor of Castile. When she died in 1290 the county went to his son Edward.

Edward II 1307-27
He was Count of Ponthieu as from 1290. In 1325 he relinquished the county of Ponthieu and the Duchy of Aquitaine to his son Edward.

Edward III 1327-77
He was Count of Ponthieu and Duke of Aquitaine as from 1325. At the outbreak of the war in 1337 he lost Ponthieu which was restored to him in 1360. In 1340 he assumed the title of King of France, which he abandoned again in 1360 as a result of the Treaty of Calais. He then obtained Aquitaine in full sovereignty and consequently changed his Aquitanian title from Duke (dux) to Lord (dominus) as the first one implied the overlordship of the French King. He gave Aquitaine as an apanage to his son, the Prince of Wales, better known as Edward The Black Prince, b.1330, d.1376, who was Prince of Aquitaine from 1362 till 1372, although he actually ruled from 1363 till 1371. In 1369, after war broke out again Edward reassumed the French title, which was henceforth used by the Kings of England until the Treaty of Amiens in 1802.

Richard II 1377-99
The son of The Black Prince succeeded his grandfather, Edward III, as King of England and as Lord of Aquitaine.

Henry IV 1399-1413
He adopted the same titles Richard II had, whom he ousted from the throne.

Henry V 1413-22
From 1417 until 1420 he used the title 'King of the French' on his 'Royal' French coins. After the Treaty of Troyes in 1420 he styled himself 'heir of France'.

Henry VI 1422-61
He inherited the title 'King of the French' from his grandfather Charles VI. He lost actual rule in Northern France in 1450 and in Aquitaine in 1453.

Louis VII 1137-80

Philip II (Augustus) 1180-1223

Louis VIII 1223-26
Louis IX (Saint Louis) 1226-70
Philip III 1270-85

Philip IV 1285-1314

Louis X 1314-16
Philip V 1316-22
Charles IV 1322-28

Philip VI (de Valois) 1328-50

John II (The Good) 1350-64

Charles V 1364-80

Charles VI 1380-1422

Charles VII 1422-61

'All Kings of England in the period 1154-1453 had interests in France. They were Dukes or Lords of Aquitaine, Counts of Poitou or Ponthieu, Lords of Issoudun or they were even or pretended to be, Kings of France itself, and, in those various capacities, struck coins. These coins, together with the French coins of their sons, and of their English vassals, are called Anglo-Gallic coins'.

So starts the introduction of the Bourgey-Spink book by E.R. Duncan Elias on this series. We would also like to thank Messrs Bourgey and Spink for allowing us to use some of the illustrations from the book, as well as the chronological table of the Kings of England and France during the period.

The Anglo-Gallic Coins by E.R.D. Elias is still available from Spink and Son Ltd, London (see Some Useful Books on page 11).

Henry II
Denier,
Aquitaine

HENRY II 1152-68	F	VF
Denier	£50	£135
Obole	£100	£275

RICHARD THE LIONHEART 1168-99
Aquitaine

Denier	£40	£125
Obole	£50	£150

Poitou

Denier	£40	£85
Obole	£65	£175

Issoudun

Denier	£225	*

ELEANOR 1199-1204

Denier	£50	£125
Obole	£350	*

Edward I
Denier au lion,
during his
father's
lifetime

EDWARD I
During the lifetime of his father 1252-72

Denier au lion	£30	£80
Obole au lion	£45	£125

After succession to the English throne 1272-1307

Denier au lion	£90	£250
Obole au lion	£175	*

Edward I
Obole au lion,
after succession

Denier á la croix longue	£70	£175
Denier au léopard, first type	£30	£75
Obole au léopard, first type	£50	£125
Denier á la couronne	£275	*

The coinage of PONTHIEU (Northern France) under the Edwards

Edward I	F	VF
Denier	£100	£250
Obole	£85	£225

Edward III		
Denier	£175	*
Obole	£275	*

EDWARD II

Gros Turonus Regem		ext. rare
Maille blanche		ext. rare
Maille blanche Hibernie	£35	£85

EDWARD III
Gold coins

Ecu d'or	£1000	£2500
Florin	£2750	£6750
Léopard d'or, 1st issue		ext. rare
Léopard d'or, 2nd issue	£950	£2250

Edward III Léopard d'or, 2nd issue

Léopard d'or, 3rd issue	£900	£2000
Léopard d'or, 4th issue	£1250	£3000
Guyennois d'or, 1st type	£2750	£7000
Guyennois d'or, 2nd type	£1500	£3750
Guyennois d'or, 3rd type	£950	£2250

Silver coins

Gros aquitainique au léopard	£175	£500
Gros tournois à la crois mi-longue	£275	£700
Gros tournois à la croix longue	£125	£300
Sterling	£85	£200
Demi-sterling	£135	£400
Gros au léopard passant	£525	*
Gros à la couronne	£150	£375
Gros au châtel aquitainique	£200	£500
Gros tournois au léopard au-dessus	£70	£200
Gros à la porte	£70	£200
Gros acquitainique au léopard au-dessous	£250	*
Blanc au léopard sous couronne	£65	£135
Gros au léopard sous couronne	£225	£600
Gros à la couronne avec léopard	£175	£475
Sterling à la tête barbue	£350	£900
Petit gros de Bordeaux		ext. rare
Gros au lion	£135	£350
Demi-gros au lion	£275	*
Guyennois of argent (sterling)	£100	£250
Gros au buste	£1250	*
Demi-gros au buste	£500	£1250

Black coins

Double à la couronne, 1st type	£85	*
Double à la couronne, 2nd type	£85	£225
Double à la couronne, 3rd type	£125	*
Double au léopard	£80	£185
Double au léopard sous couronne	£30	£90
Double guyennois		ext. rare
Denier au léopard, 2nd type	£30	£85
Obole au léopard, 2nd type		ext. rare
Denier au léopard, 3rd type	£35	£110
Denier au léopard, 4th type	£35	£90

THE ANGLO-GALLIC SERIES

	F	VF
Obole au léopard, 4th type	£35	£90
Denier au lion	£45	£125

N.B. Some issues of the deniers au léopard of the 2nd and 3rd type are very rare to extremely rare and therefore considerably more valuable.

The coinage of BERGERAC
Henry, Earl of Lancaster 1347-51

	F	VF
Gros tournois à la croix longue ...	800	£1750
Gros tournois à la couronne	£650	*
Gros au châtel aquitainque	£750	£1600
Gros tournois au léopard au-dessus	£450	£850
Gros à la couronne	ext. rare	
Gros à fleur-de-lis	ext. rare	
Gros au léopard passant	ext. rare	
Double	£1000	*
Denier au léopard	£650	*

Henry, Duke of Lancaster 1351-61

	F	VF
Gros tournois à la couronne avec léopard	£750	*
Gros au léopard couchant	£750	*
Sterling à la tête barbue	£600	*
Gros au lion	ext. rare	

EDWARD THE BLACK PRINCE 1362-72
Gold Coins

	F	VF
Léopard d'or	£900	£2250
Guyennois d'or	£1250	£2750
Chaise d'or	£1200	£2650
Pavillon d'or 1st issue	£1000	£2250
Pavillon d'or 2nd issue	£975	£2000
Demi-pavillon d'or	ext. rare	
Hardi d'or	£1000	£2500

*Edward the Black Prince
Hardi d'or of Bordeaux*

Silver Coins

	F	VF
Gros	£750	£1850

Edward the Black Prince Demi-Gros

	F	VF
Demi-gros	£85	£200
Sterling	£60	£135
Hardi d'argent...	£35	£95

Edward the Black Prince Hardi d'argent

Black Coins

	F	VF
Double guyennois	£100	£275
Denier au lion	£45	£125
Denier	£60	£135

RICHARD II 1377-99
Gold Coins

	F	VF
Hardi d'or	£1350	£3500
Demi-hardi d'or	ext. rare	

Silver Coins

	F	VF
Double Hardi d'argent	£650	£1750
Hardi d'argent...	£40	£110

Black Coins

	F	VF
Denier	£75	£225

HENRY IV 1399-1413
Silver Coins

	F	VF
Double Hardi d'argent	£425	£1200

Henry IV Double Hardi d'argent

	F	VF
Hardi d'argent...	£35	£110
Hardi aux genêts...	£175	£500

Black Coins

Denier	£50	£125
Denier aux genêts	£125	£350

HENRY V 1413-22
Gold Coins

Agnel d' or	£3000	£7000
Salut d' or	£4250	£12000

Silver Coins

Florette, 1st issue	£75	£175
Florette, 2nd issue	£125	£300
Florette, 3rd issue	£50	£135
Florette, 4th issue	£60	£150
Guénar	£275	£850
Gros au léopard	£350	*

Black Coins

Mansiois	ext. rare	
Niquet	£30	£90
Denier tournois	£65	£150

HENRY VI 1422-53
Gold Coins

Salut d' or	£300	£550
Angelot	£900	£2250

Henry VI Salut d'or, Paris Mint

Silver Coins

Grand Blanc aux ècus	£45	£110
Petit Blanc	£85	£225
Trésin...	ext. rare	

Henry V Grand Blanc, Paris Mint

Black Coins

Denier Parisis, 1st issue	£55	£135
Denier Parisis, 2nd issue	£55	£135
Denier tournois	£65	£150
Maille tournois	£65	£150

N.B. The prices of the saluts and grand blancs are for the mints of Paris, Rouen and Saint Lô; coins of other mints are rare to very rare and consequently more valuable.

Island Coinages

CHANNEL ISLANDS

From the date of their introduction onwards, proofs have been struck for a large number of Channel Islands coins, particularly in the case of Jersey. Except for those included in the modern proof sets these are mostly at least very rare and in the majority of cases have been omitted from the list. A number of die varieties which exist for several dates of the earlier 19th century Guernsey eight doubles have also been excluded. For further information in both cases the reader is referred to The Coins of the British Commonwealth of Nations, Part I, European Territories *by F. Pridmore, published by Spink and Son Ltd.*

GUERNSEY

TEN SHILLINGS

	F	VF	EF	BU
1966	*	*	*	£2

THREEPENCE

	F	VF	EF	BU
1956	*	*	*	£2
1959	*	*	*	£2
1966 proof only ...	*	*	*	£2

EIGHT DOUBLES

	F	VF	EF	BU
1834	*	£12	£40	£200
1858	*	£12	£40	£200
1864	*	£15	£50	*
1868	*	£10	£40	*
1874	*	£10	£40	*
1885 H	*	*	£12	£60
1889 H	*	*	£10	£50
1893 H	*	*	£10	£50
1902 H	*	*	£10	£25
1903 H	*	*	£10	£25
1910 H	*	*	£12	£30
1911 H	*	£15	£40	£75
1914 H	*	*	£7	£20
1918 H	*	*	£10	£25
1920 H	*	*	£5	£12
1934 H	*	*	£5	£15
1934 H prooflike ...	*	*	*	£100
1938 H	*	*	*	£5
1945 H	*	*	*	£5
1947 H	*	*	*	£4
1949 H	*	*	*	£4
1956	*	*	*	£1
1959	*	*	*	£1
1966 proof only ...	*	*	*	£3

FOUR DOUBLES

	F	VF	EF	BU
1830	*	*	£30	£150
1858	*	*	£35	£200

Guernsey 1864 four doubles

	F	VF	EF	BU
1864	*	£5	£45	*
1868	*	£5	£45	*

EIGHT DOUBLES (continued)

	F	VF	EF	BU
1874	*	*	£45	*
1885 H	*	*	£8	£30
1889 H	*	*	£5	£25
1893 H	*	*	£4	£20
1902 H	*	*	£4	£20
1903 H	*	*	£4	£20
1906 H	*	*	£4	£20
1908 H	*	*	£4	£20
1910 H	*	*	£3	£20
1911 H	*	*	£3	£20
1914 H	*	*	£3	£20
1918 H	*	*	£3	£20
1920 H	*	*	*	£15
1945 H	*	*	*	£5
1949 H	*	*	*	£6
1956	*	*	*	£2
1966 proof only ...	*	*	*	£2

TWO DOUBLES

	F	VF	EF	BU
1858	*	£30	£100	£250
1868	*	£30	£100	£250
1874	*	£30	£100	£200
1885 H	*	*	£6	£20
1889 H	*	*	£4	£15
1899 H	*	*	£4	£15
1902 H	*	*	£5	£15
1903 H	*	*	£5	£20
1906 H	*	*	£4	£20
1908 H	*	*	£4	£25
1911 H	*	*	£4	£20
1914 H	*	*	£4	£25
1917 H	*	£10	£30	£75
1918 H	*	*	£2	£10
1920 H	*	*	£3	£10
1929 H	*	*	£2	£6

ONE DOUBLE

	F	VF	EF	BU
1830	*	*	£20	£50
1868	*	£40	£100	£250
1868/30	*	£40	£100	£250
1885 H	*	*	£4	£10
1889 H	*	*	£2	£5
1893 H	*	*	£2	£5
1899 H	*	*	£2	£5
1902 H	*	*	£2	£5
1903 H	*	*	£2	£5
1911 H	*	*	£2	£8
1911 H new type ...	*	*	£2	£8
1914 H	*	*	£3	£8
1929 H	*	*	£1	£2
1933 H	*	*	£1	£2
1938 H	*	*	£1	£2

ISLAND COINAGES

SETS

1956 proof	... ...	£25
1966 proof	... ...	£8
1971 proof	... ...	£7.25

For coins post 1971 refer to the Standard Catalogue of World Coins published by Krouse Publications annually. Many commemorative pieces in various metals have been struck and therefore a full list of the complete coinage is beyond the scope of this publication.

JERSEY

CROWN	F	VF	EF	BU
1966	*	*	*	£1
1966 – proof	*	*	*	£3

1/4 OF A SHILLING

	F	VF	EF	BU
1957	*	*	*	£2
1960 proof only	*	*	*	£5
1964	*	*	*	£0.30
1966	*	*	*	£0.75

1/12 OF A SHILLING

	F	VF	EF	BU
1877 H	*	*	£7	£40
1881	*	*	£9	£50
1888	*	*	£8	£40
1894	*	*	£7	£30
1909	*	*	£8	£40
1911	*	*	£5	£25
1913	*	*	£5	£20
1923	*	*	£5	£25
1923 new type	*	*	£7	£20
1926	*	*	£5	£18
1931	*	*	£2	£10
1933	*	*	£3	£10
1935	*	*	£2	£10
1937	*	*	*	£5
'1945' (George VI)[1] ...	*	*	*	£3
'1945' (Elizabeth II)[1] ...	*	*	*	£2
1946	*	*	*	£4
1947	*	*	*	£3
1957	*	*	*	£0.40
1960	*	*	*	£0.20
1964	*	*	*	£0.15
1966	*	*	*	£0.15

The date 1945 on one-twelfth shillings commemorates the year of liberation from German occupation. The coins were struck in 1949, 1950, 1952 and 1954.

1/13 OF A SHILLING

1841	*	*	£60	£125
1844	*	*	£70	£140
1851	*	*	£75	£150
1858	*	*	£70	£140
1861	*	*	£70	£140
1865 proof only	*	*	*	£600
1866	*	*	£20	£60
1870	*	*	£25	£60
1871	*	*	£25	£60

1/24 OF A SHILLING

1877 H	*	*	£4	£30
1888	*	*	£4	£25
1894	*	*	£4	£25
1909	*	*	£3	£20
1911	*	*	£3	£20
1913	*	*	£3	£20
1923	*	*	£2	£15
1923 new type	*	*	£2	£15
1926	*	*	£2	£15
1931	*	*	£1	£5
1933	*	*	£1	£5
1935	*	*	£1	£5
1937	*	*	£1	£5
1946	*	*	£1	£5
1947	*	*	£1	£5

1/26 OF A SHILLING

1841	*	*	£45	£95
1844	*	*	£50	£110
1851	*	*	£45	£80
1858	*	*	£45	£80
1861	*	*	£40	£75
1866	*	*	£20	£60
1870	*	*	£20	£50
1871	*	*	£22	£50

1/48 OF A SHILLING

1877 H	*	£25	£65	£125

1/52 OF A SHILLING

1841	*	£40	£110	£250
1841 proof	*	*	*	£500
1861 proof only	*	*	*	£500

DECIMAL COINAGE

SETS

		BU
1957	... ...	£30
1960	... ...	£15
1964	... ...	£10
1966 (4 coins) proof	... ...	£4
1966 (2 crowns)	£7
1968/7 1 decimal coins	£2
1972 Silver Wedding (5 gold, 4 silver coins)	£400
1972 - - proof	£450
1972 - - (4 silver coins)	£25

For coins post 1972 refer to the Standard Catalogue of World Coins published by Krouse Publications annually. Many commemorative pieces in various metals have been struck and therefore a full list of the complete coinage is beyond the scope of this publication.

MALCOLM BORD

GOLD COIN EXCHANGE

16 CHARING CROSS ROAD,
LONDON WC2H 0HR
TELEPHONE: 020 7240 0479
FAX: 020 7240 1920

As one of London's leading dealers in most branches of Numismatics we are able to offer you unrivalled advice when it comes to both the buying or selling of coins or whether you wish to buy or sell coins or medals, we will endeavour to offer the most competitive price.

REMEMBER

That any offer we make is not subject to commission and we offer immediate payment.

A comprehensive selection of coins and medals is always available for viewing at our showroom.

ISLE OF MAN

Contemporary forgeries of several of the earlier Isle of Man coins exist.

COPPER AND BRONZE 1709-1839

Isle of Man, Halfpenny, proof in Silver, 1733

Isle of Man, Penny, 1786

PENNIES	F	VF	EF	Unc
1709	£20	£60	£200	*
1733	£30	£100	£200	*
1733 proof	£20	£60	£150	£300
1733 silver	*	*	£300	£500
1758	£20	£40	£150	*
1758 proof	*	*	*	*
1758 silver	*	*	£450	£700
1786	£10	£20	£90	£200
1786 plain edge proof	*	*	£200	£425
1798	£15	£40	£125	£225
1798 bronzed proof	*	*	£125	£200
1798 AE gilt proof ...	*	*	£700	£1250
1798 silver proof	*	*	*	*
1813	£10	£25	£95	*
1813 bronzed proof ...	*	*	£70	£200
1839	*	£15	£50	£125
1839 proof	*	*	*	£500

HALFPENNIES	F	VF	EF	UNc
1709	£40	£80	£450	*
1733	£25	£90	£150	£300
1733 proof	£10	£25	£80	£350
1733 silver	*	£100	£250	£475
1758	£15	£40	£100	£250
1758 proof	*	*	*	*
1786	£15	£40	£150	*
1786 plain edge proof	*	*	£250	£400
1798	£10	£40	£150	*
1798 proof	*	*	£125	£225
1798 AE gilt proof ...	*	*	*	£500
1813	£8	£30	£85	£175
1813 proof	*	*	£90	£200
1839	*	*	£15	£85
1839 proof	*	*	*	*
FARTHINGS				
1839	£10	£25	£45	£90
1839 proof	*	*	*	£300

Prices for the gold series, £5 to half sovereign, plus 'angels', and platinum 'nobels' are directly goverened by day-to-day prices in their respective bullion markets, to which reference should be made for current valuations. Since 1973 there have been many changes to the designs of the circulating coins and these have often been accompanied by special sets in gold, platinum and silver. In addition there have been many commemorative crowns struck in base metal and in precious metal. A full list of the complete coinage is beyong the scope of this publication. Refer to the Standard Catalogue of World Coins published by Krouse Publications annually.

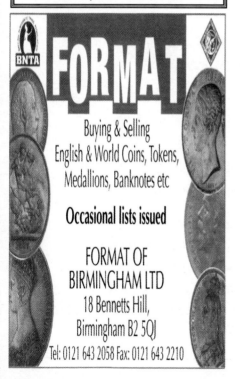

CMV INDEX

British Paper Money

THE prices listed here are only intended as a guide to values of English bank-notes. Notes with the current Chief Cashier, Andrew Bailey are generally available at a little above face, notes prior to that tend to increase in value, especially the very early notes.

Top condition is the most important factor in banknote pricing although it is quite possible to collect a more attractive selection in lower grades; some notes for example are never seen in better then Very Fine. The prices quoted here, recently updated are for EF and VF, a premium can be expected for first class notes - this is especially relevant to notes of John Bradbury and to a lesser extent, N. F. Warren Fisher.

We have not listed banknotes prior to 1914 as these are all scarce and only available in grades up to Very Fine. The past year has continued to show a healthy demand for material at every level, the emphasis still remaining on quality followed by rarity. The hobby continues to grow at a sensible pace, the shortage of good material being the only drawback.

Reference numbers are according to Vincent Duggleby's *English Paper Money*. 6th edition published by Pam West in October 2002.

TREASURY NOTES

Signed by John Bradbury

First Issue

			VF	Unc
T9	10s	Red on white. Prefix 'No'	£300	£550
T8	10s	Red on white. Six digits	£350	£800
T10	10s	Red on white. Five digits	£500	£850
T1	£1	Black on white. Prefix large letters A., B. or C.	£600	£1300
T2	£1	Black on white. As previous but no full stop after serial letter	£875	£2250
T3	£1	Black on white. Six digits	£250	£500
T4	£1	Black on white. Large serial number, 'dot' and five digits	£425	£1200
T5	£1	Black on white. Large serial number, 'dash' and five digits	£500	£1000
T6	£1	Black on white. Double prefix letters	£550	from £1000
T7	£1	Black on white. Small type face serial number	£1000	£2400

(Serial number with prefix 'No' are referred to as 'dot' if 'No' is followed by a full stop and 'dash' when a dash is used).

Second issue

			VF	Unc
T13	10s	Red on white. Six digits	£150	£325
T12	10s	Red on white. Five digits	£120	£325
T11	£1	Black on white.	£180	£250
T15	10s	Red on white. Arabic overprint	£350	£950
T14	£1	Black on white. Arabic overprint	£2500	*

Third issue

			VF	Unc
T20	10s	Green and brown on white Red serial no. with 'dash'	£120	£265

			VF	EF
T19	10s	Green and brown on white Red serial no. with 'dot'	£350	£800
T17	10s	Green and brown on white. Black serial no. with 'dot'	£180	£400
T18	10s	Green and brown on white Black serial no. with 'dash'	£180	£350
T16	£1	Green and brown on white	£50	£95

Signed by Norman Fenwick Warren Fisher First issue (overall watermark)

T25	10s	Green and brown on white, 'dot'	£80	£160
T26	10s	Green and brown on white, 'dash'	£70	from £175
T24	£1	Green and brown on white	£25	£70

Second issue (boxed watermark)

T30	10s	Green and brown on white	£65	£130
T31	£1	Green and brown on white 'dot'	£30	£60
T32	£1	Green and brown on white, sq. 'dot'	£90	£150

Third issue (Northern Ireland)

T33	10s	Green and brown on white	£70	£140
T34	£1	Green and brown on white 'dot'	£35	£80
T35	£1	Green and brown on white, sq. 'dot'	£100	£170

Unissued notes prepared during the Great War (all extremely rare)

T21	5s	Deep violet and green on white (Bradbury)	from £6000
T22	2s 6d	Olive-green and chocolate on white	from £5000
T23	1s	Green and brown on white	from £6000
T27	5s	Violet and green on white (Warren Fisher)	from £2500
T28	2s 6d	Olive-green and chocolate on white	from £4000
T29	1s	Green and brown on white	from £3500

BANK OF ENGLAND NOTES
Cyril Patrick Mahon 1925-29

			EF	UNC
B210	10s	Red-brown	£90	£160
B212	£1	Green	£60	£120
B215	£5	Black on white	£200	£400

Bank of England £1 serial no. 2 sold at auction by Spink and Son Ltd several years ago for £56,000.

John Bradbury
5 shillings.

Basil Gage Catterns 1929-34

			EF	UNC
B223	10s	Red-brown	£50	£55
B225	£1	Green (prefix: letter, number, number; e.g.E63)	£40	£35
B226	£1	Green (prefix: number, number, letter)	£100	£35
B228	£5	Black on white	£160	£250

Kenneth Oswald Peppiatt 1934-49

B236	10s	Red-brown (prefix: number, number, letter) 1st period	£40	£80
B251	10s	Mauve 2nd period	£35	£60
B256	10s	Red-brown (prefix: number, number, letter) 3rd period	£80	£150
B262	10s	Red-brown (metal filament) 4th period	£35	£70
B238	£1	Green (prefix: number, number, letter) 1st issue	£25	£40
B248	£1	Pale blue (prefix:A-D) 2nd issue	£15	£30
B249	£1	Blue (shades) 2nd issue	£9	£10
B258	£1	Green (prefix: number, number, letter) 3rd issue	£28	£50
B260	£1	Green (metal filament) 4th issue	£14	£25
B241	£5	Black on white, one straight edge, three deckled	£50	£225
B255	£5	Black on white, straight edges, metal filament, thick paper	£50	£180
B264	£5	Black on white, straight edges, metal filament, thin paper	£50	£180

Unissued notes of the 1939-45 War (very rare)

B253	5s	Olive-green on pale pink background	£4000	
B254	2s 6d	Black on pale blue background	£4000	

Percival Spencer Beale 1949-55

B266	10s	Red-brown (prefix: letter, number, number, letter)	£18	£40
B265	10s	Red-brown (prefix: number, number, letter)	£25	£45
B268	£1	Green	£5	£12
B270	£5	Black on white	£45	£150

Leslie Kenneth O'Brien 1955-62

			EF	UNC
B271	10s	Red-brown (prefix: letter, number, number, letter)	£10	£20
B272	10s	Red-brown (prefix: number, number, letter)	£50	£120
B286	10s	Red-brown, Queen's portrait	£2	£5
B273	£1	Green	£5	£10
B281	£1	Green (prefix: letter, number, number) Queen's portrait	£2	£4
B282	£1	Green (prefix: number, number, letter). Queen's portrait	£2	£4
B284	£1	Green (prefix: letter, number, number, letter). Queen's portrait	£10	£18
B283	£1	Green 'R' variety (letter R found in white space above lower BANK OF ENGLAND panel on reverse)	£250	£350
B275	£5	Black on white	£30	£100
B277	£5	Blue, pale green and orange (solid symbols)	£8	£30
B279	£5	Blue, pale green and orange (symbols for £5 white)	£8	£30

Jasper Quintus Hollom 1962-66

B295	10s	Red-brown (prefix: number, number, letter)	£2	£5
B294	10s	Red-brown (prefix: letter, number, number, letter)	£2	£5
B288	£1	Green	£2	£5
B292	£1	Green, 'G' variety ('G' in same position as 'R' as B283)	£4	£10
B297	£5	Blue	£16	£35
B299	£10	Multicoloured	£20	£45

John Standish Fforde 1966-70

B309	10s	Red-brown (prefix: number, number, letter)	£2	£5
B310	10s	Red-brown (prefix: letter, number, number, letter)	£2	£5
B311	10s	Red-brown (prefix: letter, number, number) Replacement	£5	£12
B301	£1	Green	£2	£5
B303	£1	Green 'G' variety	£4	£10
B312	£5	Blue (prefix: letter, number, number)	£16	£35
B314	£5	Blue (prefix: number, number, letter)	£16	£35
B316	£10	Multicoloured	£20	£35
B318	£20	Multicoloured	£150	£250

John Brangwyn Page 1970-1980

B322	£1	Green (prefix: letter, letter, number, number)	£2	£5
B324	£5	Blue	£20	£45
B332	£5	Multicoloured (prefix: letter, number, number). 1st series	£10	£20
B334	£5	Multicoloured, L on reverse signifies lithographic printing	£10	£20
B326	£10	Multicoloured	£10	£35

			EF	UNC
B330	£10	Multicoloured A-series	f	£40
B328	£20	Multicoloured	f	£80

David Henry Fitzroy Somerset 1980-1988

			EF	UNC
B341	£1	Green	£2	£5
B346	£10	Multicoloured (prefix: letter, letter, number, number)	f	
B350	£20	Multicoloured	£40	£80
B352	£50	Olive green, brown, grey	£70	£140

George Malcolm Gill (1988-1991)

			EF	UNC
B353	£5	Blue	f	£20
B354	£10	Brown	f	£25
B355	£20	Multicoloured	f	£80
B356	£50	Multicoloured	f	£100
B357	£5	Multicoloured (Series E) AO1	f	£25
B358	£20	Multicoloured	f	£45
B360	£50	Multicoloured	f	£45

G.E.A. Kentfield (1991-)

			EF	UNC
B362	£5	Multicoloured	f	£20
B366	£10	Multicoloured	f	£25
B372	£20	Multicoloured	f	£45
B375	£50	Multicoloured	f	£90

* Exist but no price can be quoted. f - still face value unless special prefix number, i.e. AO1. Prices on modern notes for EF or/and UNC

A recently dicovered extraordinarily rare Bank of England £100 of 1790 sold at auction by Spink in 2000 for £44,000